THE NEW OLD

PREVIOUS BOOKS

By Ronald Gross

THE LIFELONG LEARNER
HIGH SCHOOL (*with Paul Osterman*)
THE TEACHER AND THE TAUGHT
THE ARTS AND THE POOR (*with Judith Murphy*)
INDIVIDUALISM (*with Paul Osterman*)
THE NEW PROFESSIONALS (*with Paul Osterman*)
POP POEMS
OPEN POETRY (*with George Quasha*)

Edited by Beatrice and Ronald Gross

THE CHILDREN'S RIGHTS MOVEMENT
RADICAL SCHOOL REFORM
WILL IT GROW IN A CLASSROOM?

Ronald Gross is the author of *The Lifelong Learner* and other books, founder/co-ordinator of Writers in the Public Interest, and adjunct associate professor of social thought at New York University. He has been associated with the Ford Foundation, the Aspen Institute for Humanistic Studies, and the Fund for the Advancement of Education, and is currently on leave from the Academy for Educational Development which administers the Clark Foundation Program for the Elderly.

Beatrice Gross co-edited *The Children's Rights Movement, Radical School Reform,* and *Will It Grow in a Classroom?* A Distinguished Visiting Scholar of the State University of New York, she has lectured and run workshops with older adults throughout the country.

Sylvia Seidman, Ed.D., is educational gerontologist at the Institute of Study for Older Adults at New York Community College, City University of New York. She has taught and administered programs in continuing education and consults widely on curriculum design and evaluation.

THE NEW OLD

Struggling for Decent Aging

EDITED BY

RONALD GROSS
BEATRICE GROSS
SYLVIA SEIDMAN

ANCHOR BOOKS
ANCHOR PRESS/DOUBLEDAY
Garden City, New York
1978

The Anchor Books edition is the first publication of
The New Old: Struggling for Decent Aging.

Anchor Books edition: 1978
Library of Congress Cataloging in Publication Data:

ISBN: 0-385-12763-4
Library of Congress Catalog Card Number: 77-12857
Copyright © 1978 by Ronald Gross, Beatrice Gross, and Sylvia Seidman.

Grateful acknowledgment is made to the following contributors for permission to reprint the material contained in this book:

Senator Charles Percy for "Destruction of the Old," from *Growing Old in the Country of the Young,* by Charles H. Percy. Copyright © 1974 by Charles H. Percy. Used with permission of McGraw-Hill Book Company.

David Vidal for "'Healthy' Elderly Face Transfer," from the New York *Times,* March 18, 1977. Copyright © 1977 by The New York Times Company. Reprinted by permission.

Dean W. Morse for "Aging in the Ghetto," from *Perspectives on Aging,* July/August 1976. Published with permission from *Perspectives on Aging,* bimonthly magazine of The National Council on the Aging.

Vivian Gornick for "For the Rest of Our Days, Things Can Only Get Worse," from *The Village Voice,* May 24, 1976. Reprinted by permission of *The Village Voice.* Copyright © 1977 by The Village Voice, Inc.

Thomas Fox for "Fear Stalks the Elderly," from the Detroit *Free Press,* June 19, 1973. Copyright © 1973 by the Detroit *Free Press.* Reprinted with the permission of the Detroit *Free Press.*

Zachary T. Bloomgarden for "The End of the Line," from the New York *Times,* January 18, 1977. Copyright © 1977 by The New York Times Company. Reprinted by permission.

Bernice L. Neugarten for "The Rise of the Young-Old," from the New York *Times,* January 18, 1975. Copyright © 1975 by The New York Times Company. Reprinted by permission.

Judith Murphy and Carol Florio for "Older Americans: Facts and Potential." Copyright © 1977 by the Academy for Educational Development.

David Hackett Fischer for "Putting Our Heads to the 'Problem' of Old Age," from the New York *Times,* May 10, 1977. Copyright © 1977 by The New York Times Company. Reprinted with permission.

Matilda White Riley and Joan Waring for "Most of the Problems of Aging

February 1975. Published with permission from *Perspectives on Aging*, bimonthly magazine of The National Council on the Aging.

Mary S. Calderone for "Sex and the Aging." Copyright © 1976 by Mary S. Calderone.

Marc Kaminsky for "What's Inside You, It Shines Out of You." Copyright © 1974 by Marc Kaminsky. Reprinted by permission of the publisher, Horizon Press, New York.

Tish Sommers for "A Free-lance Agitator Confronts the Establishment." Reprinted with permission of the author.

Robert N. Butler for "To Find the Answers," from a speech given before the National Conference on County Resource Development for Aging Citizens. Reprinted with permission from the National Association of Counties Research Foundation.

Robert N. Butler for "Toward a National Policy on Aging." Report of the Special Committee on Aging, U. S. Senate, S. Res. 373, Report No. 95-88, 95th Cong., 1st sess., L-T 3458.

Jack Ossofsky, of The National Council on the Aging, for "Nourishing the Minds of the Aging." Copyright © 1976 by The National Council on the Aging, Inc.

Margaret Mead for "Growing Old in America," from interview with Grace Hechinger, reprinted from July 26, 1977, *Family Circle* magazine. Copyright © 1977 by The Family Circle, Inc. Reprinted by permission of Family Circle, Inc.

Lou Cottin for "The Senior Citizens' Declaration of Independence." Copyright © 1977 by Lou Cottin.

National Council of Senior Citizens for "Issue Analysis: Problems of the Aging." Published by permission of the National Council of Senior Citizens, Inc.

National Caucus on the Black Aged for "A Generation of Black People." Copyright © 1977 by the National Caucus on the Black Aged.

National Urban League for "Help for the Minority Aged." Copyright © 1977 by the National Urban League.

Merrell M. Clark for "It's Not All Downhill!" from *Social Policy*, November/December 1976, Volume 7, Number 3. Copyright © 1976 by *Social Policy*. Reprinted with permission.

Beverly T. Watkins for "Gerontology Comes of Age," from *The Chronicle of Higher Education*, March 21, 1977. Reprinted with permission of *The Chronicle of Higher Education*. Copyright © 1977 by Editorial Projects for Education, Inc.

Maggie Kuhn for "New Life for the Elderly." Copyright © 1977 by the Gray Panthers, Margaret E. Kuhn, National Convener.

Carol Mackenzie for "Gray Panthers on the Prowl." Copyright © 1977 by Carol Mackenzie. Published by permission of the author.

James A. McCracken for "The Company Tells Me I'm Old," from *Saturday Review*, August 7, 1976. Copyright © 1976 by *Saturday Review*. Reprinted with permission.

Harriet Miller for "Ageism in Employment Must Be Abolished," from testi-

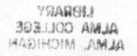

For May Schaap and Bessie Kass,
who have grown older
with grace and concern for others.

Editors' Acknowledgments

The editors gratefully acknowledge the advice of the following individuals in the preparation of this anthology: Carol Florio, Academy for Educational Development; Rick Moody, Brookdale Center on Aging, of Hunter College; Judith Murphy, coauthor, *Never Too Old to Teach;* Peter Oppenheimer, Institute of Study for Older Adults, New York City Community College; Walter Wannerstrom, Gray Panthers.

CONTENTS

Introduction   THE EDITORS   1

Part I: Waiting for the End: Our Shameful Treatment of the Aged

Destruction of the Old   SENATOR CHARLES PERCY   7

"Healthy" Elderly Face Transfer   DAVID VIDAL   12

Aging in the Ghetto   DEAN W. MORSE   16

For the Rest of Our Days, Things Can Only Get Worse
   VIVIAN GORNICK   28

Fear Stalks the Elderly   THOMAS FOX   38

The End of the Line   ZACHARY T. BLOOMGARDEN   42

Part II: The Graying of America: Demographic Perspectives

The Rise of the Young-Old   BERNICE L. NEUGARTEN   47

Older Americans: Facts and Potential   JUDITH MURPHY
   and CAROL FLORIO   50

Putting Our Heads to the "Problem" of Old Age   DAVID
   HACKETT FISCHER   58

Most of the Problems of Aging Are Not Biological, but
  Social   MATILDA WHITE RILEY and JOAN WARING   63

The Economics of Aging   JUANITA KREPS   66

Part III: Ageism: The Last Segregation

Aging: Real and Imaginary   ALEX COMFORT   77

What Is Ageism?   EDITH STEIN   89

Myths and Realities of Life for Older Americans   LOUIS
  HARRIS & ASSOCIATES, INC.   90

"Everybody's Studying Us" and "I Hate to Be Called a
  Senior Citizen"   IRENE PAULL   120

The Compounding Impact of Age on Sex   TISH SOMMERS   123

An Open Letter to a Young Doctor   SHURA SAUL   137

The System Makes It Unhealthy to Be Old   NEIL G.
  MC CLUSKEY and JODY ALTENHOF   140

Part IV: Death: The Final Confrontation

Old People Talk About Death   SHURA SAUL   151

Death as an Acceptable Subject   TABITHA M. POW-
  LEDGE   158

"I Want to Go Home": A Very Old Lady Dies in Style
  NANCY WILLIAMS   161

About the Life and Death of Rae Edith Rose   MARION
  EBNER   166

Part V: "What's Inside You, It Shines Out of You": Joys
          and Rewards of Old Age

Old People Write of Aging   171

The Crowning Years   SIEGMUND MAY   178

"The Best Is Yet to Be"   JULIA HARRIS   187

Awakening   POLLY FRANCIS   191

Greetings from Bruce Bliven   BRUCE BLIVEN   194

A Lamp at Dusk: Adjusting Puts Peace into Growing
   Old   WHITNEY WHITE   200

Sex and the Aging   MARY S. CALDERONE   205

What's Inside You, It Shines Out of You   MARC KA-
MINSKY   209

Part VI: Rallying Cries: Agendas for Action

A Free-lance Agitator Confronts the Establishment   TISH
   SOMMERS   231

To Find the Answers   ROBERT N. BUTLER   241

Toward a National Policy on Aging   ROBERT N. BUTLER   250

Nourishing the Minds of the Aging   JACK OSSOFSKY   257

Growing Old in America   MARGARET MEAD, interviewed
   by GRACE HECHINGER   267

The Senior Citizens' Declaration of Independence   LOU
   COTTIN   273

Issue Analysis: Problems of the Aging   NATIONAL COUN-
CIL OF SENIOR CITIZENS   276

A Generation of Black People   NATIONAL CAUCUS ON
   THE BLACK AGED   281

Help for the Minority Aged   NATIONAL URBAN LEAGUE   284

It's Not All Downhill!   MERRELL M. CLARK   287

Gerontology Comes of Age   BEVERLY T. WATKINS   291

New Life for the Elderly: Liberation from "Ageism"
   MAGGIE KUHN   296

Gray Panthers on the Prowl   CAROL MACKENZIE   310

Part VII: The Struggle over Retirement

"The Company Tells Me I'm Too Old"   JAMES A. MC-
CRACKEN   317

Ageism in Employment Must Be Abolished   HARRIET
    MILLER   325

The Willy Loman Complex   ALBERT ROSENFELD   331

Mandatory Retirement Is Death to Personality   HOPE
    BAGGER   339

Part VIII: Moving Toward a Better Future: Promising Programs and Projects

The Aging Are Doing Better   DAVID HAPGOOD   345

"I Am Still Learning"   RONALD GROSS   364

Senior Lobby: A Model for Senior/Student Action
    ARTHUR M. HANHARDT, JR., and RON WYDEN   370

Senior Personnel Placement   LAWRENCE HOCHHEIMER   376

An Alternative to Institutional Care in Kansas   ELBERT
    C. COLE   381

Senior Actualization and Growth Explorations (SAGE)
    SUZANNE FIELDS   387

Living to the End: The Hospice Experiment   JOHN
    KNOBLE   396

Retirement Planning Classes in Los Angeles   MARION
    MARSHALL   400

After 65: Resources for Self-Reliance   THEODORE IRWIN   408

An Inventory of Innovative Programs   VIRGINIA FRASER
    and SUSAN THORNTON   422

Part IX: Resources, Information, Help

Books and Magazines   465

Organizations, Services, and Networks   476

Index   497

THE NEW OLD

INTRODUCTION

"We are next."

ALEX COMFORT

The three of us, the editors of this book, will face the problems described in these pages eventually. So will you, if you are not confronting them already.

Being old is the one minority status we can all expect to enter. Whites may *sympathize* with the struggles of blacks, straights with gays, privileged with poor, adults with children, the "normal" with the handicapped. But they do not face the prospect of becoming part of that oppressed group themselves. But "we are next."

So, if this book is not about your present, it is about your future —how it will be for you if things continue as they are now, and how they might be if we act together. To understand aging and to struggle for decent aging in American society are to invest in one's own future.

The anxiety that many of us feel about growing older runs deep. Susan Sontag has written that getting older is "a crisis that never exhausts itself, because the anxiety is never really used up. Being a crisis of the imagination rather than of 'real life,' it has the habit of repeating itself again and again. . . . Aging is a movable doom."

This book does not espouse a beamish optimism about aging. Our thesis is not that consciousness-raising or reforms of the economic and political system—though we vigorously advocate both—will spare us the fierce fate of coming to terms with our own decline, our own vulnerability, our own limitations, our own death.

But there is not so sharp a line as Susan Sontag draws between "real life" and the way we see and feel our fate. And we have turned aging and old age into a hell for millions by adding to its inherent anxieties and challenges as a life stage, a host of vicious inequities. Old age is inevitable, but not nursing homes run like concentration camps, nor potentially productive individuals being prohibited from exercising their capacities, nor discrimination and oppression, nor starvation and decrepitude for want of minimal means of subsistence, nor isolation from the life of society or from normal sex or from the pleasures of learning and personal growth. Old age is a crisis of the imagination, as Ms. Sontag says, but it is also a crisis of social policy, a crisis of public attitudes, a crisis of community organization—crises we *must* address together, as fellow citizens. This book is about these public issues of aging in America.

Part I, "Waiting for the End: Our Shameful Treatment of the Aged," evokes the nether world of old age in which too many of our citizens are currently trapped. Vivian Gornick expresses most fully the rage that the shocking conditions of many older people's lives should properly arouse.

The next section presents more objective data, on the "graying" of the American population, suggesting that the conditions that today destroy and oppress old people must—and with growing strength in numbers and in spirit, *will*—be rectified. Bernice Neugarten's concept of the "young-old" as a new element in society strongly suggests that activism on behalf of the old may find champions in this emerging group of vigorous, successful, and concerned people.

Part III, "Ageism: The Last Segregation," explores that peculiar form of institutionalized prejudice by which we convince ourselves, and many of the old themselves, that they are worth less in every respect simply because they are aged. In this section the old begin to speak eloquently for themselves, and their voices will be heard often in the ensuing pages. Again, it is older *women*—Edith Stein, Irene Paull, and Tish Sommers—whose voices rise in protest.

Part IV concerns death, a vivid fact of life for old people. We have focused here on the variety of responses to death, merely to suggest that its shadow need not blight the life-affirming impulses of the human spirit.

Now for the good news. Part V celebrates the joys and rewards of old age, largely in the words of elders themselves. Old people are here seen experiencing life to the full—working, serving, expressing themselves, making love.

Part VI, "Rallying Cries," provides some of the basic documents of the movement to liberate and serve older Americans. Here are the programs of such organizations as the National Council of Senior Citizens, the National Caucus on the Black

Aged, the National Institute on Aging, and the Gray Panthers. The other major activist groups, such as the American Association of Retired Persons and The National Council on the Aging, are represented elsewhere in the book, and all such organizations are described in the "Resources" section.

Part VII, "The Struggle over Retirement," presents the tough issues in this crucial area. We share the conviction that it is intolerable to throw seasoned workers on the scrap heap—merely because of a certain birthday—to their detriment and society's, too.

Part VIII, "Moving Toward a Better Future," offers profiles of some promising programs and projects around the country that are making things better for older people. These are seedbeds of change, and every one of them—plus a good many more for which we lack the space here but to which the readings listed in the "Resources" section provide leads—needs to be replicated a thousand times.

Finally, Part IX, "Resources, Information, Help," provides practical information on where to start your own activisim, including a highly selective list of the best books and magazines, an inventory of the network of organizations in the field, and other leads to promising sources of strength.

As editors, we have viewed our task as simply to place in the reader's hands a varied and representative selection of the best that is being thought and done in this nascent field. We have not been afraid to include viewpoints that, if not contradictory—for we believe virtually all the contributors take a basically progressive, reformist view of the problem—are quite different in emphasis.

We hope this book will help create bridges, make connections, strengthen common bonds between different individuals and groups involved in this effort. People and organizations that have perhaps never been in contact before will see their words side by side between these covers, and perhaps, finding the company congenial, feel impelled to go further in direct communication and collaborative action. All too often, major efforts at social change are pressed by people isolated from each other, organizations unaware that their over-all aims are consonant. The whole movement will gain strength from a keener awareness of common commitment.

PART I

WAITING FOR THE END:
Our Shameful Treatment
of the Aged

DESTRUCTION OF THE OLD

Senator Charles Percy

"What is it that compels us to discard virtually anything that is old
—including human beings—as if the signs of age mark one worthless?" asks Senator Percy. He describes how we abuse the elderly
because they have become non-productive—economic "burdens"
in our youth-oriented society.

To Mrs. Jean Rosenstein of Los Angeles, to be old means being
"so lonely I could die." Mrs. Rosenstein, an elderly widow who
lives in a cramped, $60-a-month apartment near a freeway, wrote
a letter to the Los Angeles *Times:*

"I see no human beings. My phone never rings. I feel sure the
world has ended. I'm the only one on earth. How else can I feel?
All alone. The people here won't talk to you. They say, 'Pay your
rent and go back to your room.' I'm so lonely, very, very much. I
don't know what to do. . . ."

Mrs. Rosenstein enclosed $1.00 and six stamps with her letter.
"Will someone please call me?" she asked. The dollar was to pay
for the call; the stamps were to be used if anyone would write to
her. As the *Times* pointed out, in that city of nearly 3 million people, Jean Rosenstein, age eighty-four, had no one.

In some primitive societies, the aged, seen as an economic burden, are killed. With too many of our own elderly we achieve the
same effect more subtly.

We value productivity. If someone is not "productive" (is that
word to be measured only in terms of Gross National Product?),
he or she has little value. "The minute we meet someone, we ask,
'What do you do?'" says Dr. Jack Weinberg, director of the Illinois State Psychiatric Institute. "That places the person within a
framework we can understand and cope with. But if you meet a
man and ask him what he does and he says, 'Nothing,' you're
stymied, as if he seems *to be* nothing." Too often, that is precisely
our attitude toward the aged in America.

"To our nation's shame, many are hidden in the slums of urban centers, barely surviving," reports one observer. "Eventually they face placement in a substandard nursing home or a state mental hospital. Or they die alone, unnoticed."

In Miami not long ago, two elderly men—critically ill, homeless, penniless—were put into wheelchairs to sit in a jammed aisle of a hospital until nursing-home space could be found for them. Both men died in those chairs, and it was hours before anyone even noticed they were dead. One man had been sitting in his chair for three days and the other man for two.

As the hospital told of the deaths of these men, ten more just like them were still sitting in that aisle.

Indifference toward older citizens pervades our national laws. Jacqueline Hosanna, sixty-seven, and Samuel Pell, seventy, of Albuquerque, New Mexico, both lost their spouses to serious illness a number of years ago. Candidly, they admit they live together. "We'd like to get married," Mrs. Hosanna says, "but our government penalizes us if we do. I'm now getting 85 per cent of my late husband's Social Security check. If I remarry, I'll receive only half of Mr. Pell's. And we can't afford that loss." Rather than be concerned about two basic human needs—companionship and love—we force many of our elderly to live a lie.

If they are timid, they turn away from this closeness in their last years. "I'm writing to ask a favor," a recent letter to me began. "I am sixty-five years old. My friend is too. We want to get married. I can't afford to give up my income, $393.60 a month. This Social Security was rightfully earned by my deceased husband. Why should I have to forsake this income if I get married? Living alone is miserable. Can't you do something?"

At a time in their lives when they need more, rather than fewer, services, older people suffer drastic drops in income. Just when they discover that their bodies are less nimble, they find that transportation costs are rising—if the service has not disappeared altogether. When they find it necessary to buy more medication and to visit doctors more frequently, they see medical costs climb out of reach.

And finally, at an age when, because of decreased mobility, inadequate income, and declining health, they feel the greatest need to live in comfortable, familiar surroundings, close to the people they know and love—something that could be made possible if the community provided the barest of home services—older Americans frequently are forced to give up their homes or are shunted off to institutions.

"We seem to believe that every 'problem' has some sort of institutional solution," wrote nurse Sharon Curtin in *Nobody Ever Died of Old Age*. "Now that we are beginning to realize that the aged in our society are a 'problem,' we respond by creating new institutions. New nursing homes and new retirement centers are all places where the aged are segregated from the rest of the community and, thus, invisible. It is a ridiculous response to the needs of the elderly. They need more, not less, involvement with the community."

It's little wonder that people over sixty-five make up almost 30 per cent of the residents of public mental hospitals and constitute almost 20 per cent of all first admissions. "Much of their mental impairment springs from the reduction of opportunities for human contact," says The President's Task Force on the Mentally Handicapped. "Boredom is frequently a contributory factor." The Committee on Aging of the American Medical Association studied "aging" for fifteen years and reported, "There is no mental condition that results from the passage of time."

Too many people believe too many false things about the elderly. "As far as we know, nothing says biologically that at age sixty-five somebody should not be as active as he was at fifty-five," says Dr. Carl Eisdorfer of the University of Washington Medical School, Seattle.

There are a number of myths we clutch as truths:

Most of the aged are disabled.

Eighty-nine per cent of all men and women over sixty-five live in the community and are totally self-sufficient. Only 7 per cent are confined to their beds or to their homes. Just 4 per cent live in institutions.

Most of the elderly suffer from serious mental deterioration and senility.

Intelligence, as measured in tests of comprehension and knowledge, shows little or no decline for the average elderly person. "Mental deterioration rarely occurs among normal older people before the eighties," says Dr. Robert E. Rothenberg. Evidence indicates the ability to think and reason *increases* with age if those faculties are given sufficient use.

Older people cannot cope with change.

They give up jobs, a way of life, move to a different community or into a smaller house. These changes are greater than those faced by many younger men and women.

Most men and women over sixty-five have no sexual interest or activity.

"Approximately 60 per cent of married couples remain sexually active to age seventy-five," says gerontologist Edward W. Busse. For many, sexual interest and activity continue into their eighties and beyond. Lessened sexual capacity often is psychological, caused entirely by current beliefs of society. Elderly men and women who would like to continue sexual activity frequently feel that society disapproves, so they stop. "Let *your* biology, not your neighbor's, be your guide," urges one authority.

All older people are alike.

The aging process spans two and three generations. The differences in characteristics and needs are as great between sixty-year-olds and eighty-year-olds as the differences among any other age categories.

Old age is a disease.

No one dies of old age, according to the AMA's Committee on Aging. "There is no such disease," says *Prevention* magazine. "What we do die of is some infection or degeneration of a vital organ. The more we use every muscle, organ and gland—the more we use our minds—the less likely they are to deteriorate."

Physical limitations imply an inability to function.

A disability need not be a handicap. Many older people adjust to biological changes normal to the aging process and continue to function as vital, interesting men and women.

Admittedly, our culture thrives on youth, but that is no reason for us to be insensitive to the aged among us—to the often harsh reality of their lives, to their needs, to their dreams.

How long are we willing to tolerate the abuse of older, vulnerable people for the sake of avoiding the inconvenience and cost of caring for them properly?

What is it that compels us to discard virtually anything that is old—including human beings—as if the signs of age mark one worthless?

Why do we place so little value on that one quality that only an older individual can offer: wisdom gained from decades of experience and contact with several generations?

When will we begin to devise an intelligent, compassionate, and comprehensive approach to the elderly among us?

"In the country of the young, old people move like shadows," notes the *Vista Volunteer*. "They have preceded us as travelers in the land of youth, but we rarely stop to ask them the way. To remember that they were young is to realize that we will be old."

A witness before our U. S. Senate Special Committee on Aging put it more tersely one day: "If you don't die young, you are liable to get old; and if you get old, you had better think about what's going to happen to you."

"HEALTHY" ELDERLY FACE TRANSFER

David Vidal

It is known among professional workers that moving elderly people out of a familiar environment causes anxiety, depression, and even death. Yet the United Presbyterian Residence was forced to transfer patients to another adult home because . . . "the state has decided they are too healthy to remain there. . . ." Unbelievable? Read on!

WOODBURY, L.I.—For fifty years Anna C. Schreiber worked as a saleswoman in a Manhattan department store. She retired on a pension of $48.50 a month and Social Security. She soon realized that inflation had eaten up the value of her only income. So Miss Schreiber, who was an elder in the United Presbyterian Church, sought refuge in a church-sponsored home. She entered it two years ago, thanks to Medicaid.

"All these years I have only had the Man upstairs to keep me going," said Miss Schreiber, who is now seventy-two years old. "I have no one, not a relative in the world."

The only security she felt was that the United Presbyterian Residence would be her lasting home. But now that security has been shattered. She has been caught up in a drive by the $3.2 billion New York State Medicaid program aimed at saving $12 million. The drive, which undoubtedly will affect more of the ninety thousand patients in 650 nursing homes in the state, is forcing Miss Schreiber to move out.

Her destination is an "adult home" on Long Island, one that will cost the state less money because it offers no medical supervision. And the reason she and fifty-seven others at the "health-related facility" are being moved is that the state has decided that they are too healthy to remain there.

"We really are in the business of performing a balancing act," said Donald Davidoff, assistant commissioner of the division of facilities standards of the State Health Department. "We are aware that the dislocation of patients is very risky and sometimes fatal.

Our problem in the Health Department is that we are concerned with patient care and safety but we are also charged with moderating Medicaid costs."

Miss Schreiber said: "I am hard of hearing, I have scars on my cornea. I have a heart condition, I have angina pectoris. Otherwise I'm healthy, too healthy to stay."

As she spoke with a visitor, she swallowed one of the several nitroglycerine tablets she takes every day for her heart condition.

"I've had a hard life," she said, "and now to be put out like this. . . ." She sobbed.

Others living at the private, 610-patient home have become sick after being informed they would have to move.

Miss Schreiber's fate and that of the other patients, most of whom pay their own way in the $994-a-month home, have been determined by a system of rating patient needs that went into effect March 1. Because the state licenses nursing-home operators, its regulations affect the seventy thousand patients on Medicaid as well as the twenty thousand who are not.

Patients seeking entry into nursing homes or virtually any other type of geriatric facility will likewise be affected by the procedures governing placement, which have aroused strong criticism in professional circles.

"There is nothing to protect the patient's rights in all this," said Gerald Beallor, the director of social services at Montefiore Hospital, in the Bronx.

"It is crass and dehumanizing," he added, reflecting a view that professional, hospital, and nursing-home associations have voiced to the state. "We made a long struggle to provide professional care, but the state now is moving back to the concept of warehousing patients and creating a custodial system."

Under the new system, which reflects policies promulgated over the past year to reduce Medicaid expenses, each patient at a nursing home receives a kind of scorecard. Points are given for the needs and disabilities of a patient. If, for example, a patient needs total help in feeding, he or she gets fifty points; if no help is needed, no points are given.

To be eligible for placement in a skilled-nursing facility, the patient must receive a total score of 180 or more points. To be placed in a health-related facility, the score must be at least sixty.

Miss Schreiber scored too low. She said her medical history was not consulted. No one, she said, saw her in connection with the relocation that officials outside the nursing home had determined after computing her score.

"They don't even know what we look like," Bessie Conklin, eighty-seven, a resident of seven years at the home who must also move, said as she packed cartons.

John Eadie, director of the Health Department's bureau of utilization review, said the purpose of the new grading system was to make patient placement more efficient and to "assure that patients receive the type of care they really need."

Of the $3.2 billion Medicaid expense of the state, he said, one third goes to provide nursing-home services.

The state has already frozen reimbursable rates paid to nursing homes through Medicaid at the 1975 level. The power to impose such retroactive cuts has been upheld by the Appellate Division of the State Supreme Court. Nursing-home operators, meanwhile, have complained they need rate increases, not cutbacks, and some have said they face bankruptcy if this ruling is upheld at a higher level.

"GLOOM OVER THE WHOLE PLACE"

According to Andrew P. Zweben, a lawyer for Legal Services for the Elderly Poor, in November the state put into effect a formula that tied the reimbursing of nursing homes to a rating based on the quality and efficiency of its services.

"They're using a hatchet instead of a surgeon's knife," said Mr. Zweben.

The Reverend Herman L. Heim, executive vice-president of the United Presbyterian Residence, which celebrated its fiftieth anniversary a decade ago, said the state's measures would effectively further weaken the financial condition of the home.

He said Medicaid covered $766 of the monthly $994 cost for the 230 patients who rely on it. He said the home was already $750,000 "in the hole" because of the freeze in Medicaid rates and because of the outlay and interest for an adjacent plot the home had purchased to build another facility. Ironically, that facility would have been suited to the fifty-eight patients being moved to three different residences.

"But the state said our long-range plans were inadequate and mandated immediate corrective action," Mr. Heim said. "There is fear among remaining patients who feel they are going to be next. This has set a gloom over the whole place and people come in and say it's like a morgue in here."

Before the meal began, Mr. Heim read a Psalm which included the words: "Wait, wait I say on the Lord."

A woman at the table said later: "What they should do when people get old is to put them out in a boat in the middle of the ocean, and sink it."

AGING IN THE GHETTO

Dean W. Morse

Based on life stories told by some one hundred urban older blacks, Dr. Morse, a senior research associate with the Conservation of Human Resources Project at Columbia University, distills some major themes that were expressed. While the elderly of most groups share some of these concerns, such as loneliness, Social Security benefits, and the education of their children, the pervasive discrimination they faced throughout their lives caused incredible hardship and deprivation. Whatever the elderly suffer in our society, the black elderly suffer more.

Americans tend sometimes to be overwhelmed by social statistics, indices and indicators of all manner and shape. We seem to know so much about the part of our social existence or economic life that can be expressed in numbers, described by trend lines, measured by the month, the quarter, the year or the decade. Prices and profits, wage and welfare rates, income and idleness, birth and death rates—the list of items we collect is almost endless.

And the various items making up the list usually receive the most diligent attention. Analysts and computer put the figures together in myriad ways. Anything that can be correlated with anything else has, it sometimes seems, already been subjected—usually more than once and in several different ways—to the ingenuity and insights of the social analysts and the computer's power and appetite.

The content of this article is at the antipodes of large-scale social statistics. It is based on the life stories of a relative handful of people, stories carried as much as possible from early recollections up to the recent past, and is concerned with their experiences, attitudes, emotions and beliefs. It is an example of "oral history," but the kind that concentrates on the so-called "small people" rather than prominent individuals.

The "small people" in this case are a group of older black men and women who live in a large industrial and commercial city in

the Northeast. It is a city that has suffered decay and economic decline, undergone successively urban riots and urban renewal. The
scars of both experiences are evident. Parts of the city's center are
in a state of devastation, and they happen to be where the older
black community has been concentrated for many decades.

MOST LEAD LONELY LIVES

About 100 people talked with us, some for hours. A few were
willing to talk only a short time about their lives; these shorter accounts, almost all by men, came from older men whose experiences closely resembled the lives of people described in Elliot
Liebow's "Tally's Corner." They were for the most part unat-
tached individuals living in rooming houses, spending most of their
time either in their rooms or among others like themselves, sitting
on door stoops or standing in small groups in front of houses and
stores.

We have distilled from their stories what we feel are the major
and minor themes that emerge from their lives. Insofar as possible
we have tried to present the themes in their own words. After all,
the point of talking with these men and women was to give them
some chance to make their voices heard, to allow them to speak
freely about their experiences and concerns.

PRIDE, SELF-RELIANCE PRIMARY

A pervasive theme encountered in our interviews can be summed
up in the expression "self-pride." Clearly the idea of "black
pride," often used today by the young in relation to terms like
"black power" and thought by many black youth to be somehow
more or less newly born in the sixties, was at the heart of their existence. It was engrained in the older black men and women from
their earliest years.

References to their own parents often contain expressions of
wonder at and admiration for their strength displayed in the midst
of adversity, hardship and humiliation. Mrs. B., remembering her
father, recalls:

> He always went off to work no matter how bitter the weather, no
> matter how tired and sick he might be. He said to us children, and I
> can remember it as clear as a dead tree against the sky, he said, "It's

the heart and strength of a man that counts, and how long he lasts against his troubles, not how he's treated by those as may be less than he is, if you really could see their innards."

I suppose he got this from his understanding of the Scriptures, that a man's strength is somehow inside and doesn't always show. You know it by what he does.

Self-reliance, self-possession, making it on your own and making do, never to be beholden to others—these are essential parts of this quality of pride. But it is also manifested in knowing how to give and receive gratitude and support when they are due. These people were raised in communities where charity was traditionally a personal matter. Ambivalence toward public charity is among the most frequently expressed themes, arising usually as a response to what organized charitable aid does to an individual's sense of self-worth.

JUST "A NUMBER AND A FILE"

"Oh, Lord," says Miss L., "they just never know you for anything but a number and a file. And they expect that you lie and cheat and are just nobody at all, that you never have been anybody. Of course, there are exceptions, but you have to sit all day in one of those offices to know how it feels to be nobody; you have to hold on to yourself to keep from believing that you are nameless as they treat you. You just do, I'll tell you."

And Mr. W., recalling his first and last experience in a welfare office, tells about his feeling of powerlessness and his anger that a life of hard work would end with questions about whether he had any savings or property:

I decided that I would get out of there no matter what and make do even if it meant not enough to eat because Lord knows you can't really live on what I get from Social Security. They always told us that Social Security would take care of us when we couldn't work no more and that we had a right to it because we done paid for it. I wonder what happened to all that money that I was supposed to have paid into it. Sure enough, what I get isn't enough for a skinny cat, must less than a dog, to get by on. But I'll make do so long as I got friends and kin.

EQUATE COURAGE, MANHOOD

Being a man, several older black men emphasized, means having courage, fighting square and fair. A number relished telling of battles with each other when they were boys, trials of strength and courage that did not have to mean victory. More important was the capacity to take a bloody lip without flinching. A mode of manliness was inculcated by older brothers and friends.

One of the most vehement criticisms of the younger generation was that they no longer fight with their bare fists. The horror that many older black men feel about attacks by teenagers on older women and men is rooted in a sense that the youth who engage in such attacks are cowardly. One of the more elderly black men snorted:

Them, if I was to say "boo" loud to them, they would all go running down the street. What kind of a kid goes around stealing old women's purses and tripping up men old enough to be their grandpappy? It beats me. Who ever learned them things like that? We would have been ashamed to even think such a thing.

The importance of World War I in the memories of several men stands out. They or other blacks had offered themselves as soldiers, with their performance on the battlefield a testimonial to their courage. They had stood up to Hindenberg's best. They were as good and better. For one it was "a glorious day when we marched in that uniform and showed them how to march. But they weren't ready for the colored soldier then. They had to keep us hid."

TRIED TO DO WHAT'S RIGHT

Pride was often expressed in such terms, but there was another kind, perhaps most often voiced by older women. It was the outcome of looking back at a life for the most part already lived, a summing up and finding:

I'se just human and I done things that I wishes I hadn't, but mostly they're little things. I don't think I been mean or a bad person. I always tried to do what's right, what my mother and father told me was right, what I felt was right to do. That's the most important, how you feel about yourself. Did you try or not, and I can say that

I tried, and now that I'm not too far from being took up by my Lord, I can hope that His mercy will wash away the spots, and He'll see that I tried to follow His way as best I could.

Or in another voice, male:

We colored people couldn't expect to lay up very much in this world. Big houses and all that goes with them, that wasn't for us, not in our time at least, but perhaps it wasn't all too bad. It maybe kept us out of temptation and kept our mind on what was important, how you treat people. You know, I think we generally were good to each other. We had to be. Course there were some who weren't, but I do say that most of them are gone now. The ones of us who are left, we generally were good to each other. And they can say it about me, too.

WORK CROSS TO BEAR

A sense of worth is closely related to the meaning of work and activity in the minds of the older blacks we talked with. There were no illusions about work. It was never supposed to be pleasurable or self-fulfilling. With a few exceptions, almost always women, work was viewed as instrumental, a necessary cross to bear. It kept you alive and it fed and clothed children. It is unavoidable; a person tries to find the best work he or she can. But expectations of career were very rare among this group.

For some, however, work permitted avocations that were the primary source of satisfaction in life. A conspicuous example was a man who was an elevator operator, later a receptionist, in an office building. As a young man he had been trained as an organist at a leading school of sacred music. During his lunch hour he played the organ in a prominent Protestant church in the heart of the city, with a regular, if small, audience.

He also had a small music school. His job at the office building seemed to be taken as a matter of course. It was not possible for him, as a black, to make a living as a church organist and choirmaster. His job permitted him to perform Bach and Handel on a good organ during his spare time. It was the best he could arrive at. He was part of the musical life of the city and that was his contribution. "Music is color blind," he said.

KIND OF JOB MOSTLY CHANCE

Work was a trial for most of the persons interviewed, but it was also something over which an individual often felt he had little or no say. This is connected, naturally, with the absence of anything that could be thought of as a career. What kind of job you had was often a matter of chance. A casual acquaintance might tell you about a job; a sign in the window might mean employment. Jobs began and ended abruptly.

A central point in the work experience of most individuals was the awesome fact of the Great Depression. The one thing most important in life in one sense, work itself, was the thing over which a man frequently had least control. Opportunity had to be caught on the wind, so to speak. Reflecting on what you might like to do was worse than useless.

You had to be ready to take what was available. Only a few men could afford the luxury of turning down jobs because they were dangerous or extraordinarily demanding in terms of physical effort. Moreover, many jobs ordinarily not considered dangerous or physically debilitating—like laundry worker or garage attendant—turned out to sap a man's health insidiously over a period of many years.

SHOESHINING LOWEST ECHELON

More obviously dangerous jobs were the lot of others: Steel mills, chemical plants, heavy lifting and hauling—dirty jobs, jobs under conditions of intolerable heat (because the black man "stands heat better than the white man, that's what they always said"). These industrial jobs and their counterparts composed the working life of a large number of the black men. Some of the others did what they felt was trivial work, service work where little was asked except a willingness to perform a service for white men and women. At the bottom of it all was the job of shoeshiner. Other jobs were measured by their distance from that.

While it is difficult to find any obvious pattern of a career in the working life of the great majority, a fairly frequent development was movement from an occupation or industry into quite a different field, sometimes representing a step upwards in income and job status. A man might have spent many years as a laborer;

then, through a combination of the demand for skilled workers and training opportunities that emerged during World War II, make a jump into a different industry and occupation. In rare cases, that jump was followed by a final one into a white-collar job or political position.

As one individual said:

> You got to take advantage of what comes. You can't stay stuck in the mud, but you got to get out into new fields if you want to get ahead. You're never going to get to be promoted if you are just at the bottom of the heap. If you're digging a ditch by hand, you're not going to be given the job of the bulldozer that is going to bulldoze you right out of that ditch. You got to be looking for the main chance all the time.

> If I had stayed on that dock, I'd still be toting these boxes. You think I would be operating that hiloader? That would go to some young kid who knew the boss, leastwise when I was there.

MANY WOMEN REMAIN ACTIVE

Many of the women were eager to find some activity to occupy them after their active working life ended. Indeed, for a good proportion it was hard to determine just when their work lives did or would terminate. Part-time work opportunities were plentiful for many. An eagerness to help out less fortunate friends and neighbors, to keep active in the community and home, to keep busy somehow, these attitudes were often emphatically asserted.

In contrast, a number of men—particularly those with lives spent in demanding occupations—looked forward to a minimum of activity:

> I've had enough of running around and scrounging and getting up early in the morning. What I wants is to feel that I have nothing to do but put my feet up if that's what I want to do. Even if I rest all the remaining days of my life, I don't know whether it will be enough to make up for those times when I wanted to get some rest and the boss told me to get my ass moving or else. It would take a long time to rest bones that got as weary as mine did.

> And I don't know a colored man my age who went through what I done who don't feel the same. We don't need any activity, like they always planning at the Senior Citizens for old folk. We need to be

left alone to play checkers and chat with each other these days that we got left. They can't be too many for a lot of us. You know, a black man, I heard he doesn't live too many years compared with the white man. I read that somewhere, and I said to myself, wouldn't that just figure! So don't talk to me about whether I want something like work or what those social workers call a constructive hobby. That's just what I'm trying to avoid.

On the other hand, older black men who had white-collar jobs on occasion expressed a desire to keep working as long as they could, certainly past normal retirement age:

So long as I can get around easily, I want to be able to go in to work in the morning. Maybe not a whole day. But at least something to fill the time. Maybe it would be different if I had a place down in the country to keep me busy, but what's a man to do in a small apartment in the city. And he can't go outside because the kids won't let him walk up and down the streets without him getting hit over the head or something. Better to be doing something, and earn some income doing it.

That Social Security isn't going to mount to a hill of beans when you come to it. That's what I envy those old fellers who got some place to go back to down South. That's where I would go in a minute, but I don't have any roots there any longer. I was a baby when we come. And, as far as I know, there's no kin down there, and, anyway, I wouldn't know their faces. Course there's got to be some, but I don't know where they are nowadays, and so I'll have to stay up here in the big city. And that's why I want to be able to work as long as I can.

SCHOOLING NEGLIGIBLE

Discussion of work was often closely linked to education. A sense of lifelong handicap or disability due to a lack of education, particularly if a person attended Southern schools, was often voiced:

How could you learn in a school like that? We were all bunched in together; there weren't enough books, and the teacher was just a young girl out of high school herself. What do you think us boys did? Now, I learned some reading after I came up North and I was already growed. I made a practice of doing that. But I tell you, if it had been just for those years in that school in the back country of Alabama, I would be as ignorant as a babe. They just didn't mean for you to get an education at all; they just went through the motions so they could say they had a school for the colored.

And us boys, we just got out of it as soon as we could. I sometimes wonder whether young folks today can really imagine what a country school for the blacks down South was like when I was a kid. I tell my grandchildren about it, and I tell them to take advantage of what they got here, even if it is not so perfect. But I don't know whether or not they listen.

Conversely, a number of older black women who were educated in the South recounted stories of extraordinary efforts to get an education, to go to college, to get nurse's training. Many of the women, when they were young, were motivated by a sense that, if an education could be gained, it would make possible a life different from the pattern of household service that their mothers confronted. It was often possible for them to combine education with part-time domestic work, even though the hours worked were sometimes equivalent to a full-time job today.

Where older brothers would long since have given up school and be working full time on the farm or as a laborer in a sawmill or on the roads, the younger daughters might be encouraged to finish high school, even to go on to college. It was understood in many families that the boys could not; college was just not in the cards. Who ever heard of a farm boy getting himself through a college, and what would it get him? A girl could teach or go into nursing. What was a strong, healthy boy going to do with a college diploma, particularly if his family needed his work or he wanted to get married?

WANT CHILDREN'S EDUCATION

At the same time, a profound respect for education and a desire to make it possible for their children to have the education they didn't have were almost invariably expressed by parents. They mentioned the educational achievement of their children with pride and satisfaction. They pointed out the struggle to put sons and daughters through college, but the sacrifice and effort were ungrudging. In a world where they encountered obstacles and barriers at every turn, education, they strongly believed, was the single most powerful weapon to overcome and undermine obstacles.

For many, there was nevertheless a deep ambivalence toward higher education. True, it opens doors and provides some of the most important credentials, but it is also associated with barriers that have held the black man down, part of a game and a charade. An education does not mean that you are more qualified or a better man. It simply leads to a piece of paper, a badge of entry, something that the white man uses to exclude the black man.

Some of the men said that as soon as a large number of black youth had achieved college degrees, the degrees would probably cease to open employment opportunities for them. So long as there were just a few black college graduates, it might mean advancement, but that could not be true for the average black person:

You just wait and see. They'll find some other way to keep us out, specially if jobs are hard to come by. You think that a college degree going to make all that difference for a black boy? You think it was because we didn't have a college degree we couldn't get to be a plumber or a carpenter and a member of the union? So long as you don't compete with them, then it's all right, but what happens when there are a lot of black college graduates knocking at the doors of banks and corporations alongside the sons of bosses and owners? You think they're going to be so happy to see you? That I got to see.

But many expressed another attitude towards education. The black man needs to know; he has been kept in ignorance. As soon as he gains educational equality with the white man, he will be able finally to compete on even terms:

They don't want our boys and girls to get a college degree or to go to law school, because one of these days they are going to find that we do as well there as we do on the football field or the basketball court. They know that when the competition is fair, they won't be able to talk about the black man being inferior. Maybe we are going to show that we are superior! Maybe that's what they are afraid of.

And that's why we have to get ourselves educated. My generation, we just couldn't do it. Most of us, we didn't have the money or the opportunity, but we have made it possible for our children. And they are going to show the world something, that I know. It's coming, and I hope I live to see it.

DISCRIMINATION PERVASIVE

The web of discriminatory practices, pervading every aspect of life and daily encountered, the constant irritation of barriers to carrying out sometimes the simplest activities, the weight of arbitrary and unreasoning discrimination in a society that lays claim to equality and fairness of treatment—these are things men or women can never get accustomed to. They may know what to expect—that a particularly offensive or petty act of exclusion or prohibition because of their black skin will occur—but the fact is always galling.

Somehow, all the petty acts taken together mean more than single incidents can reveal. And the absurdity of it all, the fact that the black gets caught up in the same web, sometimes forced even to discriminate against his fellow black to comply with the discriminatory code, is truly maddening.

A black man tells of driving a white man down to a city in southern New Jersey. The black man takes along his bride. The white man, a lawyer, goes off to finish his business, and the black man and his wife go into a restaurant near the railroad station. It is early; they are alone in the restaurant. They wait and wait. Nobody comes to serve them.

Finally, a white couple comes in, and a waitress—a black woman —takes the white couple's order. The black man protests. The waitress says that she will call the restaurant owner, who turns out to be a black woman. She is sorry, but she cannot serve blacks. She says they can get something to eat in the railway station lunchroom. They go there and discover it contains only stools at a counter.

"I wasn't going to put my bride on a stool," the black man said. "So we just didn't eat at all until we got back home. Would you believe it was a black woman who wouldn't serve us? That's what it was like only a few years ago."

Numerous older black men feel that younger blacks do not really understand what their parents and grandparents had to face.

How could they? How could anyone who didn't live through it? It's easy enough to hear tell about it. But the South, it wasn't just that you had to get into the mud to let a white man pass. You never knew when it was going to come and hit you. Why, I remember when white kids, they couldn't have been more than about 15 years old, they used to ride through the black section of the city I was raised in. It wasn't one of your small towns, but a regular city, and you would think that this couldn't have taken place in a city.

But I tell you, they used to ride through the colored area on Friday night with shotguns loaded with birdshot, and they would just fire at any black who happened to be out on the streets. And they was laughing all the while, like it was some kind of harmless bit of tom-foolery. Boom, the gun would go, and then a lot of guffaws. And there was nothing you dared to do about it, because it would have cost you your life to muss the hair of one of them white brats.

FOR THE REST OF OUR DAYS, THINGS CAN ONLY GET WORSE

Vivian Gornick

Vivian Gornick visits a senior citizens center in Brooklyn and talks to six people between the ages of sixty-five and eighty. Struck by their vitality and responsiveness, she nonetheless reports that despair, loneliness, and boredom infuse their lives—including that last terror, "of being thrown into a home."

One cold, rainy evening not too long ago, I climbed aboard a bus in midtown Manhattan, dropped my fare in the box, and sat down three seats from the door. It was late, the bus was crowded, most of the passengers looked tired. At the third stop the bus seemed to stand for an inordinately long time without closing its doors and moving on. Restless, I looked toward the front to see what was happening. We were halted because an old woman was climbing very slowly up the front steps of the bus. One hand clutched the railing beside the front seat, the other was wrapped around the head of a cane. The woman's hair was white and wispy, her eyeglasses thick; a black coat that seemed as old as she hung loosely from her thin shoulders. Her face looked dim and unseeing, concentrated on the task of climbing the stairs, oblivious to all the people on the bus trapped into waiting for her. Oh, God, I thought, we'll be here forever.

Then a young man sitting beside me said between clenched teeth: "Come *on,* old woman. Get up on this bus, God damn it! Don't you know we got things to do, and places to go?" I swung around to stare at him; then I turned back to the old woman at the door. By now she was at the top step and I could see her swollen feet. Suddenly a shock went through me. I thought: That's *me* in thirty or forty years. That's not some "old woman" who has nothing to do with me. Once she *was* me, young and strong, leaping up on the bus, causing no one any trouble, paying her own way through the day. And someday I'll be her, old and weak, arousing hatred and irritation in everyone around me, isolated, a pariah in a world where I have spent my entire life being unobtrusively useful.

America is one of the worst countries in the world in which to grow old. This is a country in which the only value of a human being is the ability to produce. If you can produce you are respected and have power; if you can't, you are despised and shunted aside. Many different kinds of people can't produce, for one reason or a hundred, and are vulnerable to the contempt engendered by this primitive ethic of the most modern of modern societies. The young, for instance, can't "produce"; neither, supposedly, can blacks or women or those on welfare. And the old, the old can't produce either.

I have been a couple of these "non-producers"—I have been young and I have been a woman—and I know what it feels like not to have the right to an opinion. And someday I will be old and I will have to experience the sensation all over again. It seems to me the worst of it is being old. To pass from being young and "useless," to being mature and "useful," and then back again to being old and "useless" is to know the pain of a rejection that is tantamount to annihilation. To become a statistic, deprived of the individual self you have carried around with you all those years you were being "useful," to be either uniformly ignored or else surrounded by the false smiles, the false concern, of a society that at best condescends to its old—as though by becoming old you have become retarded or interchangeable; as though by accumulating the skill of endurance for sixty to seventy years you now have nothing to teach, nothing to say, no real space to occupy—that is truly to be wiped out. That, in a sense, is to have lived almost for nothing.

There are today in the United States more than 22 million people over sixty-five years of age. More than a million of these people live in institutions—nursing, convalescent, and old-age homes. More than a third of them live alone. Millions of them are indigent —more than 15 per cent of the poor in this country are old. The proportion of old people living with their families decreases rapidly with advancing age. Nearly all old people are experienced by their families and the society around them as a burden, a social problem, a thing to be dealt with (preferably by being put away, out of sight). Almost no old people are experienced as vital human beings in whom an entire human history resides and whose place in the social scheme of things is natural and desirable.

What does it actually feel like to be one of these people? What is it like, in its *dailiness,* to be old on the streets of a large American city? What is it like to be inside the skin of that old woman on the bus? To what extent does she feel included in or excluded from the life around her?

In search of some answers to these questions I spent an afternoon at a senior citizens center in Brooklyn. I talked to six people between the ages of sixty-five and eighty, whom I shall call Doris Everts, Ephraim Oldinger, Gerald Reiss, Sarah Durkin, Sophie Karlinsky, and Lizzie Brauner. Each of these men and women lived alone in apartments near the center. All of them were widowed with grown children living either in distant parts of the city or the country. Three were American-born, three immigrant citizens. All have worked their entire lives, most since early childhood. They had been, variously, a bookkeeper, a businessman, a librarian, a teacher, a sewing-machine operator, and a commercial artist. They were not easy with each other; there was no real rapport of personality, interest, or experience among them. They were there only because they are old and alone. Yet it was clear that although this affliction of lonely old age had reduced them to the lowest common denominator of human need, each of them had a separate inner life to which he or she clung tenaciously.

What struck me immediately about all six of these people was their vitality. (Perhaps secretly, I had expected them to be doddering and inarticulate with depression.) They were alert, well dressed, and intensely responsive. They had opinions on everything, and collectively, their opinions revealed a sharp grasp of the condition in which they now found themselves living.

We spoke together for many hours, these six people and I. Now, when seven animated strangers are gathered together in a room to discuss a live issue, the conversation rambles, digresses, bounces off the walls, takes a spin in the corridor, shoots back in through the window, loses the point, makes another point, miraculously returns to the original point, and if you're all lucky, you eventually emerge with a measure of shared understanding.

I can't duplicate those hours of talk at the Senior Citizens Center. What I can do, and have tried to do, is to "summarize" the es-

sential bit of understanding with which I left those people in
Brooklyn. What follows is a compacted version of hours of talk,
laughter, silences, and pauses during which six people between the
ages of sixty-five and eighty tried to give me a sense of what it is
like to grow old in America today.

"Well," said Sarah Durkin, smoothing her dress over her knees,
"in many ways it's quite good, growing old in America. We have
pensions, Social Security, Medicaid, things our parents never had.
We have better health longer; we have this center. This center is a
godsend, I don't know what I'd do without it." Sarah Durkin's
eyes gleamed within a network of wrinkles, her body had the sag-
ging shapelessness that comes with long years of hard work, her
hands were blotched and broken. She was clearly the determined
optimist in the crowd.

"Right," said Gerald Reiss, "this center is a godsend. If you
didn't have this center you might as well go home and kill yourself.
Because, let's face it, Sarah, what else have you got?"

A round of snickers, nods, and protests followed this exchange.

"Well," said Ephraim Oldinger slowly, gravely, "to a large extent Sarah is right, but to an even larger extent Gerald is right."
Oldinger was eighty years old, his body was terribly frail, his eyes
swam behind thick lenses; but the philosophical mien of the
teacher, which had been his all of his life, remained.

"It is true," he continued, "that the center is a godsend. Most of
us have absolutely no place else to go to, no other way to make
human contact, and without human contact, as you surely know,
dear lady, a human being shrivels up and dies. So we are grateful
to the center. At the same time, the center *reminds* us, also, of
how terribly reduced our lives have become, how bitter our loneliness is, and how cut off most of us are from the life around us."

How is the loneliness of old age different from the loneliness of
youth or middle age?

"It's more isolating than the loneliness I have known at any
other time in my life," said Doris Everts simply.

The words and the dignified quiet with which they were spoken
were a bit shocking, coming as they did from this particular
woman. Doris Everts looked ten years younger than her seventy-
five years. She was very well dressed, her face and hair were care-

fully made up, and her voice was tinged with the kind of educated accent that one associates with human options.

"When I was lonely as a girl or as a young woman," Doris Everts went on, "I could distract myself in a hundred ways. I'd call a friend on the spur of the moment and go out, or I'd clean the house, or go to a movie, or take a walk in the park, or share my loneliness with my husband. Now it is a terrible effort to fight loneliness. My husband is dead; most of my friends are dead; the friends I have left live so far away. It didn't seem so far away when I was young, but now it does. I haven't the strength to clean the house; I'm afraid to walk in the park. I feel hemmed in on all sides."

"Yes," said Ephraim Oldinger heavily, "the loneliness is the killing factor. For me the loneliness began the day I stopped working. I never realized how much I'd thrown myself into my work, what a *world* my work was, until the day the work stopped. On that day I began to be lonely. But I mean *lonely*. My wife was already dead, and [he nods toward Doris Everts] most of my friends were also dead. Suddenly the world had become narrow as a coffin. I sat and stared at the four walls. My eyes were beginning to go, soon I wouldn't be able to read so much either. That was when I began to want to die. . . ." Oldinger's voice began to trail away; his head bobbed toward the floor. Suddenly he pulled himself together, held his head erect, and laughed. Life came crowding back into his lined face. "But," he said, "I'm not dead yet, not yet. I force myself to go out into the street every day. Every day, no matter what's happening out there. I know that if I don't, I really *will* die. My legs will get stiffer and stiffer, the circulation in my body will go, and I'll become a vegetable."

"That's *my* great fear," said Sophie Karlinsky. "That my health will go. I live in terror of the day when I can't dress myself, go shopping, and keep up my apartment. On the day they cart me off to a home, that's the day I want to die."

"Oh, those homes, those homes," moaned Gerald Reiss. "The thought of being thrown into a home! The fear of being segregated, sealed off from the world. And perhaps being abused. Some of those homes are like Victorian institutions. And then, talk about a leveling of life. Can you imagine this man here [he points to Ephraim Oldinger], he's talking as intelligently as he does, and he turns to look at the person he's talking to, and he's *dribbling*. Because that's what it's like there. You're surrounded by a silent, drooling depression, everyone waiting to die. I swear, I'll put a bullet through my head first."

I stared at Gerald Reiss as he spoke. He was sixty-eight years old. His hair was white, his skin hung in chicken-like folds from his narrow frame, but his eyes! His eyes were dark and alive, full of urgency.

"Well," said Sarah Durkin, still the brave optimist, "it's not as bad as all that. People are very kind to me here at the center, and my children, God bless them, they do the best they can. Of course, I don't see them that often but, then, they're busy, you've got to understand that. They've got their own lives. But they try, they try. For instance, my son, last year he said to me, 'Ma, let me take care of your money; then you won't have any money on the record and you'll be eligible for Medicare. So that's what we did. He takes care of everything for me now, everything."

Lizzie Brauner seemed suddenly galvanized. She strained forward in her seat, forgetting her polite posture, her eyes sparkling. "Let me tell you," she said to Sarah Durkin, "the day you can't sign your own checks is the day you should really shoot yourself!" She turned to me: "I did exactly what Sarah is talking about. I signed over all my money to my daughter. Listen, my daughter is a wonderful woman, good as gold. But all of a sudden I was like a little child. I had to ask her for every little thing. I was no longer a *person*. I had to explain to my daughter if I wanted to draw out a hundred dollars. Oh, it was terrible! And let me tell you, it ended in a mess." Lizzie Brauner flushed and her eyes wavered, but she decided to go on. "I had to take my daughter to court. She was so upset when I said I wanted my money back that the only way she could explain it to herself was to tell herself I wasn't right in the head any more. I had to get a lawyer. Against my own daughter. Oh, it was terrible. But, thank God, we're all right now. And let me tell you, they can *keep* Medicare. If it means I have to turn myself into a beggar or a child because I'm seventy years old and not entitled to free medical care in this country because I'm not a welfare case—listen to how crazy it sounds!—then the hell with this country. I'll die fighting, the way I've always had to live here."

"You'll die fighting, all right," said Gerald Reiss, "probably fighting a mugger." He turned to me. "That's another thing that keeps us prisoners in our houses. The fear of being mugged."

"I know," I said, "I know."

"You *don't* know!" he said passionately.

I looked at him. He's right, I thought, I don't know. I have my fears, but I don't know what it's like to be sixty-eight years old and feel utterly helpless. I remembered all the stories I'd heard in the past few years of old people being knocked down on the streets in broad daylight by marauding teen-agers, robbed and beaten, their frail bodies making them natural targets for terror and humiliation.

As though he were reading my mind, Ephraim Oldinger said, "It's not just the fear of being killed or even badly hurt by the muggers, it's the powerlessness you feel when these things happen, the sheer *insult*. Once, I was waiting at a bus stop. A bus pulled up. It wasn't my bus, and I continued to wait at the stop. Some young boys were gathered in the back of this bus, and one of them hung out the window and called to me. I looked at him, and he nodded at me as though to say yes, it was me he wanted to speak to. I stepped off the curb and went up to the window. The boy leaned way out, and then he spat full in my face. I stood there, stunned. I couldn't believe this was happening to me. And behind him all his friends were laughing wildly. And I remember thinking: What can *I* do? I'm just an old man."

My God, I thought, the Eskimos put their people out on ice floes when they get too old to work, and the nomads simply leave them behind when they move on, but here we hunt them in packs.

"What it is," sighed Sophie Karlinsky, "is the helplessness of it *all*. It isn't any one thing in particular. It isn't *just* the loneliness, or *just* the fear of illness, or *just* the muggers, or *just* getting poorer. It's all of it together. What makes you so damned helpless when you get old is all of it happening at once. And the realization, finally, that there's no relief coming. This is *it*. For the rest of your days things can only get worse, they are never again going to get better. That's what old age means to me."

Was it better to grow older forty years ago than it is now?

"Oh, yes!" nearly every one of them said.

"My mother didn't grow old the way I'm growing old," said Sophie Karlinsky.

"There's no family life now; there was a family life then," said Sarah Durkin. "Things were altogether different."

"Yes," said Doris Everts. "My children come to visit me, but we have nothing to say to one another. We are strangers. They live in a world where there's no room for me. My mother's world was not that different from mine."

"People were kinder to one another years ago. They cared about each other. No one cares now, not about anything, or anyone," said Gerald Reiss.

"They've given us Social Security, true," said Ephraim Oldinger, "but in return they have taken everything from us that Social Security was meant to be applied to. What a term! *Social Security,* indeed!"

"The thing is," Doris Everts says, a painful little smile on her face, "we need love now more than we ever needed it before. And we have less chance than ever before of getting it. People think love is a thing of the past when you get older. Let me tell you, even *sexual* love is not a thing of the past. Most of us are dying just because, physically, we're all locked up inside ourselves. And certainly ordinary affection is not a need of the past. In a funny way, it's like being a child all over again. When you're a helpless child in the world, what you need in order to flourish is love, simply love. And when you're old the thing that can prolong your life is love, just a sense of love coming in at you. . . . But where does one get it, ordinary affection? When I think back on it, the way we all lived forty years ago, even if you didn't love your mother and father that much, just being together the way we all were, that *passed* for love. And as far as I'm concerned now, that's as good as the real thing."

I don't know if Gerald Reiss was right about people having been kinder to one another forty years ago, but certainly Sarah Durkin and Doris Everts were right when they said that forty years ago there was a family life that made an enormous difference in how one grew old. And, God knows, Ephraim Oldinger was right when he called attention to the irony of social benefits bestowed upon the old at a time when the old have less of a place in society than ever before.

My grandmother endured a life of working-class poverty in this country; for her, the streets of America were never paved with gold. Many of her children died in infancy; those who survived struggled in vain for an education and spent their lives working hard just to make a living. My grandmother's life teemed with turmoil and social neglect. But all of her children and grandchildren lived within blocks of her house, she saw most of them every day of her life, and she died at home at the age of seventy-four in her oldest daughter's arms.

My mother is now the age her mother was when she died. The differences between her old age and her mother's old age are great. On the one hand, forty years ago, at seventy-four, my grandmother was a broken old woman; today, at seventy-four, my mother is strong and healthy, her body ten years younger than her chronological age. On the other hand, my mother endures a social isolation that was unthinkable for my grandmother. She lives alone in a high-rise building in a section of New York City that in no way resembles a "neighborhood." Her children are educated beyond her wildest dreams; they are also much married and divorced beyond her wildest dreams; and they are scattered around the country and available to her only for visits, not for a daily sharing of life.

These past forty years have made America the most powerful, most technologically advanced nation in modern history. Along with that power and that technology has come a devotion to production never before known. The industrial revolution of the nineteenth century has come into its own in the American twentieth century with a vengeance. At the same time, the human uprootedness that from the very beginning accompanied industrial production has also come into its terrible own. Affluence and mobility have disintegrated family ties, the stability of lifelong marriage, the connectedness that comes of growing, marrying, and dying in the same place. There is now in America almost no sense either of the past or of the future. Our lives, to an extraordinary degree, are dominated by an intense and furious present. When a disc jockey plays a record that was made five years ago and says, "Here's an oldie but a goodie," he wipes out the past. When people enter weekend encounter therapy in droves, they wipe out the future. A hysteria of immediate gratification—one that belies the natural maturation process of intimacy, real work, genuine growth—fills the void of institutional loneliness in which we have come to live.

There is cause, in this condition, both for excitement and despair. On the one hand, the emphasis on "self-realization" comes directly out of the *now*-ness of life, and is certainly at least partially responsible for the tremendous social revolution—the liberation movements—now under way. On the other hand, the now-ness of life tempts us to place no value on the past, not only the past in our society but the past in ourselves.

To be old is to be the past in ourselves. Every day of our lives, that past accumulates inside us. If we dissociate from the old around us, we are dissociating from ourselves: from the future of our own pasts. One day, each and every one of us will reap the bitter harvest of the disconnected lives we are now sowing.

Human dissociation—not to see yourself in others, not to have others see themselves in you—is the worst condition in which to live. It is the condition in which most old people live today in this, the most advanced nation in the history of the world.

FEAR STALKS THE ELDERLY

Thomas Fox

The Louis Harris & Associates survey found that the elderly ranked fear of crime as the most serious problem they experienced. In his article, which was part of an award-winning series on the elderly in Detroit, Fox discusses two other fears that stalk the elderly.

When Marie Munch, eighty-one, was stabbed to death on her bed in her two-story brick home three weeks ago, she became the twelfth person over sixty to be slain by intruding robbers in Detroit this year.

The bricks of her home are tarnished now. They have lost the brownish-red glow they had when Mrs. Munch lived there with her husband and children years ago.

Her children married and left. Then her husband died. Like many other elderly women, she was left alone in a house too big for her needs, yet too dear to leave.

"We asked her to get out, but knew she wouldn't," her daughter recalled. "The house was too much a part of her."

Three women in their twenties are being questioned by police in connection with the murder. One has allegedly said they needed money and that Marie Munch was an easy target.

The death has cast an uneasy shadow over the 1000 block of Van Dyke. Many other elderly people live in the neighborhood and lament that it has deteriorated so much during the past twenty years.

They live in constant fear now.

"I don't go outside anymore. I just sit around," a sixty-nine-year-old woman said as she glanced out her door to retrieve her mail. "You never know what's going to happen.

"It's frightening, all this killing," she added before disappearing behind a quickly locked door.

A seventy-six-year-old man said he fears for his life, but will never leave the area.

"There is no place to run," he said.

It is fear more than any other emotion that controls the habits of the 330,000 Detroiters over the age of fifty-five.

There is the fear of being robbed or mugged, the fear of being cheated or misunderstood, and the pervasive fear of being isolated and cut off from human contact by illness or weakened limbs.

A Detroit police inspector said recently that the elderly are victims of more street robberies proportionate to their numbers than any other group.

Twenty-two per cent of Detroit's population is over fifty-five, but 34 per cent of all unarmed robberies are committed against them, a report revealed.

"It's a problem for them [the elderly] to come in and look at a lineup or mug shot. The thugs know this," Inspector Richard Boutin said recently. "Their powers of perception are not fine. They are powerless to defend themselves.

"Sadly," he added, "an assault against an older person is usually more serious than one against someone younger."

One of the most common forms of robbery committed against the elderly, police say, occurs on the third of each month when they return from local or downtown banks after cashing Social Security checks. Robbers hang around public housing projects waiting for their victims to return with purses and wallets filled with cash.

Also, many older couples who live together insist that one person stay at home at all times so that their house is never left unprotected.

"There's always someone out there looking to rob you," said a seventy-five-year-old east side man who lives with his wife in a private home. "But we're always here waiting."

But robbery is not the only crime that elderly people fear. It is common for many older people to feel out of touch with rapid change around them. This adds frequently—and with justification—to their suspicion of all strangers.

A newsletter issued to elderly citizens by the Mayor's Senior Citizen Commission said that "the nation's aged are the number-one target for an almost limitless variety of con games and frauds."

It listed "home repairs," "debt adjusting," "chain referral selling," "dance studio rackets," "model home swindles," and the "pigeon-drop swindle" as some of the most common schemes by which the elderly are "bilked of hundreds of millions of dollars each year."

In addition, the elderly lose large parts of their savings by more legal methods.

A recent confidential study by the U. S. Senate Small Business Subcommittee revealed that pharmaceutical firms soak older Americans and other patients up to thirty times too much for lifesaving drugs. The elderly use more drugs collectively than any other segment of the population.

"At the heart of the problem is the lack of transportation," Margaret Hossack, director of the Mayor's Senior Citizens Commission, said recently. "The senior citizens are simply not able to get around, compare prices, and find out what things really cost. So they become easy victims."

She added that many con men play on the loneliness of the elderly by listening sympathetically to them before peddling their schemes.

To help combat the crimes against older Detroiters, a task force for the elderly was formed recently to investigate what might be done by private groups and the police to protect the elderly. The task force has gotten off to a slow start, but has the potential of improving the lives of many senior citizens.

In some cities, other programs have been initiated to seek out elderly men and women living alone to assist them. Whether they are called "Operation Outstretch" or "Project Find," their goal has been the same: to find the dispossessed and assist them.

In Detroit, the Mayor's Senior Citizens Commission has laid the groundwork for a nutrition program for the elderly. It would establish perhaps as many as forty centers where senior citizens could gather to eat and associate with friends. But federal funding for this program has been held up for several years already.

Dr. Eve Kahana, a gerontologist at Wayne State University, recently investigated the lives of some elderly persons living alone to see what they felt their needs are.

"I was surprised at first to find," she said, "that one of the most pressing needs older people feel is the proper care of their feet."

She explained that her finding really should not have been so startling, saying that for many elderly persons, their feet become a symbol of their mobility.

"If their feet break down, they see themselves losing their mobility—and translated, it means increased isolation."

Figures show that 8 per cent of Detroit's elderly are bedridden. Twenty-seven per cent more are ambulatory but ill, and thus their movements are somewhat curtailed.

The fear of isolation haunts many older men and women. It comes on slowly and methodically: friends die, sons and daughters move away, transportation costs rise, and inexpensive public transportation is inadequate.

And personal disabilities—aching feet, arthritic joints, cracked hips, and weakened spirits—add to the loss of human contact.

So, in addition to the fear of crime, violent and otherwise, the elderly hold within them a fear that is less obvious, but no less real.

One social worker who assists the elderly of Detroit summed it up:

"You can understand the fears they have. But feeling them, that's another thing."

THE END OF THE LINE

Zachary T. Bloomgarden

"One out of three people die within a year of entering the home."
Dr. Bloomgarden, resident in internal medicine at Montefiore Hospital, questions how this can be avoided. His conviction, shared by many professional workers, is that most of the elderly should remain in their own homes and communities. He points out the devastating effects a nursing home's medical structure can have on a person's self-image.

More than 10 per cent of the population are older than sixty-five, and this figure may double over the next twenty-five years. A steadily increasing number of these people are spending, and ending, their lives in institutions. As the physician caring for a group of forty residents of a "health-related facility" over the past year, and having been involved in placing perhaps one hundred elderly people in nursing homes after a hospitalization, I have come increasingly to question this way of channeling the lives of our older people.

Nursing homes are not, of course, homes. They are large institutions most of whose residents must share a small bedroom with others, must eat their mass-prepared, high-carbohydrate meals in a large, linoleum-floored dining room with others, watch television in a communal room with others. From bedroom to dining room to television, several times daily, the residents spend their lives.

Are nursing homes, then, for nursing? A tremendous structured system goes to convince one that this is so. Much of the day-to-day running of these establishments is supervised by nurses: when to awake, when to eat, when to sleep. Medications of various sorts are distributed four or more times daily. Each resident is required (by law) to be examined regularly by a physician to renew his "diagnoses" and "orders"—not only for medications but for diet and activities as well.

Is this complicated process actually *medically* necessary? Is our society actually producing this many chronically and severely ill people? Or does this medical system serve rather to legitimize, to the residents of the nursing homes as well as the remainder of the society, this mechanism of "putting away" the elderly?

We should ask, further, whether the "homes" are even effective in what should be the goal of medicine—that of decreasing the amount of illness.

One out of three people die within a year of entering the home. One might suppose this to be due to their underlying physical ailments. But isn't the burden of proof on us to show that it is not due to the fact of institutionalization?

A few small studies have shown, in fact, that if an intensive effort is made to adjust people to the idea of entering a home, this mortality rate is reduced.

A number of related disorders can clearly be traced to entering the nursing home. A relatively small number of persons, perhaps one in ten, become profoundly depressed. Somewhat more often, one sees a previously mildly confused person become disoriented, agitated, unco-operative.

But most common of all is the effect of the nursing home's medical structure on the individual's self-image. He does not merely live in the nursing home—he becomes a patient, profoundly dependent on the medical personnel around him. Gradually and progressively, there is a somaticization of many psychic troubles until he becomes entirely submerged in this role.

How much of this process could be avoided? Published studies support my impression that only about one third of nursing-home residents require full-time nursing. Most of the elderly could, and should, remain in the community—in their own homes, with their relatives, or in communal facilities maintained by the residents themselves.

In order to do this, support must be available for centers for the elderly to meet in during the day, for transportation, for home visits by medical personnel.

Yet we are trapped by the fiction that the problems of the elderly are medical disorders. A housekeeper must be "ordered" by a physician. For lack of transportation with a driver who can help him up the steps to his home, the elderly citizen must remain in his apartment until he becomes sick enough to need an ambulance. Rather than being helped down the steps every day by his neighbors, he must be placed in a nursing home. And the cost of the nursing home now exceeds ten thousand dollars per resident per year in New York State.

Our elderly population need not, and should not, remain a burden on the society. We can benefit from their knowledge and experience. They can help care for the community's children. They can help maintain the environment. Rather than stripping away their dignity and individuality, we should, and must, include them in the community, to enrich our lives as well as theirs.

PART II

THE GRAYING OF AMERICA:
Demographic Perspectives

THE RISE OF THE YOUNG-OLD

Bernice L. Neugarten

An emerging age group, those between fifty-five and seventy-five, is appropriately dubbed the young-old by Bernice L. Neugarten, professor of human development at the University of Chicago. They are healthier, better educated, more active politically, and less economically disadvantaged than their predecessors. These young-old "may well become major agents of social change in moving toward a society in which age is irrelevant."

The United States population is rapidly changing, particularly with regard to older people. These changes may produce a society liberated from outmoded stereotypes of the so-called declining years. Two important elements are a lengthening life span and the rise of the young-old.

Because of increased longevity and improved health, and also the changed timing of family events, middle age has recently become a well-delineated stage in the life cycle.

Because marriage and parenthood were occurring earlier after the turn of the century and because children are spaced closer together and then grow up and leave home earlier, there is now a period when parental responsibilities diminish, when work continues but specific work roles may change, and when most people consider themselves middle-aged, as their last child leaves home.

Another meaningful division of the life cycle is now appearing with the rise of the young-old, a group drawn mainly from the fifty-five-to-seventy-five age group. The young-old are distinguished from the middle-aged primarily by retirement, and distinguished from the old-old by continued vigor and active social involvement.

We are not yet accustomed to thinking of fifty-five to seventy-five as an age group, for since the beginning of our Social Security system we have used sixty-five as the economic marker, then as the social and psychological marker, of old age. A set of stereotypes has grown up that older persons are sick, poor, enfeebled,

isolated, and desolated. While these stereotypes have been greatly
overdrawn even for the old-old, they have become uncritically attached to the whole group over sixty-five.

These stereotypes are now beginning to yield to reality. For one
thing, the general drop in age of retirement makes fifty-five a
meaningful lower age limit for the young-old. Many workers are
voluntarily retiring as soon as they think they can live comfortably
on their retirement incomes. In industries where over-all employment is declining, the downward trend in retirement age is dramatic. Most observers predict that the downward trend will continue over the next few decades. Thus the young-old will become
increasingly a retired group.

It is already a relatively healthy group, with fewer than one out
of four limiting any of their major activities because of health.
While the number of widows is high, the intact family is by far the
most common pattern, with couples living in their own households, owning their own homes, and seeing their children frequently.

The economic position of the young-old relative to other age
groups is less easily summarized. While income drops sharply for
most persons upon retirement, current money income is only part
of the total economic resources for retirees; government in-kind
transfers such as Medicare, value of rent to homeowners, net-
worth holdings, tax adjustments, and intrafamily transfers must
also be included in assessing economic welfare.

The young-old are already much better educated than the old-
old, but the more significant fact is that they will soon be in a less
disadvantaged position in comparison to the young. By 1980, the
average fifty-five-year-old will be a high school graduate, and by
1990 this will be true of all of the young-old as a group.

The young-old are already very active politically as compared to
younger age groups. There is no evidence that an age bloc or a
politics of age is developing in the United States; yet over-all political participation, when corrected for income levels and educational levels, is highest for persons fifty-one to sixty-five, and it
falls off only a little for persons over sixty-five. Thus the young-old
are disproportionately influential in the electorate as a whole.

The young-old can be expected to develop a variety of new

needs and will want a wide range of opportunities both for self-enhancement and for community participation.

Some will choose early retirement, some will want to continue in their jobs after sixty-five, some will want to undertake new work careers after forty. Some will want to move to retirement communities, some will want to move from the suburbs back to the inner city, some will want to "age in place." One trend already accelerating is the return to education.

Like the young, the young-old are likely also to want a society in which arbitrary age constraints are removed and all individuals have opportunities consonant with their needs, desires, and abilities, whether they be young or old.

As the young-old move away from work roles, in the sense in which we have usually used that term, and become the users of leisure time, they may be the first to reach the society of the future, a society in which freedom from work is coupled with freedom from want.

If so, they may become not the neglected or the isolated or the expendables of the society but, instead, the social contributors, as well as the self-fulfilled. They may become the first age group that on a large scale creates new service roles and gives service to the community without direct financial remuneration.

Finally, if the young-old do not form a strong age-group identification of their own, they may well become major agents of social change in moving toward the society in which age is irrelevant.

If they create an attractive image of aging and thus allay the fears of the young about growing old, if they help to eradicate those age norms that are meaningless and those age attitudes that are divisive, they will do the society an untold service.

OLDER AMERICANS: FACTS AND POTENTIAL

Judith Murphy and Carol Florio

Who are our old, what is their current status, and what could they contribute to their own and society's well-being if their potential were recognized? On the basis of the demographic data and the Harris poll, Judith Murphy and Carol Florio of the Academy for Educational Development envisage that "an indeterminate, but large, number of these older Americans are equipped and willing to make life better for themselves and others through a great diversity of roles."

The key to sound social policy on improving the lot of older people is to keep firmly in mind that "older people" are first of all people, individuals each in his own right.

With these warnings in mind, let us review some familiar statistics that provide a useful framework in which to consider these millions of individual men and women.

- More than one out of every ten Americans is sixty-five years of age or older.
- According to mid-1976 Census Bureau estimates, the sixty-five-and-over population numbers about 22.9 million—an increase of 2.8 million since 1970—or 10.6 per cent of the estimated total U.S. population of 215.1 million. Of the 22.9 million, nearly 60 per cent are women.
- By the year 2030, if the present low birth rate and declining death rate hold steady, these older Americans will account for over 17 per cent of the population, or one in every six Americans.
- Most men sixty-five and over are married and live with their wives. Only one out of seven is widowed; only one out of seven lives alone.
- By contrast, more than half the women in this age group are widowed, and more than a third of the women live alone. Only one third are married and living with their husbands.

- Contrary to popular opinion, only a small proportion of the elderly population—about 5 per cent in 1974—lives in institutions. (Over 80 per cent of these are seventy-five and over.)
- Life expectancy for a boy born in 1973 is 67.6 years, for a girl 75.3 years, as against forty-six years for a boy and forty-eight for a girl born in 1900. Most of these extra years of life expectancy have been achieved not through control of the process of aging but through improved sanitation and the conquest of the major fatal childhood diseases. A woman reaching sixty-five today can expect to live an additional 17.5 years; a man, another 13.4 years.
- The annual income of older households averages $7,500. Because the typical household is now quite small, per capita income comes to $4,100, or 95 per cent of the national norm. Twenty per cent of older households have incomes in excess of ten thousand dollars. Yet some 3.4 million elderly persons, most of them single women, live in poverty, with annual household incomes of less than $3,500.
- Of all people sixty-five years old or more, about 3 million (or only 14 per cent) were part of the work force in 1976. Of the total at work, close to 2 million were men, 1 million women. Since 1900 the rate of participation in the work force by older males has decreased steadily—from two out of every three men sixty-five years and older in 1900 to one out of five in 1974. The female rate in 1974 was one in every twelve, as it was in 1900, after rising slightly in 1972.
- In 1974, the working men and women were found preponderantly in three low-paying categories: farming, self-employment, and part-time occupations of various kinds.
- The rate of unemployment for both men and women sixty-five and older is low—under 4 per cent in 1974. The figure is misleading, however, since so many older workers have become discouraged and stopped looking for work, thus counting themselves statistically out of the labor market.
- As to formal education, the attainment of older people is still well below that of the over-all adult population. In 1975, only about 35 per cent of persons sixty-five and older were high school graduates, compared to about 62 per cent of all adults twenty-five years old or more. But the level is rising for all

adults, and by 1990 about half the people sixty-five and over are expected to be high school graduates. (As recently as 1952 it was only 18 per cent.)

This basic statistical profile of Americans aged sixty-five and over indicates that, *on the average,* they are not working or looking for work, that they include substantially more women than men, and that the women are much more apt to be widowed and living alone. Only a minority finished high school. The picture thus far is primarily derived from census returns, and is necessarily painted in broad strokes.

For more revealing detail about the sixty-five-and-over population, it is necessary to look elsewhere. Thanks to the work of physicians, psychologists, and a variety of scholars, it is possible to understand much better than before what aging means and what it does *not* mean. This understanding has been further enhanced by that quintessentially modern tool, the scientific survey, notably the 1974 poll completed by Louis Harris & Associates for The National Council on the Aging. It is the most extensive study of attitudes on aging ever conducted in the United States.

The Harris study is aptly called *The Myth and Reality of Aging in America.* Myths about old age are persistent and hard to eradicate; they persist among all age groups, including the aged themselves, who, after all, were but lately young. Thus, a person sixty-five or older tends to consider himself the exception and, along with the rest of the population, to lump all *other* older people together as not terribly bright or alert, adaptable or resilient or open-minded, although usually warm and friendly and wise from experience. Studies made in the 1960s and 1970s suggest that society's view of the aged has its roots in childhood. In 1976 a University of Maryland study of children's attitudes toward the elderly produced such responses as "sick," "sad," "tired," "dirty and ugly," "wrinkled," "crippled," "chew funny," and "haven't any teeth." The same children, however, tended to view old people as "friendly," "good," "kind," "rich," and "wonderful."

One of the most persistent myths, very slowly losing its grip, is the notion that senility is somehow inevitably linked with aging and that mental and temperamental vigor and capacity are bound to decline with physical vigor. We know now that there is no such correlation. A minority of old people do become senile, for reasons still unknown. The unhappy denouement may be the product of particular genetic and/or experiential causes, perhaps even diet. It is not the automatic outcome of years lived. Alex Comfort, author of *The Joy of Sex* and a leading gerontologist, is not one to mince words. "Crazy" is his word for "senile," and he has written: "Old people become crazy for three reasons: because they were crazy when young, because they have an illness, or because we drive them crazy," and he points out that "rather fewer old people are crazy than at earlier ages."

According to Dr. Daniel T. Peak, a psychiatrist at Duke University's Center for Aging, successful aging most often follows successful youth and middle years. But even without this felicitous prologue, a person is not condemned to an unsatisfactory old age. Stressing for the later years what commentators from Erickson on down to Sheehy have been saying about the whole of life, Dr. Peak discounts the "social delusion" that "growth and development stop when one reaches early adulthood." Change is possible at almost any age. It depends on the individual. "Old people," as Jack Ossofsky, director of The National Council on the Aging, recently told the St. Petersburg *Times*, "are usually what they were when they were younger, only more so. What we need to do is to begin separating out those older people with problems instead of thinking of older people's problems."

Over all, certain mental capacities do tend to diminish with age; for instance, the capacity to immediately recall new facts or events as well as one remembers the more distant past. In part, however, even this failing is mythically induced, in young and old alike. Samuel Johnson makes the point: "There is a wicked inclination in most people to suppose an old man decayed in his intellect. If a young or middle-aged man, when leaving a company, does not recollect where he laid his hat, it is nothing; but if the same inattention is discovered in an old man, people will shrug up their shoulders and say, 'His memory is going.'" And of course, the old man is inclined to agree and help perpetuate the myth.

In combating the myths and fears and prejudices that becloud old age, however, it is essential to avoid the opposite danger, of idealizing and thus equally falsifying this time of life. We might do well to eschew Browning and his "best is yet to be, / The last of life, for which the first was made," in favor of Maurice Chevalier and his commonsensical view ("Am I looking forward to old age? Yes, considering the alternative!").

Frank Reissman, editor of the bimonthly *Social Policy,* in his introduction to a 1976 issue devoted to "older persons," struck a good balance on this particular question:

> . . . In their genuine efforts to eliminate negative stereotypes, too many "gerontophiles" have tended to deny the real difficulties associated with aging. My own personal experience of aging has shown me that reflexes slow down, mental functioning is at least different, a subtly more conservative outlook emerges, and death becomes a more important concern.
>
> Although I have an extremely active intellectual and athletic life as well as a fulfilling family life, I do experience aging in my bones, in my mind, in my emotions, and in my attitudes. It takes me longer to recover from illnesses, my reflexes on the tennis court are not as sharp, maintaining a desirable weight is hard, learning new games and new ideas is not as easy.

Again, this is the view of one man, obviously a member of the "young-old" generation, who is well off, active, and variously blessed. The Reissman statement illustrates once more how critical it is to bear in mind that "older people," or "senior citizens," or "the aging," are *not* a bloc, not a monolith, not a census abstraction. Like blacks or Hispanics or youth, they have only certain things in common. As a group, what they chiefly share besides age are the by-products of the aging process and—extrinsically—the assets and debits of society's arrangements for the sixty-five-and-over population. Carolyn Setlow, of Louis Harris & Associates, makes the point lucidly:

> Above all else, the sixty-five-and-over group have lived longer than the rest of the public. More than any other factor, older people share with each other their chronological age. Yet the research shows that factors more powerful than age alone determine the conditions of one's later years. Instead, the aspirations and disappointments, the life satisfactions and dissatisfactions, the personalities and problems, that defined them as individuals when they were younger continue to make them unique in their later years.
>
> In short, there appears to be no such thing as the typical experience of old age or the typical older person. At no point in one's life

does a person stop being himself and suddenly turn into an "old person," with all the myths and stereotypes that that term involves.

The fallacy of overgeneralizing about the elderly is clear from the statistics already cited, whether the specific is health or education or marital status or income or living arrangements. On any given aspect of later life, one can often say "many" persons but seldom "most" and never "all" or "almost all." This diversity also prevails in the picture derived from statistics of the older American's attitudes toward work and retirement. As figures cited earlier show, only a small fraction (14 per cent) of people sixty-five and older were still part of the work force in 1976.

The Harris poll discovered, in questioning retired or unemployed older people, that the majority expressed no interest in returning to work. But the minority expressing a desire to work was sizable: nearly 7 million people, or more than three out of ten. Least happy with unemployment were the members of the lowest income group.

Poor health was the major reason cited for not working despite the expressed desire to do so. More than twice as many people (57 per cent) named this obstacle as did the next-most-cited obstacle (the 28 per cent who simply said "too old"). The Harris study, however, reached the interesting conclusion that the pre-eminence of "poor health" among reasons for not working may well be "a learned excuse to cover up for other reasons such as 'nobody wants me,'" a more acceptable and less embarrassing justification for not working. The study went on to suggest another interpretation of health problems among the aging: "a causal relationship between enforced idleness and health." According to a 1972 study by the American Medical Association:

> There is ample clinical evidence that physical and emotional problems can be precipitated or exacerbated by denial of employment opportunities. Few physicians deny that a direct relationship exists between enforced idleness and poor health. The practitioner with a patient load comprised largely of older persons is convinced that the physical and emotional ailments of many . . . are a result of inactivity imposed by denial of work.

The Harris survey probed some of the social and economic facts of life behind older people's assertion of being "too old" to work, making it apparent that often this was less a self-diagnosis than a reflection of prevailing attitudes and mores and, to some extent, law. Most pension policies set age sixty-five for mandatory retirement. Even more influential in making sixty-five synonymous with the onset of old age was the quite arbitrary decision, in 1935, to gear full retirement benefits to that age in the new Social Security system. Moreover, even the Age Discrimination in Employment Act of 1967 protects persons only up to the age of sixty-five, not beyond. So no matter how well a man or woman of sixty-four realizes that the next birthday is not going to change him from middle-aged to elderly overnight, it is difficult to buck the combined weight of all these social forces.

Discrimination among employers against older people is widespread and incontrovertible. The barriers, in fact, loom larger than those facing any other age group, and this despite well-documented evidence that older people perform well on the job and that most of the public believe they do.

What the ground-breaking Harris survey showed about older people and work was, in sum, that the population of persons sixty-five and over who want to work extends far beyond the 14 per cent now gainfully employed (most of them part time) and beyond the more than 20 per cent engaged in volunteer work. These millions of men and women constitute an important source of manpower. Many of them feel that they have particular skills or capacities that they would like to use, given the chance. Nearly 3 million people expressed an interest in learning new skills, taking part in job-training programs, and embarking on new or renewed careers; the figure would doubtless be higher were it not for the well-known barriers to the employment of older people.

In real numbers, the present volunteer force among older people is 4.5 million. According to the Harris study, however, the figure understates the potential. Another 10 per cent of the public aged sixty-five and over and not now engaged in volunteer work say they would like to be, thus suggesting a volunteer force (actual and potential) of nearly 7 million older Americans.

Not every or almost every older American would, given the chance, opt for working, at "real" jobs or as volunteers. Many are beset by poor health, lack of mobility, and assorted cares; some of them really are "too old." Others, after a lifetime of drudgery or unrewarding work, are disposed, now that they can, to take life easy. Still others are happily endowed with absorbing friends, family, avocations, and interests. Not everybody subscribes to the bad press that retirement now gets. Nor are all the elderly as down on leisure and as gung-ho for work as some of their more doctrinaire apologists seem to assume. A cautionary analogy could be drawn to an early and malign by-product of the women's movement whereby reasonably contented wives and mothers were made to feel uneasy or even guilty for not entering or wanting to enter the work force.

Nonetheless, an increasing number of men and women who have retired or are about to retire and who no longer bear heavy family responsibilities want to play active roles in life for as long as possible, whether in paying or unpaid jobs. They are not resigned to an endless vista of knitting, model building, bingo, TV, or competitive valetudinarianism. It is clear that an indeterminate, but large, number of these older Americans are equipped and willing to make life better for themselves and others through a great diversity of roles.

PUTTING OUR HEADS TO THE "PROBLEM" OF OLD AGE

David Hackett Fischer

Some two hundred years ago, the elderly in America were venerated, says David Hackett Fischer, Professor of History at Brandeis, because there were few of them who lived that long and those that did had power. The author of *Growing Old in America* analyzes the shift from veneration to neglect of the aged, to what he sees as "A new era in age relations . . . now beginning in America . . . ," which puts an "end to age discrimination in all its forms. . . ."

In seventeenth-century America, there were few elderly people, but their authority was very great. At a time when about 20 per cent reached the age of seventy (compared with 80 per cent today), young people were trained to regard the survivors with veneration, a feeling of religious awe.

Calvinist writers exalted age, which they took to be a special sign of grace. Their image of Jesus was a man with hair "as white as snow." And their idea of an angel was a man in his seventies. In New England meeting houses, the seats of highest honor and authority went to the oldest, rather than the richest, inhabitants.

Respect for age was not entirely voluntary. It was forced when it was not freely forthcoming. In an agrarian society, old people controlled the land and were slow to surrender it to their seeking children. "Better it is," the moralists taught, that "thy children should seek to thee, than thou shouldest stand to their courtesy." Young people were often exploited, bullied, and economically repressed.

Elderly people rarely retired to make way for the young. Old men worked until they wore out. Public leaders clung to office until death removed them—90 per cent of New England's ministers and magistrates died in office. That society's "rulers" were younger than today's because of differences in life expectancy, but they ruled with the authority of age, as so many of their titles tell us: elder, alderman, presbyter, senator.

Not all elderly people were venerated in early America. There were many exceptions—poor old men who hunted their dinner like dogs in the streets of towns; old slaves who were sent into the woods by callous masters; penniless widows who were driven out of town by neighbors mindful of the pauper tax.

In seventeenth-century America, *most* old people were honored, but it was not a "golden age" even for them. More than today, old age was filled with physical and psychic pain. Elderly people were so few that they felt as strangers among their own kin. Beneath the surface of respect there were deep currents of resentment against their authority. Satirists attacked the vices of the aged, which were mostly the vices of power: arrogance, cruelty, greed, lust. The irony was striking: The social power of the aged was linked to psychic vulnerability.

People were not very kind to the aged in early America. There was respect without affection, veneration without love. Old age was exalted by law and custom, but it was wounded in the heart.

From 1607 to 1780, those two sides of its condition were combined in a system of age relations that grew steadily stronger through time.

In a society where age conferred authority, people tried to make themselves seem older than they actually were. Today, Americans sometimes subtract a few years when reporting their age to the census taker. But, in the eighteenth century, they pretended to be older. They tried to look older by powdering their hair and wearing clothes cut to imitate old age. And they gave their eldest sons important advantages that grew greater with time.

Then, late in the eighteenth century, the direction of change suddenly reversed. The social status of the aged, which had risen for two centuries, began to fall. Between 1775 and 1830, elderly Americans lost their seats of honor in the meeting houses. New laws forced them to retire at a fixed age—the first, in 1777, was for judges in New York State. Primogeniture was abolished in law and custom during the American Revolution. Fashions began to flatter youth rather than age during the French Revolution. The direction of age prejudice reversed in census reporting and showed a bias toward youth from 1850 to 1950.

All the evidence suggests that a great transition occurred in American attitudes toward old age between 1780 and 1820. It was not a period when one static system replaced another, but a "deep change" in the pattern of change itself, a break between change processes.

The transition happened in America before industrialization and urbanization. It came at a time when nearly 95 per cent of Americans lived in the country and 90 per cent were farmers. Its cause had less to do with the Industrial Revolution than with the great social revolutions in America and France.

The ideal of equality undercut the hierarchy of age; the ideal of liberty dissolved its communal base; the decline of deference diminished its political authority; the growth of wealth stratification lessened its economic strength.

During the nineteenth century a spirit of gerontophobia grew steadily stronger in America. Where the Puritans had made a cult of age, the Transcendentalists made a cult of youth instead. "Age is no better, hardly so well qualified for an instructor as youth, for it has not profited so much as it has lost," wrote Thoreau in *Walden*. "I have yet to hear the first syllable of valuable or even earnest advice from my seniors. They have told me nothing, and probably cannot teach me anything." That attitude grew more intense, from the Transcendentalists to the generation of Hemingway and Eliot.

As the status of the aged fell, their numbers began to rise. The drab statistics tell a poignant story. Americans over sixty-five increased from 2 per cent of the population before 1810 to 3 per cent in 1870, 5 per cent in 1930, and 10 per cent today. Retirement rapidly became common. As late as 1870, more than 80 per cent of men over sixty-five were still working; by 1970, fewer than 25 per cent were. Pauperism among the old grew inexorably: 23 per cent in 1910, 40 per cent in 1930, 65 per cent in 1940, its high point in American history.

In the nineteenth century, as social and economic conditions grew worse, bonds of intimacy between the generations may actually have grown strong; Tocqueville commented upon the warmth of relations between old and young in America. Anthropologists have found that in cultures where the authority of grandparents is weak, affection is strong. Here was another irony: As the social status of old age declined in the nineteenth century, its psychological status improved.

Early in the twentieth century, a second great transition began, when old age was suddenly discovered as a serious "social problem." In 1909, the first Commission on Aging was appointed, in Massachusetts; the first Federal Old-Age-Pension Bill was proposed, in Washington; and a new discipline named geriatrics was invented, in New York—all within a single year.

Private pension plans grew rapidly after 1900. Arizona established the first state pension system, in 1915. After twenty years of controversy, Social Security was established in 1935 and enlarged in almost every federal election year thereafter. An academic field called gerontology was created largely after 1945. The cult of youth reached a climax in the 1960s and began to be attacked by a large polemical literature. Pauperism among the aged declined dramatically after 1940. And many social services were established for "older Americans," or "senior citizens" as they began to be called.

A new era in age relations is now beginning in America. Its nature will depend upon what we wish to make of it. Our historical experience tells us what it should *not* be. In early America, the young were often victims of the old. In modern America, the old have been victims of the young. We might try to build a future without victims altogether—a world without gerontophilia on the one hand or gerontophobia on the other.

Those who seek to solve the "problem" of old age today by reversing the age bias of modern America might learn from our historical experience that reversal is not the best of remedies. The cult of youth was preceded in our history by a cult of age that was equally destructive of human relationships.

Our goal for the future should not be the creation of new forms of age discrimination more favorable to the old, but an end to age discrimination in all its forms: an end to formal age stratification and rigid age classes, which have grown so inflexible in the modern world. Prejudice by age is as unjust as prejudice by sex, race, and religion. Many changes must be made—chief among them the abolition of forced retirement at a fixed age.

We might also observe in the past a tendency for the material and ethical status of old age to be inversely related. When one was high, the other was low—and vice versa. The "problem" of old age in America today must be solved both ways at once. It is both a material and an ethical problem. The nature of the material problem is clear enough: Our Social Security system is fundamentally unsound. We must create a better system that offers more dignity and prosperity to the old without imposing an increasingly heavy and regressive burden on the young.

At the same time, we must deal with aging as an ethical problem. The values of our society rest upon a work ethic—an ethic of doing—that gives highest value to people in the prime of their productive years. We should encourage a plurality of ethics in its place—not merely an ethic of doing but also an ethic of feeling, an ethic of sharing, an ethic of knowing, an ethic of enduring, and even an ethic of surviving.

We must make room for all of these values. For only on that broad basis can a just and free society be built.

MOST OF THE PROBLEMS OF AGING ARE NOT BIOLOGICAL, BUT SOCIAL

Matilda White Riley and Joan Waring

Matilda White Riley's classic *Aging and Society* is one of the foundations of the scientific study of aging. Here she sharply summarizes some of the principal findings of her career-long concern. This statement is the best brief distillation of the sociologist's understanding of aging in American society.

SUMMARY

1   Age and aging cause problems for individuals at all stages of life and for society as a whole. Most of these problems are social, not biological, in origin.

2   A new field, *the sociology of age,* is concerned with understanding the social causes of age-related problems and finding ways to alleviate or prevent such problems.

3   One set of social problems arises from *age stratification*. Both people and roles in society are stratified by age. As a result there are age inequalities, age segregation, and age conflict. Age differences among people intensify these problems. The young, middle-aged, and old differ from one another not only in life-course stage, but also in past experiences and in the birth cohort to which they belong. (A cohort consists of people born at the same time. Members of the same cohort age together and share the same historical context.)

4   *Age inequalities* occur when people in some strata have less access than other people to valued roles and their rewards. For example, many teen-agers and people over 65 are denied work roles and the associated income and social esteem. Age inequalities are a source of obvious deprivation, hidden but widespread suffering, and various forms of deviance.

5   *Age segregation* pervades our social institutions. For example, children in age-graded schools are discouraged from interacting with children older or younger than they. Old people in retirement

communities are shut off from younger relatives and friends. Although it has certain advantages, age segregation interferes with the flow of mutual support and mutual influence (socialization) between age strata.

6   Age inequalities and age segregation breed misunderstandings, cleavages, and potential *conflict* between age strata. For example, negative stereotypes often develop from misunderstanding of young people as "too inexperienced" or old people as "no longer able" to work, and negative stereotypes can become self-fulfilling prophesies.

7   Another set of social problems accompanies the *process of aging* from birth to death. As people grow older, they move through a socially structured sequence of roles. Age is a criterion for entering and leaving these roles and for evaluating role performance.

8   Problems of aging are intensified during *life-course transitions* (such as entering the first grade, finding the first job, retiring, or losing a spouse). A transition involves relinquishing a former role as well as assuming a new one.

9   Life-course transitions present two types of problems: (a) the strains of learning the new role and adjusting to it and (b) the pain associated with loss of the former role. Relinquishing a valued and familiar role often invokes a period of grief, especially when the self has been deeply invested in the lost role.

10   Role transitions can be positive experiences when the new role is socially valued and when people (for example, *significant others* or professional counselors) provide adequate social and emotional support during the transition. For many transitions there is *no* adequate support—as in becoming a husband or wife, starting a job, becoming a parent, dying alone in a hospital, or facing widowhood.

11   *Social change* continually affects age and aging, sometimes causing new problems but sometimes eliminating old ones. For example, the tenuous balance between age-graded roles and people of the appropriate age to fill these roles is constantly being undermined by war, economic fluctuations, changes in the state of science and the arts, etc.

12   The age structure of roles is subject to special disturbances when *successive cohorts differ markedly in size,* as the outsized

"baby boom cohort" first increased the demand for schools and teachers and then left in its wake an oversupply of educational facilities.

13   Because of social change, *members of different cohorts age in different ways* and are less likely than in a comparatively stable society to share and understand one another's experiences. By creating cohort differences in life-course patterns, social change exaggerates age differences and the problems of age cleavage, misunderstanding, and potential conflict.

14   The impact of social change on the age structure of people and roles exacerbates social problems but also gives continuing *opportunity to correct problems of age and aging*.

15   Some problems can be reduced or prevented through changes in the aspirations or capacities of *people* at particular ages. For example, middle-aged doctors or lawyers can be retrained to be on a par with recent graduates, or old people can be made to realize that not all of their physical handicaps are untreatable.

16   Some problems can be alleviated by dispelling negative stereotypes and by bringing to the attention of policy makers the hidden, but widespread, difficulties of age and aging.

17   Judicious interventions are also possible in the age structure of *roles*. Unplanned changes are continually underway as some roles disappear, new ones emerge, and others are redefined. Deliberate changes can aid in solving particular problems through role redefinition, or through raising or lowering age criteria for entering or leaving a role.

THE ECONOMICS OF AGING

Juanita Kreps

Juanita Kreps, Secretary of Commerce, has long been concerned with economic problems confronting the aging. She has served as consultant to the U. S. Senate Special Committee on Aging and as vice-president of The National Council on the Aging. Focusing on the economic prospects and the concept of retirement as the new reality, she challenges: "What do we intend for ourselves when aged and what are we to provide for those who are already old?"

Every American—whether poor or rich, black or white, uneducated or college-trained—faces a common aging problem: how can he provide and plan for a retirement period of indeterminate length and uncertain needs? How can he allocate earnings during his working lifetime so that he not only meets current obligations for raising children and contributing to the support of the aged parents but has something left over for his own old age?

The economic situation of the aged today speaks ill of the solutions to this problem in the past. But people now old were hampered in their efforts to prepare for their future by two world wars, a major depression and life-time earnings which were generally low. The important question persists: what are the prospects for the future aged?

What do we intend for ourselves when aged and what are we to provide for those who are already old? How are older people, now and in the future, to share in our economic abundance?

If you were born in this century, you are likely to take your retirement for granted. For several years prior to retirement you have prepared for this new phase of life, and throughout your working years regular deductions from your paycheck have contributed to the retirement income you will receive.

However, this concept of retirement is relatively new. The possibility of living for eight or ten years on accumulated savings, annuities, and other assets was remote when your grandfather reached 65. His life expectancy was lower than yours, so living to be 75 was less likely. Also, he probably had no monthly income from a pension fund or annuity. With no source of income except his earnings, he continued on the job as long as he could. Because a much larger proportion of the labor force was engaged in farming, most older men could find work for as many or as few hours as they wished.

During the first half of the twentieth century this picture changed markedly. The industrial pace quickened after the Civil War, gaining further momentum in the early decades of the new century to transform the nature of our economy—and the type of work men did. The transformation continued through two world wars.

By 1950 these changes were reflected not only in the way men worked but also in the way they did not work—that is, in their retirement from work. Between the beginning of the century—when two out of three men 65 or over were in the labor force—and its midpoint—when only one out of three older men worked—retirement came to be the established pattern. Now among the 65 and over males, only about one in four continue work.

Other changes have taken place. The birth rate has declined and life expectancy has risen; the result is an aging population. This aging leads to new considerations of the special problems of older persons. The capacity to deal with these problems has emerged from another economic factor in the transformation: the increasing output and income of our economy. The first half of the twentieth century witnessed such vast improvements in national product level that the American economy can now "afford" to retire workers at 65 (or even 62) without jeopardizing output. In fact, our economy not only can afford retirement; it apparently requires it.

I

The practice of retirement, as well as the shortened workweek and later entrance into the labor force, are basically the result of increased productivity. Each development is made possible by the growth in output which enables man to produce enough goods and services to meet his family's needs in less than a 12-hour day and in a working life considerably shorter than that which began at age

14 and ended with death. It is possible, with modern production techniques and capital equipment, not only to provide for your current needs, but also to acquire claims against goods in the form of retirement income.

In a less productive economy, retirement is not possible. With lower productivity, it is not possible to subsist on the product earned in a short workweek, nor is it possible to keep children in school until 18. Output per manhour is so low that all persons are required to work practically all their lives. Leisure in any form invites starvation.

The contrast between these two extremes points up the advantages of living in a technologically advanced economy: higher productivity, hence higher living standard; a lowered workweek and thus more leisure; elimination of child labor and improved education. The dual effect in all cases is more goods and services and more free time in which to enjoy them.

But leisure time provided by retirement, although arising from the same set of circumstances that creates the shorter workweek and postpones age of entrance to the labor force, may not be greeted with quite the same enthusiasm. For many reasons, a sudden and complete withdrawal from work may prove a difficult adjustment. Full-time leisure may strike the new retiree as a dubious blessing, and the accompanying drop in income may restrict his leisure activities.

Ideally, if the retiree could balance his desire for leisure with his desire for earned income and continued participation on the job, he would probably retire gradually rather than suddenly at 65.

II

Complete withdrawal from work at age 65—or earlier, in many cases (about half the men who have retired in recent years have done so before age 65)—presents one with an abundance of free time but often, also, a dearth of income. This sharp drop in income that accompanies retirement is hard to adjust to. For although living expenses may fall a bit, they surely will not decline as much as income.

Needless to say, many of the elderly who are now poor were poor during their working years as well. Their education and skill levels were low, their job opportunities scant. For those persons who are disadvantaged in their capacities to earn adequate incomes, society must make an important decision: how much will it contribute to their economic well-being? Are we willing to guarantee some minimum family income, in order to assure all persons the basic necessities, whether or not they "earn" these necessities by working? This question is one of the key domestic issues of the moment.

But such a minimum guarantee, even if it comes about, does not resolve the issues relating to income in retirement. Retirement income will be a problem to all of us. And there is no reassuring evidence that those of us now in middle age, and at the peak of our earnings, will be any better off, relative to these present incomes, when we retire. It is true we will all have a social security benefit, and that it will be higher. But in comparison with the standard of living we are now accustomed to, the contrast may well be just as extreme.

The problem lies, not just in low earnings during worklife, but in the allocation of one's total income throughout life. We are paid for working, and our tendency is to assume that all we earn in a year is available for consumption that year. We may save, true: we pay for homes, we save for children's education, for next summer's vacation (or more likely, for last summer's vacation). But we save very little, privately, for retirement and even when we do, we must have some investment know-how in order to have the savings grow with the rise in living costs.

Payroll taxes for social security purposes are a form of saving for retirement, of course. We pay for the benefits of today's retirees; in return our own benefits will be financed by those who work when we are in retirement. But the amount we save is limited, and the benefit is accordingly low. Moreover, we resist a higher payroll tax because we are reluctant to forego today's consumption in favor of tomorrow's.

Until we do smooth the income a good bit more, retirement incomes will continue to be substantially below earnings. The smoothing can occur in any one of several ways: by spreading work into the later years, particularly through part-time jobs; by private savings and annuities; by heavier contributions to public retirement benefits. Different people would elect different options.

But they amount to the same thing in one sense. They all recognize the need for considering some reasonable balance of work and income through the lifespan, as opposed to a concentration of work and earnings in the middle years. Recognition of retirement as a relatively new lifestage, which requires its own financial arrangements, is obviously necessary, and just as obviously lacking. The implications of this lifestage for public policy have not been fully accepted; similarly, each of us needs to reexamine this perception of what lies ahead. In economic terms, the best summary of intergenerational relations comes from Kenneth Boulding: "One of the things we know for certain about any age group is that it has no future. The young become middle-aged and the middle-aged become old. . . . Consequently, the support which the middle-aged give to the young can be regarded as the first part of a deferred exchange, which will be consummated when those who are now young become middle-aged and support those who are now middle-aged who will then be old. Similarly, the support which the middle-aged give to the old can be regarded as the consummation of a bargain entered into a generation ago." It is this bargain that we made a generation ago that we are as a nation, sometimes guilty of neglecting.

III

Suppose we are concerned here with the handling of a man's own earnings through his worklife, and with making arrangements for these earnings to be apportioned in some optimal fashion, given the timing of his family's consumption needs. To make it simple (and to spread a bit of cheer), let us suppose that we are all young —so young, in fact, that we are just now entering the labor force. Suppose further that we are all male (which is a less cheerful assumption, at least to those of us who are not male; I trust it would be an equally unsatisfactory arrangement for those of you who are). This eliminates the sex difference in length of worklife, and allows us to speak of, say, a 40- to 45-year working period, from age 20 or 25 to 65.

The problem is one of accommodating the necessary variations in consumption that go with changes in family size and composition, and eventually, with retirement, subject of course to the overall constraint imposed by total earnings.

Imagine a two-dimensional diagram in which the vertical axis measures income, or consumption, in current dollars. Horizontally, visualize that we are indicating age, from the point of entry into the labor force, to death. By assumption, all of us are age 20, and have just taken our first jobs. You will see also that we all die promptly at age 80, thereby lending a certain order to things, which the actuaries may find reassuring.

What is the usual relationship between age and income level? We know from the data that the average income of the 30- to 40-year-old male in most any occupation or profession is higher than the average income of the 20- to 30-year-old; and that in most cases, the income of the 40- to 50-year-old is higher still. But alas, the average money income of males who are in the last decade of worklife, 55 to 65, is lower than that for the age group just younger. Thus, it is often pointed out that our incomes rise until we are in our 50s, then decline gradually until retirement, at which point they fall to perhaps one-half or a third.

But this conclusion is incorrect. It is true that at any point in time, a picture of average money income in an occupational group is an inverted U, that slopes upward more gently than it declines, then drops sharply and levels out for retirees. But this does not describe the usual behavior of a particular man's income through his lifetime. His income is likely to rise throughout his worklife, reflecting the impact both of experience and economic growth.

How, then, can we expect our money incomes to behave—those of us who are now a mere 20—as we move through worklife? Not, surely, as the cross-sectional data indicate. Rather, we can reasonably expect that our highest incomes will accrue to us at the end of worklife. True, when we are receiving our highest income (at age 64, or thereabouts), that income will be lower than the income of our colleagues of age 60, if things continue as they are. But their incomes are higher than ours, on the average, not because ours have declined, but because they entered the labor force in a later, more productive era than we, and thus they will have higher incomes at any age, than we did at that age.

If our income does in fact continue to rise up to the point of retirement, what will happen to our consumption expenditures? Will we raise our living standards to absorb the rise in incomes as these increases occur? Turning to the two-dimensional diagram, will the consumption line follow along with the income line, rising gradually up to age 65, when both drop to some fraction—say, half, of their previous levels? Or is it more likely that a significant portion of the income in late worklife will be saved for consumption during the nonworking years?

The latter would seem reasonable, at first glance. In most families, the last child has finished school and left home by the time the father is in his early 50s, leaving a 10- to 15-year period of high earnings and somewhat reduced living costs. It would be possible to spread these earnings into the retirement period, thereby reducing the extent of the drop in consumption which now marks the withdrawal from the work force.

In model terms, we might suppose that the couple who has reached age 50, and sent their last child off to seek his fortune, might choose to hold their consumption levels fixed at the level reached at that age, in order to spread their next 15 years of earnings through the remainder of their lives. If one saved all increments in income after age 50 (in addition to whatever he was able to save during the earlier periods of heavier expenses), he would have approximately 15 years of saving and 15 years in which his income was supplemented by those savings, plus interest.

Depending on his time preference for consumption goods, he might elect to take an even more stringent position. He could say, for example: "My wife and I want to suffer no drop in our level of living at retirement; we want to expend our income in such a way as to allow the same standard during each of the last 30 years of our lives, even if we must reduce our expenditures at present. The question is then, what annual outlay is appropriate, given our projected earnings during the remaining 15 years of worklife, the expected level of social security benefits and private pensions, and the value of any equities, such as a home, on which we might draw?"

Long-range budgeting is indicated by a new consumption curve which rises along with income (although lying slightly below income) up to age 50. Then, whereas income continues to rise for another 15 years and then drop to one-half or one-third, where it is stable for the remainder of life, consumption levels off at age 50 (or even drops somewhat at that age), remaining constant through the remainder of the lifespan.

Needless to say, such an attempt would be impeded by many uncertainties. At what rate will earnings rise? What is a reasonable guess on the level of social security benefits? What of the differences in expenses as between working and nonworking years? How much must one allot to each successive year in order to offset price change and thus allow real income to be stabilized? Perhaps most serious of all is the implied assumption that such a reallocation of consumption expenditures would solve the income problems of the low income elderly, whose earnings late in worklife are meager, as during their earlier years. No amount of retiming of consumption is effective in these cases; transfers of income, or improved job skills and job opportunities are the only alternatives.

None of us here are in that position. I suspect, moreover, that none of us expect to have any real income squeeze in our retirement years. This expectation may be borne out, of course. I would argue only that most people do in fact face such a crunch which, along with the other infirmities of old age, seems more than we should accept without protest.

Biologists and medical researchers are constantly improving the physical quality of life in the 60s and 70s. And despite the common complaint that they are merely keeping the very old alive longer and longer, thereby creating problems for the families of the aged, the primary thrust of their research would add life to years, not the reverse. Without adequate incomes in old age, however, physical stamina and intellectual vitality will have limited outlets. It follows either that worklife must be extended or some substantial reapportionment of the income earned in prior years must be arranged.

PART III

AGEISM:
The Last Segregation

AGING: REAL AND IMAGINARY
Alex Comfort

Dispeller of myths and champion of old age, Dr. Alex Comfort, author of the best-seller *A Good Age,* is always a joy to read.

Aging comes in two forms: physical and sociogenic.

Physical aging expresses itself with the passing of time in limited physical changes—skin wrinkling, hair graying—and a growing liability to system failure, that is, ill health. The muscles weaken somewhat and there is a real but practically unimportant slowing in some mind-body reactions, which the older person more than compensates by the use of experience. In the absence of ill health, such as untreated high blood pressure, aging has no adverse effect on intelligence or learning power; sexual response is normally life-long in both sexes; and working capacity, unless it is impaired by ill health, is retained and performance in it is high.

We do not know the cause of the physical aging process in mammals, including man, and I will discuss it here only to make one point. Its rate of progress, measured by the changes just mentioned and by the mortality curve, is highly stable, and when decline occurs it is multiform. The characteristic pathological change of aging is an increase in the number of pathological changes. A man who dies at 40 will usually have one cause of death, a man who dies at 90 will have 13 to 15, on the average. Over the last 100 years, the mean length of life has vastly increased through medical and economic advances, but the life span has not altered. What has happened is simply that more people reach the age of systems failure. We get old at the age that Moses and Pharaoh got old, and in much the same way.

Science may affect human longevity favorably in two ways—by suppressing causes of premature death or by postponing the aging process which causes our liability to disease and death to increase logarithmically with the passage of time. The first of these two influences has already meant that in privileged countries more people reach the so-called "specific age" (75–80 years), but it does not alter that age appreciably. The second, which is now in the stage of active research, aims at postponement or slowing of the aging process itself.

Advanced societies are now approaching the practical limits of public health in prolonging life. While the expectation of life at birth has increased steadily over the last century, the expectation at 65 years has changed little if at all, having risen by only two years since 1901. It is computed that the total cure of the three leading causes of natural death in the United States (cardiovascular, cerebrovascular, and malignant disease), while greatly beneficial to those who contract them young, would only increase the mean expectation of life at age 65 by 2.5 years. The same applies to all piecemeal therapeutic, supportive, medical, or social measures. The patching-up of single age-dependent conditions is accordingly both costly and of limited usefulness in producing further years of full-quality life.

Biological interference with the actual rate of aging, however, has already been carried out in rats and mice and is now ready for test in man as soon as aging rates can be measured nonactuarially in the individual and in the short term, thereby avoiding impracticable 70 to 80 year experiments. We know how to do it, though not precisely why it works or what it works on. It is virtually certain that such experiments will be begun within the next decade. A lot depends on the funding of the new National Institute on Aging, which will be the equivalent in this field as NASA is in space research. The effect of success in transferring existing rodent techniques to man would be that a treated man of, say, 80 would have, for a 10-year gain, the same health and the same disabilities as he would have had at age 70.

We can expect that within the lifetime of some of us, and given adequate funding for experimental gerontology, and in particular of the new National Institute, physical aging in man will be susceptible to some—perhaps considerable—postponement. This would be not by removing single diseases, but by integral interference with a rate mechanism. Some of us will be Moses rather than Joshua at the present rate of funding.

SOCIOGENIC AGING

Physical aging of the kind which can be attacked in this way accounts for perhaps 25 per cent of the picture of aging that we see in American society. Seventy-five per cent is accounted for by another type of aging, sociogenic aging, which has no physical basis. It is the role which our folklore, prejudices, and misconceptions about age impose on "the old." It requires no scientific discoveries to abolish this aspect of aging, simply a change of attitude, and that, in a society in love with the technological fix, is harder to obtain. It is on this kind of aging—imaginary or imposed aging—that I intend to concentrate.

If we insist that there is a group of people which, on a fixed calendar basis, becomes unintelligent, asexual, unemployable, and crazy, the people so designated will be under pressure to be unintelligent, asexual, unemployable, and crazy. The fact that no person becomes any one of those things by virtue of age alone is beside the point. The fact that many if not most older people obstinately fail to be as we describe them is beside the point. As they are well known to be unemployable we don't let them work; as they are known to be asexual, and it is embarrassing if they are not, we can herd them into institutions which deny them elementary privacy; as they are known to be liable to go crazy, symptoms due to infection or overmedication or simple exasperation with a society which demeans the older citizen are interpreted as senility. In fact fewer old people are crazy than at earlier ages: about nine per thousand over 65 need psychiatric hospitalization, and that includes chronic brain disease, alcoholism, the whole lot.

Old people become crazy for three reasons—because they were crazy when young, because they have an illness, or because we drive them crazy. Prejudice not only has a bad effect on its victims; in this case it corrupts us all. Other victims of vulgar prejudice suffer from it lifelong, but we all become old. One wonders what Archie Bunker would feel about immigrants if he knew that on his 65th birthday he would turn into a Puerto Rican. White racists don't turn black, black racists don't become white, male chauvinists don't become women, anti-semites don't wake up and find themselves Jewish—but we have a lifetime of indoctrination with the idea of the difference and inferiority of the old, and on reaching old age we may be prejudiced against ourselves.

Most of our institutions are unwittingly geared to age prejudice as in the past they were geared to race prejudice and sex prejudice. In determining needs and abilities, age is quite as irrelevant as is race. The old have earned entitlements, certainly—the right to a pension which doesn't require idleness as a condition of payment is one of them. Administratively the right way to handle the "old" is to stop treating them as a problem, when they are in fact a resource, and begin treating them as people, the same people they were, and which they now are. The only relevant administrative feature of oldness is the increased risk of ill health and decreased mobility which goes with it. However, ill health is, after all, not confined to age, and the needs of an old sick person do not differ from those of a young person who is equally sick. It would be both scientifically and politically sound to strike age out of the reckoning, except for purposes of earned entitlements, and to concentrate on needs.

There are in fact encouraging signs that the obnoxious stereotype of age, at least when put, as we have put it, at its blackest, is already out of date. In the study conducted for The National Council on the Aging by Louis Harris & Associates,* 74 per cent of the public now see "the old" as friendly and warm, 64 per cent as wise from experience, 41 per cent as physically active, 35 per cent as effectual and proficient, 29 per cent as alert, but only 21 per cent as adaptable and only 5 per cent as sexually active. This implies a substantial shift from myth to reality. Unfortunately, many public attitudes are still predicated on the myth. Significantly, while 82 per cent of people between 18 and 64 reckoned 65-and-over seniors to be friendly, only 25 per cent over 65 thought their contemporaries to be so, and while 5 per cent of the young thought them "very sexually active," the figure only rose to 6 per cent among the old for their view of old people generally but 11 per cent for themselves! In fact, although the poll showed a surprising proportion of American seniors to be contented and happy, both socially and economically, with the latter years of their lives, there is a hint that others have been imprinted with the negative attitude to their own age group which fear of aging generates.

All in all, however, the image that the public has of oldsters is generally much more negative than that which oldsters have of themselves, as individuals, whatever they think about the old as a group. Other people are openminded, bright, active, adaptable, and sexually active, but look upon "old folks" generally as not—

* *The Myth and Reality of Aging in America*, National Council on Aging, 1975.

"I'm fine, but then, I'm an exception." Individuals have as much confidence in themselves as do the young—it's "the others" who follow the stereotype. On the same line, one in three over 65 find their present life better than they had expected it would be, while only one in 10 find it worse, and then often because of unanticipated boredom, sickness, or bereavement.

So there are two put-down and alarmist views of aging in America, one generated by thoughtless ageism and the other by overstating the injustices inflicted on the old in order to reform them. I don't personally subscribe to either. Old age in America, except for those to whom society has never given their due share as human beings, is indeed more prosperous than in many, and perhaps most, other countries. On the other hand there are countries where the standard of living of the old is far lower but where their involvement in society and their sense of worth are greater. The changes which could remedy this deficit and evoke the full powers, intellectual and physical, which human beings possess lifelong, are changes of attitude. I can only reiterate that once an older person is seen, not as old first and a person second, but as a person who happens also to be old, and who is as he or she was, plus experience and minus the consequences of certain physical accidents of time, "social gerontology" will have made its point.

To remain in optimal health, old people need what people need —work to do, money to live on, a place to live in, and other people to care whether they live or die. At present they tend to get denied some or all of these by virtue of age.

Work is probably the biggest preservative of all. What we call retirement is in fact compulsory unemployment. Jefferson said that a man should not too long occupy the same ground, and there is a case for that view. He did not say that a man or woman should be excluded from working society into an unvalued, uncivic idleness which, with 20 years to kill, is as onerous to the rich as it is to the poor. If we persist in the fiction of the unemployability of the old, we shall shortly have 20 per cent of the population of some states compulsorily unoccupied for that reason alone—I leave you to do the cost-benefit analysis. In two world wars old people went back to work with excellent results to their health and to the national economy. In both those wars, other prejudices gave way to necessity—blacks and women gained new recognition as citizens, and kept some of it after the peace. The old gained little, because they alone of the victimized groups have a turnover, and each old generation has to start again.

Work—useful paid work, not dilution, make-work or cheap labor—is also a way to ensure that old people have enough to live on, except of course for the sick, who at any age, need public aid. Numerous senior employment schemes have shown that new jobs—often needing experience as a special qualification—are capable of creation for seniors without depleting the supply of jobs at earlier ages. Oldsters excel in reliability and teaching ability. The White Plains agency found 7,400 newly created jobs for seniors in three years. One big problem at the moment is the Social Security deduction, which penalizes work for many in low-income brackets. Even with this, most fit people would sooner work and remain in the community than be idle and drop out of it. But I want to stress the point that for modern gerontological planning, real lifelong employment, not play-work, is the key operation in preventing many of the social deficits of age, such as loneliness, boredom, mental disturbance, poverty, and deterioration. We would all deteriorate on the dole. Treating the old as a resource is also the answer to cost-effectiveness—and they are a resource.

TWENTY YEARS OF LEISURE?

I am frankly disturbed by the emphasis by some on "leisure" as the prescribed state of later life. Leisure is a con. It's like saying someone has been recycled by a shark. Leisure should occupy an occasional afternoon, not 20 years. I know that it is easy for successful academics, who will never retire so long as they are capable of lecturing, to underrate drudgery, but what the victim of drudgery wants is not Disneyland-type leisure, not compulsory leisure, but worthwhile work with dignity. We now have talk of leisure centers, even degree courses in organizing the leisure of others. I think we should be talking about occupation.

That obviously does not mean that occupation till death should be compulsory, either through financial pressure or social convention. I spoke of age as determining entitlement, and oldsters who are infirm or who merely choose to be unoccupied have their rights. Old citizens have as much right as the young, if not more, to sit on the porch or be hippies (in India they may traditionally elect to become religious contemplatives). But both those alternatives are occupations—they have goals, for even secession from the world is part of the world, and they rest upon choice, not rejection by society. Leisure in our culture means activity which is by definition goalless and irrelevant, and our emphasis on it childrenizes older people. In addition to the word "aged" I would suggest we try the practical effects of striking the word "leisure"—leisure facilities, leisure activities, leisure organizers—out of our planning vocabulary and substitute "continuing employment," "non-waste of human resources," "second career," "community service." As we age we do get nearer the end of our lives, and our toleration for triviality (which is what leisure means in our culture) should get less, not more.

As to income, the vast inequalities we see may disguise the fact that in America sheer poverty is not the leading curse of oldness. It is one leading curse, because people who have always been poor stay so when old, and many who were not poor become so with all the attendant subcurses of bad health, bad housing, low self-esteem, and exploitation which descend on poor people and can be remedied only by money. The percentage of statutory poor over the age of 65 has indeed tended to fall for some time. Social Security payments alone have gone up by 70 per cent in five years, though this does not allow for inflation, which has hit both savings and fixed-level interest and pensions (some of the worst distress recently was in retirees who were well off when they retired but are now on welfare). At retirement, income is on the average halved.

This, of course, assumes only statutory poverty standards. Between 25 per cent and 30 per cent of those over 65 are in social fact "poor." But the real curse of being old is still what amounts to ejection from a citizenship traditionally based on work—in other words, it is demeaning idleness, non-use, not being called on any longer to contribute, and hence being put down as a spent person of no public account, instructed to run away and play until death comes out to call us to bed. To this, chronic shortage of money is ancillary. This is something the Supplemental Security Income plan can't deal with—in fact, there is marginally more chance of useful social involvement for an old person in a ghetto than for a retired executive pitched into a life of uninterrupted golf or reading paperbacks, who may not recognize that he has been sold a second, non-civic, childhood along with the condominium key.

There is a school of thought which has argued that we can deal with all of the problems of age by making money available directly or indirectly to the old. I don't want to understate the poverty component in aging, especially in the case of those—minorities in particular—who having never had economic equality get even less in old age. Economic injustice is real. But the inequality of the old has another component which comes from the attitudes, the folklore, and the ejection which I've outlined, exactly as in the case of other prejudices: being poor and black has differed from being merely poor, and exactly the same applies to oldness, to the point where the richest of the old can't entirely buy their way out of penalties exacted by society. We need both social justice and a specific change of mind. If we have the attempt at one without the other we shall have the usual welfare and pacificatory approach which can aggravate the sense of exclusion from society under which the old labor. They may need some special programs to cover the decline which occurs, statistically, in health and mobility, but the right program is one which leaves them in their places doing their work, in their homes occupying their customary social space, buttressed in sickness by the same social support mechanisms which are required for sickness at any age. Organizations are sometimes against encouraging employment of oldsters for fear of dilution and risk to the job market. I think this is unfounded, because second-trajectory jobs will in most cases be new uses of the person, often in a teaching capacity, while continuation in work, against the present trend to early retirement, could benefit wages by reducing the need for tax-financed subsidies and by maintaining health to higher ages.

WORK AND DIGNITY

If old people were really socially incompetent, it would be reasonable to provide them with minimal care in institutions; if old people were really non-people, it would not matter that the institutions provided for them are often a disgrace, a ripoff, and generally run in a manner which would lead to prosecution if they were advertised as animal hospitals. Care of the old is rapidly becoming one of the fastest growing branches of organized crime.

Between 4 per cent and 5 per cent of seniors actually live in institutions. Some of these are excellent, but for the majority I doubt if "live" is the right word. California has a special team of gang-busters assigned to nursing home abuse.

We need some nursing homes, and these will undoubtedly have to be reformed—often by the prosecution of the people who run the existing institutions. Draft legislation to effect this reform is a great advance, but the right place for a person of any age is in his or her own home, and that is where most old people now live until overtaken by their final illness. Of those now institutionalized, a high proportion need not be so if they had minimal services available at home and were housed in suitable premises—the services needed are a dining hall, a shop, hairdressing, home-making, nursing, and a sickroom, or some combination of these. Senior groups could create these, given some low-interest capital, plus Titles V and VII. Top-income projects of this kind are already in being, and low-income projects cover about 150,000 Americans in varying degrees of adequacy.

Since sickness multiplies with age, old people are the major consumers of health care. They need accessible medical centers, public transit which makes it possible to visit those centers, accessible walk-in clinics or mobile offices—docmobiles—and doctors who make house calls. Of all citizens, they most need a health service. Their needs cannot be met, and are not being met, by a commercial sickness industry, and in-home care of this kind would vastly improve service while limiting medical fraud and costing a good deal less.

Another corollary is the high-priority introduction of geriatrics as a speciality in medical schools. In the past geriatrics has been defined as "treating old folks who don't pay." Now it is undergoing popularity as an easy and lucrative way of tapping Medicare. In fact, proper geriatric medicine is a highly skilled branch of internal medicine, in which diagnostics, therapeutics, and pharmacology differ significantly from that for younger ages. It requires to be learned, but once learned it is one of the most medically rewarding fields of practice. Every old person, already entitled to Medicare, should have access to a primary care physician, part of whose training has been in geriatrics, and to a geriatric specialist for referral, backed by a geriatric assessment hospital of teaching standard. There are few places in the United States where this is now true.

In sum, enough money to live on is partly a consequence of employment. American seniors are among the better off in the world income league, but mostly through entitlements. Being valued, remaining a person and a citizen, is also employment-linked and dependent on non-segregation, especially in a world where the family no longer provides a constant context for the old. We sometimes lament this, and forget that a resentful or uncaring family can be as bad an environment for personhood as the worst institution. Contrary to belief, as we get older we need relatives less and friends more.

ACTION BY LEGISLATION

I do not wish to deliver homilies. State government officials have practical concerns related to policy and how it can be implemented and financed. What I'm asking those officials to do is to shed, if they have it, any previous image of oldness, and concentrate on "old" persons simply as persons, who have been around for x years, and to see those persons as unchanged, unaffected by any rite of passage, and normally expecting them either to continue at their occupation for life, making changes if health obliges them, or to enjoy a retirement of two weeks and then commence a second trajectory of employment which will last them until they die. I want officials to see them continuing in education and experience; I want officials to see them living in their homes, in the community, with any federal or state support facilities they need on health grounds, or to support physical mobility, and with reference made to their age solely for census purposes. This is the norm of aging. Special programs will be for the exceptions.

There are strong political reasons to think this way. The "old" over the years, like the population as a whole, have become steadily healthier and more educated. The last generation included 1 million functional illiterates. The next lot of "old" will be more accurately informed about aging (what it does and does not involve), more educated, more vocal, and higher in expectation than those now old—they will, incidentally, include most of us. They will make up as much as 20 per cent of the electorate in some areas. Unlike women, they will not have to demand a vote; unlike blacks, they will not have a struggle for registration—they are voters and they are registered. They also, once they realize it, have at present the chief requisite for campaigning, namely compulsory leisure. There is one employment one can recommend now to every senior American unemployed by reason of seniority, and that is political activity. One cannot as yet predict whether they will act through the party they have always supported or through ad hoc organizations.

One medical fact—that we now treat even minimal hypertension throughout life—will probably reduce even the relatively small number of mental incompetents we now find among the old. We shall not really have reached an ideal condition with regard to age until sectional action by the old is no longer needed. At present it is needed, consciousness-raising is needed, and education is needed to correct ingrained superstitions, some of them, like the supposed decline in intelligence with age, still enshrined in old scientific literature.

Action by legislation is also needed. Educational change is needed—we need to turn around the education industry to make education lifelong and geared to second trajectories. Reorientation of the media is needed, if only to inform older people.

Reformers are people who want to alter the attitudes of society. Radicals are angry people who want to alter the attitudes of society. American institutions have the immense advantage that they are alterable, albeit slowly, through democracy and legitimate "direct action." Attitudes require other means of reform, but when they change, societies change with them. There is basically no rational interest which would be infringed upon by western society recognizing the irrelevance to a person's rights of the length of time he or she has lived; rather the reverse is true and in times of external emergency we adopt that position, only regressing to folklore in times of business as usual. It is inevitable that older citizens to come, who will be ourselves grown old, will alter this backsliding. Prudent forecasts will recognize this certainty, whether they are the forecasts of business, government, or the political parties. Like racism, ageism has had its day. "The old" to come will not acquiesce in it. The reforms they demand will not disrupt but strengthen the society on which they are imposed, and will add to its economic wealth and democratic legitimacy, however little that society likes them at the time.

WHAT IS AGEISM?

Edith Stein

Ageism has been called the ultimate prejudice, the last discrimination, the cruelest rejection. Edith Stein's crisp, succinct poem says much about the consequences of this social sickness.

It's when an older person falters for a moment because s/he is unsure of herself and is immediately charged with being "infirm."

an older person is constantly "protected" and her thoughts interpreted.

an older person forgets someone's name and is charged with senility and patronized.

an older person is expected to "accept" the "facts of aging."

an older person misses a word or fails to hear a sentence they are charged with "getting old," not with a "hearing difficulty," which many young people have.

young and old have a power relationship.

an older person is called "dirty" because s/he shows sexual feeling or affection to one of either sex.

an older person is called "cranky" when s/he is expressing a legitimate distaste with life as so many young do.

an older person is charged with being "like a child" even after society has ensured the fact that s/he shall be dependent, helpless and powerless as are kids!

MYTHS AND REALITIES OF LIFE
FOR OLDER AMERICANS

Louis Harris & Associates, Inc.

How do Americans perceive and feel about older citizens, and how do older Americans regard themselves? These questions form the basis of an extensive study undertaken by Louis Harris & Associates, commissioned by The National Council on the Aging.

Here is an invaluable source in helping to separate the myth from the reality of aging in America today. Among the revelations of this pioneering study are:

Most older people feel that their condition in life is *better,* economically and socially, than the general public believes it to be (despite the fact that millions of older people are in desperate straits).

Most older Americans have both the desire and the potential to be productive, contributing members of society.

Old people are themselves primary victims of stereotyped ways of perceiving aging and the aged.

Eighty-six per cent of Americans agree that people should not be forced to retire because of age.

To understand the image which both younger and older Americans have of the elderly and to assess the reality of old age in our society, The National Council on the Aging, Inc. (NCOA), commissioned Louis Harris & Associates, Inc., to conduct a major, in-depth survey. The survey, conducted during the late spring and early summer months of 1974, was funded by a substantial grant from the Edna McConnell Clark Foundation, with additional funding from the Florence V. Burden Foundation.

As an important part of NCOA's program aimed at improving the public understanding of what roles of 65-plus Americans are and can be, the survey had a twofold purpose:

1) To examine the public's attitudes toward older Americans and their perceptions of what it is like to be old in this country today.

2) To document older Americans' views and attitudes about themselves and their personal experiences of old age.

For the study, trained Harris interviewers conducted a total of 4,254 in-person household interviews, including a representative cross-section of the American public 18 years of age and over. Interviewees were selected by random probability techniques, so that every household in the continental United States was guaranteed an equal chance of being drawn into the survey.

Scientific survey techniques, to provide adequate numbers of older people, both black and white, were used for detailed analysis of the group's conditions and attitudes. An additional cross-section of people 55 to 64 years of age was drawn into the sample, allowing an in-depth analysis of the group approaching retirement age. Where groups were sampled beyond their proportions in the U.S. population, they were weighted so that their natural proportions were represented.

The public 65 and over comprise 15% of the total adult population in this country, or approximately 21 million people. Compared to the 18–64 population, the older group has a higher proportion of women; considerably lower household incomes (a median of $4,800 compared to $12,400); numbers fewer blacks proportionately, and is far less well-educated (63% never graduated from high school compared to 26%). The Harris study showed like proportions of both groups in major metropolitan areas but a higher concentration of the 65-plus in rural areas.

OLD AGE AND PUBLIC ATTITUDES

THE BEST YEARS OF A PERSON'S LIFE

Few in the general public single out the later years as the most desirable period of life. Instead, substantial numbers (69%) chose the teens, twenties or thirties. Very few feel that way about the sixties (2%) and less than 1% about the seventies. A higher percentage of those who have reached the later years themselves see the sixties and seventies as an optimal period, though still not many; overall, only one in 50 consider the later years as the prime of life.

Each period in life is valued for its own reasons: The teens for limited responsibility, a time to enjoy life and have fun; the twenties for these reasons as well as a time to develop ambitions and set goals; the thirties as a time of greater wisdom and maturity, to enjoy family life and settle down; the forties and fifties as a time to enjoy the family, of stability and financial security, to enjoy the wisdom and experience of maturity.

Those who singled out the sixties as "best" cited retirement, relieving pressures of productive roles, and fewer family responsibilities allowing for more individual freedom.

Leisure, Independence Among "Best"

Though few single out the later years as the best time of a person's life, the vast majority (all but 16%) could volunteer some positive aspects of growing old. According to both old and young nationwide, having more leisure is foremost, i.e., more free time to enjoy life, "do the things you've always wanted to do," travel, enjoy your spouse, family and friends. Independence and freedom from responsibilities are next, followed by retirement.

The 18–64 group mentions leisure and retirement significantly more often than the older group experiencing it, and responses varied dramatically by income, education and race.

THE WORST YEARS OF A PERSON'S LIFE

Though most of those surveyed did not identify the sixties and seventies as the *worst* years, about a third of both the younger (33%) and older (35%) named these as the least desirable periods. Second only to the seventies (21%), the 18–64 group saw the teens (20%) as the most difficult period.

Just as certain decades were valued, those who singled out the teens through fifties as the worst periods had their reasons: The teens as unsettled and tending to overestimate your own wisdom; the twenties as also unsettled, of financial problems, difficulties in adjusting to married life and raising children. The thirties' drawbacks were seen as the responsibility of raising children and financial problems; however, the precursors of aging, such as bad health and feeling older, were seen as the worst aspects of the forties and fifties.

Have Common Drawbacks

Those in the younger group choosing the sixties and seventies as bleak periods associated those years with common drawbacks of "bad health, illness," financial problems and "not being able to get around, do much or be involved." Particular problems were given for each decade: For the sixties, bad health (40%), retirement and difficulty in finding jobs (31%) and financial problems (20%); for the seventies, bad health (41%), loneliness (20%) and being dependent, a burden.

Those over 60 who designated the sixties and seventies as the worst periods cited such things as "not much to look forward to with the kids gone," "not enough money to get what you need, not to mention what you want," "too feeble to go out and have any fun" and the death of loved ones.

Bad Health, Loneliness Among "Worst"

While only one in three singled out the sixties and seventies as the worst years of life, the public as a whole (excepting 6%) could describe what they consider the "worst things about being over 65."

For those under 65, such feelings were expressed as "perhaps loneliness, facing the fact of the inevitable," "boredom and limited income," "no longer feeling productive," "your health starts to get bad," "you don't have as many friends as when you were younger," to be "left alone and have to be sent to a rest home."

From personal experience, among the worst things about being over 65 are:

"At 65, I could do as much work as I could at 35 but no one wanted me."

"I wanted to work but my heart gave out."

"The younger generation just doesn't care about the older generation."

"Not having a husband to take you around."

"Financial problems are the worst."

When the responses were coded and tabulated, poor health came out far ahead of other responses as the major drawback of old age, followed by loneliness, financial problems, lack of independence, being neglected or rejected by the young and boredom. Yet, with the exception of poor health and forced retirement, those under 65, compared to those 65 and over, overstated every problem, indicating that young people's negative perceptions of old age are perhaps worse than the actual experience.

Women mentioned loneliness far more than men, not surprising since most outlive their husbands (53% to 15% of widowed men). Better educated (and therefore perhaps younger) people were more concerned with loneliness, financial problems, boredom and being neglected in old age than the less well-educated.

WHEN DOES OLD AGE OCCUR?

Is there some arbitrary cut-off point at which a person stops being middle-aged and becomes old? About half of those interviewed thought so, but nearly as many used functional criteria related to health, employment status, etc.

Notions of the average age at which a man or woman becomes old do not vary substantially by the age of the public. While those under 65 are slightly more likely to feel that 65 is the turning point than those 18–64, differences between the two age groups' responses were minimal (29% to 21%).

Staying active and involved may not keep a person young, as the old saying goes, but it can safely be said that it keeps a person's *image* young. Those who expressed the feeling that most people over 65 are useful in their communities were less likely to expect a person to become old before 65 than those who felt people over 65 were useless in the community.

Those who gave a fixed base for aging also attributed other conditions apart from chronology, primarily the visible signs of aging, such as getting sick, slowing down, wearing out, gray hairs and wrinkles (70% for men, 77% for women). Other reasons given were state of mind (feeling old), retirement, reaching a turning point, family and social changes. The latter were considered more responsible for old age among women, and retirement was felt to age men more often than women.

Very Serious Problems Seen

Poor health. Fear of crime. Loneliness. Not enough money to live on. Feeling neglected, dependent or burdensome. Boredom. Lack of adequate medical care. Too little education. Not enough to do to keep busy. Too few friends. Poor housing. Not enough job opportunities. Lack of transportation. Inadequate clothing.

That these problems, and a host of others, do indeed exist for many older Americans was substantiated by the survey of people 65 and over. However, in addition to measuring the experience of old age in America, a major purpose of the survey was to measure the expectations; that is, what the public, young and old, think life is like for "most people over 65."

Show Wide Discrepancies

When the problems attributed to the 65-plus were compared to what older people themselves identify as very serious problems, there were in most cases enormous discrepancies in degree:

Fear of crime (23% to 50% of public)
Poor health (21% to 51%)
Not enough money to live on (15% to 62%)
Loneliness (12% to 60%)
Not enough medical care (10% to 44%)
Not enough education (8% to 20%)
Not feeling needed (7% to 54%)
Not enough to do to keep busy (6% to 37%)

Older people may have been reluctant to identify their problems as "very serious." Yet, when the analysis went a step further and included definitions of "somewhat serious" in personal experience, there still remained, in most cases, considerable differences between the actual experience and the severity of problems expected by the public at large.

Lack of Mobility Sore Point

In another area, that of mobility, substantial minorities of the 65-plus complained of limitations imposed by danger of being robbed or attacked on the street (24% to 46% of public expectations); difficulty of walking and climbing stairs (22% to 44%); general health (20% to 41%); no buses or subways available (15% to 39%); not having a car or being able to drive (14% to 38%); cost of buses and subways (9% to 33%).

Most striking of the findings is that, while the public 18–64 and the public 65 and over do not disagree substantially in their evaluations of the problems of "most people over 65," many of the

65-plus group do not consider these problems as very serious for themselves personally but for others of their peer group.

When the 18–64 group was asked to rate the same questions personally as very serious, somewhat serious or hardly at all a problem, with only a few exceptions the responses were nearly identical to the older public. Putting myths aside, the personal testimony shows that the problems for older people, except for health and fear of crime, are comparable to those of younger people.

The message emerges here that the older public, like the young, has bought the negative images of old age, apparently assuming that life is really tough for most people over 65 and that they are really exceptions to the rule.

The conclusions: Problems do exist for older people. But the same problems do not exist for all older persons, substantiating the fact that the aged are a mixed group. Nor should having a problem be confused with *being* a problem.

Generalizations about the elderly as an economically and socially deprived group can do the old a disservice, presenting them merely as a problem and not as part of the solution of society's problems. As a group for whom there is little social and economic demand, the older population also may lose self-esteem, with deleterious effects to society.

An exclusive emphasis on problems of old age can do the young a disservice, as well, turning them away from an appreciation of the talents and energies that older people can still contribute and, perhaps, giving a false image of what life will be like for them in the future.

PREPARATION FOR OLD AGE

As shown earlier, not only the young take a negative view of old age; the older public has also bought the myths. Yet older people, who see old age as related to having problems, consider themselves as individual exceptions to the rule, since life is not so bad for them.

A third of persons 65 and over in the survey said that their life now was better than they had expected it to be when younger; almost half said it was about the way they expected, and only 11% reported it worse than expected.

However, income and race more than age affect the tendency to feel that life hasn't measured up to expectations. Twice as many people with incomes $7,000 and below as those with incomes $15,000 and over feel life is worse than expected. Among the black elderly, only 22% felt life was better than expectations as opposed to 37% of the whites.

Reasons for believing that life is better than expected included financial security, good family and/or marriage, generally a good life with few problems and health good or better than expected.

For those who felt that life had turned out worse than expected, reasons are primarily separation from family and spouse or poor health; only a small percentage cite financial problems. Of the wide variety of other reasons given, total percentages were minute.

STEPS TO PREPARE FOR LATER YEARS

Majorities of the total public, young and old, agree on seven "very important steps people should take" in preparing for their later years:

Ensure medical care is available (88%)

Prepare a will (81%)

Build up savings (80%)

Learn about pensions and Social Security benefits (80%)

Buy your own home (70%)

Develop hobbies, leisure-time activities (64%)

Decide whether you want to move or stay where you are (50%)

In addition, three in 10 (31%) feel it is very important to "plan new part-time or full-time jobs."

By and large, the older public has taken the steps they consider are very important to prepare for later years. In four areas, however, the older public seems less prepared than it would like to be.

Regret Lack of Savings

More people said they felt it was important to build up savings than had been able to do so (85% to 73%). The same was true of preparing a will (79% to 65%), planning new part-time or full-time jobs (26% to 16%) and enrolling in retirement preparation or counseling programs (19% to 8%).

Only half considered deciding whether you want to move or

continue to live where you are as a very important step, yet many (72%) report already having taken that step, a response showing the greatest net difference. Perhaps having already done so, the step becomes less important in contrast to other steps and decisions still to be made.

The lower the income, the less prepared an older person appears to be for later years. Leisure-time activities have not been developed throughout life, savings have not been built up. A fairly substantial percentage of elderly with incomes of $3,000 and under (79%) feel sure of having medical aid available, though fewer than in the higher income bracket immediately above, $3,000 to $6,999 (90%).

Blacks in general are less well-prepared for old age than older whites; less than half as many blacks as whites have built up savings, 25% more older whites than blacks own their own homes. Two areas where the black elderly appear better prepared for their later years than older whites: Higher number of blacks than whites have talked to older people about what it's like to grow old and have moved in with their children or other relatives.

Recognizably, a number of variables are related to being comfortable and secure in later life: Income alone is not a sufficient indicator; total assets and measures taken in preparation for later years are equally important. Many of the steps relating to preparation for making old age better are part of younger life as well. But being well-off in younger life does not insure being well-off in later life.

Would Have Done Differently

While substantial numbers of those 65 and over surveyed did take important steps to prepare for their later years and many (43%) doubted they could have done more, more have regrets that they couldn't foresee well enough what it would be like today to prepare differently.

They would have tried to save more, held on to medical insurance, made investments or bought property, tried to get more education or a different or better job for higher pay, better pension and Social Security benefits. Some regret retiring too early.

Of those who feel they could have done nothing differently in preparing for old age, it was frequently *because* family responsibilities precluded getting a better education or training that would have turned the courses of their lives.

Yet, as previously mentioned, only one in 10 think old age has turned out worse than they expected, and three times that many that it turned out better.

THE EXPERIENCE OF BEING OLD

For comparative purposes, older people have been treated in this study as a homogeneous group with one factor in common: They all had passed their sixty-fifth birthday.

Yet, while society tends to view older people as a homogeneous entity, the findings of this study underscore not their homogeneity but rather their differences. While older people as a group may not suffer as seriously as the public thinks from a host of problems, both economic and psychological, certain subgroups of older people suffer far more seriously than others.

Similarly, while the 65 and over themselves have a far better self-image than the image attributed to them by the public at large, certain groups of older people have lower self-esteem than others. Measures of general life satisfaction among older people and over-all psychological well-being differentiate older people rather than unite them, in the same way that these same measures point out the differences among various groups of young people.

In other words, there appears to be no such thing as the typical experience of old age, nor the typical older person. At no point in one's life does a person suddenly stop being himself and turn into an "old person," with all the myths and stereotypes that the term involves. Instead, the social, economic and psychological factors that affect individuals when they are young often stay with them throughout their lives. Older people share with each other their chronological age, but factors more powerful than age alone determine the conditions of their later years.

SERIOUSNESS OF PROBLEMS FOR 65-PLUS

Income plays a key role in determining the degree of security and comfort in which older people live. The elderly poor (the 23% with household incomes under $3,000) understandably have a far harder time coping with life than those with higher incomes. Not only do the older poor have more difficulty making ends meet financially or securing adequate medical care, housing and clothing, their low economic position also appears to increase dramatically their sense of loneliness and rejection by society.

Increased fear of crime, serious health problems, limited budgets, etc., also severely decrease the mobility of the older poor, heightening their feelings of isolation. For about one in three of the elderly poor, serious health problems, not enough money and fear of crime make life a difficult struggle indeed.

Share Many Problems

Further study shows that the elderly poor share with younger persons of their income group many identical problems, except for a poorer health level. The older group does not, however, report experiencing the impact of financial problems with the intensity the younger group does. Older people appear to be less dissatisfied, perhaps because their expectations are more modest.

In every problem area except one (not enough education), the elderly black feel far more burdened by very serious problems than do the elderly white. They report more fear of crime (twice as much as the white group); more poor health; more than three times as many say not having enough money to live on is a very serious problem. The same proportions are shown in respect to not having enough medical care when compared with the white group. Of the 65 and over blacks, 23% report loneliness as a very serious problem, while only 11% of the whites in the same age group mention this.

Though income difference may partially explain this, even when income is equal for black and white groups the black group reports far more serious problems, twice as much in many cases and increasing with age. In three areas, problems stand out as more serious for the 80-plus group than for those in their sixties: Poor health, loneliness, not feeling needed.

Fear of Crime High

In only three areas does the over-65 group as a whole appear to suffer more serious problems than the young: Fear of crime, poor health and loneliness. Yet, even where results vary somewhat by age, they vary far more dramatically by income and race.

The older public has more problems in mobility than the young.

Obstacles which keep the old from getting where they want to go include danger of being robbed or attacked on the street, difficulty in walking and climbing stairs and general health. The lack of public transportation and not having a car or being able to drive affect the older public substantially more than the younger group. Among the 84 and over group, mobility problems appear more serious than among those in their late sixties.

The conclusions: Poverty, not old age, creates more very serious problems in people's lives; the poor young suffer just as much as the poor old, if not more. In the same way, race appears to generate more very serious problems than does age. With the exception of poor health, afflicting older blacks more than younger blacks, 18–64 blacks are afflicted with the same problems as those 65 and over, sometimes more seriously. In every area, blacks of all ages suffer problems more severely than whites.

Just as low-income groups suffer more seriously from every problem than the more affluent do, so do the less well-educated suffer more on all counts than the college-educated. The college-educated in today's 65-plus population represents a small proportion (7%); however, they report experiencing very serious problems less than the high school/some college category.

Education Prime Factor

Consistently, there seems a correlation at all ages between the level of education and the severity of problems experienced, holding true into older ages with different emphases: Health, fear of crime and loneliness predominate, while in younger ages severe problems relate to money, housing and education.

In only a few areas does a sex differential appear to affect the degree to which older people suffer from various problems:

Older women tend more than older men to report fear of crime as a very serious problem (also true of the younger group).

Loneliness appears to afflict older women more than older men; however, more women than men over 65 are widowed.

Older men complain slightly more than older women about lack of job opportunities, though differences at all ages are minimal.

Poor housing seems to affect younger women more than younger men, though older men and women appear to suffer in comparable numbers.

Thus, on the whole, key demographics such as income, race, sex and education are more important indicators of serious problems than age, though for the 80 and over, three problems are more serious than for those in the late sixties: Poor health, loneliness and not feeling needed.

SELF-IMAGE OF THE 65 AND OVER

While the public 65 and over generally tends to see itself individually in a far more positive light than the public at large, the self-esteem of older persons varies noticeably by key demographic variables.

In four of the seven image areas tested, income (and race) have very little effect on how older people view themselves; comparable numbers of the least affluent see themselves as very warm and friendly, very wise from experience, very bright and alert, very open-minded and adaptable. In determining their self-image about physical capabilities, income plays a more important role. The more affluent older people are more likely than the less affluent to see themselves as being very good at getting things done, very physically and sexually active, possibly showing a relation to good health as a functional result of better care concurrent with higher income.

The pattern holds in the younger group to a lesser extent: Those 18–64 with incomes under $7,000 view themselves as somewhat less physically active than those with incomes of $15,000 or more in the same age category (60% to 69%). Differences in physical activity between the less and the more affluent vary more dramatically in the 65 and over group.

Younger Blacks More Positive

Generally, older blacks tend to have a less positive self-image than older whites, coming closest in the image area perceptions of being very warm and friendly (69% to 73%), very wise from experience (63% to 70%) and very sexually active (11% to 10%). They rate themselves lower in being very bright and alert (54% to 69%), very open-minded and adaptable (51% to 64%), very good at getting things done (45% to 56%) and very physically active (31% to 50%).

Some of these same differences exist between younger blacks

and whites, to a much lesser extent. In some areas, younger blacks match younger whites in self-esteem, suggesting that recent movements toward raising black consciousness have successfully helped the self-image of younger blacks.

Better educated older people appear to have more positive self-images, both in the areas of mental and physical activity, than do the less well-educated. A lower percentage of those whose education ended with some high school or less see themselves as very bright and alert or physically active. Retirement tends to wash out income differences, while differences in educational background remain. However, the key variable of education also operates in younger groups.

More Women Widowed

In only one area does sex differentiation appear to have an impact on older people's self-image, that of sexual activity. More of the 65-plus men report they are very sexually active than the women of the same age group, who are more likely to be unmarried or widowed.

With 11% of the group 65 and over calling themselves very sexually active and 28% somewhat sexually active (and another 15% not sure how to answer the question), the myth of older people losing interest in sex is dissipated.

Social and Family Involvement

For the Harris study, the degree of contact those 65 and older had with relatives or close friends was compared to that of younger persons. With a range of 0 to 30 points given for responses, interviewees were asked if they had family or close friends and when they had last seen them in a stipulated period. A third question asked if there was someone they felt close enough to talk to about things that really concerned them.

Length and quality of contact were not measured, nor numbers of individuals, and casual social contacts or those related to community or job setting were omitted. The median scores for the 18–64 group and the 65-plus group were all nearly the same, with indications that the elderly are not nearly so isolated as the myths portray them to be.

In the true loneliness gauge, the third question, only 8% of the older group and 5% of the younger said they had no one "close enough to talk to" about things of real concern, and many of these said it wasn't necessary.

The responses indicate that younger people turn to their spouses, while older people talk to their children about what really bothers them.

COMMUNITY INVOLVEMENT

The public expected older people to spend far more time at sedentary, passive activities than older people say they do. Though older people from their responses are as equally involved as those under 65 in many activities, economic and physical limitations make the facilities providing leisure time or recreational activities out of reach for many of the 65-plus.

Far fewer older people report having a library convenient, for instance, than do young people. Public parks, movies, sports events, live concerts or theater and museums all were mentioned as convenient places to go by younger people in large percentages. There was a marked difference in the older age group seeing any of these as "convenient."

Both old and young agreed the home of a neighbor or relative, church or synagogue and places to shop were convenient. With a higher level of education, more places were seen as convenient; still for the younger group parks, movies, sports events and live performances are more convenient than for the old. Location is less of a factor in accessibility than economic mobility, physical mobility and education.

With the younger public having substantially higher incomes than those 65 and over, it would be easy to attribute the lower attendance rate to income factors. However, the young with the same income level as older people attend cultural or artistic events far more often than older people. This is particularly true of movies, where attendance was reported at half the rate for the old compared with the young. The older group's lower attendance apparently is because they view facilities as less convenient.

RELIGIOUS INVOLVEMENT OF 65-PLUS

When questioned about church or synagogue attendance in the last year, the percentage of responses for the 18–65 group and the

65-plus group were close. Attendance at a church or synagogue, however, is slightly higher among the older public than among those under 65. Attendance is lowest among the very young, peaks among those 55 to 79 and falls off somewhat at 80 and over.

Responses of the older group surveyed indicated that while attendance at a house of worship does not increase steadily with age, the importance attached to religion in people's lives does. Seventy-one per cent of the public 65 and over feels religion is very important in their own lives, compared with only 49% of those under 65. Fewer of the older group identify their religion as "none" than do the younger public.

INTEREST IN SENIOR CITIZEN CENTERS

For half of the public 55 and over, a senior citizen center or golden age club is convenient to attend. Senior citizen centers are apparently least accessible to blacks, to older people in the South and to people in rural areas.

There is a relationship between higher income and a senior citizen center or club being "convenient," matching findings about other facilities being more accessible to persons with higher income and less so for the lower income group. One-fifth of the public 65 and over and 13% of the 55 to 64 group say that they have attended a senior citizen center or golden age club in the past year or so. A 57% majority of the public 55 and over have not attended a senior citizen center or golden age club in the past year, saying they have no interest in attending or are too busy.

Poorer Attend More

While such centers were considerably less convenient to blacks, black attendance among those 55 and over is comparable to that of whites. The lowest income group (under $7,000) attended more frequently than the higher income groups. This is especially noteworthy in view of the fact that the lower income groups report that the centers or clubs are less convenient to them than do the upper income groups.

While 13% of the public 55 and over have been to a senior citizen center in the past year or so, 19% of the total public 55 and over said that they would like to attend. Interest is highest among blacks; an additional 39% of blacks said they would like to attend.

The 19% of people 55 and over who would like to attend but have not done so give the following reasons: No time, too busy (33%); no facilities here; don't know where there are any (21%); transportation problems (13%), and poor health (12%). The more affluent are apt to give "no time" as their reason, while the less affluent mention frequently that there are no facilities or transportation problems.

THE IMAGE OF AGING

Aside from the economic and social conditions of the older American, the public view of the elderly as human beings and contributing members of society was surveyed. As before, the public expectation of old age differed from the view of older people themselves.

When judged on a list of attributes associated with productive, active and effective individuals, "most people over 65" received positive ratings on only two counts: Substantial majorities of the public 18–64 consider them "very warm and friendly" (82%) and "very wise from experience" (68%).

But most people over 65 are not viewed as very active, efficient or alert: Less than half (41%) consider them "very physically active" and lesser percentages as "very good at getting things done" (35%); "very bright and alert" (29%); "very open-minded and adaptable" (21%), though larger percentages on all counts conceded they were "somewhat" all these things.

In one area, being "very warm and friendly," the 65-plus (25%) were far more critical than the younger group of their peers; they were only slightly more generous in other aspects. They have apparently also bought the stereotypes of older people as being unalert, close-minded, nonproductive members of society, though older people tend to see themselves as more adaptable and open-minded than they're given credit for being.

Self-image High

While the public at large, young and old, may question the efficiency, mental alertness and flexibility of the older population, the 65 and over do not question their own attributes as individuals:

Very bright and alert (58%/29%);
Very open-minded and adaptable (63%/21%);
Very good at getting things done (55%/35%).

The image that the public holds of most people over 65 varies only slightly from one demographic group to the next, with age appearing to be the most significant determinant of attitude; the youngest group of adult Americans seems to harbor the most negative attitudes toward the oldest and the more affluent somewhat more positive attitudes.

ACTIVITIES OF OLDER PEOPLE

The public at large thought the older group spends more time at passive, sedentary activities than the older group says it actually does.

The public judged television to be the number one pastime of the older group; it actually was reported fourth by the older group.

The public thought of sitting and thinking as the second most favorite pastime of older people; the 65-plus group reported it as their fifth most common activity.

Older persons seem to spend the same amount of time on most pastimes as those under 65. Except for more television watching in the older group and the younger group's spending more time on caring for family members, working and participating in sports, involvement in activities mentioned was nearly comparable.

Though the 65-plus group was far less likely than those 18–64 to exaggerate the amount of time most people over 65 spend sitting and thinking, sleeping or just doing nothing, older people are still more likely to attribute to their peers the sedentary pastimes in which they are themselves involved.

The 65-and-over population reported spending "a lot of time personally in socializing with friends" (47%); followed by raising plants or gardening (39%); reading (36%); watching television (36%); sitting and thinking (31%); caring for younger or older family members (27%); participating in hobbies and recreation (26%); going for walks (25%); participating in organizations or clubs (17%); sleeping (16%); just doing nothing (15%);

working part-time or full-time (10%); doing volunteer work (8%); in political activities (6%); participating in sports (3%).

Not Absolute Measures

With time seen as a relative and subjective measure, what may be seen by one person as a "lot of time" may seem like "hardly any time at all" to another. Therefore, these results should not be interpreted as absolute measures; they are valuable as indications of the kinds of activities people see themselves involved in and the degree of involvement.

With the public at large seeing older people spending more time at sedentary activities, it is no wonder that it considered older people as "not having enough to do to keep busy," though those 65 and over deny that this is a serious problem.

USEFUL COMMUNITY MEMBERS

In the minds of the general public, being a useful member of one's community involves, primarily, taking part in community activities, organizations and politics and helping or serving others.

The 65-and-over group has a relatively high self-image of being useful members of the community, a more positive view than the 18–64 age group has of them. Also, many more of the older group (40%) thought of themselves as "very useful members of their community" compared to what the younger group (29%) felt about themselves. This shows the satisfaction and sense of usefulness which those 65 and over find in community involvement and the importance attached by older people to the role of helping others.

COMPARED TO 10/20 YEARS AGO

Most of the public agrees that today's older people are better educated and live longer than those of 10 and 20 years ago; more older people now live alone and are independent than before; older people are healthier now than they used to be. The public believes that older people in general are better off financially than one or two decades ago and recognizes that there are more of them now. Generally, the 18–64 group agrees with the 65-plus group, except that the latter sees itself even more positively as better off financially than older people used to be.

It became apparent that an older person views the economic status of his peer group according to his own economic conditions. There was a relationship to income level and agreement within a group about economic conditions: The higher the economic level, the more people tended to agree with each other about conditions.

Under the $7,000 income level, the 18–64 age group largely agrees older people are worse off financially than they used to be; the 65-plus group of the same income level disagree. Thus, the view from "outside" seems very different from the view of the group experiencing the economic situation.

All in all, as a group, the 65-plus population sampled recognizes that the status and conditions of the older group have improved over the 10 or 20 years: That the elderly population is a growing one, healthier, more apt to live alone, better educated and in better financial shape than it used to be.

THE YOUNG'S RESPECT FOR PEOPLE OVER 65

The survey showed a substantial proportion of those 65 and over (45%) feel they get less respect from the young than they deserve, not surprising considering the variety of negative perceptions the young have about old people. Older blacks reported too little respect from the young in higher percentages than whites. However, the under-65 public seems more aware of the lack of respect than the older group, with a full 70% feeling that people 65 and over get too little respect from young people these days.

Respect is by no means a one-way street; just as the old expect respect from the young, so do the young expect it from the old. Forty-two per cent of the 18–64 group felt they get just about the right amount of respect from people over 65. A third disagreed, believing young people in the 18–64 age group get too little respect from older people. There seems to be an increase with education in feeling that younger people do not get enough respect.

LIFE SATISFACTIONS

To compare the general life satisfactions of those 65 and over to those under 65, both groups were asked to agree or disagree with a series of 18 statements, *The Life Satisfaction Index Z,* developed by Dr. Robert Havighurst, professor of education and human development, University of Chicago, and NCOA board member.

Majorities of the older group responded similarly to the younger group on all but one of the positive statements, showing differences of at least 10 percentage points on only seven statements overall. Older people, like younger, agree that they:

Expect "some interesting and pleasant things to happen to me in the future." (57% to 86%)

Feel "things I do now are as interesting as they ever were." (72% to 82%)

Have "made plans for things I'll be doing a month or a year from now." (53% to 71%)

Feel "just as happy now as when I was younger." (56% to 68%)

Less than a majority of the older group (32% to 56%) agree that "these are the best years of my life." Differences on two of the negative statements also emerged, with more of the older group members agreeing that they feel:

"Old and somewhat tired." (46% to 21%)

"This is the dreariest time of my life." (23% to 13%)

An index based on the 18 statements scored on a scale of 0–36 by the following procedure:

two points for agreement with a positive statement or disagreement with a negative statement.

one point for each "not sure" or "no" answer.

0 for each disagreement with a positive statement or agreement with a negative statement.

The median score for the public 18–64 was 28.3, only slightly higher than the mean 26.0 for the public 65 and over. However, median scores dropped by increasing age: 27.4 for those 65–69, 25.7 for those 70–79 and 23.8 for those 80 and over.

Equates Positive View

But other demographic factors appear to have a greater influence than age on life satisfactions, including income, level of education and racial differences. The portion of the public with the highest life satisfaction scores are also more positive in evaluating other people, especially so for the older group.

General life satisfaction is higher for those of all ages who are employed than those who are not, becoming most noticeable among the older group: A full 72% of the 65 and over still employed expect "interesting and pleasant things to happen," compared to only 52% of the retired 65-plus.

Overall, the older public seems to be only slightly less satisfied with their lives—past, present and future—than are those under 65, though those 80 and over are somewhat less satisfied than those who recently turned 65.

THE POLITICS OF OLD AGE

Thirty-six per cent of this country's working people say their place of business has a pension or other employee benefit plan with a fixed retirement age. Thus, a third of all working people can expect to be told to retire from their jobs at a fixed age.

Apart from the required retirement age in many organizations, a variety of pressures are exerted on workers approaching the mid-sixties to move over and make room for the young. With increasing frequency, these pressures are beginning for many workers before 60. The elderly seem less aware of these policies than those involved in the hiring and firing.

Such policies can be interpreted as being discriminatory against older workers. With the pressures of inflation, such discrimination is likely to increase.

Oppose Mandatory Retirement

The public is largely opposed to putting people out to pasture at a fixed, inflexible age; a large majority (86% to 12%) agree that "nobody should be forced to retire because of age if he wants to continue working and is still able to do a good job." A majority also agreed (58% to 36%) that "most older people can continue to perform as well on the job as they did when they were younger." However, nearly half of the public (49% to 46%) recognize some advantages to fixed retirement policies, feeling that "older people should retire when they can, to give younger people more of a chance on the job."

Many are aware of the administrative difficulties involved in retirement decisions on an employee-by-employee basis: They agreed (49% to 43%) that "since many people are ready to retire at 65, and it's hard to make an exception for those who are not ready, it makes sense to have a fixed retirement age for everyone." However, the findings suggest that most hiring and firing decision-makers would not oppose some kind of individualized method for determining who should be forced to retire.

Many Shun Retirement

Another prevalent myth: That all workers are ready to retire at 65. While nearly half of retired or unemployed people 65 and over said they looked forward to stopping work, nearly as many said they did not (48% to 45%). A full 61% of those with incomes under $3,000 did not look forward to stopping work.

Retired and unemployed people 65 and over report missing the money work brought in; just as important as the income were the coworkers. Majorities of those retired or umemployed said they missed the work itself, the feeling of being useful and things happening around them.

With the country moving toward even younger retirement ages, the public is divided on whether or not this is a positive trend. The 18–64 age group agreed by a plurality (47% to 39%) that younger retirement is a good thing; those 65 and over disagreed (47% to 33%), and 20% were not sure.

Those who opted for earlier retirement reasoned: It gives people a chance to enjoy life and do things before they get too sick or too old; it also makes more jobs for younger people.

Those under 65 are much more likely than those 65 and over to feel that earlier retirement gives people a chance to enjoy life. Those opposed to earlier required retirement felt that work makes people feel useful and needed, that retirement precipitates illness and old age; that people should be able to work as long as they want to. The 65-plus group felt more strongly than the young that retirement ages people.

The results of the survey represent a strong public mandate for the roll-back of mandatory retirement guidelines and practices to make fuller use of the resources older workers represent in our society.

Government Support of Retired People

Those who choose to retire or who are no longer able to continue their work should have the right to retire, the public feels, and to turn to the government for financial support.

Asked, "Who should provide income for older people when they are no longer working?" 68% of the total public responded that the federal government should, through Social Security. Further findings underscore the idea that the government, with its powers of taxation, has the responsibility and means to support older people (81% to 14%). The under-65 agree even more strongly than the retired themselves.

The total public (76% to 19%) also feels that "no matter how much a person earned during his working years, he should be able to have enough money to live on comfortably when he's older and retired."

Agreeing almost unanimously that older people have the right to live comfortably, the public also endorsed support of older people in line with rising prices, recognizing that persons on fixed income may be victimized by inflation. By an overwhelming majority (97%), the public, both old and young, supported cost-of-living escalators in Social Security payments.

SUPPORT FOR OLDER PEOPLE: A POLITICAL FORCE

From the young and the old, the survey disclosed potential support for a movement to improve the conditions and social status of those over 65. The under-65 are most conscious of the need for such a movement; 81% of this group feel people need to join together to work toward improving conditions for people 65 and over, and 70% of the older group shared this feeling.

Substantial numbers would be interested in joining a group with these goals: The percentages from the survey who said they would "certainly" or "probably" join and take part represent 44.5 million of the 18–64 group and 6.7 million of the 65-plus potential for such an organization.

Thus, both young and old can identify with other older Americans as people sharing the same needs and problems of all humans.

What Should Older Americans Be Called?

What's in a name? The 65 and over Americans in the survey sampling generally expressed strong likes and dislikes, indicating that, for most, they had rather it not be "old man" or "old woman" (67%); "aged person" (50%); "old timer" (45%) or "golden ager" (36%). Majorities preferred, instead, to be called either a "mature American" (55%); "senior citizen" (50%) or "elderly person" (38%). However, 38% didn't like the appellation "elderly," either.

Asked to choose *one* name by which they preferred to be called, "senior citizen" topped the list of responses, followed by "mature American" and "retired person." About one in three, especially in the poor groups, volunteered that "it doesn't matter," and minute percentages weren't sure.

THE MEDIA'S PORTRAYAL

Information in the survey seems to indicate that the media's coverage of the elderly—the poor, the sick, the institutionalized and the unemployed or retired—may protect and reinforce the distorted stereotypes of old age. By playing up what exists for only a small segment of the old, the media may be perpetuating the myths of old age.

On the whole, the public is uncritical of the media for the way it projects old people. Majorities of readers, watchers and listeners feel that newspapers, magazines, books, television and radio usually "give a fair picture of what older people are like," or even "make older people look better than they really are." Only one in five recognizes that television programs may be "making older people look worse than they really are."

Younger More Critical of Media

The younger public is somewhat more critical of the media portrayal than the older group; heavy watchers tend to be less critical than light watchers. Most agree, however, that television shows young people, not old.

The total public looked up to or admired the following older people in television programs or commercials: The Waltons (21%); Bob Hope (9%); Jack Benny (8%); Robert Young

(8%); Buddy Ebsen/Barnaby Jones (6%), and Redd Foxx (6%).

Those under 65 are most apt to admire the Waltons and Robert Young than those 65 and over, who are more likely to admire Lawrence Welk.

Blacks were less likely to find television personalities to look up to, and when they did, it was other exponents than the whites admired. Highest on the blacks' list were Redd Foxx (20%), followed by the Waltons (11%), and Bea Arthur as Maude (6%).

PRESENT AND POTENTIAL ROLE
OF THE MEDIA

There are no indications that television, the medium which reaches the broadest audience, has had either a negative or positive effect on the way the public views older people. It may be that television reflects societal attitudes toward old age, reinforcing the myths.

If the overall image of older people is to be changed, it could be done perhaps most effectively through the use of television. Groups in every income and educational level, black and white, spend more time watching television than reading books, newspapers, magazines or listening to radio.

The youngest adults (18–24), revealing the least positive attitudes toward older people, unlike other age groups, reported spending as much time listening to the radio during the previous day as they did watching television. Thus, the use of radio as a medium in addition to television could be an effective tool to bring about changes in the younger population's attitudes in respect to the elderly.

STILL A LOT TO GIVE

Few of the 65-plus appear to be willing to be relegated to the sidelines of society; three of four in the survey prefer to spend most of their time with other people of all ages, not just their own, and the 18–64 group expected this to be true.

And the older generation is by no means as isolated from the young as myth would have it; a substantial majority have living children (81%) and grandchildren (75%), and most see them on a fairly regular basis.

The interaction between the young and the old extends far beyond regular visits, however. The 65-plus make it clear that they perform some valuable functions for the younger generation: Giving gifts (90%); helping out when someone is ill (68%); taking care of grandchildren (54%); helping out with money (45%); giving advice on how to deal with some of life's problems (39%); shopping or running errands (34%); fixing things around the house or keeping house for them (26%); giving advice on rearing children (23%) or on jobs or business matters (20%) and taking grandchildren, nieces or nephews into their homes (16%).

Though all ages and economic groups help in some ways, the level of service is higher for the 65–69 group than for those 80 and over; the more affluent give gifts, help out with money and advice on business matters more frequently; the less affluent are more involved in giving advice on rearing children, particularly older blacks, who are also much more likely to take grandchildren, nieces or nephews into their homes.

Agree in Many Areas of Help

The group under 65 agreed, in like percentages in four areas, that parents and grandparents over 65 assist with gifts, shopping or running errands, fixing things around the house or keeping house and taking children into their homes. In three areas, the younger generation credit the older with less assistance than parents and grandparents say they give: Helping out when someone is ill, taking care of grandchildren and helping out with money.

In giving advice, however, the younger generation reports their parents or grandparents give far more advice than the older generation feels they do.

In economic terms, the contribution that older people make to younger members of their families is substantial. Besides gifts and money, the services performed by older people for their children and grandchildren represent substantial monetary savings. As nurses for the ill, as babysitters for small children, as shoppers and errand runners, as home repairers and housekeepers or as surrogate parents, the older Americans offer assistance to children and grandchildren that would cost dearly otherwise.

Without the free services of older family members, the younger ones would either have to hire outside help or, more likely for many, sacrifice income by taking off from work themselves to perform these same tasks. Older people play a critical, even indispensable role in the lives of their children or grandchildren that may be largely taken for granted.

Gainful Employment of People 65 and Over

The economic contributions of older Americans is in no way limited to the family level; 2.5 million 65 and over provide paid service (3% full-time, 9% part-time). An additional 6% is part of the labor force but currently unemployed; another 17% identify themselves as housewives.

Employment rates are much higher for those 65–69 (4% full-time, 14% part-time) than the 70 and over and higher among men than women (17% to 9%). An equal number (12%) of blacks and whites 65 and over are employed.

At the time of this survey, the rate of those 55–64 reporting they were employed was high (38% full-time, 10% part-time); however, so was the unemployment rate (10%), suggesting that people in their late fifties and early sixties were having serious difficulties in finding work even before the recent recessionary period.

It is likely that many of these unemployed, when they reach 65 or so, give up looking for a job and consider themselves "retired." This would explain the drop-off in the retirement rate after 65 (6%).

The occupations in which those 65 and over continue to work full or part-time include managers, officials or proprietors (18%); service workers (17%); operatives or unskilled laborers (15%); skilled craftsmen or foremen (11%); professionals and sales workers (each 10%); clerical workers and farmers (each 8%).

Occupation a Factor

Judging by the retirement rate, one occupation stands out from the rest as having far less room for older employees: A full 22% of retired people were skilled craftsmen or foremen while they worked. The occupational distribution of three age groups, 18–54, 55–64 and 65 and over, show that besides skilled craftsmen or foremen, professionals and clerical workers have a lower representation of older workers than young. More old people than young are employed as managers, officials or proprietors, sales or service workers and farmers. Though people 65 and over do compete for and hold jobs in all categories, those occupational categories where part-time work is possible become increasingly important with age.

The potential manpower among older Americans appears to extend far beyond those who are currently employed; the survey shows substantial numbers of those retired or unemployed would welcome the opportunity to work. Among those of the older public who are retired (63%), the equivalent of 4.4 million (37%) say they did not retire by choice; almost half of older retired men with incomes under $3,000 and half of the retired blacks reported mandatory retirement.

While poor health was volunteered as the major obstacle keeping those who would like to work from actually working, other reasons were reported: Too old (28%); no work available (15%); other interests (8%); would lose Social Security or pension benefits (4%); lack of transportation (2%).

Though a comparative few blamed their unemployment on no work available, additional probing revealed that many more would consider working if asked back to their old jobs or offered new, suitable employment. It is reasonable to assume from these results that reasons given for not working are learned responses to cover up for the fact that "nobody wants me." In short, with over four million older unemployed or retired individuals who want to work, there exists a massive untapped source of manpower.

Feel Skills Unused

Not only would many older Americans like to work who are not currently doing so, one in 10 of those 65 and over feel they have specific skills which no one gives them a chance to use. This feeling exists not only among the retired; a like number of those still employed feel they have unused skills. However, this is not a problem exclusive to older Americans; many others in our society feel they have no chance to use present skills or would like the chance to learn new ones.

In the 65-plus group, both working and retired persons (44%) expressed interest in participating in a job training program or learning new skills. In the preretirement age group 55–64, a high percentage are interested in job training.

Neither the government nor the private sector aims job training efforts where this survey demonstrates the demand: For people in the preretirement and retirement years. With forced retirement and lack of job opportunities, preparation for an occupation in demand may provide the chance to work or the possibility of change and advancement. As older people are deprived of the opportunity to work, society is deprived of the energies and talents of many capable older workers with great potential.

"EVERYBODY'S STUDYING US"
and
"I HATE TO BE CALLED A SENIOR CITIZEN"

Irene Paull

While most of those working on behalf of the aged hail the Harris poll as a welcome clarification of the realities of aging in America, some activists have attacked it as obfuscating the real issues. In "Everybody's Studying Us," Irene Paull, veteran writer and editor for the California Association for Older Americans, expresses her reservations with characteristic wit. After that, enjoy another piece of vintage Paull: "I Hate to Be Called a Senior Citizen."

"EVERYBODY'S STUDYING US"

We are living in the Age of the Image. We have exchanged substance for image. It is not necessary for a politician to be an honest man. All he need do is project an image of honesty. Sincerity? Who can recognize it? All we can go by is the "image," carefully studied, packaged and delivered. This is the heyday of the advertising man and the pollster.

We, the old, it seems, are projecting upon society a most unpalatable image of age. It frightens little children, offends the young, and terrifies the middle aged. After all, we are the vanguard, and when we fall in our tracks it is the middle aged, inexorably moving up, who will be standing in our place. It is so terrifying to them that they are bustling about trying to provide a pleasant image to conceal our nakedness.

So everybody's studying us. At the cost of $335,000, they have just come up with a brand new image for us, researched, packaged and delivered by the Harris poll. And the Harris poll, dear friends, is sacrosanct. According to this poll, only 15% of us haven't enough money to live on comfortably; only 12% of us are lonely; only 21% are concerned about poor health; only 23% worry about being victims of crime; transportation is no problem; only 7% feel we're not needed.

Isn't that beautiful? We're a well heeled, well fed, well protected, mobile, well adjusted lot. Don't let anybody tell you we live on the lowest income of any other section of the population. Or that we are prime victims of crime. Or that we're lonely, heaven forbid, although the majority of us are single widows. Or that failing eyesight, slower reflexes or poverty have forced most of us to give up driving; and buses have become targets for hit and run muggers. Or that inflation has eaten away our savings or taxes undermined the foundations of our homes.

We may not exactly have it made, but Lord be praised, we have an image! A neat, presentable, respectable middle class image, scrubbed with Ivory soap, deodorized with "Ban," and perfumed with Chanel No. 5. Hail to the image! And if we're hungry, we can always eat it. It's concocted like cotton candy from sugar and hot air.

"I HATE TO BE CALLED A SENIOR CITIZEN"

"Those who profess to favor freedom and yet depreciate agitation, want crops without plowing up the ground. They want rain without thunder and lightning. They want the ocean without the awful roar of its waters. This struggle may be a moral one; or it may be both moral and physical; but it must be a struggle. Power conceded nothing without a demand. It never did, and it never will. Find out just what people will submit to, and you have found out the exact amount of injustice and wrong which will be imposed upon them; and these will continue till they are resisted with either words or blows, or both. The limits of tyrants are prescribed by the endurance of those whom they oppress . . ."

—FREDERICK DOUGLASS, Black abolitionist and ex-slave

I've heard that over and over. I've said it over and over. "Elderly"? "Retired"? . . . "A rose by any other name, etc." What we really hate is BEING a senior citizen in a society that does not value us. It has the connotation of being shelved, retired, passive, powerless, even senile. I remember going unwillingly to my first "senior citizen" gathering. It didn't reassure me. A group of quiet old women outnumbering five to one a group of quiet old men. A young woman from one of the colleges was in charge of the meeting. She was what I believe is known as an "ex-tern" doing her field work in helping old people. She discussed volunteer work we could do. There was no discussion. Then we drank coffee and ate carrot cake with plastic forks and it was a very sad and very dull experience.

I went to another group and the highly motivated paid worker in charge pounced on me to enlist me in teaching old women to crochet. It wasn't until I joined a group oriented toward action that I found myself accepting both the term "senior citizen" and the status it describes. I recognized that what obtained when I was young was still the rule of life now that I am old. No one expressed it better than the ex-slave, Frederick Douglass, in the statement quoted above. I regard the aged as an oppressed group. I see no cure for the oppression but what Douglass called "The thunder and lightning of struggle." Struggle is the law of life and when one ceases to struggle in one way or another . . . it doesn't have to be MY way . . . he folds his hands and waits for oblivion.

Yet the particular struggle which we must wage for our simple dignity should not even be necessary. I heard a young Indian remark the other day in reference to some problem, "We'll call upon our elders." I turned the words over in my mind. "Our elders." There was honesty in the words. Respect. No effort to be cute or to give them a euphemism. It was the value placed upon the concept, "Our elders" that made them as beautiful as any words I've heard in any language.

THE COMPOUNDING IMPACT OF AGE ON SEX

Tish Sommers

As co-ordinator of the Committee on Older Women's Rights of the National Organization for Women, activist Tish Sommers wears two hats: she struggles and speaks against both ageism and sexism, as analyzed in this definitive treatment of "another dimension of the double standard."

As with other inequities, the double standard of aging between men and women is so obvious that it is taken for granted. It is a pervasive fact of life—rarely questioned and never taken seriously as a possible subject for government concern.

Men generally marry women younger than themselves; when they remarry the age gap increases; employers usually prefer younger women; a love relationship between a young man and an old woman is a source of ridicule. When the producers of *Harold and Maude* were seeking the most bizarre symbol possible to illustrate the absurdity of our values, they picked that shocking combination. (The same age gap between an old man and a young woman is far too common in real life to have any impact.)

Even feminists have not given serious attention to the implications of this double standard until recently, since younger women have been in the forefront of the movement. In addition, so many assumptions were simultaneously under attack and so many issues required action that the aging question had to wait. We noted that women moved rapidly from sex object to obsolescence, that a billion dollar industry fed upon our efforts to slow down the process, and that we must provide for our own futures.

But we held out little hope for the older generation, already socialized to different standards than ours, and we pinned our hopes on the young. We have only recently begun to consider the serious impact of age upon sex, and to see that beside the mating differential exist problems of societal concern which are not going to go away without special analysis and attack.

One reason that the compounding effects of sexism and ageism have not been sufficiently recognized is that the aged are desexed. At the chronological cutoff of 65, a new status is acquired which falls within the purview of different laws, bureaucracies, and disciplines. These bureaucracies and disciplines tend to see their field, the elderly, as separate and distinct. They view their constituency as an undifferentiated category especially in regard to sex, so that the specifics are blurred. Older women tend to become invisible in statistics, theories, and social programs in the aging field.

To understand how aging affects women, and some of the serious gaps in coping with the consequences, examine first the male patterns: society's norms are established in terms of men.

"If we analyze this country as a white male club, committed to technological superiority and dominance on the world scene," said Robert Terry in the spring 1974 issue of the *Civil Rights Digest,* "much of what has happened and continues to happen in America can be understood more completely." Although relatively few white males run the club, all are offered benefits, he says. Minorities and white women are relegated to secondary status and are exploited for club purposes.

One fact of that club membership Terry failed to mention was age. When members reach 64 they come up for review; if they have become one of the select who run the club they may stay in. Otherwise, out they go.

As for minorities and women, who were never eligible, they are new doubly excluded. At age 65 the officers of the club, who are in such seats of power as corporation board rooms, on Capitol Hill, in prestigious university positions, or in courts of law, can continue to enjoy the material and psychological benefits of club leadership. The ordinary member must remove himself from the mainstream, lose most of the status he possesses in his community and often in his own home.

Rep. Paul Finley of Illinois pointed out that if mandatory retirement at age 65 were suddenly imposed on Capitol Hill, six Supreme Court Justices, about 60 Representatives, and at least a quarter of the Senate would have to go. John Sparkman at 75 is taking on a new job as chairman of the Senate Foreign Relations Committee. Two 75-year-old economists, Gunnar Myrdal and Frederick Van Hayek, still working, have just shared the Nobel

Prize in economics. And age is no barrier to corporation leadership, as the photos in any annual report reveal.

DOUBLE STANDARDS

There is, in fact, not only a double standard of aging between men and women, but also a double standard for men themselves—those who run the club and those who don't. The result of that membership check at 64 is a sudden influx of white males who formerly had a privileged position into the ranks of the "other." In discussions of aging, this is the group generally referred to.

As Simone de Beauvoir said in *The Coming of Age:*

> As a personal experience, old age is as much a woman's concern as a man's—even more so, indeed, since women live longer. But, when there is speculation upon the subject, it is considered primarily in terms of men. In the first place, because the struggle for power concerns only the stronger sex.

Considering the sex and race of most of those who write, plan, and speak in behalf of the elderly, it is not surprising that the aging problem is traditionally seen in white male terms although there are far more elderly women than men. It is also typical of our culture to be more concerned about those who rise and fall then those who never rise at all. The unemployed aerospace engineers caused some concern, while there was none at all for clerical workers laid off at the same time. They had just as much trouble getting new jobs, especially if they were over 40.

When the Labor Department finally won a landmark case in support of the Age Discrimination in Employment Act (the Standard Oil case), it was predictably in defense of white males in middle management, forced out of their positions by ageist corporation policy. No matter that members of the board of the corporation were older than those weeded out.

As members grow older, the club rules become more and more selective. Some may drop out of their own accord, but most of those permitted to remain hold onto their membership—for economic benefits, status, and prestige, as well as for the exclusive right to remain productive. For a very few, there are seniority privileges. But the bulk of those forced out suffer a humiliating fall from favored positions, and in many cases, introduction to the life-style of poverty.

What then of women? In a society that practices a youth cult, when do we become old?

Clearly the youth cult extends to both sexes but the timing is quite different. Whatever progress has been made in laws regarding equality, in real life customs change more slowly. In the marriage market, a woman reaches her peak at about 20 or 25. Despite the understandable fury of younger women over the use of the term "girl," the older we get the more we try to remain girls. If that were not so the billion dollar business which tries to help us maintain that illusion would not exist.

At an age when men are at their most attractive, a woman is usually a has-been. A man's peak usually coincides with his economic opportunities or the height of his power, somewhere in the 40s or even older. He becomes a man. She remains, or tries to remain, a girl. Even the young woman who most protests the term will peer in the mirror for the trace of a wrinkle or a gray hair.

The difference between the term "boy" as used derogatorily against blacks and "girl" against women is that a black wants to become a man—that is where the rewards are—while a woman secretly wants to stay a girl, because so many of her rewards are there. The much ridiculed image of the overweight middle-aged clubwoman "girl" is based upon a deeply-felt defense mechanism. When we are young and sure enough of our physical girlhood, we can resent the term, but the older we get the more we hang on to it.

Sixty-five is that standard mandatory retirement age for men, but women often face the same crisis at an earlier age, complete with economic, physiological, and psychological trauma. The dependent homemaker has little status on her own account at any time, but what she pulls together to create her selfhood usually crashes in the middle years. The empty nest syndrome, usually coupled with menopause, is a crisis of identity similar to the one men face on retirement.

Yet neither this identity crisis nor the menopause have been taken seriously, although suicide rates peak for women during these years. The lack of medical research on estrogen replacement therapy and other aspects of menopausal care is reminiscent of the slow start on research on sickle cell anemia. While almost one-half of the population will suffer with discomfort, sometimes of a serious nature, club members of the medical profession exhibit a shocking lack of interest. Those in the aging field do not consider it within their purview.

Widowhood is another form of forced retirement—a change of status for which there is no preparation and little opportunity to find a new identity. Since the traditional role of the wife in marriage is to create her identity through her husband as supporter and adjunct, when the husband dies she loses herself as well as her mate. Such women usually look for another husband, with limited success. Since youth and beauty are equated, especially for women, men remarry down in age. Over twice as many bridegrooms are over 65 as brides, and four times as many widowers are past that age.

A factor adding to the growing number of nonmarried women (separated, divorced, widowed, or single) in the older population is the increase of divorce, especially in "no-fault" states. For older women, in most cases, divorce is another form of forced retirement for which they are economically and psychologically ill-prepared. Especially in those states where unilateral "no-fault" has been instituted, the risk of divorce in later years has been dramatic. In Nebraska, for example, within 6 months after the new law went into effect in 1972, a 59.4 per cent increase in divorces occurred among those married 31 or more years; a 49.5 per cent increase among those married 26–30 years; and an 18.2 per cent increase among those married 16–20 years.

Women, especially those trying to reenter the job market, generally face the "over the hill" syndrome earlier than white men. Because it is difficult to face aging, most of us don't recognize age discrimination when it first hits us. After we have made the rounds and have been turned down repeatedly, even for the traditional "female" job for which we formerly were eligible, we become convinced that we are unemployable. Soon that is the way we do become, in the manner of all self-fulfilling prophecies.

Thus the patterns of aging for men and women have significant differences. Some men can remain in the club, and in a manner of speaking their wives can maintain an auxiliary status. Most women hit "mandatory retirement" earlier than men, but live longer. For nonmarried women especially, the heavy impact is already upon us in our 40s and 50s—yet at that age we fall between the cracks of all social programs.

In order to devise remedies for the problems of older women, aging must be redefined in a way that is more functionally accurate for women and is not based upon male chronology. Clearly women are not going to beat on the doors asking to join the ranks of the elderly at an earlier age than they have to, especially since aging in our society is synonymous with being sick, dying, poor, dependent, useless, and "over the hill." On the other hand, until sexism is eradicated and women really become self-sufficient, the period between early "forced retirement" and social security is a particularly dangerous one.

THE BLACKOUT

There are 21.8 million women between ages 45 and 64. Two million live in families headed by females. Another 5.1 million nonmarried women live alone or with unrelated persons. Of nonmarried women 45 to 54, 72 per cent are working outside the home, but the percentage drops to 63 between ages 55 and 64. Among married women 45 to 54, 45 per cent work; between ages 55 and 64, 35 per cent work. Increasing numbers live without men. Although 81 per cent of women 45–54 are married, only 66.5 per cent of women 55–64 are still living with husbands.

These middle years are an age bracket for which exists a virtual blackout of services or benefits. In the state of California nothing is available for those who do not qualify for the disabled or blind program under Supplemental Security Income, or who live in a county without a general relief program. In 1973, 12 counties gave no benefits for one person cases, while of those that did, the average award was $85.34 per month.

Older black women are even worse off economically than whites. Those who work are virtually limited to domestic and service jobs, all low paying and low status. While they may have learned to cope better than new-poor white women, many black women also experience the hazardous period when Aid to Families with Dependent Children is no longer available. Although younger black women have made some progress in moving out of domestic work—primarily into clerical fields—the same is not true of older black females. Such jobs have declined and many vacated spots are filled by white women over 50.

Typically, material on aging pictures a sweet old couple sharing their twilight years. Yet only 38.1 per cent of women over 65 are married. Except for that small, powerful minority of club members, the economic situation for the majority of the aged is bad. In 1971, half the couples had annual incomes under $4,931; 69 per cent of nonmarrieds under $3,000. (In typical fashion these HEW statistics define 65+ by age of "head of family," although two-fifths of older married men have wives under 65 years of age.)

But for nonmarried women it is worse. Of the 4.3 million (22 per cent) of older persons living below the poverty threshold in 1971, almost 2.6 million or 60 per cent were living alone or with nonrelatives. Of these, more than 2.1 million were women, mostly widows. The older we get, the more likely we are to be on our own. In the age bracket 70–79, 21 per cent of the men are widowers, and 61 per cent of the women are widows. When speaking of the elderly poor, sex is seldom mentioned, yet the vast majority are women who have outlived "the woman's role" and who are now reaping the fruits of a lifetime of sex discrimination—and in the case of minorities, racial bias as well.

ONLY A DEPENDENT

Society manifests its values most vividly in the rewards received after the job is done. Members of the club all give careful attention to retirement benefits, annuities, and "transition expenses." While a woman is encouraged to stay at home and care for a family, when she grows old she is penalized for not having "worked." While a massive child care bill was vetoed on the grounds that home care of children is essential to the fabric of American society, a homemaker receives not one penny in retirement benefits of her own. She qualifies only as a dependent.

Nor will her volunteer efforts, which are extolled as essential to maintain worthwhile charitable programs, provide one penny in social security or pension benefits. Economically speaking, women are punished for doing what society expected them to do.

A good part of the problem for older women is that officially we don't yet exist as a problem. Each group that has emerged on the civil rights scene has come out of invisibility by making a public fuss. Until that happens, a conspiracy of silence reigns, without even statistics to bear witness.

At the magic figure of 65, women are lost in the sexless classification of senior citizens for all intents and purposes. Suddenly we disappear even from the concerns of civil rights activitists, not even winning a nod in the list of "forgotten women" carried in the *Civil Rights Digest* issue on sexism and racism. The problem is no longer seen as one of "sex," but as one of "age." But can the two be separated, any more than sex and race?

Margaret Sloan stated in that *Digest,* "It would be very easy for me if the oppressor would split up the week and say from Monday to Wednesday we are going to put her down because she's black . . . but it doesn't happen that way."

Nor can oppression be divided by sex and age. Laws may separate the two but life does not.

This becomes painfully apparent when one examines laws governing equal opportunity for employment. Title VII of the 1964 Civil Rights Act does not cover age. The Age Discrimination in Employment Act does not cover sex. But a woman who is turned down for a job because she doesn't fit the employer's youth-oriented criterion of beauty is discriminated against as much for sex as for age. If the Equal Employment Opportunity Commission would investigate the matter, it would surely find that age discrimination is differently applied to men than to women. Age bias against women is in practice another covert form of sex discrimination.

Sex and age discrimination are a poisonous combination, because employers look for qualities in most female employees which have no bearing on the job per se, but which reflect their own or community prejudices. One such prejudice is that a woman should be pretty (i.e., young) for certain jobs, such as bank teller, airline hostess, or receptionist. Yet such work could be done just as adequately by a woman 40 or over, and a reentry woman at that. To hire women exclusively for such positions is now considered discrimination against men. It is equally discriminating toward older women, because the custom of hiring only young women for such positions is based on a sexist interpretation of the job. The validity of this charge could be proved by adding age to the EEO-1 forms required of employers.

Employers often argue that in the case of reentry women, it is not their age which disqualifies them, but the fact that they have been out of the job market a number of years. "Recent experience" is the most devastating question on an employment application. In the celebrated *Griggs-Duke Power* case, the Supreme Court ruled that employers must prove the validity of tests designed to predict job performance which also have the effect of excluding blacks. Similarly, no proof exists that reentry women cannot perform adequately in many job categories. The insistence on "recent job experience" while discounting responsible unpaid work may not seem like sex discrimination, but it just happens to eliminate older females.

Through feminist efforts, Office of Federal Contract Compliance (OFCC) guidelines consider a refusal to rehire after child bearing discriminatory. Why not then after child rearing? If it is sex discrimination to force women to retire at an earlier age than men, why is it not sex discrimination if women cease to be hired at an earlier age?

SOCIAL SECURITY

Jobs and pay rates take on double significance as retirement approaches, when women frantically try to get in enough quarters to qualify for social security. Under present law, a person needs at least 10 years (40 calendar quarters) of "creditable work" to meet the length-of-service requirement to earn "fully insured status." For disability benefits the person must have worked in half the quarters during the 10 years immediately prior to disability. This can be a bitter trap for single women unable to find employment in these crucial years.

Social security law is a prime example of efforts to straddle woman's shift from dependence to self-sufficiency. When adopted in 1935, man was presumed to be the breadwinner and woman the homemaker. The plan—a compromise between the insurance principle and a recognition of society's responsibility for the aging— provides benefits for dependents at retirement, disability, or death of the wage earner.

This sets up two kinds of inequities. If a married woman is employed, and "contributes" her monthly payment, she may receive more as a dependent of her husband, considering the wage differential between the sexes. She feels cheated, receiving nothing extra for her "contribution." On the other hand the woman who works at home, making it possible for her husband to earn his salary, receives nothing in her own name. If they are divorced, she may be left out entirely.

A recent amendment permits women married 20 years to the same man to collect on the same basis as a wife when the man retires or dies. This is not only degrading to the woman, but opens the way for many "catch 65s." One newspaper account from New York described the case of a 73-year-old woman whose husband of 40 years died several years ago. She will no longer receive widow's benefits because he was previously married and never divorced. According to the Social Security Administration, she was one of 119 widows who lost benefits this year because their husbands had not obtained divorces.

Another pitfall of dependency is the assumption that the woman could not be older than her husband. If a divorced woman is 10 years older (and it is not that rare, just hidden), she would be 75 before she could collect as a dependent if he retired at 65. Or a woman might be married to one man for 10 years and another for 15 and collecting nothing.

According to some, as the law now stands it discriminates more against men than against women because of the dependency features. But this is a strictly legalistic viewpoint. As of October 1972 the median social security payment—for women both workers and dependents—was $138 per month, while the median for men was $214. In June of 1973, retired women workers were paid an average monthly benefit of $144 while men received an average of $181 per month. These reflect, and continue into old age, the inequities of employment opportunity.

Still more basic is the lack of credits for homemaking and voluntary community work mentioned above. Here is the largest body of workers still uncovered in what purports to be a universal retirement system.

Social security is not the only area in which the economic value of homemaking is yet to be recognized. Economist John Kenneth Galbraith has stated that the economy hangs on the housewife's apron strings. The consumption tasks of the homemaker are essential for the well-being and continuing growth of the economy, but the homemaker's contribution is systematically ignored. No accounting of it is made, and if something isn't measured, it isn't noticed—as with social security.

So homemaking is carefully kept out of the realm of statistics, although an occasional estimate surfaces. In New York City a jury recently awarded $56,000 to the husband of an injured woman for "loss of services" for over 2 months. A Chase Manhattan Bank report of 1972 conservatively computed that the marketplace value of a typical homemaker's labor is $257.53 per week. None of this labor is included in the Gross National Product, but if it were suddenly to disappear, the GNP would take a disastrous dive.

As laws are made more "equal" to reflect the changing status of women, they can adversely affect those whose roles were defined in an earlier day. The white male club members (who are also the lawmakers) are far more receptive to those charging unequal treatment of men than to those seeking economic security for homemakers.

FACADE OF PROTECTION

Changing divorce laws are a case in point. The tragedy of the new "liberal" no-fault laws, especially those which allow either partner to terminate the marriage at will, is that they superimpose a legal facade of equal protection upon very unequal situations. They are another example of prohibiting the rich and poor alike from sleeping under bridges.

Many women who did not have the choices of the present (such as they are), assumed that marriage was a viable contract which would provide security in later years. Whatever the disadvantages of homemaking as a career, our mothers taught us, we would be taken care of in later life if we performed our part of the bargain. On the whole, other options for women provided much less.

When the contract suddenly is rescinded after 20 to 40 years of unpaid labor, opportunities for remarriage or employment are severely limited. If the woman has saleable skills, they are rusty, her self-esteem probably has taken a nosedive with the divorce, and employers don't want the reentry woman anyway.

When a middle-aged man leaves his wife of many years for a

younger woman, the ex-wife is psychologically and socially committed to the junk heap even when her economic situation doesn't take a sudden dip—but it usually does. The publicized cases of women who have "taken their husbands to the cleaners" are in the financial upper brackets and have little bearing on the majority. In setting spousal support for homemaking wives, judges are now quick to cite women's liberation. "We're taking women at their word; they say they don't want anything from men," said one San Francisco judge.

Even in community property states, the division rarely includes the all-important fringe benefits such as health insurance and retirement. The job resume and experience that make an employer take notice go, of course, with the breadwinner. Spousal support is too often awarded as a gesture and then not paid, so that more assertive ex-wives are forced to fight for a settlement in court and the timid ones give up. A woman who expects to continue being supported is considered without pride, although financial support was, she believed, a condition of her marriage contract.

It is just such results from the backlash to equality that make some older women resist the Equal Rights Amendment. However, a careful look at the fate of elderly women in the traditional dependency role should dispel any illusion that there is much to lose. In fact the impact of sexism is most sharply illuminated by the conditions of older women in contemporary society. If gross inequity between the sexes did not exist, why are so many of us poor when we grow old?

The fate society allocates to aged females exposes the myth of special protection. Legal equality will only supply the underpinning for a continued struggle for authentic protection. The status of dependency, of working without pay, of early obsolescence, of rules of marriage changed midcourse, and the final lonely years all cry out for new solutions. Neither maintaining the status quo nor winning equality under the law will solve them, but the ERA will give a constitutional handle for that struggle.

Once the principle of equality is established, opportunities for revising legal structures in ways that will not eliminate protections for women without substituting meaningful reforms will be increased, not diminished. Just as in the cases of protective labor legislation, which has ambivalent value for working women, dependency protections for older women are eroding in both law and custom whether we like it or not. The only way out is to move forward, seeking new answers which pave the way for self-sufficiency. Whether those answers are application of the community property principle to social security, insistence upon the right and opportunity to work (including effective compliance machinery), legally viable marriage contracts which provide real safeguards, workman's compensation coverage for homemakers, unemployment compensation for divorced women whose ex-husbands default on spousal support, or other extensions to women of protections won through collective effort—new answers will be hastened by passage of the Equal Rights Amendment.

A NEW LINK

On the positive side, the emergence of a new wing into the ranks of those who see themselves excluded from society's benefits opens fresh possibilities. Older women are just beginning to define their self-interest, as other groups have done before. Restive older women can help to link reviving senior activism to women's fight for equality—on the one hand bringing a feminist viewpoint to elders, and on the other, interpreting the realities of aging to younger women. Gray Panther leader Maggie Kuhn is already doing just that, and NOW's Task Force on Older Women, as well as other feminists, are beginning to speak out in these terms.

The current economic situation underscores the need to find common ground. The depression is already here for the elderly, complete with indoor bread lines in federally-financed meal programs. This past month, St. Anthony's Dining Room in San Francisco called in reporters to celebrate its 11 millionth free meal. The person so honored was an 86-year-old woman with an income of little over $100 a month, who confided that she was "absolutely dependent" on the balanced meal served by the Catholic agency. The deputy director of the project told reporters, "The old stereotype of some wino as the usual diner doesn't hold any more." Elderly women on fixed incomes now are the main customers.

In that same spring issue of the *Civil Rights Digest*, Lucy Komisar pointed out that the feminist movement holds possibilities for social change that have hardly been considered by those that view it from the outside. One such potential for change relates to age and poverty, especially as they affect women—for once we have a clearer view of the causes, we can proceed to find the cures. The vigor of the woman's movement and its widespread impact will suggest new strategies. Understanding the interconnections, as well as the compounding effects, of sexism, racism, and ageism will lead us deeper into the body of the monster.

Once there, we can launch a combined attack.

AN OPEN LETTER TO A YOUNG DOCTOR

Shura Saul

Without condescension, Dr. Saul skillfully informs an attending physician ministering to an elderly patient about a commonly held notion of old people and aging. It should be included in medical training for all doctors-to-be and required reading for those already in service.

Dear Doctor,

This letter is by way of thanking you for your attention to a patient and, also, to ask you to consider further the subject on which we exchanged a very few words in the hall at the hospital, namely, old people and aging.

I watched you attend to your elderly male patient. I watched your skill. I appreciated the humor with which you accepted his angry retorts and his sheer cussedness. I admired the patience in your treatment of him, and I was grateful for your efforts to explain to him what he should and should not do. I realize that all of this behavior, on your part, reflects your skill as a doctor and your real caring about, and caring for, people.

Then, I thanked you in the hall and said, "The man is a free soul. He cannot bear to be restrained."

To which you replied that that might be so, but that the real problem was his disorientation which, you went on to assure me, was a consequence of and associated with his old age.

To this viewpoint I must take exception. Yes, this patient was somewhat confused as to time, place, etc. But I cannot accept this as a function of his age. To do so is to affirm a common stereotype of old people and aging: that is that old people must, by sheer virtue of their years, become confused and disoriented.

Doctors, psychiatrists, psychologists and others who have studied aging (with the same intensity and dedication that you studied medicine) have disputed this stereotype. I refer you to works published by the Group for the Advancement of Psychiatry (GAP), to works by Dr. Stanley Cath and Dr. Martin Berezin, material by

Dr. Robert Butler, Dr. Robert Fulson, Dr. Alvin Goldfarb, Bernard Kutner, Muriel Oberleder, N. W. Shock, and Simon and Epstein—to mention just a few. All of these experts suggest that *all* the circumstances of the person, rather than his age alone, are considerations in determining diagnosis and treatment.

Consider this patient you attended today. When he was 55, he underwent a prostate operation. He manifested much of the same behavior as today. He tore at the tubes, the dressings, raged and ranted, etc. No one attributed his behavior to his age, then. He was simply a very difficult patient!

This man's wife died 25 years ago, very suddenly. His response to this trauma was confusion, disorientation—to the point where he did not recognize his own children when he met them in the street. He was about 62 years old then—hardly old enough to be called "disoriented because of aging." Yet it took many months after his wife died for this man to pick up the threads of his life. He did— and held down a job, ran his own household, and took care of an invalid son for the next 24 years! He worked at his job until he was 80 years old.

Within the past 24 years, whenever this man became ill, he manifested the same confusion and behavior that he does now. Yet, he recovered, both physically and mentally, from several major episodes . . . at 72 from a serious attack of Ménière's syndrome; at 80, and, again, at 82 from cardiac infarction. Tell me, at what point during these past 25 years was it correct to attribute his disoriented behavior to his agedness? At 62, when he lost his wife? At 70, at 80, at 82—each time during severe physical illness? Yet, each time, he recovered, and continued to function at a level that made younger people, observing him, say, "Wow, wotta man!" *At which point, then, doctor, would it have been accurate to have diagnosed his confusion as inevitable and, possibly, irreversible?*

One cannot know all such things about a patient one is treating. That is what makes it so dangerous to apply a stereotype . . . a rigid, universalized concept that negates the quality of the individual and consigns him to a useless, meaningless generality! (This, we have all learned, is true of all stereotypes—isn't it?)

How about other aged people, aged 90 and over, whom I have known both personally and professionally, who underwent all kinds of surgery; cataract, mastectomy, surgery for cancer in various parts of the body, and who returned to their homes to live with no signs of disorientation at all? What does that do to the idea that "he's old, therefore he is disoriented." Or, "he is disoriented because he is getting old . . . there comes a time. . . ."

I do not dispute the fact of your patient's current confusion. I submit merely that such a state cannot be attributed to the "inevitable consequences" of his aging process.

I suggest further, that those of us who serve, help, and care for people (doctors among us) need to understand older people. Before we can even do that, we must dispel the effects, on our thinking, of these unfounded and unscientific stereotypes of old people—especially those that suggest the inevitability and irreversibility of given states.

You are quite young, and I am middle-aged. Both of us, I think, want a chance to live and work for many years to come. Both of us will, I hope, reach a ripe old age and, perhaps, will need some kind of professional assistance. Neither of us would want our possible states of depression, confusion, and/or anger, which might conceivably manifest themselves in some form of unrealistic behavior, written off as consequences of our aging. Rather, we would want the professional's attention directed to the human condition and circumstances underlying our behavior in a stress situation. In fact, that is exactly what you (young) and I (middle-aged) want now from anyone who assists us!

There is no intention in this letter to criticize the quality of professional, medical attention that I witnessed given to your patient today. I do believe, however, that the attitude you expressed afterward about aging and disorientation may have a negative effect on a service you may give an old person someday. And I promise you that, unless it is eradicated, this same stereotyped view may well affect (negatively) some professional service to you and yours today and tomorrow.

I am sure that you are as unwilling for this to occur as I am.

Thank you again for your very kind attention, and please do think about this note.

Most sincerely,

Shura Saul, Ed. D.
Consultant on Aging

THE SYSTEM MAKES IT UNHEALTHY
TO BE OLD*

Neil G. McCluskey and Jody Altenhof

Neil G. McCluskey is professor and director of the Office of Gerontological Studies in the Center for Advanced Study in Education of the CUNY Graduate School. (See "Resources" section, p. 463.)

Jody Altenhof is a research assistant at the Center.

The health of the elderly is of less value to society than the health of other people. That is a shocking but seldom articulated premise of our current health-care policies. These policies sharply skew effort and expenditures toward the health problems and solutions of other segments of the population. The old are discriminated against.

Now, however, health care has become a powerful thrust of the new activism by and on behalf of the old. The goal is to influence public policy toward a greater concern for their health needs. The way the present "health pie" is cut up is being questioned by young and old alike.

The contemporary American assumption that the health of the elderly is of less worth than that of the young is echoed in many other cultures.

Whenever its food supply neared exhaustion, the Masai tribe, of East Africa, used to make a farewell feast for the non-productive elderly and then leave them behind as they moved on to a new campsite. Eskimo tribes of Alaska and northwestern Canada long followed a similar practice, of abandoning the frail elderly to the ice floe. Stark survival lends a semblance of sense to this type of euthanasia. Primitive nomadic societies are keenly aware of a fundamental fact of economic life; namely, that the food-gathering

* This article was largely inspired by the Brookdale Social-Health Center on Aging Workshop at The Doris Siegel Memorial Colloquium on "Value and Ethical Dilemmas in the Delivery of Social Health Care," at the Mount Sinai Medical Center, May 5–6, 1977.

and -sharing systems are intimately related. He who produces, shares; he who does not produce, does not. How differently the Gauls, Angles, and Slavs acted toward their elderly in the fourth century B.C. is pretty much a matter of conjecture, but the custom of disposing of the non-productive elderly was known elsewhere. In his delightful *The Honorable Elders,* Erdman Palmore tells us that, although we have no evidence in over a thousand years of recorded Japanese history of the abandonment of the aged as a matter of custom, the *Obasute* (meaning "to discard grandmother") theme is traceable through tales dating from the sixth century to the present.

In contemporary society mankind seems generally to have risen above the survival equation, which remains a constant within the packs and flocks of other animal species. In theory, we still honor the dignity and worth of each individual human life. The law still protects every life no matter how precariously housed it be in a body. The human person is protected because of a spiritual quality that seems to transcend the vicissitudes of physical existence. Consequently, lameness, blindness, feebleness of the body—whether acquired at birth or as the result of an accident—do not put an individual beyond the pale of human society, but, uniquely among age groups, today the state of health of the elderly seems to come under a different dispensation.

Two years ago the case of Karen Quinlan and the national attention it provoked were a strong reminder of how our society esteems young life and, conversely, how little heed we give to the parallels that regularly involve the infirm elderly. When a twenty-one-year-old brain-damaged woman lay in a coma for weeks, her vegetative life sustained only by machines, there was a national debate over the ethics of "pulling the plug." During that period, several hundred thousand dollars were expended to prolong Karen's life. Yet how little concern is directed to similar situations daily across the land wherein the machines are quietly unplugged to release elderly persons from a comatose state.

In 1968 an extensive analysis of the literature indicated that the medical care of elderly patients in the United States was characterized by "negativism, defeatism, and professional antipathy." Somehow this state of affairs was received with complacence and even considered partially justified in dealings with the old, explained the survey, with the result that "therapy for the aged sick is often little better than palliative procrastination." Yet, as City University's Charlotte Mueller testified at a 1973 Senate hearing, "elderly persons suffer from more illness, have more disabling chronic conditions, and receive more personal health services than younger persons."

A 1973–74 survey of over one hundred medical schools in the nation indicated that 87 per cent offer no geriatric speciality and do not plan to add one; that 74 per cent lack an apprenticeship experience for students, interns, or residents to fulfill requirements through work in nursing homes; that 53 per cent provide no opportunity for contact with nursing-home patients. Student interest in old age is rarely intrinsic but almost always stimulated by job opportunities or study stipends, although in several instances an opportunity to work directly with old people has led to what one student referred to as "a conversion experience."

The medical profession's negative attitude toward the elderly is further reinforced by the fact that only one out of five cases of true organic senility, as opposed to "pseudo," or functional, senility, have a treatable cause. Some budget-conscious officials in our health system have seized upon this situation to question the cost-effectiveness of spending up to five hundred dollars for extensive series of diagnostic laboratory tests on all elderly patients when they may have only a few years to live.

Yet even in the face of such odds, many physicians would disagree, emphasizing the severity of a diagnosis of senility. According to Leslie Libow of the Jewish Institute for Geriatric Care:

> Senility is one of the most serious medical diagnoses that can be given to a patient, because the prognosis is so serious and the effectiveness of treatment is not clear. If we value our older people, how can anyone seriously argue that every physician should not do the tests to make sure a treatable cause has not been overlooked?

The elderly person does not fare much better with the psychotherapist. Looking over the previous fifty years, M. Powell Lawton wrote in 1974 that "during the heyday of psychotherapy the older person was totally excluded from the company of those thought to be suitable for individual therapy, and things are no better today." He cited statistics from the National Institute of Mental Health that report that only 2 per cent of all patients treated in outpatient clinics are sixty-five and over.

Since 1964, when Kastenbaum coined the phrase "the reluctant therapist" to describe the therapist who is loath to make his couch available to the elderly client, this situation has been documented at intervals in the journals. The latest studies now indicate a somewhat more positive attitude among analysts relative to treating the elderly client. Moreover, René Garfinkel, in *The Gerontologist* for April 1975, has suggested a new factor that might have been or still is the chief rationalization for their disdainful attitude: namely, that "old people usually don't talk much." Verbal interaction is the *sine qua non* of analysis therapy, and the presumed lack of it or enhanced difficulty in eliciting it presents a ready justification for an attitude still prevalent in the profession.

But what of the attitude of other professional groups toward the aging elderly? Attitudinal studies among dental students made by Beth Hess (Research in process on attitudes toward the elderly. Department of Social Science, County College of Morris, Dover, New Jersey, 1976) found much the same attitude within dentistry. Understandably, the dentist has to be concerned with the traits that make an individual easy or difficult to handle in the chair, but her survey revealed an astonishingly large number of negatives with which beginning dentists tag the elderly. According to dental students, the elderly patients are set in their ways, hard to please, less adaptable, self-centered, slow in thought and speech—in addition to having co-ordination lapses, sensory problems, and communication difficulties.

Even among the clergy, ministering to the aged is regarded as not among the most enjoyable tasks but not the most unenjoyable either. While clergy do not turn their backs on the elderly, they feel that they are better prepared to deal with younger parishioners.

There is, however, an increase in the demands for ministries to the aging despite what is still a lag among theological institutions in creating special training for work with the elderly. In *The Gerontologist* for April 1975, David Moberg compares a survey of catalogues in the mid-1960s with one done in 1972. In the earlier study only fourteen of twenty-four theological schools indicated any course material on the aging process or the aged. There were seventeen courses in which the elderly figured as part of a larger group, but only one was specifically devoted to aged parishioners. By 1972, a survey of 124 schools indicated that twenty-four now offered a special course on ministering to the aged, with two schools requiring it. Some twenty-eight listed continuing-education courses related to the elderly, while seventeen offered graduate programs allowing a gerontological specialty.

Comparing articles written a decade ago with those from the latest meetings of the Gerontological Society, it is clear that some progress has been made in preparing practitioners to deal with old people. It is even clearer that many of the "old" problems remain: negative stereotyping, inadequate preparation, and lack of consensus on what kind of training should be initiated and at what phase of practitioner education. Attitudes are the key question here. They are two-faceted: to what extent do stereotyping and prejudice make work with the aged less desirable to the practitioner than comparable time and effort spent upon the young, that is, the population who will, with luck, get better or respond to treatment in a way that rewards the practitioner; and in what manner do negative attitudes influence the professional's behavior so that they lessen the probability of success with older patients/clients?

One of the justifications for poor health care for the elderly is the tradition of keeping the elderly in the family. If the elderly person is kept in the family, then it is the family's responsibility if he gets sick and not society's. And indeed, keeping the elderly person within the family seems to be the norm. While traditional family theorists such as Burgess and Parsons have postulated that the nuclear family exists in relative isolation from its extended kin, there is considerable evidence in both major and minor studies since the late 1950s for a continuation of family relationships throughout life. Since three- and four-generation families are a relatively recent development, the norms governing relationships between middle and older generations are unclear. Among the many changes resulting from these multigenerational families is a reorientation of society from an emphasis on supporting children to one concerned with the support of the elderly—especially non-married females.

Studies focused on the second half of the family cycle or what has been called the contracting family are few. These studies are concerned with patterns of adaptation as well as practical information on family versus public support in later life and most show that family members of all generations prefer to seek help from other family members than from any other sources. If family members are continually expected to be responsible for the elderly, this takes the responsibility away from the professionals, who can refer the problem back to the family—a practice that runs the danger of simply begging the question.

One cannot examine health values in this country without taking into account that health involves more than adequate biological functioning. According to the charter of the World Health Organization, "Health is a state of complete physical, mental and social well-being and not merely the absence of disease or infirmity." Further, the WHO document states that "The enjoyment of the highest attainable standard of health is one of the fundamental rights of every human being without distinction of race, religion, political belief, economic or social condition." Quite obviously "socal condition" was meant to include "age."

There is no doubt that the negative stereotype of the aged person in society strongly affects the health of its elderly. Among the many reasons cited for this stereotype are the elderly's inability and lack of opportunity to reflect the American values of productivity, achievement, and independence, as well as the association of old age with illness and death.

Many studies have shown that the status of the elderly relative to other age groups diminishes with a shift from an agricultural to an industrialized society. Such a decrease in status is intimately tied to the high value placed on productivity in an industrialized society and what is considered to be the necessary institution of mandatory retirement.

In 1930, when mandatory retirement was first being introduced, only 5.4 per cent of the population were over sixty-five, but today the figure is 10 per cent, and by 2020 may become 15 per cent. However, despite this growth, the proportion of older people in the labor force has declined dramatically. Whereas, in 1900, 39 per cent of the over-sixty-five population were working or actively looking for work, by 1950 this figure had fallen to 25 per cent. Today it stands at 16 per cent.

If these trends continue unabated, our society is faced with the possibility of a decline in the percentage of workers as compared to the percentage of non-workers and retired persons. Already, many of those concerned with this problem have proposed that the nation begin encouraging people to work for as long as they are healthy and capable. A lengthened work life increases the period of time over which citizens pay taxes and contribute to the growth of the economy. A number of Western European countries have chosen to promote flexible retirement practices out of recognition of this basic fact.

But keep in mind that retirement, except for reasons of health, is a condition imposed upon the elderly by corporate regulations, Social Security requirements in particular, and a social practice of recent origin. Nearly a third of America's over-sixty-five retirees would still be at work if given the choice, according to the Harris poll made for The National Council on the Aging in 1975. Moreover, in a 1972 study the New York State Division of Human Rights found that "workers over sixty-five have better attendance records than younger workers, are seldom late for work, have fewer accidents, and are as productive as, and in some instances more productive than, younger workers." Yet mandatory retirement, in spite of the fact that it is arbitrary in many ways, still exists with virtually no probability of being substantially changed.

This forced retirement of competent and healthy workers comes in for strong denunciation in Alex Comfort's most recent book, in which he writes: "The things which make oldness insupportable in human societies don't at all commonly arise from . . . biological aging . . . [but] from sociogenic aging—the role which society imposes on people as they reach a certain chronological age." And the reviewer of the work in the New York *Times* extends the point: "It is *we* who 'retire' people at sixty-five—meaning we render them unemployed, useless, and often impoverished. It is *we* who define the elderly as crazy, asexual, unpeople, spent persons of no public account, instructed to run away and play until death comes out to call them to bed."

One of the most consistent findings in the gerontological literature is that negative attitudes toward poor health are correlated with high devaluation of old age. This had been found to be true of all ages, young and old alike. The current "health boom," while beneficial in that it basically encourages optimum health for all ages, has in a rather insidious way added to the already existing norm of regarding old age as a "second-rate" period of life by promoting vitamins and exercise to "preserve youth" and "retard aging."

Although gerontologists have not explicitly explored the relationship between attitudes toward aging and association with death, the relationship is assumed to be a powerful one. Death and dying are still taboo subjects in our culture. The more this is true, the less we want to accept or even acknowledge our older people. Nowhere is this attitude more pronounced than within the medical profession, where the death of a patient is regarded as a failure. Until we re-examine our attitudes toward death, it will be difficult to turn around the present negative stereotyping. Is it a marvel at all, then, that our professionals—no different from the rest of us— are more comfortable with younger population groups? Is it at all strange that American talent and money have always been poured lavishly into research into solving the problems and bettering the health of every other group in society, with the forlorn exception of the elderly?

Is it any wonder, then, that the elderly feel both devalued and ignored? Their treatment by society often has much to do with mental and attitudinal changes that are not directly biological and, in turn, increase their dependence on health professionals for psychological as well as medical reasons.

One might conclude from the foregoing somber recital that the situation is all bad. Yet the very fact that more and more voices in American society are talking loudly and clearly about the problems of the elderly and, more important, are working to uncover the underlying causes surely indicates that things are beginning to turn around. Back in 1961, the year of the first White House Conference on Aging, some 250,000 Americans held membership in the various professional and consumer organizations with a particular concern within the field of aging. In 1977 that number had reached 14 million.

The myths about aging that have fogged our minds and the stereotypes about the elderly that have blinded us are only slowly fading away. The 1959 report of the American Medical Association's Committee on Geriatrics, insisting that there are no diseases of the aged that are specifically the result of the passage of years, did open a new and more hopeful avenue of study. We have no right, they said, "to assume that the shaky hand, the wobbly step, and narrowing of physical and mental horizons are inevitable. We have the hope of prolonging life and living by modifying environment—including housing, family relationships, social life, employment, educational opportunities, spiritual life, and recreation, as well as sanitation, diet, and improved medical care."

This emphasis on modifying the environment implies the co-operation and effort of all generations in addition to the present generation of older people. Those who are young will become old. Young and old are simply the two sides making a single valuable coin. No one has expressed the thought better than the ever-sensitive Goethe, whose poems and stories still warm our civilization today: "Each generation helps the other see life as a whole. We need one another." If our society, in fact, did not place different values on youth and old age, but saw old age as a different, but not less desirable, period of life, the differential and unequal treatment of the elderly in our health system would no longer exist. This requires more than just a change in attitudes by and toward the present generation of elderly; rather, it requires a basic change by all generations of attitudes toward aging. The solution to the unequal delivery of health care to older people, and related problems of old age, must be intergenerational in nature and will require the attention and co-operation of people of all ages.

PART IV

DEATH:
The Final Confrontation

Only recently have we begun to see death as a part of the process of living, and to learn something of the myriad of attitudes and responses to this ultimate phase of life. "To study dying . . . is to fear it a little less," says one of these contributors.

Note: The editors would have liked to include in this section a representative piece by Elisabeth Kübler-Ross, but her work was not available for reprint at this time.

OLD PEOPLE TALK ABOUT DEATH

Shura Saul

The scene is the thirtieth session of a mental health group led by a trained psychotherapist in a nursing home. The group consists of five women, their ages ranging from 75 to 88 years. They are all ambulatory and alert; each suffering from a physical ailment requiring some level of nursing care. Within a range of capacity for ego functioning, each of them is related to reality and is competent in some decision making concerning her immediate needs and problems.

This group experience is part of an interdisciplinary treatment program that is consciously aimed at keeping these women reality oriented through such problem solving and decision making as may be possible within the severely circumscribed circumstances, physical and emotional, of the nursing home setting.

The psychotherapist had recently returned from a trip to England, which he had discussed with the group the preceding week. Among other things, he had reported that many small towns now use crematoria instead of cemeteries. This had occasioned interest in the question of burial versus cremation, and the group had decided to pursue the subject at its next session. During the week between the two sessions, there had been two deaths of some significance to these women. A resident had died, and also the sister of another resident.

The psychotherapist has had to deal with depression, a continuous condition of residents in an institution. Knowing of their suppressed fear of death, and their repression of feelings about the death of others, the therapist felt that it would be valuable to offer an opportunity for expressing these feelings through a discussion like this one.

The five group members include:

MRS. HOWARD: A very bright, alert woman of 75, active in all phases of the nursing home program.

MRS. ROSE: A smiling, well-dressed woman who usually denies problems; was friendly with Mrs. Robbins before coming to this home.

MRS. ROBBINS: A calm, alert woman who had been Mrs. Rose's neighbor when they both lived in the community.

MRS. RIKER: A tall, angular woman with a deep voice and quick laughter.

MRS. MORAN: A soft-voiced, quiet, visually handicapped woman who functions well and always dresses up for this meeting.

As usual, after the initial greetings, the discussion begins very slowly.

DR. S.: Do you remember what we said we'd be talking about this week?

MRS. HOWARD: I remember, but it's better to talk about life, not about death.

MRS. ROSE: Talking about dying is a sad thing.

DR. S.: Do you think we shouldn't talk about it?

MRS. ROSE: I realize you can't bring the dead back. . . . It depends how you talk about them.

DR. S.: Remember, last week we planned to talk about burial or cremation?

MRS. ROBBINS: She (pointing to Mrs. Rose) had her husband cremated. Do you remember that? (She turns to Mrs. Rose)

MRS. ROSE: That is right. That was how he wished it.

DR. S.: What do you think about it?

MRS. ROSE: Well, if it happened to me, I'd just as soon go that way.

DR. S.: So your wish is to be cremated?

MRS. ROSE: Yes!

DR. S.: How do the rest of you feel?

MRS. ROBBINS: I'm Catholic. I don't believe in cremation.

DR. S.: How about you, Mrs. Moran?

MRS. MORAN: I don't like to hear that story.

DR. S.: What story?

MRS. MORAN: I want to be buried just like my husband . . . my father. (Very softly)

MRS. RIKER: (Very matter of fact) I wonder how much it costs to be cremated. It must be cheaper, I'm sure.

DR. S.:   That's not why they do it in England. It's because there, they have no space.

MRS. RIKER: Since Peggy (Mrs. Rose) has had experience, maybe she will tell us more about it (cremation), some little thing.

MRS. ROSE: (Schoolteacher style) You should go to such a funeral, then you'll know more about it.

DR. S.:   I think Mrs. Riker wants to know your experience.

MRS. ROSE: Well, it was my husband's wish . . . he always said when it happened to him . . . that's why I had it done. That's how I felt at the time, and you can imagine that yourself.

MRS. ROBBINS: They had a wake the night before the cremation.

DR. S.:   How did you feel about it?

MRS. ROBBINS: I didn't mind. When you're dead, you're dead.

DR. S.:   What would you want for yourself?

MRS. ROBBINS: No, I don't want it. I want to be buried with my husband and my family.

DR. S.:   Do you think there is a hereafter?

MRS. ROBBINS: Yes, you have to account for your sins . . . and then you will get together.

DR. S.:   Then you have a religious reason for preferring burial?

MRS. ROBBINS: Yes, that's right.

DR. S.:   Mrs. Moran, what about you?

MRS. MORAN: Me? Poor, blind me?

DR. S.:   What would you want?

MRS. MORAN: I want my sight back—if I can have what I want.

DR. S.:   What about cremation or burial?

MRS. MORAN: All I want is to be buried with my husband, my friends, and my people. I want to be with the people I love so much, and with the baby that died, too.

DR. S.:   So you, too, believe in a hereafter?

MRS. MORAN: That is right.

DR. S.:   Mrs. Riker?

MRS. RIKER: Oh, it wouldn't make any difference to me. I

think I'm going to be buried. A lot of people think that the worms won't eat you if you're not buried. Some people think they'll hate to lie there—the worms will eat them. It makes no difference to me. Whatever goes on after I'm gone, I won't know anyway! They can throw me over the fence and I'll lay there and I can rot there. It won't make any difference!

(She laughs. . . . There is general laughter . . . and some relief)

DR. S.:   Well, we finally got a laugh out of this. Mrs. Howard, how about you?

MRS. HOWARD: I'd like to be buried where my husband is.

DR. S.:   So, you want to be buried too?

MRS. HOWARD: I have a plot there. (She is suddenly thoughtful). . . . I have the deed . . . but I didn't pay my dues . . . I don't know what I should do now . . . if they are very scarce with the plots (Suddenly defiant) . . . I don't care. Whatever the children want!

DR. S.:   Whatever your children want?

MRS. HOWARD: I gave them the deed to the plot.

DR. S.:   So you want to be buried?

MRS. HOWARD: I don't know what I want. (Sadly) I suppose so.

DR. S.:   Any particular reason?

MRS. HOWARD: (Very softly) No reason . . . no particular reason . . . I belonged to a society . . . where I got the plot and then I couldn't pay dues . . . I paid a little, then I stopped. Maybe I lost the plot because of "off-payment."

DR. S.:   Well, we could find out for you, if you wish.

MRS. HOWARD: Yes, I would want you to do that.

DR. S.:   Do you ladies think about death?

MRS. ROBBINS: Yes, I think of it . . . sure!

MRS. MORAN: By golly, I do! I wish it very bad sometimes!

DR. S.:   Mrs. Riker, how about you?

MRS. RIKER: I don't so much now, as when I was a kid. When you're a child, you are afraid of death. But now, when you know it is coming, you can't stop it.

MRS. ROBBINS: I'm not thinking about it, because I don't want to go there.

MRS. RIKER: Where?

MRS. ROBBINS: To the—uh—crematorium.

MRS. MORAN: (Her voice suddenly pitched high) I think of it, off and on, I speak with my daughters.

DR. S.:   Are you frightened by it?

MRS. MORAN: (Soft voice again) No, I'm not frightened.

MRS. ROBBINS: Sometimes I just wonder what will happen to me after I die.

DR. S.:   Does anyone else think of that?

MRS. ROSE: Sometimes I just hope that they'll put me where I want to go, that's all. I want to be cremated.

MRS. ROBBINS: She wants to be with her husband.

(There is a long silence)

DR. S.:   Did you leave any papers to that effect? Any message with anyone?

MRS. ROSE: Oh yes, to the people who are concerned.

DR. S.:   How many of you have made arrangements for burial?

(There is another long silence)

MRS. RIKER: I have a grave from my husband's insurance.

(Suddenly there is an active hubbub among the ladies . . . they have begun small buzzing conversations between themselves . . . finally Mrs. Robbins turns to Dr. S.)

MRS. ROBBINS: I just say I'm old, and they'll have to bury me.

MRS. HOWARD: Don't they have plans here in the nursing home?

DR. S.:   Why, do you think I'm selling plots?

(There is general laughter which relieves the tension)

MRS. RIKER: It feels good to laugh . . . we all needed that laugh.

DR. S.:   Does this whole discussion disturb you?

MRS. RIKER: No, not me.

MRS. HOWARD: Now, I have the occasion to ask, why such a discussion? Why did it come up here?

DR. S.:   Well, did anything happen in the home here this past week involving someone who died?

(Silence)

MRS. HOWARD: Yes. Rose, Mrs. Ellis' sister, she died. I wanted to go to the funeral, but then I made another plan and I stayed away.

DR. S.:   *I* think Mrs. Moran doesn't know what you are talking about. Would you like to tell her?

MRS. HOWARD: (Suddenly overtly hostile) She doesn't know what I'm talking about, so she's gonna be without it.

DR. S.:   Who died?

MRS. HOWARD: The sister died. Mrs. Ellis' sister.

MRS. ROBBINS: (Interrupts suddenly) Mrs. Leland died.

(Nobody pays any attention to her at this point)

DR. S.:   Is this news to anybody? About Mrs. Ellis' sister?

MRS. HOWARD: A few people from this place went to the funeral with Mrs. Ellis, that's all. I wasn't there.

DR. S.:   Who else, did you say, died this week, Mrs. Robbins?

MRS. ROBBINS: Mrs. Leland.

(There is another buzzing of interest over this bit of information, above which emerges the slightly Irish brogue of Mrs. Moran)

MRS. MORAN: Oh, did she die?

MRS. ROBBINS: Yes, she did.

MRS. MORAN: I didn't know she died.

MRS. ROBBINS: She was sick a long time.

MRS. MORAN: (Incredulous) The lady on my floor? That Mrs. Leland?

DR. S.:   Yes. Does that upset you, Mrs. Moran?

MRS. MORAN: (Amazed) They took such good care of her!

MRS. RIKER: She was supposed to be very wealthy . . . many years ago. Mrs. Leland, one of the Leland dress house family.

MRS. HOWARD: Money doesn't pay off the death. Money doesn't pay off not to die.

DR. S.:   Um . . . um. . . .

(There is a deep, long silence)

Well, if I'm quiet will everyone else be quiet too?

MRS. HOWARD: (Sarcastically) Maybe somebody should start dancing. Mrs. Moran should play the music, then we wouldn't be so quiet.

DR. S.:   You want us to play some music and everybody dance?

MRS. HOWARD: (Softer tone) They won't dance. I'm just joking.

DR. S.:   You're angry with me, Mrs. Howard?

MRS. HOWARD: Because you picked such a topic today . . . we got to have a little bit of fun.

DR. S.:   I have upset you.

MRS. HOWARD: Of course, the topic upset me! It doesn't make me happy. It doesn't make me sad.

DR. S.:   Shall we stop the discussion now? I'm asking everyone.

MRS. RIKER: (With a laugh) You're the boss.

(There are murmurs of general concensus)

MRS. HOWARD: (Pleased voice) Well, let's ask the group to do the memory exercises. Let's see if we know the names of the people here, the live ones. . . .

The group accedes and begins their weekly name game to exercise their memory faculties.

NOTE: Two weeks after this discussion, Mrs. Rose died suddenly. She was cremated as was her wish. In the session that followed her death, the group members talked freely with each other and with the therapist about their feelings at her sudden passing.

In sharp contrast to earlier situations when such feelings had been repressed, and conversations had ignored the fact of death, Mrs. Riker opened the session by asking the therapist, "Do you notice that someone is missing from our group?"

DEATH AS AN ACCEPTABLE SUBJECT
Tabitha M. Powledge

The pretty, solemn face has been staring out from magazine covers, newspapers, and television sets for the better part of a year now, forcing each American, as no public event ever has before, to see not just the consequences of today's technology, but his own inevitable end.

But though everyone will ultimately meet the same fate as Karen Quinlan, most people will not face it unknowingly, in a coma, as she does now. Many people have months, sometimes years, to live through even after they have been handed a certain death sentence. And in the past few years, it has become clear that people who know they are dying have special needs that have been largely ignored.

Death is now, as one recent book put it, a fact of life; it has, since Geoffrey Gorer characterized it only a decade ago as a form of pornography, burst out of the closet along with many of our other shameful secrets. The magazine *Psychology Today* noted with astonishment a few years ago that more than thirty thousand readers had replied to its questionnaire on death, ten thousand more replies than it received to its questionnaire on sex.

Indeed, this new openness has already produced signs of a death backlash. A New York psychologist titled a recent journal article "Is Dying Being Worked to Death?" and Princeton theologian Paul Ramsey has inveighed against "the indignity of 'death with dignity.'"

Much of this new interest in the dying process was triggered by the pioneering work of psychiatrist Elisabeth Kübler-Ross, who in 1969 published "On Death and Dying," which told of her work with dying patients. She identified five psychological stages of dying, beginning with denial and ending (if the patient was lucky) in acceptance. To look at dying as a developmental process, like pregnancy or puberty, was a new and startling idea for most people. Dr. Kübler-Ross transformed the way dying is seen, and made it clear how badly society was doing at assisting people through that process.

One of the reasons for this failure is that, in the past few decades, more and more people have been dying in hospitals instead of at home. Hospitals are not organized around dying; they are organized around curing. Each death, no matter how old and ill the patient, is a failure for the hospital and a cause of anxiety for the staff. Dying patients have therefore often been either the targets of superhuman, futile efforts at resuscitation and maintenance (as in the Quinlan case) or shunted off into the furthest room and ignored as much as possible. The hospital staff is in the business of saving lives, not watching lives lost. One study has shown that physicians are not only more afraid of death than other people are, but also that they fear death even more than people who are terminally ill.

In some places, the hospital situation is improving. Dealing with death is starting to become part of the training of hospital personnel, and the need has even given rise to a group of people who might be called "dying counselors," although it is not by any means a formalized profession. They are simply people who concluded that dying was being rendered more painful and horrifying than it needed to be, and who were determined to do something about it.

They have often come from the ranks of the clergy, although many individual health professionals, such as nurses, have also made care of the dying a specialty. They have worked hard to see that hospitals are more responsive to the needs of their dying patients, and they have also worked with the patients and their families, helping them get their lives in order, helping them openly express their anger and fear.

From Britain has come the idea of the "hospice," an inpatient facility specially designed for the dying: cheerful, homelike, full of plants and families (including young children). There are about thirty such places in Britain now, but the idea has been slower to take root in the United States. The hospice in New Haven, for instance, has been in operation with a home-care program for more than two years, and has on paper a striking design for a building, but has not yet begun construction.

The emphasis will remain on home care even after the building is built, because most of the dying are happier at home for as long as it is possible to remain there. For all the hospices, the central therapy is the relief of pain, emotional and physical. Strong drugs are given on a schedule designed to prevent pain, rather than alleviate it, although they also try to maintain thinking processes on a level as near normal as possible.

Most people will not die in such a place, but their going may be made easier because of things learned there. Courses and seminars on death and dying are becoming part of the training of the health professional but are also widely available to the general public, even on television. Many hospitals are revising their treatment of the dying. The trickle of books and articles on the subject became a torrent long before Karen Quinlan was part of the national consciousness; in less than ten years, one bibliography on death grew from four hundred to twenty-six hundred items. Research on college students early in this decade found them more preoccupied with thoughts of death than a group of students surveyed in 1935.

The source of the new fascination with death has itself become an object of speculation. Is it because of the continuing threat of nuclear annihilation? Is it because of increased street crime, the world-wide wave of terrorist activities, the Vietnam War, the parade of assassinations? Is it, most of all, the window on mortality provided by television, which dangles before the audience fantasies of violent death in prime time and reinforces the fantasy with the bloody reality between six and seven-thirty?

Whatever the reasons, the fascination is there, and many people think it is a healthy development. French social historian Philippe Ariès argues that such concerns not necessarily only foreshadowed the collapse of the Middle Ages but may also have indicated a new flowering of love of life which followed.

In that sense, to study dying, to know its stages and its demands, is to fear it a little less. In his influential book *The Denial of Death,* Ernest Becker argues that human heroism has its roots in the common human terror of death. The hero was the man who could visit the underworld—and return. "When we see a man bravely facing his own extinction," Becker says, "we rehearse the greatest victory we can imagine." If that is true, then the new open curiosity about death, the new techniques and skills aimed at helping the dying to the "good" death, far from constituting a resigned acceptance of inevitable mortality, is actually another show of human heroism, another human way of overcoming death.

"I WANT TO GO HOME":
A VERY OLD LADY DIES IN STYLE

Nancy Williams

Anna Grace Péquignot died in 1976, age ninety-six. Nancy Williams wrote this account of her mother's brief final illness and death in a letter to her daughter Christina, who was living overseas.

Dearest Chris,

What I want you to know surely about Grandma is that her death was a triumph of spirit. We wished so much that you had been there so that you could have seen that for yourself. The boys didn't stay at the hospital to be dutiful, they really wanted to be there; nor were any of us depressed at watching her die. She did it exactly the way she had lived, with style and humor and incredible courage. I want to describe those hours to you because you belonged there. If it's too much, darling, just read it in bits.

Mother had the sense to phone me at twelve-thirty on Sunday afternoon, saying in a rather burbly voice that she hadn't been able to dial my number but had had to ask the operator, and that she was the most confused person in Ann Arbor. So we went right over. She was sitting in her chair in the living room and did seem confused and uncomfortable. Her first Grandma-like act was to refuse to let me feed her soup and toast or to have a tray on her lap. After she had eaten she said she needed to go to the bathroom and, thank you, she did *not* need us to help her with that either.

When she was through she allowed us to help her to bed. Daddy and I have the feeling that from that moment she turned things over to God and to other people; she'd done all she could and now it was up to others. During the last month or so she had gradually and oh so reluctantly let go of the last of the duties that made life bearable to her: ironing for me, bringing over to Daddy her business matters, watering her plants. On the other hand, the preceding Friday night she had come over to supper all decked out in her shocking-pink sweater and skirt and matching hair ribbon, to help celebrate Rhys's being accepted into graduate school, and enjoyed her dry martini and shrimp salad and mince pie.

We phoned Dr. Payne to see if there was anything we could do to make Mother more comfortable; neither of us was particularly alarmed, feeling she was just fading a little more. We discussed asking her to come to our house but agreed to hang on as long as possible to everyone's desire to have her be in her own house, since Mother's independence was all-important to her. After Daddy had gone home to do some work, Mother said I should turn off the lights when I left, a typical energy-conserving remark. When I said I was staying, she protested.

I felt uneasy in the living room, so I sat beside her bed. She was able to talk, though with increasing difficulty, and her eyes were mostly closed. She said this prayer: "Dear Jesus, sweet Jesus, forgive me all my sins. Not my will, but thine be done. I'm not afraid to die. Dear God, let me go." Then she thanked Him for her children "and all the kind people who have helped me all my life." Later she seemed to think I'd said something about a "cardinal" when we'd talked of calling a priest. I said if we were going to try for a cardinal, we might as well shoot for the Pope. At which a nice smile went over her face.

Soon Dr. Payne arrived. After checking Mother he told me in his kind, plain way that she was very seriously ill, that she had congestive heart failure, probably renal failure as well, quite possibly pneumonia. He added, "You know, she will be very mad at us if we bring her back." So I told him that we all wanted Mother to do what she most wanted now, to die as soon as possible, and that we wanted her to be comfortable. We decided that it wasn't feasible for me to try to care for her at home (her home), that nurses at the hospital would be able to move her, change her (renal failure), administer oxygen. After Dr. Payne had called an ambulance and left, I sat by Mother and she roused herself to say another prayer: "If I were to make my last statement, it would go like this. This is what it would be like. 'Dear Jesus, not my will but thine be done. Forgive me for my sins. And please, *please,* don't let me be too much trouble.'" At which, needless to say, I nearly dissolved, and kissed her and said she had never been a trouble. She looked at me and said, "Is this it?" I wish now I'd said that perhaps it was. I think I told her that I didn't know but I thought everything was going to be all right.

Rhys and young Lloyd arrived just before the ambulance. The five or six young men who came with the ambulance were just darling with Mother. They called her "Anna," which she might not have appreciated if she'd been her old self, one of them, "Anna dear," and they each described to her what they were about to do. I thought Mother by then did not hear or care much. I was wrong. She told the ambulance squad not to make too much commotion and alarm the other apartment dwellers, and not to use the siren, because there was enough noise pollution around already.

Then began the final eight hours. We got to the hospital at 6:25 P.M. Sunday, and Mother died at about one-fifty the next morning. As the four of us sat by Mother's bed, nurses administered oxygen and tried to make her a little more comfortable. She kept the plastic gizmo around her head and in her nostrils for an hour, maybe, then decided that was enough; every time any of us or a nurse would try to reinsert it, she would firmly, very firmly, remove it. About eight or so, Dr. Payne came and said to forget it if she felt so strongly. Rhys holds that it wasn't just the discomfort, that she didn't want any delaying tactics.

One of the most wondrous moments was when the boys returned from making phone calls and I said, "Mother, Lloyd and Rhys are here now." She opened her eyes and said, "Thank you for coming to help me die." At which point Lloyd knelt down by her bed and kissed her hand and said, "I love you, Granny," and Rhys stood on the other side and held her other hand. And Mother smiled, quite fleetingly, but she smiled.

During Dr. Payne's visit, he sat by her bed, and she tried to talk to him. What finally came out after laborious minutes was, "I'll give up smoking if. . . ." Dr. Payne just sat there quietly, his chin on the bedrail, waiting, not trying to interpret, just waiting. Mother never did finish her sentence, but Dr. Payne told me the next day that he knew beyond a doubt that what she was trying to say was, "I'll stop smoking if you don't stop me from dying." A long and fond admirer of my mother in all her stubborn independence, he observed that he didn't consider her offer a very good bargain under the circumstances.

Then there was the time when Mother opened her eyes and

said, "Am I dead?" And I said, "Not yet, Mom." At which point
she said, with fierce intensity, "Oh, God." The boys both thought
she looked beautiful. I think they hadn't seen her hair down in a
long time; it was indeed very long. They said she looked like an
American Indian and were especially moved when she asked
whether she was dead, because an old Indian man in the movie
Little Big Man had said just those words and looked just like her
when he was dying and the rain had fallen on his face and roused
him. Rhys told Mother how pretty she looked. Again that fleeting
smile went across her face, and she blew him two kisses, that familiar ironic gesture of hers when somebody paid her a compliment.

When we made these little jokes we were pleased when Mother
understood and smiled. But after a while I think we all sensed that
perhaps we were pulling her back to life in the same way as the
oxygen and that we needed to let her go. Afterward Lloyd quoted
Ram Dass to the effect that when a person is dying it's important
for him to know it's all right to let go, that he doesn't have to hang
on.

A splendid episode: Mother had had the bedpan, but almost
immediately afterward needed it again. She tried to tell us she
wanted it by making the letter "p" with her index finger and
thumb and the index finger of her other hand (either for "pot" or
"pee"). When we didn't get it, she pointed to her crotch, and
when we still didn't understand, she finally managed to really spit
out, "P, as in Piss!" And when the nurses were putting the bedpan
under her, she pulled down her hospital gown and whispered,
"Modesty, you know." The boys loved that.

I guess the last little joke we had was when a nurse wiped
Mother's lips with a cool cloth. She grimaced and drew back and
my husband said quickly, "That's a dry martini, Bobby." The little
smile appeared.

There isn't much more to tell. From time to time Mother would
say, "Oh, God," as though pleading with him. At one point she
said, "I want to go home." When I made some feeble explanation
about the hospital's greater comforts, she shook her head impa-
tiently. And I belatedly knew what home she was talking about.
Hallelujah! We all held her hands and stroked her hair and said,
"Hi, Granny." About midnight the nurses moved her to a private

room. About one o'clock Daddy and the boys left, to get some sleep before work the next day. I lay down on some put-together chairs, relieved that Mother seemed to be really resting for the first time. I could hear a little breath once in a while. After a few minutes a nurse came in, checked Mother's pulse, and said, "I think she's gone."

I just stayed there a bit, saying good-by. When a very brisk young night nurse appeared, I said, "What will you do with my mother's body tonight?" She replied, "The eye man will be here in fifteen minutes to remove her cornea and then we'll put her in the cooler till morning." Can you imagine? She should be held for a witness, as my mother used to say. I just packed up my things, pulled the sheet up around Mother (saying to myself that it was so damn hot in that hospital she'd probably enjoy being in the cooler), and went out.

ABOUT THE LIFE AND DEATH OF
RAE EDITH ROSE

Marion Ebner

Last week, Rae Edith Rose died in Bellevue Hospital. To the best of my knowledge, she was over 102 years of age. Because she was a patient of Bellevue's Home Care Program, Mrs. Rose was able to maintain herself in her own home until approximately a week before her death.

When I first met Mrs. Rose, she was well into her nineties. Her body was failing her, and she was angry. She had been trying to cope with the bureaucracy of the clinic, and that only made her more aware of her own vulnerability. A small, meticulous woman, she wore a neat veiled hat and white gloves, the trappings of a lady of another era. Her speech was precise; her words were right to the point. She needed help. She was added to the list of patients in the Home Care Program.

Mrs. Rose was not easy to work with and would react with sharp words to anything she interpreted as threatening her independence. At first, the nursing staff had difficulty in accepting her, labeling her "unco-operative." She rejected social workers as "do-gooders," even though she needed the services only they could provide. For a while she was not comfortable in relating to our nurse's aides, because they were black and her contacts with this group had been very limited. They sensed it but never let it interfere with the way they responded to her.

As time passed, mutual respect and real affection developed between her and all the staff. We became her family. She learned to accept our help without being threatened, and we learned to look at the aging process and its consequences with less fear.

A very independent woman, Mrs. Rose never revealed too much about herself. We knew she came from the New England region and was very proud of her "Yankee know-how." Widowed when she was nineteen, she was left on her own. She told us how she became a dressmaker and milliner: designing, sewing, draping heavy laces and velvets, putting on fashion shows, and traveling to sell her work. Once, she showed me a picture of some of her dresses. They had the look of the World War I period.

Apparently her business thrived until the Depression, when illness struck and her financial problems began. That was the start of her long relationship with Bellevue Hospital (she would have been in her fifties at that time). When her health stabilized, Mrs. Rose resumed her craft, but she was never able to regain her former status.

The memorial service in the Bellevue Episcopal Chapel was attended by a few friends and the staff of the Home Care Department. The minister who officiated was one of her Bellevue "family." It was a very meaningful experience for all of us.

A goal had been established at the time Mrs. Rose was placed on the Home Care Program: to assist the patient in her efforts to maintain her independence in her own home for as long as it is safe and practical.

The goal was reached. Because of the Bellevue Home Care staff, Mrs. Rose was able to live and die on her own terms—with dignity.

MARION EBNER
Elmhurst, N.Y., March 3, 1977

PART V

"WHAT'S INSIDE YOU,
IT SHINES OUT OF YOU":
Joys and Rewards
of Old Age

OLD PEOPLE WRITE OF AGING

GETTING OLDER ... OLDER ... OLD

Rose Rudin

You don't get old all at once. You notice the first wrinkle, the first gray hair . . . but you are too busy living to really think of "when you'll be old."

Then, one day, you are "over 75!" Out of habit, you continue doing all the things you did all your life.

You take care of your husband with constant concern for his health and well-being. (I am fortunate to have a husband who is a great comfort and help to me in all ways, even in the process of becoming, and being, old.)

You keep house—with more effort, of course.

You still do little things for those around you.

You also do your small share toward peace and a better world.

You anxiously watch the progress of your children and grandchildren—and hope that they will have a better life in a world at peace and real brotherhood.

You think of the past, and you are sorry for all the wrong things you did. You regret not to have done more of the right things.

You long for all the dear ones who have gone.

You cherish the ones still around and want to see more often.

You try not to "push time" unless a dear one is ill or you have a sleepless night.

You plan for tomorrow . . . next year . . . and next . . .
And you know that there are not many of those left for you at your age so you feel a little sad!

HOW AN EIGHTY-THREE-YEAR-OLD MAN LOOKS AT LIFE
Froim Camenir

My few words on this topic will not be a resume for all old people because each one of us looks differently at life. I'll describe my own view of life.

Since elderly people die before younger ones, I do not worry about death. Since death comes "willy-nilly" I am not sure of tomorrow's day—so I appreciate every day of my life. I regard each, not as the forerunner of my tomorrow's day of death but, rather, as the continuation of my yesterday of life. Like any other day, it is welcomed because it brings life, pleasure, and the power to think.

My daily routine as an 83-year-old man (except for a change in the quantity of physical work) is no different from when I was age 73, or 63, or 53. It is true that, physically, the body becomes weaker, and we cannot perform the work or activities that we could in our younger days. Personally, however, I am in quite fair physical condition.

Some elderly people are afraid of death. I am not. Death is another form of existence, which is not known to us. I am not a religious person—however, I think that some sayings in the holy scriptures are correct—for example, "From dust thou cometh to dust returneth." I surely do not believe in resurrection!

A number of philosophers have discussed life and death. Some have praised the stage of youth—"De Juventute." Some have praised the stage of old age—"De Senectute." Leo Tolstoi wrote a nice little story about death, called "The Three Deaths." He describes the death of a rich, capricious old lady who dies in the middle of a journey between Moscow and the Crimea; the death of an old driver dying peacefully on an old peasant oven; and the death of a tree that is cut down to become a cross on the grave of the old driver. It all takes place early at dawn, a beautiful description!

However, I do not always think of death. Since I am an optimist by nature, and since death is not such a pleasant topic, I think mostly of life's problems, which we each face. I do not work any longer in my profession, so I don't have to think about earning a living. I am the secretary for a few fraternal organizations so I am quite busy with some actual secretarial work. I am also always thinking of ways to improve our work there. It is quite a problem to maintain these groups because I deal with old people who are faced with many problems such as health, income (most of which is based on social security payments or union retirement pensions), and family relationships.

Of course, I think about my family. How will my wife feel when I die? (She is quite a bit younger than I.) I think of my only daughter and her husband, who drive about in their cars daily. I am concerned about possible accidents. I think of my grandchildren and hope that they will be able to keep their various jobs.

I read in the newspaper how many teachers, engineers, and others are being fired. I think of the unhappy people (unemployed in many states) and how they could be helped. It breaks my heart to see the condition of our country, which has come to such a state that our "almighty dollar" has fallen so low on the international exchange. When I came to this glorious country in 1913, carfare was 5 cents with two transfers; the price of a letter only 2 cents, a postcard was a penny; the best meat was 35 cents a pound; a pound of bread was 8 cents. These concerns cause me to think about other serious social conditions—such as a person being afraid to go out alone in the street at night.

I think of the ignorance of many of our people, so many of our legislators who allow this unnecessary war in Vietnam. Our young boys die for nothing, tens of thousands dead and injured . . . billions of dollars spent and the question arises: "Why all these losses? In the name of what?" It seems that it is easier to ask the question than to get a logical, reasonable answer—and I, as an old man, am shedding silent tears, helpless to do anything to change the situation.

The only consolation I do have is to see the protests of our young generation. Their work, their protests follow the work of my generation. We taught them to work toward a better life without wars and without unemployment.

I am glad, and proud, that members of my generation were actually instrumental in achieving unemployment insurance, social security, teaching and enlightening the younger generation about the structure of our society, about minority groups.

All in all, old people play an important role. We are consumers, which is good for the economy. We are a political power—through our millions of votes we can elect a government more sensitive to our needs and the needs of all people.

We can offer support and guidance to the young generation. There are quite a few youngsters in my own family—nephews, grandchildren, nieces—who always ask me about my life, my studies, my teachers—in general, about the customs and life of my young days. They are interested in knowing what my world was like when I was young.

Some old people who are scientists, musicians, doctors, lawyers, actors, do still practice their professions, and the young generation can learn a great deal from them.

When this 83-year-old man gets up in the morning, he observes the sky is blue; the trees and grass are green; the sun shines; the birds sing; the city is in motion; people (most of the time) work and are happy. Children of all ages attract my attention. I see them grow nicely, strong. I believe they are willing and anxious to learn from the old generation—and the old generation is only too glad, happy, and also anxious to give to them.

This is the way I, an 83-year-old man, look at life.

OLD PARENTS

For reasons we could not control
This Home has now become our home,
We may not live amongst our own
We who are blind and aged grown.

Our children must their own lives lead,
Their own tasks do; their own times need.
Here we live in calm and rest—
Indeed, for us, this is the best.

To God nor man bemoan our fate
But join in friendship; cast out hate.
Let peaceful living be our goal
As befits a human soul.

(*Translated by Shura Saul from Yiddish Verse Written by an 83-Year-Old Resident of a Home for Aged People*)

MY ADVANCING YEARS

Frieda Laufgraben

My advancing years? Very much like my early years!

Curiosity and involvement have been part of me as long as I can remember.

I think a good starting point would be at the age of 54 when a piece in *The New York Times* attracted my attention. "The Academy of Medicine would have an all-day seminar on the need for Licensed Practical Nurses."

I attended, became carried away with the idea, and enrolled for the one-year intensive course, but was met with humorous harassment from my family and close friends.

Back to discipline and study at the YWCA and clinical practice and training at Beth El Hospital, now known as Brookdale. It was definitely one of my roughest years, but without the cooperation of my husband, I know I could not have done it! He relieved me of almost all the family chores for that year.

Seven weeks before graduation I very suddenly found myself a widow!

My impulse was to drop nursing, but with the encouragement of my instructors and director of nursing, I completed my course. "You have so much to give," is what they insisted.

Shortly after, the State Board Exams came up and still in my dark hours, I was shocked to learn that I came through with 93 per cent. This was my green light that I must carry on.

I worked at Maimonides for about 10 years on a per diem basis only so that I could continue to maintain contact with my family, friends, and community.

I continued my membership in two organizations, always in some active capacity, including the presidency of Kings County Jewish Veterans, Ladies Auxiliary. This consisted of 30 auxiliaries —over 2500 members.

At present, 15 years later, I am president of the Friendship Club, over 300 members, serving on several committees, and the nearest thing to my heart is the NRA (Neighborhood Resources for the Aging).

Not at all easy! Many mornings it would be so nice to stay in bed—a pain here, an ache there, but with a little struggle, get the curlers in the hair, dress slowly, put the lipstick on, and miraculously you're ready to go!

I'm satisfied with small daily blessings and with helping one person if I can.

A regimen, conducive to good health, is worth trying.

I have worked for six summers as a nurse in children's camps —work four days each year on the Board of Elections—took a 31-day trip abroad, occasional shorter trips, weekends with family or friends, their homes or mine, and manage to squeeze in a luncheon, book review, a bit of reading and knitting, and a weekly game of Canasta.

Yes, I do my own housework and enjoy my own cooking. Actually there is always "something to do."

My thanks to my personal friends and family, especially my grandchildren who understand when Grandma is busy.

ON BEING INVOLVED
Pauline Affronti

When I was young my involvements were mostly being a wife and mother. It was a very happy involvement. But time passes so quickly, and soon the family has grown and left home, and then you're left with just your husband. It also comes to pass that he has gone and I'm left alone.

I felt so sad and lonely for a while until my son insisted I take a trip cross country to California by bus. I had traveled plenty with my husband, and my son said I should continue, so I did. I didn't know a soul on the bus, but soon we became one big happy family. By the time I got back home I began to realize that I had to be with people. Thank God, I'm an outgoing person. Soon I joined the AARP and heard about a club being started for Senior Citizens in Maimonides so I became involved.

My whole life and being became exciting to me again. I started with people, with older adults, and enjoying it very much, soon I became president of this club. For two years I was very active with the club and outside activities, that never did I have a chance to think in terms of loneliness and sadness.

Any person who feels lonely when left alone, man or woman,

should join an organization with their age group and become involved. It is the most rewarding thing that can happen.

Growing old? Never! Moving around makes you feel younger, look younger, and even eases health problems.

THE CROWNING YEARS

Siegmund May

A compassionate and perceptive physician asks, and attempts to answer, an intriguing question: "What makes some old people so brave and content, so interested, so intensely humane—and what makes others so sour, cranky, and demanding?"

The advent of septuagenarians, octogenarians, and nonagenarians in large numbers is a new phenomenon in the history of man. Naturally, it has attracted enormous attention everywhere and notably in the sciences of biology, medicine, and sociology. Many previously held assumptions concerning old age have had to be discarded, some drastically revised, and new revelations absorbed. Altogether, today, we have a better chance of analyzing the magic formula for longevity than ever before. We may even find out how we all can achieve a long and good life.

Of the greatest importance is the study of the inner resources which lead people to long years of usefulness and enjoyment. what makes some old people so brave and content, so interested, so intensely humane—and what makes others so sour, cranky, and demanding?

It accomplishes nothing to shrug off these questions with the stereotyped answer that we are all made from different molds. Every human being is in a state of developmental flux—in fact, of aging—from birth to death. Old age implies an adjustment to a set of altered circumstances, but we have been meeting new conditions and unexpected situations all through life. Adjustment is not automatic when we are old, as it may have seemed to be in youth. We are capable of bringing it about, but only if we ourselves direct the aging process wisely.

My belief in this human capability is not merely wishful thinking. I have had many occasions to observe the rebuilding and the revitalizing of people who had been deteriorating in idleness and self-pity. Sometimes this has happened after a thoughtful self-

search. Sometimes the shock of a traumatic experience seems to
have been necessary.

One friend of mine was plunged into semiretirement while still
a healthy, wealthy, and life-loving man of fifty after a most strenu-
ous quarter of a century. Only too soon he realized that all the
pleasures now available to him would not only bore him but sap
his ego and demoralize his character. Defying warnings of his family and friends, he embarked upon a new experimental and risky
enterprise. He succeeded in creating an industrial empire. Today,
at ninety-four, he still is active, though his eyesight has failed him;
he has a remarkable memory and radiates cheerfulness and humor.
He is extraordinarily modest. Nothing delights him more than to
surprise his friends with all sorts of comforts and pleasures. His
age has been blessed by a devotion to people and the devotion of
others to him.

An excellent plumber, an immigrant from Central Europe to
America in his youth, he refused to yield to the urging of his family
to retire at sixty-five. When a serious automobile accident crippled
him so that he no longer could be active in his trade, he sank into
the deepest despondency. For several months he was completely
inactive and in despair. Then one day he shut himself up in a small
room off his former workshop, coming out only for lunch and the
night, locking the door behind him. Every day thereafter he disappeared into this tiny place, but kept silence for a long time about
what he was doing there. However, his family saw a rapid return
of his former cheerfulness and optimism. Finally he confessed that
he was working on an invention which he hoped would improve a
detail of plumbing practice. For a long time he would tell no one
what it was, but his eagerness to get back to it every day was very
obvious. Finally, he told his son, also a plumber, so that it could
go forward in case of his own death, but swore him to secrecy.

With the invention perfected and a model and application for
patent sent to the United States Patent Office, he again found time
on his hands and once more began to sink into depression. Then
he had another idea. He sent word to all the plumbers in the area
(all of whom respected him) telling them that he was starting a
weekly class for plumbers' helpers, free of charge, in order to pass
on to them the knowledge he had gained. Soon a dozen would-be
master plumbers were spending an evening a week absorbing the

knowledge and human wisdom of a man whose skill and integrity had become a byword in his community. And their teacher? He still walked on crutches, as he would the rest of his life, but his eyes were once more bright with the joy of living. He had met the challenge of age and partial disability successfully. Satisfaction he had never dreamed of had come to him through his own courage and intelligence.

Twenty years ago I was called into consultation to see a man who had suddenly collapsed with a serious heart attack. Though it was nip and tuck, he recovered. But his former intense drive and energy had left him; he turned into an anxiety-ridden, self-centered invalid with nothing left but self-pity. Some years later his only son succumbed to a heart attack. The catastrophe opened the older man's eyes. He suddenly realized the emptiness of his languid existence. Instead of inconsolably grieving, he dedicated himself to exhausting communal and charitable activities, as well as to profound self-education. Today, at eighty, he is healthy, respected, and beloved.

Must we be shocked by a tragedy to discover and use our hidden resources? Probably not. But in some cases it may, as in the case of this man, dramatically change one's attitude and, therefore, one's conduct of life.

Too many people, convinced that five or six decades of hard work entitle them to rest on their laurels, discover too late that they cannot sit back and be content. No one should ever presume that he has earned the right to laziness and luxury. It is a universal gerontological experience that this kind of fool's paradise leads inescapably to physical, mental, and probably also to social decline. A secret belief that one may remain at a given summit of performance, or of security, or of status in idleness is futile. If achievement is not made a continuous performance, it atrophies. To stay still is to retrogress and become rigid. Adaptation to change is the secret which preserves the forward-looking aspect of youth.

There is no one whose later years are not eventually marred by setbacks of one sort or another. Aging inevitably demands certain sacrifices of health and happiness. When these demands jolt us out of passive submission, they vitalize our powers of adjustment. They can lead us to uncover our real resources and to steel our courage. The prevention of many disadvantages in aging depends solely upon our ability and determination to call forth our defensive strength.

But what about those who evade and refuse all challenges? They enact the true tragedy of old age (and, I think, the only tragedy), those countless disintegrating old people whose miserable existence is a burden to their families and to themselves. For many years I have been in daily contact with such lost souls who were unable to cope with the problems of old age. They have been crushed not only by physical conditions, but also by inner struggles they could not resolve.

Certain neurotic attitudes, like feelings of insecurity or inferiority, are probably always at the base of unresolved inner struggles. Others are even more deep-seated, complicated, and difficult to unravel. We are restrained from self-expression by the social pressures of living in a herd. We clash with other personalities, but we must conform and acquiesce. We are frustrated by an environment unsuitable to the ways in which we wish to live. Our conflicts are intensified in the face of our own failures, of unsatisfied ambitions, of shattered dreams, or of real or imagined offenses committed by others.

In later years smoldering inner conflicts sometimes burst into a consuming conflagration; it may totally wreck mental sanity. (The victims are stored away as the "unreachables" in nursing homes or in institutions for the insane.) These lamentable but often preventable end stages develop in many ways. They are foreshadowed by certain peculiarities in attitudes and behavior.

In our modern society the fight for identity is all too often lost in escapist flight. Instead of facing and resolving conflicts many people simply avoid them. They allow themselves to be caught up in all sorts of distractions which lead nowhere. Monumental industries have been built up to prevent us from thinking unpleasant thoughts. Frantically people bathe in amusements, soak up pleasures, play with gadgets and trinkets, excite themselves by watching televised sports, westerns and extravaganzas. In short, they "kill time." Taking refuge in an avalanche of products designed for their consumption, they penalize their thinking power, memory and learning facilities, their critical judgment, and their intuitive capabilities. Dr. Erich Fromm has characterized our whole establishment as a consumer society and the aged as superconsumers.

"This is the attitude of the eternal suckling." Yet most older people do reach a saturation point sooner or later. They become sated, fed up. Then they may make the right turn into constructive thinking and creative activity.

Many people ignore their conflicts by busying themselves with their physical discomforts. Their closed minds concentrate on primitive functions or real or imagined dysfunctions. In earlier life they may have suffered from a variety of minor complaints, headaches, backaches, insomnia, allergies, and all the rest. The older they get, the more self-centered, hypochondriacal and dependent they become. Outside interests and objectives dwindle. Sooner or later the whole personality disintegrates.

Other people incapable of solving their problems, when getting on in years, "revenge" themselves on their families and the world for their many inadequacies and dissatisfactions. They drop the more or less agreeable façade behind which they have struggled through their decades of mediocrity. Nobody has described them better than Dr. J. Chernus: "They present a picture of bitterness, cantankerousness and demandingness; their feeling and thinking are narrowed down to a small circle, in the center of which they sit in their wheelchairs, thoroughly nasty old people with few or no saving graces."

Many people are inclined to take refuge from their anxieties, deficiencies, and resentments in withdrawal. Many were hardboiled or loners to begin with. Now they crawl into their shells and dream their morbid dreams. They shy away from contact with the outside world and doggedly neglect their appearance and hygiene. Their flight from society and reality often ends in mental illness. The untidy tired old person staring at nothingness in a corner, more often than not, is paranoiac and suffers from hallucinations.

Recognition of the pathways to mental deterioration will give us ample warning. It is the first step to alert us that we ourselves must seek to remedy the situation through a serious effort to reconcile the flagrant conflicts within us. The second step is to search for those positive qualities which can essentially contribute to avoiding the pitfalls of mental corruption.

Let us therefore, happily, now return to the victors who have successfully met the crises encountered at the onset of old age and have proceeded into their later years in unostentatious triumph.

From whom else can we learn more than from those who have achieved and perfected the art of aging? In studying their ways and personalities, we find clues to achieving a similar good fortune.

These masters in aging can be found in all walks of life. They do not have to be educated, high up on the ladder of social success, or even well equipped with physical health and vigor. The blind man who gives freely of his friendliness, love, and humor is an artist in aging. The lively grandmother whose grandchildren compete for the privilege of her attention is an artist in aging. How did these people and others like them use the resources at their disposal in achieving their success?

One common characteristic strikes me particularly—the awareness and constructive use of time. They do not harbor fears that their time grows short, that time passes them by too quickly, and as a consequence pressure themselves into inhibiting time schedules. The experts in aging have made their peace with time.

It is ironic that the people who are most afraid to die usually appreciate time the least. Time is wasted if used only for the prolongation of life. Those who do not comprehend that it is a precious gift are likely to misspend it.

The well-adjusted who are making a success of their old age have learned to muse over life and memories not as a means of evading the present but as a source of enrichment, an opportunity to settle things with themselves. Age gives them a chance to consider all aspects of life in a wider perspective and more objectively than ever before. They are able to view the past and the future calmly. They use their days much as an artist uses his brush, to cover his canvas with his own personal vision.

Let me list some other qualities which, I believe, contribute to the making of an artist in aging, since I have found them in so many who have aged successfully but not in those who have aged without grace.

It is easy to notice that men and women who excel in the art of aging love life intensely. They have the gift of enjoyment and the ability to give joy. They acknowledge the positive side of life. They are lovers of nature; a gorgeous rose is a thing of beauty for anyone, but a blade of grass, a tiny insect, a cloudburst can be just as beautiful for them.

They love people more than they love gadgets and love them unselfishly, as people need and want to be loved. They are not quickly disappointed, nor do they let love turn into hate. They are deeply concerned; their love is compassionate. These old people always stand ready to understand and forgive. A wise old lady used to say: "The old should understand the young; they have been young themselves, but why expect the young to understand the old? They have never experienced age."

They lack the compulsion to rule people around them; they are not inclined to be dictators, manipulators, or pompous authoritarians. They are modest. Usually, they belittle their own desires, needs, problems, and difficulties rather than emphasize them. They do not ask for sympathy. They do not want others to suffer with them, or for them. They have courage.

They are curious and forward-looking. Probably their curiosity is one of the things that makes them seem so young. Or perhaps it is the other way round; because their minds retain the resilience of youth, they are curious. In any case, the degree of their curiosity seems to me a better yardstick of their real age than the dates on their birth certificates.

Generally they are optimistic in their views and outlook, and they love fun. A Frenchman once said that age puts more wrinkles in the mind than in the face. However, I am sure for people who have mastered old age the opposite is true; they have more wrinkles in their faces than in their minds. Why? They laugh harder and more often.

They are not overly tolerant, nor are they aggressively intolerant. They are not always unbiased, but do not argue violently against opinions that differ from theirs. They usually have some prejudices stored up, but seldom press them very hard. To tolerate too much and too easily often makes fools out of people. The artists in aging are seldom fools.

They are seasoned and they are mellowed. They have no need to be rude or stubbornly antagonistic. They are not impulsive; they have learned to control their tempers. If they have disagreements with families or friends, as sometimes they must, they would rather keep silent than upset others or themselves. They may be a bit hurt and a bit sad, but the pain and the sadness pass.

They usually have certain definite values, likes or dislikes with which they are identified, and which may concern ideas, politics, social institutions, the arts, clothes, or personal possessions. No matter how controversial their values may be, they cling to them and are proud of them. They may do things differently, and perhaps in ways that seem outmoded to younger people, but they like to hold onto the methods to which they are accustomed, and this also is an expression of their individuality. Yet they do not become obsessed with their ideas or material possessions, or become slaves to them.

This profile of the artists of aging is neither complete nor entirely accurate. Neither is it a caricature. It is a picture that more or less reveals the healthy human who has grown old and has achieved what we all aspire to—satisfaction and fulfillment in life.

I believe the essential difference between those whose aging exhibits a superior quality and those who age unsuccessfully is that the former possess a deep-rooted feeling of responsibility to themselves, as well as to their fellowmen while this quality is missing in the latter.

Responsibility is a somber word. Many rebel and ask why assume further responsibility if one has worked all through life to free himself of it? Is not freedom from responsibility the goal for which we are striving? These are futile questions. No matter how totally irresponsible we imagine we would like to be, none of us can escape responsibilities as long as we have the power to think and to act. The word "responsibility" derives its meaning from "respond," and response to the challenge of living is everybody's lot and duty as long as life lasts. What becomes of us if we renounce responsibility? We fall into a void. The totally irresponsible man or woman is a shaky fragment, socially and mentally bankrupt.

In an attempt to formulate guiding principles for aging successfully, we should be fully aware of what we are striving for, and why. Which leads us right back to the original question of all mankind: What is the meaning of life? I am afraid that the reluctance to face this question and all the other escapist tendencies in us are caused by a certain despair spread by our modern concept of living—or of philosophy, if you will. For many, the faith in protection by supernatural forces is waning. The new creed is that man is alone in the vast universe without help and without aim. Dr. Irvine

Page, the eminent physician and author, remarked on today's philosophy: "Man, with his greatly increased powers over the universe, now finds himself rudderless and at sea—the individual stands spiritually naked before this awesome universe."

The purpose in facing up to life is to find ourselves. If the ups and downs—triumph and failure, fortune and tragedy, joy and pain —in a life story could determine our fate we would, indeed, be rudderless at sea. It would mean that our ideas and ideals, our love and fear, our resolves, have no hand in helping us find satisfaction with our final years of life. What nonsense! Probably the greatest revelation in the study of aging has been that it is not so much that physical health adds strength to our age as it is that determination and motivation enforce its vigor and vitality.

Common sense tells us that it is we, ourselves, who must become masters of our destiny. The crux of the matter is to recognize and to accept this responsibility. Let us compare age with the space missile, from which the first rocket stages have dropped off. Now we are in flight; to avoid aimless wandering off into the gloom of the universe we must have direction and purpose.

The enigma of life is not solved and probably never will be. As disturbing as this thought may be, it furnishes no excuse for resignation. If anything, it should enable us humbly to acknowledge human limitations.

The artists in aging are aware of the mysteries in which life is shrouded as well as of its inevitable hardships. But this does not distract them from an appreciation of all its riches and exhilarations. Their steadfast optimism commits them to lead a meaningful and purposeful life and stimulates the resourcefulness which they demonstrate in their accomplishments. Their efforts are rewarded by grace and serene happiness. The masters of aging prove that one's later years can truly be the crowning years of life.

"THE BEST IS YET TO BE"

Julia Harris

Nearing my seventy-eighth birthday is a kind of success in itself. That exceeds by thirty-two years the life expectancy of forty-six at the turn of the century. I was five years old at the turn of the century. Physically, in every way, I have tried to live adequately by avoiding excessives in food habits, in recreation, in dress, in personal care, excessives of any kind. Few illnesses have overtaken me, but these were overcome and I have learned to live with a few past and a few present illnesses. The annual examination here at Duke (physical, emotional, mental, everything) for use in the gerontology study has been helpful to me. The examiners discover and also help me realize somewhat my own aging process. A report of the physical examination comes to me (in laymen's language, of course); also, at my request, a report goes to my personal physician. In addition, for the past twenty-five years I have had regular checkups with my personal physician. I neither smoke nor drink; however, some elderly people have done and are still doing both. Possibly my wise choice of grandparents has helped. My paternal grandfather reached eighty-seven. My maternal grandmother reached eighty-one. My mother reached eighty-five, so I have to keep going awhile in order to keep up the family record. Wholesome mental and emotional outlooks, I think, contribute to physical well-being. Always I have considered good health something to be proud of and was determined to have my share of it. My sisters and brothers were hale and hearty, and I was the puny one. "Puny" to me is still the ugliest word in the English language. I intended that it should not always be so. Twice when I was ill, once as a child and once in later years, I lived, I think, simply because I refused to die. Though I occasionally miss my guess, I expect to feel well and refuse to dwell on my illness.

Hobbies help too. They bring relief from tensions. Feeding and watching the wild birds, growing plants (nowadays they are in pots and boxes), listening to the music that I like (generally on records), and reading. Reading was always my favorite pastime. I find too little time for it now. Co-ordinating a group of senior citizens including myself has come to be not just a service but a hobby also.

Socially, I try to maintain a medium between introversion and extroversion. I suspect I am more naturally inclined toward introversion, but my friendships are broad, including all age groups from babies to the hundred-year-olds. Nor is race or religion any deterrent to friendship. Membership in social groups—a literary club, a social civic group, a sorority, a bridge club, the church altar guild, and the senior citizens club bring a group together. These help to keep me socially alert. Though I still do enjoy group recreation, I like to think that a certain amount of poise is gained through reserving some time through reading, thinking, reflecting all alone and, occasionally, just loafing.

Economically, conscious economy was always a part of my earliest teaching. At first my family consisted of both parents, one grandparent, two uncles, my five sisters and brothers, and me—a farm family. There was plenty for all, but plenty because of careful frugality: raising most foods on the farm, some hunting and fishing, then drying, canning, preserving, storing, for the fall and winter seasons. Sewing, too, was an important part of our family economy. Never has there been a time in my life when economizing was not a necessity. Having started with mud pies and doll clothes, I learned cooking and sewing very early. When I was twelve years old, the immediate family left the farm; then there was the somewhat different way of economizing, but frugality prevailed. Even in town we had fruit trees and a vegetable garden—flower garden in the front, vegetable garden in the back. Whenever extreme frugality has been needed, it seemed a kind of game, rather than a hardship, to see how much we could do with so little. I had learned budgeting long before I knew that word. Not to be able to budget would be tragic. Some conditions in our country today are making it pretty nearly impossible.

Emotionally, I have been capable of pride, joy, delight, from the days of Santa Claus through school days, courtship and marriage, middle age to senior citizens clubs, parties, and trips. Also, I have always been capable of the opposite emotions: I can be angry, sometimes moderately, sometimes intensely—angry at work, at play, at civic, social, and political events. Occasionally, I have not been proud of my reactions. I think that I still run the whole gamut of human emotions. A stabilizing influence, I think, has been my religious upbringing. Not extreme orthodoxy but emphasis upon regular attendance at Sunday school and church, having studied the Sunday-school lesson on Saturday evening, then living daily by the golden rule. Ability to keep on a fairly even keel is attributable, I think, to several things:

One is a sense of humor. This sometimes can turn would-be tragedy into fun. I can smile at the follies and idiosyncrasies of others, and I can laugh at my own blunders.

Two. Appreciation of beauty. Nature's beauties, man's art, beauty in people as beings, art forms (i.e., music, dance, and painting); I enjoy them all. Nature's beauty is utterly inexhaustible —flowers, trees, birds, rivers, clouds, lakes, mountains, sunrises, sunsets, rainfall, snow, rock formations—there's no end. I still enjoy them. Some of my childlike enjoyments remain with me. I find four-leaf clovers, I see figures in the clouds, gaze at a hummingbird sucking nectar or bees on the clover, show a child how to find the honey in the honeycomb, how to catch lightning bugs and butterflies.

Three. Knowing the pleasure derived from helping others. This I learned very early. Before my fifth birthday I greeted my third little sister. Helping the younger ones, showing them, teaching them, playing with them, gave me as much pleasure as it did them. At all ages and with all associates it has been so. Great joy is derived from making others happy, and there are many easy, inexpensive ways to do it.

Four. Praying sincerely the familiar prayer for "Serenity to accept the things I cannot change, courage to change the things I can change, and wisdom to know the difference."

Five. Living by the "Other Than That" philosophy. This experience I am about to tell explains what I mean by "Other Than That." Some years ago on visiting an elderly, very elderly, uncle, I found him walking in the street just outside of his house. He was walking without a cane but carefully touching each railing of the fence as he went along. To my question "How are you?" he answered, "Well, I'm taking a little walk (his voice was high, tightened with age). I can't walk very far, but I walk; and my digestion, well, Mary (that's his daughter) has to be very careful what she lets me eat; and my hearing is a little dim; my eyesight's not so good, I do not read so well any more; you have to speak up to make me hear you; and my memory, it's like good pastry—short." But then his whole face lighted up and he said to me, "But you know, Julia, other than that, I'm just fine."

I live by the "Other Than That" philosophy. Doing things for myself, keeping house, and the "Prayer for Serenity" have helped. Since I could not halt the passing years or disregard their lessening of physical powers, I gradually gave up trimming the hedges, mowing the lawn, and doing the heavier household tasks. I have help only where I need it. I do all of my own cooking, some sewing, the lighter housekeeping jobs, and I do my personal laundry by hand. I have learned gradually to increase the time allotted for a given task, and I heed the stop sign by sometimes letting an anticipated activity just wait awhile.

Success? Well, seventy-seven years, ten months, and two days. I live by living, not merely existing. With Robert Browning, I still say, "The best is yet to be."

AWAKENING
Polly Francis

Polly Francis shares her philosophy and perceptions at a later stage in life. The author, who will have "lived out her ninety-second year and entered her ninety-third" on February 8, is a former fashion illustrator for the Condé Nast publications based in Paris. She arrived there from New York on Christmas Eve 1911, a free-lance artist with facile pencil, adventuresome spirit, and no knowledge of the native language, whose work was destined to catch the eye of one of the era's ranking magazine publishers (*Vogue, Vanity Fair,* and *House and Garden*).

With my autumn spent and the barriers of winter closing in, I contemplate my harvest. Old beliefs and habits have blown away with the leaves of my years. Some of the less obvious aspects of aging are now seen clearly and simply. This awakening has brought me added peace and a stronger faith in a guiding force.

The basics now stand out like the skeletons of trees, stripped of their blazing autumn beauty. I now seem better able to evaluate what fate has tossed to me. Some of the things I struggled hardest to get I could very well have done without.

As my sense of detachment grows and I feel less earthbound, a new kind of freedom, a release, settles over me. Strife fades away. This new kind of serenity is not resignation; it comes from a deeper understanding of man's frailties and limitations.

What a little bit of the world's knowledge an individual mind can hold! I no longer feel the least embarrassment at having to say, "I don't know."

As the pendulum of life swings, it throws satisfactions and frustrations in our way. These are the warp and the woof of the fabric of life, pulling in opposite directions to build up resistance.

This late release is not a *"giving up"* or a *"dropping out."* It's a casting off of encumbrances. The serenity that comes, as our character is tempered by time, can help us through the turbulent tide of life's tribulations. It is the counterbalance to our woes.

An inexhaustible source of satisfaction lies within the framework of fantasy. Things as fragile and as fleeting as butterflies endure in this domain, immune to changes of circumstances or environment. This invulnerable inner life can buttress us against all threatening storms. Memories, with their abiding comfort, can brighten the dark hours as the stars brighten the skies of night—gently and unobtrusively.

Within my heart I hold a glowing imprint which lights my way through the darkness and gloom of life's sad moments. It's my richest treasure. It can't be lost or mislaid or stolen. It will be mine to the very end. The power and influence it wields is one of my life's greatest blessings. This imprint is my shield against the blight of bitterness, which cannot survive in a climate warmed by an inner glow.

What an incomparable joy it is to know that an insight of ours sparked a similar response in another soul! This kind of closeness can survive great distances in space for long periods of time. Our vision clarified by the mist of distance, we see one in all his appealing humanness, unobscured by the shadows of those around him. The distant perspective diminishes his flaws. But, in the end, even his flaws endear him to us.

As we grow very old, our world of fantasy becomes our world of reality. The rest diminishes in importance. Fatigue of the very old is something that no one who is not that old can quite understand. Minor problems multiply, and little anxieties become burdens. Together these can rob us of sleep and routine rest. Our fatigue is caused, not by activities, but by the little anxieties surrounding them.

The normal bent, of even the shy, is to want congenial companionship. As the years pass, we become more sensitive to emotional fatigue and so must protect ourselves against intrusion—painful as it sometimes is to do so. A relaxed intimacy, without troublesome involvement, would be ideal for those whose pace is faltering. We can't love everybody, but we should keep our compassion alive.

In time, it becomes our tendency to lean more and more towards the intangibles. Our world of fantasy makes no demands, but we must not let it take over completely. While we are earthly beings, we need earthly things. Much of the tangible beauty around us represents the outpourings of man's inspired genius. The products of this earth have their purpose, which cannot be ignored.

The basic needs of man have not changed all that much that we need to keep ourselves in a fever of exhaustion trying to keep up. There are too many people running in too many directions for us to follow. So we jog along at our comfortable pace.

Old age is not an affliction which blights the end of life. *Don't* pity us; we are not forlorn old people. *Don't* be oversolicitous and patronizing. We cling to our independence and our dignity. At the same time, it is heartening to know that people want to help us, even though we don't want to appear helpless.

Life is to be enjoyed, not merely endured. It is serious, but it need not be solemn. The pleasure that comes from the awareness of little things—the perfume carried on the breeze of spring, the freshness in the garden after rain, the birdsong in the quiet of the dawn—is among our greatest blessings.

Don't grieve over mistakes. Life is a matter of meeting the challenges that fate throws in our way. Decisions of fallible man are always a matter of chance. Regret is futile—it changes nothing.

GREETINGS FROM BRUCE BLIVEN

Bruce Bliven

Bruce Bliven's Christmas letters have become prized possessions for the five hundred friends who received them each year. About these letters the author said, "Every year I make fun of myself, and of old age in general, for a couple of reasons. One is that most Christmas letters are deadly dull. The other is that my friends, who are the only normal recipients, include a lot of people of my own age who take a gloomy view of their situation. I try to suggest to them that it is better to laugh than to cry. I also try to deal lightly and casually with the fact that we are coming close to living on borrowed time."

CHRISTMAS, 1968

Another year, another dollar (reduced by inflation to 50 cents). The Blivens have survived 12 months more. We are surprised and gratified. But also optimistic. To paraphrase an old saying, inside every elderly man is a young man crying to get out—and thinking he might make it, too. At 79-plus, I walk with a cane so that I won't stagger into the path of a car. I go down a short flight of steps like an elephant crossing a bamboo bridge in a typhoon. I lower myself into an armchair the way they set down a Michelangelo statue with a derrick. But in my heart I'm sure I'm only pretending these expedients are necessary, that I'm just imitating someone old, and could start gamboling any minute.

The superannuated milk-wagon horse, left to his own devices, would faithfully follow the familiar route, stopping at every house. I run a clipping file on a hundred subjects I am unlikely ever to need again; I read a ridiculous number of newspapers, magazines, and books. I carefully correct typographical errors in printed matter before I put it into the wastepaper basket. I go to speeches, make full notes, and then throw them away. I am like the exercise fanatic who said he felt he must keep fit, but, "Fit for what?"

CHRISTMAS, 1969

Bruce here, reporting at the end of another year. We always knew we would end with a whimper, not a bang; but this is becoming ridiculous. Young people are not much interested in the old, and the old are not much interested in each other, encapsulated as they are in the narcissism of age. But we are interested in ourselves. I still sign my letters with a flourish. When I stagger while walking, I pretend I was going that way anyhow. When I forget the name of someone I know, or some famous figure, I say to my wife, as Emerson said to his, in old age: "What's the name of my friend, who was buried today? Thank you, of course, Henry Wadsworth Longfellow."

If you live long enough, people become markedly amiable toward you; everyone wants to pat the toothless tiger. What you achieve is evaluated, as Dr. Johnson said in a different connection, of a dog walking on its hind legs, not with regard to its quality, but to the fact that you can do it at all.

We still take pleasure in living on this campus of heavenly beauty, where we met and fell in love 60 years ago. Rosie enjoys many section meetings of the Faculty Women's Club, and I'm forbidden to mention the ice cream and cake, or even tea and cookies. We have some good friends among younger people here, and a few old ones. But increasingly people of our own age or older seem to be waiting with benign patience for some unspecified thing to happen, like cows at milking time.

If a prophet lives long enough, a lot of his dire predictions of 50 years ago come true, and this has happened to me. The world has plenty of troubles—war, the threat of the hydrogen bomb, pollution of air, water and soil, the alienation of youth, and most of all, burgeoning population, doubling every 30 years. But I have the faintly grim optimism of old age; most governments are at last aware of these dangers, and are taking steps. I think mankind has enough sense not to commit mass suicide. Just barely. So, Merry Christmas!

CHRISTMAS, 1970

Another 12 months, and four-fifths of the five Blivens, New York and California, are in good health and spirits. The other fifth, in good spirits, is me, Bruce Sr. (this is no time for correct grammar). My heart attack is now 12 years behind me, and I am still going. Maybe not strong, but going. My ambition used to be to live until my bald spot covered up my cowlick. With mission accomplished, my sunny hope now is to die of something else before I starve. My chances seem good.

People are tired of hearing me tell what old age is like; but that never stopped a Bliven yet. It is a rerun of a prize-fight film when you already know that your favorite gets knocked out in a late round. It is the time when you don't buy winter clothing at the bargain sales in February, just in case. It is when young people you knew in the cradle are the heads of big corporations, presumably keeping discipline by shaking a rattle at recalcitrants. It is when, if you can wheedle a compliment out of anybody, it always begins with that melancholy phrase, "for one of your years." It is when I remember the names of my friends by carrying an alphabetized notebook and putting them under the appropriate letter—G for Garrulous, etc. And how did my own name get there under S for Senility?

CHRISTMAS, 1971

Of 1971 the five Blivens, New York and California, can say what the Abbé Sieyès said of the French Revolution—"We survived." On balance, we are slightly better off than a year ago, and so is the world, if I keep my thumb just a little on one side of the scale.

The family motto is, "Let Father write the Christmas letter; he loves to whimper." (Rosie never whimpers; she doesn't know what she is missing.) At 82, I feel perhaps it is time I picked out a life career for myself, but I don't want to choose the wrong one by being too precipitate. For years my motto was taken from the old Scottish ballad, "I shall lay me down and bleed awhile/Then rise and fight again." This is still my favorite, but I have dropped off the second line.

Rosie is blessed with eternal youth; I don't feel like an old man, I feel like a young man who has something the matter with him. I repudiate those who say, "You have aged terribly since I last saw you." "When was that?" "A week ago."

CHRISTMAS, 1972

And 1972 is nearly gone, but not the five Blivens, Fred, Naomi and Bruce Jr. in New York, Rose and Bruce Sr. in California. We remain. The family agrees to let Bruce Sr. write the Christmas letter, to keep him from pouting.

A year ago, when I was only 82, I wrote somebody that "I don't feel like an old man, I feel like a young man who has something the matter with him." I have now found out what it is: It is the approach of middle age, and I don't care for it.

I walk with a slight stagger, thus acquiring a lot of new friends; everybody welcomes the approach of what they feel is an amiable, elderly drunk. I forget a lot of words, thus reducing the size of my whaddayoucallit. The floor is covered with memos to myself, that I hope I'll be able to reach down and pick up. Looking back, I see my past littered with fearful mistakes and weaknesses, all the way to the horizon, but before me I see only a broad smooth road. How stupid can you get?

What have I learned in 83 years? I have learned, if you are mugged on the street, don't yell "Help!" yell "Fire!" Nobody wants to come to a mugging, but everybody is interested in a fire.

We have lost some dear friends the past 12 months; and actuarial tables being what they are, more of us will go in the next 12. But, "we accept the universe," as Margaret Fuller once said. (To which Carlyle snarled when he heard it, "Egad! She'd better!")

CHRISTMAS, 1973

Here's another example of that dreadful thing, a Christmas letter, this one from the California Blivens, Rose and Bruce Sr. Written by the latter, scribbling furiously in a corner before they take away my pencil.

At 84, Rosie and I feel we are doing pretty well. One of us now has to do the remembering for two, but she very sweetly reminds me why I went into the bathroom. (To clean my teeth.) She assures me she doesn't worry when I leave the TV running. (Only the bathtub.)

I am thinking of becoming an old man. If I decide to, I'll send out cards and wear a lapel pin. There are several advantages, the first being that my native cowardice won't show quite so much; if they saddle up the meanest horse in the corral and invite me to get on, I can say "No." Another is that maybe I shall stop running downhill frantically as I have been doing for 65 years, ahead of a snowball of my own creation, calling pitifully for help. The snowball melted long ago; it is time I slowed to a walk and looked around. I'll try to face bravely the humiliating fact that I don't now really need a pocket computer.

We all slow down with advancing years; I now know how tortoises used to feel when I passed them. A word the elderly hate is "still"—"he still drives"; "she still gives those delightful little dinners," etc. We know that old age is endemic, and fatal; but for now, we are like passengers in a balloon with a slow leak (we hope it is slow!): The world seems to move, but we don't. I have calculated that the diseases I don't have outnumber those I have by 20 to one, so I am only five per cent ill.

CHRISTMAS, 1974

And at 85, Rosie and I are still able to answer *"Adsum!"* (A touch of Anglophile snobbery there, Bruce; watch yourself!) Rosie is ageless; she tenderly helps down steps old women of 60. As for me, I bear in grim silence the fact that the part in my hair has overflowed its banks and is threatening to inundate the lowlands behind my ears. I find I am a little more absent-minded; but if while driving I forget who I am and where I live, there is always a friendly highway patrolman to radio in my car license to the computer, which instantly responds with my name and address. I am older than it is; so why do I think of the computer as my father?

A handful of my friends (that makes about half) suggest I stop trying to be funny once a year about old age. They point out that I have made all the jokes there are, they are not very good and the subject isn't really so comical. I suppose they are right, though I feel it is better to laugh than to cry. But even of this I'm not sure. People have been known to say to me, "Excuse me, are you laughing? Would you mind trying to cry? No, that's worse; can't you put your face in neutral?"

Rosie and I know of course that at 85, time is no longer on our side; the Senior Blivens are an endangered species. Like the whales, only smaller.

If the elderly seem somewhat less concerned than the young about the terrible world drama of dwindling natural resources, and of famine that is just beginning, perhaps it is because we know we shall be going home at the end of the first act. Or perhaps we cheer ourselves a little by reflecting that successive generations of men and women very like ourselves survived about 88,000 years of the latest Ice Age, and came out stuffed with baked mastodon, and wearing sealskin.

CHRISTMAS, 1975

And at 86, Rosie and I are still able to say, with General Pershing landing in France, *"Lafayette, we are here."* (Pershing never said it, of course; an Army press agent hung it on him.) We celebrated our 62nd wedding anniversary last May; ours has been that wonderful marriage possible only when a hypochondriac is wedded to a girl who never heard of illness. We avoid the unhappy spectacle of two enpurpled people hurling symptoms at each other.

We live by the rules of the elderly. If the toothbrush is wet you have cleaned your teeth. If the bedside radio is warm in the morning you left it on all night. If you are wearing one brown and one black shoe, quite possibly you have a similar pair in the closet. . . . Try not to mind when a friend tells you on your birthday that a case of prune juice has been donated in your name to a nearby retirement home.

I stagger when I walk, and small boys follow me making bets on which way I'll go next. This upsets me; children should not gamble. . . . Like most elderly people, we spend happy hours in front of our TV set. We rarely turn it on, of course; if we do we see a whole nation of people in a panic about how they smell, or smaller groups solving the anguished conflicts of the human heart by crashing automobiles together.

A LAMP AT DUSK: ADJUSTING PUTS PEACE INTO GROWING OLD

Whitney White

Mary Whitney White, in her mid-eighties, informed *National Observer* Editor Henry Gemmill she prefers her middle name, Whitney, as a byline because "Mary White sounds like applesauce," and that, since she likes articles on aging, she decided to write one herself. Widowed in 1972, she is a 1911 Vassar graduate, has four great-grandchildren and lives in Upper Montclair, N.J. For a hobby, she likes to "read, read, read."

Dear Daughter:

Your visit gave me a big lift and, despite our no-stop chatter, I thought of a dozen other things we should have discussed. I *am* sorry you dread old age so much. I confess it is not my most favorite of life's chapters, but as Samuel Hopkinson Smith once said: "Old age? There is nothing one can do about it, and, after all, one is only old once." This is probably the most factual thing that can be said about it; much nearer the truth than calling it the "Golden Age" or other Pollyanna names, trying to make it sound like a glorious romp.

You asked me to write down some thoughts I have on it. So here goes. I know full well that anything I say will soon be dated, as doctors will find new drugs to keep the octogenarian agile on the tennis court and decreasing for many old people the crippling discomforts and poignant experience of growing old.

THOUGHTS TUMBLE AROUND

Many thoughts are tumbling around in my head, asking to be expressed. If I tried to voice them all it would make a 1,000-page tome covering such subjects as belief in life hereafter, health, habits, hazards, financial security and on and on. I will spare you much of it.

Throughout life there are crisis moments when tough decisions have to be made. How and why to live this last chapter is one of these decisions. Here are some alternatives: (1) Move in with one's children; (2) stay in one's own home; (3) move to an apartment; (4) go to a retirement home.

As I discuss these with my contemporaries, all but a few seem to agree *not* to live with one's children. That is not because you are not charming and hospitable and that we do not love you, but your pace is too fast, your household too active, your space too limited. Besides, you have enough responsibilities without taking on us old crocks.

I wobble as to what to do with our house, where we have lived for 50 years. I know now I should have given it up when my last birdling left the nest. Then it would have been easier to adapt to a new environment, and I would not have the luxury of empty rooms into which I could toss things and decide later what to do with them.

Yes, I might as well admit it. I am a space addict. I like to roam from room to room and out into the yard where little things that gave me a backache when I planted them are rewarding me now by blossoming. I like to come into the house and see my cherished possessions standing in their familiar places, so many reminding me of the lives of my ancestors. Until I tangled with this problem, I did not realize what a hold the old homestead has on me, each inch harboring fun-filled—and some tear-filled—memories. Like a turtle's shell, it is part of me. I can draw into it and let the world go by or, when feeling sociable, emerge.

DIALOGUE WITH A GREMLIN

I wish the gremlin that keeps needling me to solve this problem with my head and not my heart would cease its noisy chatter. I keep telling it how like Paradise it would be to stay put. It chuckles sardonically and says, "*No,* not *like Paradise, with its host of ministering angels. Face it, old lady.* (It knows how I hate to be called senior citizen.) *Just because some of your friends have been lucky and found helpers does not mean you will be. So who will talk to you when the winter's icy sidewalks isolate you? With your unsteady legs, who will market for you, bank and do your sundry errands or pick you up when you fall and break your hip?*"

This dialogue between my gremlin and myself makes vivid the intense silence of the house as the snow piles up on the windowsills and the frustration of wanting things and not being able to totter up to the village to get them. It is amazing how distance lengthens as the years ahead grow fewer.

The argument for an apartment is that I can still maintain, more or less, my independence. I will have a door I can close and people to summon in an emergency. I know that I will miss space and a garden plot, and that with the present cost of apartments I will not save any money, but at least you kids will not have me on your minds and you will inherit some nice pieces of furniture while you are still in the social whirl.

I know you asked me to consider a retirement home. There is much to be said for them: Perpetual care, people constantly around, release from responsibility and planned activities and entertainment. However, I am not sure I am the type to enjoy all those goodies.

NEEDS SOME SOLITUDE

You are a child of the herd. You like noisy cocktail parties, crowded ballroom floors and droppers-in for coffee. I, however, am more like your sister. Remember when she wanted to leave college because she hated eating in the noisy dining room with a hundred "chewers and chatterers"? She and I have to have some solitary days just to mooch around in and the independence of choosing the people we want to see and the places we want to go. Don't think I feel our type is superior to yours, for goodness knows it would be a drab, colorless world without people with bounce like you.

The number of words I have devoted to this dwelling problem may lead you to think that, having settled it, old age has no other adjustments to make. Far from it, dear daughter. As I sit here and write I am aware that my body is grown creaky with wear. Never having been afflicted with chronic ills, I have not been conscious of it before, and always expected it to do the things I asked of it.

Today, however, trying to get going in the morning is much like trying to crank our old Model T Ford. I have to crank and crank it, and several times during the day's travail it sputters and falters, crying out for bed rest. My doctor is sympathetic as I tell him how my knees buckle and my legs wobble. He, however, has no advice to offer and ends by saying, "What do you expect at your age?"

FRIENDS' LOSS LEAVES VOID

I know I must learn to live with this dissipation of my bodily strength and accept a less active life, but I do deplore it happening to my friends. It is sad indeed to see them failing: First giving up walking, then driving, then growing homebound, finally going to a nursing home for their last days. There are lots worse things than death for those who experience it; for those they leave there is an aching void, difficult at our age to fill.

When I was a youngster my nurse taught me a hymn sung to a jolly little tune. "Count your many blessings, name them one by one," were the words of the chorus. We sang them in duet, I beating time with a comb on the bedposts. Now in my advanced age I find it good therapy to do just that, and the blessings really mount up when I put my mind on it. Old age certainly has its compensations: Freedom from being responsible in this day of the new morality; from committee work, from caring about status, from outside pressures.

RESIGN OR ADAPT

There seem to be two ways of meeting old age. One is to resign to it, letting it take over your life; the other is to adjust to it, still keeping in the stream of life and prodding oneself gently into the activities one can still do.

My grandmother chose the former. I can still see her, sitting and rocking on her porch in Brookline. She wore frilly caps, thus hiding her hair (or the lack of it; I never knew which) and abolishing the need to struggle to a beauty shop and sit for a precious hour under a dryer. A lace shawl took the curve of her bent shoulders, and I always smelled a faint fragrance of lavender as I kissed her. To all appearances there was no turbulence in her soul. And thanks to not having television shouting daily of the agonies of the world, she was able to say, and often did say, "This is a good, good world." She went to her creator from the house in which she had lived 60 years and in which she had brought up eight children, rather than having been toted off to a nursing home to spend her last days among strangers. I think hers was the easier way.

LIVING EASIER IN 20TH CENTURY

As I said in the beginning of this all-too-long letter, this is not my favorite chapter in life. I do realize, however, that the twentieth century grandmother has a better life than any previous ones. With discrimination she can have pleasant entertainment on television or radio; with the telephone she can share her doings or the lack of them with her friends, or listen to theirs. The Government is concerned with her and gives a slight but welcome boost to her finances. Many communities have committees that plan ways of getting her out and amusing her, as well as sending in hot, nourishing meals to her. Who knows what will be offered you when you reach this chapter!

Ulysses, returning home from the Trojan wars tired and grown old, is reported by Tennyson to have said, "Though much is taken, much abides: and though we are not now that strength which in old days moved heaven and earth, that which we are, we are: One equal temper of heroic hearts made weak by time and fate but strong in will to strive, to seek, to find and not to yield."

So now, inspired by those words that I say often to myself, I must go out for a short walk, thus helping my heart—which feels less than heroic—do its pumping job. When I come in, there will be the Philharmonic to listen to. I will light the fire, take up my knitting and, shutting out the world, I will agree with my grandmother that there are moments in this chapter when I can say this is a good world.

I hope I have not exhausted you. Keep cheerio, and with love,

Mother

SEX AND THE AGING

Mary S. Calderone

Mary S. Calderone, veteran expert on human sexual behavior and champion of liberated approaches to sexual matters, speaks authoritatively but warmly about sex and the older person.

There are just as many myths and clichés about the sexuality of aging as there are about sexuality of other age groups. Through sheer ignorance, physicians themselves can pass on these destructive attitudes when they become aware of a sexual problem with an older person. Women after hysterectomy or menopause have been informed that their sexual lives are over. So have men in their fifties who have experienced one or two episodes of impotence and gone to their physicians in anxiety. We now know, of course, that these myths are not true at all, and that simple preventive and immediate psychotherapy can usually restore sexual function. It has been stated by many that the largest and most important sex organ in the body is the brain, and this is absolutely true. Very rarely can any sexual problem be shown to have a purely organic origin.

Other incorrect attitudes make fun of sexual or dating activities in the elderly, very much as we tend to tease and make fun of children in the early grades for their love friendships. This kind of attitude is totally damaging to the self-esteem of the person involved, and Dr. Alex Comfort has remarked that such attitudes are an impertinent intrusion on the privacy of the older person.

Another myth relates to the sexual interests of old men. Except in cases of true senile deterioration, there are very few cases of the "dirty old man" that can be substantiated. Indeed, many of the advances that old gentlemen make to young children have as their basis pure and simple loneliness, because it has not been made possible, by those responsible for their welfare, for them to have any kind of normal social experiences that could lead to rewarding companionship at their own age levels.

The Dirty Old Woman syndrome is applied almost automatically to any woman over fifty who forms a friendship with a man five or ten years younger. Many psychiatrists and others are beginning to suggest that marriage of women at any age to men some years younger, rather than older, than themselves might result in a better-balanced male-female married population after the age of sixty.

Women tend to lose their sexual drive, or to transmute it into primary interest in touch or communication rather than in genital sex, less than and at later ages than do men. One important finding is that continued sexual interest and activity in the later years is "substantially greater for persons who have been highly interested and highly sexually active in their younger years." (This is one bank account that, the more you spend it, the higher is the balance left!) I realize of course that in any institution there is a certain proportion of guests who are deteriorated, either physically or mentally, or have intercurrent illness, such as severe arthritis of the hip, that may make sexual activity painful or impossible. But I have seen several articles in medical journals pointing out that physicians can help even such patients, by showing them positions that may make intercourse more comfortable, by helping to orient the partner as to the patient's special needs, and perhaps by prescribing that medication be taken within a given period of time before intercourse in order to achieve maximum comfort.

The medical profession has, in this society, indeed taken the lead in recognizing that sexuality and sexual expression are integral to the integrity of the personality from infancy through old age. This means, as I remarked earlier, that all of us must deal realistically and generously with the true needs for intimacy of the aging people whose care is confided to us, if only because they have less time left than the rest of us in which to find joy in such companionship. There is a general feeling among most medical people that persons in institutions, whether they be the elderly or the handicapped of any kind, should be helped to achieve as fulfilled a sexual life as possible within the limits of their disabilities. Administrators of institutions are beginning to provide residents wth opportunities for privacy, and many meetings are being held on behalf of the mentally retarded, not to discuss what kind of sex education these individuals should have to make them less annoying but, rather, to consider what kinds of lifelong marriages and companionships they might be educated and helped to achieve, with such concomitant protections as appropriate contraceptive or sterilization measures. We can do the same for older people—without contraception of course—but must work with their families as well.

People in institutions need life and laughter around them in order to stay alive—spiritually and emotionally as well as physically. They need fun, stimulation, a glass of wine, a hairdo, becoming clothes that suit their personalities, opportunities to be productive, even to discovering new or disused talents. They also need plenty of opportunity for the formation of such relationships as will make them happy. Children and grandchildren often worry that a formal marriage may interfere with their inheritance, yet they cannot bring themselves to accept a non-formalized relationship. We need to rethink our beliefs about this dilemma, if only out of charity and generosity for people whose lives are ebbing yet who seek to feel alive during each and every one of the ebbing days.

What else is there to say? Much. Most times when I go to an institution to lecture to the staff caring for older people, I shudder when the word "sterile" comes to my mind. Not for nothing does its medical meaning apply to an environment in which bacteria have been killed or cannot grow. In these institutions something else has been killed or cannot grow: the human spirit, the human sense of being alive, an individual, worthwhile. Whether in guests or in attendants, the same principles apply.

I saw in England, fifteen years ago, a community's home for older people. And that's just what it was. A series of two-story home units, with each unit having its own living room, complete with the wood paneling, the chintz-covered furniture, the coal grate so dear to English people. Outside each unit were garden plots, tended by those residents to whom gardening meant carrying on dear and familiar activities. In such a setting friendships and even intimacies might develop, although at that time it would not have been considered proper to discuss either the word sex or the word intimacy.

But, without question, intimacy is something that each one of us seeks, hungers for, throughout life. But this hunger is greatly intensified as one gets older and precious intimacies may be lost, while, at the same time, opportunities for the creation of new ones are diminishing. Families as well as institutions need to understand this on behalf of our older people, and in particular, we should be aware of the components that go into the formation of intimacy. These components are, in order, *choice, mutuality, reciprocity, trust, delight*. We choose quite consciously those few with whom we can or shall be fully intimate. A choice made unilaterally would itself exclude intimacy, hence *mutuality*. Mutuality must be equal, one person cannot be more intimate than another; hence *reciprocity*. The critical step is the establishment of trust, the mutual and reciprocal development of which is a most delicate and vital part of the achievement of intimacy; the steps taken by two individuals toward trust involve multiple small revealments as each one carefully opens his or her innermost self to the other and tests the safety of the opening. Like the sculptor building up his work with tiny finger bits of clay, successive experiences of trust, safely engaged in, serve to build up the intimacy to its ultimate expression, which is open *delight,* one in the other. And this, to me, is the ultimate meaning of the word intimacy, for when two people delight each other and delight *in* each other, in an atmosphere of security based on mutuality, reciprocity, and trust each in the other, whatever their age or sex, this surely is what we all seek in human relationships yet do not all achieve, certainly never in quantity, in our lives. And in this kind of a relationship it is entirely possible that sexual needs can be fulfilled without compulsion, and in particular the aging can discover that these sexual needs need not be defined in terms of the younger years but in much simpler experiences that may perhaps involve only warmth, stroking, loving gestures, and comforting proximity.

No one can possibly put a price or a value on such opportunities as we can make available to our older citizens to fill their ebbing hours not with busywork and little cheer but with quiet opportunities of shared time together in peace with someone one has chosen for one's self. I believe that there is a great humanitarian movement abroad in which professionals in the health field, in the social-work field, and in the field of religion can interpret to families and to institutions that theirs is the great opportunity and therefore privilege of resexualizing and therefore rehumanizing those who are dependent upon them—whether it be the handicapped or the aging.

WHAT'S INSIDE YOU, IT SHINES
OUT OF YOU

Marc Kaminsky

Marc Kaminsky has conducted poetry workshops with old people as a group worker with the Jewish Association for Services for the Aged, starting in 1972. He is a poet himself, of course, and out of the works of his students and his own perceptiveness he fashioned a wonderful book whose title we have borrowed for this selection.

At the first meeting of the first JASA senior citizens' club in Brooklyn, Dina Rosenfeld, my co-worker, announced that I would be holding a "poetry group" in my office. It was Dina, not I, who first used the term. She had come straight from social work school, and so everything to her was a group. The senior citizens' club was a group; it was a group that contained many little groups—a sewing group, a singing group, a Jewish studies group, a discussion group, an arts and crafts group, a women's group. So why not a poetry group?

Later, I adopted the term. It was clear to me, almost at once, that the work I was doing was different in character from the workshops I had done in the past. At first, I considered my sessions with the old people unrealized workshops—workshops with holes in the middle. But the holes seemed very interesting to me. They were occupied by living persons who weren't always so excited by the poem ideas I brought in, and who wandered off in their own direction.

Since my own inclination was to follow the flow of talk wherever it might lead, I did not have much difficulty in abandoning my idea of a model-workshop and working with the situation as it actually was. I was as much concerned in the people I was working with as I was in the poems, and my instinct in the workshops of the past had been to allow things to develop of their own accord, with a minimum of pushing around by me.

I had never thought it proper for me to shove the poem into shape, but rather to let the shape of what we made emerge out of the process of our working together. Then, too, I had come to working with old people with something like a basic faith in the group process itself. The emphasis of the early sessions was not solely on the making of poems. It naturally came to include the growing and suffering creatures who composed the group and were the makers of the poems they spoke.

If I clearly saw that I was no longer doing workshops, it was also clear to me that what I was doing with the old people was not quite the same thing as the poetry therapy of Dr. Leedy and his colleagues. It had a great deal in common with poetry therapy, and yet it did not fall easily into that category. It was true that we spent part of each session talking to each other about the dreams, memories, thoughts and feelings that were touched off by a catalytic text, and that this was a vital part of our work. But we also studied poems as poems, and we also spent a considerable amount of time in the group dictating—and later, writing—poems.

When I realized that I was doing neither poetry workshops nor poetry therapy, I became very curious—and very interested. I began to observe the sessions with growing vigilance, and to jot down notes on what was happening among us. I knew enough just to go ahead and follow my instinct; and, equally important, to trust the group process itself. It was all right to work in the dark, feeling out the way slowly. But I was actively seeking to know more precisely what I was doing with these old people. After five months, I made an exciting discovery. I was doing poetry groups!

And they were quite definitely poetry groups. They were the place where we found the person in the poem and the poem in the person.

After Dina's announcement, three old women showed up in my office. "So," said Bella Jacobskind, "here we are." There we were —sitting in a small circle at the JASA District Office in Brooklyn, looking out onto an enormous male flexing mountainous biceps: the sign of the health spa across the street. The male's over-developed and Alpine musculature, zooming in through the picture window of the office, caught my eye. I wanted to laugh. There we were: three old women, a somewhat rabbinical-looking poet—and an all-American giant came maundering in. I had a funny sense of dislocation. This time, it was not accompanied with the *angst* on the floating dance floor. My eye for the incongruous now filled me with a sense of possible discovery. It was a good sign: no doubt many antithetical and rejected images would find their way into this place.

There was a long silence. The old women were eying me, with a similar sense of the incongruous. Their looks clearly asked: What are we doing here? Would you kindly tell us already? What, in God's name, is a poetry group? And I could also see them sizing me up, moving rapidly from mild dismay to provisional acceptance: And what sort of person are you—with your rings and your necklace and your long black hair? You're not one of those *mishuganeh*[1] hippies, are you? Well, well, that's how you young people dress nowadays, and you can't be all that bad, if you're here with us.

Bella looked particularly eager. She looked like a passenger with a first class ticket, ready to go on an adventure. First stop: the land of dreams. Where else? I naturally started out with the first poem that had come from my work with the old people.

Dreams

I dreamed that my husband all dressed up
  in his gentle voice came back to me
  and told me: Take care of yourself.

I dream all the time of water, always
  in my dream there's water—muddy water,
  pools, but there's always water.

I dreamed that when I was alone in this
  country my parents appeared before me,
  and my father blessed me, and I knew
  it was their last time, I knew they
  were perished, this was just before
  Shavuos, 1942.

I dream about the beautiful things—the
  colors of nature, and music, and I see
  Haifa and Israel and the mountains
  of Switzerland.

[1] *mishuganeh:* crazy.

> I dreamed when I was sleeping at a window
> near the fire escape a hand came and
> choked me, and in the morning I saw
> the watch was there and no one had come.

> Whenever I dream of my folks, I know I have
> to call the rest of the family.

"Well," said Bella, "if you'll look in the Bible you'll see the story of Jacob. All night he wrestled with the angel, and he got the blessing."

Speaking of the last line, Bella said, "This is a signal, maybe she didn't call up in a long time and something is happening by her sister, her parents are giving her a reminder to keep in touch."

Vera Rosenfeld said, "I like the line about the husband. It means he was only wearing his gentle voice, he was dressed like Adam—a *nakitter*.[2] He was probably a handsome man, a good man. The woman is telling herself to go on, that's what it's all about, you have to go on, no matter what. This woman had a good marriage, so it was a loss, but now she has to go on, I guess her dream helped."

Hilda Glick said, "I had a dream like that, but I didn't know what it meant, and it hurt me. I didn't realize my mother was really telling me to take care of myself, my friend had to explain it to me."

It was at this point that I began taking dictation. The poem that came out, "Mourning," is what I call a "conversation poem." It is a verbatim transcript—with only transitional comments deleted—of the conversation that took place when Hilda began telling us her dream.

> I dreamt about my mother after her death.
> I wanted to kiss her but she pushed me away,
> I was hurt.

> My friend said that she didn't want me yet,
> she wanted me to live.

> How many years did I spend with my parents?
> But I spent fifty years with my husband. And
> how long do you get with your children? They're
> so far away.

[2] *nakitter:* a naked one.

It took me three years to come out of the
dilemma I was in.

I went to Israel and it brought me out—
the heroes of the Bible I saw before my eyes.

I suddenly lost my only sister and there
was an unveiling.[3]

My brother said: Here comes the sentimental one.

I said: I want to be alone now.

I sat on the family plot. There was my father,
there was my mother, there was my brother, there
was my sister, and I was the only alive person
here.

I thought: all these people were once alive,
all these people once ate and laughed and danced
and wept, and I was the only alive person here.

You know, it did me good.

For a year you mourn, and after that you
have to go on with your life, that's the Law.

The rabbi told me: If you go on crying
and mourning, there is no peace. The year is up.

The year is never up.

This morning I was going to bake some
potatoes and my sister came back to me, how she
used to brush the potatoes.

It never stops.

—HILDA GLICK, BELLA JACOBSKIND, VERA ROSENFELD

Most of the poems made by this poetry group—because it met
on Thursdays we called it the Thursday Poetry Group—came
about in this way. After I presented the catalyst-poem, the initial
conversation would often circle warily about it. And then a moment of concentration and power came, and behold! there it was—
the poem, the persons in the group speaking the poem to each
other, and I, my hands racing across my composition book, trying
to catch every word of it before it vanished. The women were usually deeply engrossed in what they were talking about—regrets,
Florida, anti-Semitism, rejecting children, wonderful or tyrannical

[3] unveiling: a ceremony held within a year of the burial. The monument is ritu-
ally "unveiled" to the family and friends of the dead one.

husbands, loneliness, loss of kin, the injustice of life, the "dilemma" of death—and they would rarely take notice of the moment when I started writing. Then Vera would suddenly realize I was taking down all their words, and she would say, *"Gib a kook, er shreibt, er shreibt!"* (*"Gib a kook"* is the Yiddish equivalent for a Spanish word that will soon pass into New York City English: *"Mira! Mira!"* combines the same nuances of excitement, alarm and pleasure. Vera wasn't only saying, "Look, he's writing, he's writing," she was also saying, "Look out!") Once she had "caught me at it again," she would chuckle to herself, and go on with the discussion.

At first, they were perplexed and amused to see me acting as their faithful scribe. They thought it odd and funny that at a certain point in the group, I would grab my notebook, and become suddenly silent, invisible, just attentive. Once, in discussing this, they asked me why I wasn't more of a disciplinarian. Hilda, in particular, wanted to know why I let the "old ladies" go on and on, just as they pleased, and didn't try to keep everybody more in line.

"Let me tell you a story. Once a child was walking through a wheat field, and his father came up to him and said, 'Why are you wandering around like that? Don't you see the rows of wheat? Why can't you stay in line?' And the child answered, 'Oh, but I *am* staying in line.' He pointed to a fine line on the ground, the barely visible trail that a garter snake had made before it disappeared. The father was so accustomed to his rows of wheat that he couldn't see the line which his child was following."

This was the first of many tales I found myself making up in the group. I was a great reader of Hasidic tales, Zen parables, and the like, and much of "the teaching" that mattered to me had come by way of tales I had heard or read. My way of finding and naming the meanings of things was changing, spontaneously, without my quite realizing it. I was no longer so inclined to do as much explaining as I had done in the past, and so of necessity I had to find other ways of transmitting my thought, ways that would help people learn without imposing the jargon that worked for me. Each person had his own experience and vocabulary to work with, and each could be left to put things together for himself in a way that would be significant and valuable for him.

Vera, in interpreting the story, said that the poetry group wasn't like a class, that everyone in it had something to learn, that everyone was a teacher, but that the great teacher was experience, and that they, the old women, had had a great deal of it, and they also had good stories to tell.

Bella reminded Hilda of the time that I had cut her off after she had cut Hilda off. No matter how many times Bella thanked me for "teaching" her "how to listen," she was always a bit sore about it. She referred to it as "the time he told me to shut up." I had said, "Why can't you listen to what Hilda is saying?" She told Hilda, playfully, "And you remember the time he told me to shut up? When he wants to keep someone in line . . ." She didn't finish the sentence. She pressed her hands against her cheeks, rocked her head to and fro, her non-verbal equivalent for: *"Oy vay!"*

I said that very often "the line" wasn't known in advance, and the only way you could find it was by keeping your eyes open and waiting, and if you were interested in finding the line it was distracting to try to keep other people inside of it. The mistake of the father in the story had been to believe that he knew what the line was, and he could only find the child's line of reasoning by watching him carefully.

I said I was interested in following the lines that they came up with. What I wanted was to get at the moment when the people in the group were truly talking to each other, and that moment could not be legislated by anybody, it could only come when we all helped create a positive situation.

"So you see," Bella said, "silence *can* be golden."

I said I thought that the group members were too disposed to addressing themselves only to me. They tended to get to the moment of truth when they forgot about classrooms and teachers and discipline and started speaking to each other. I obviously did my share of the talking. My silence was an equally important way of allowing the group to get to the moment when the poem was being spoken, the moment of high energy, deep feeling, honesty, and vivid speech: the moment when Hilda got up and started dancing and narrating her physical gladness; the moment when Bella recalled her encounter with death at the Yad V'Shem;[4] the moment when Lilly Palace, Bella's close friend and a newcomer to the

---

[4] Yad V'Shem: Literally, Garden of Names. A memorial to the victims of the Holocaust in Jerusalem.

group, began to speak of her "crazy wisdom," of finding beauty in things that others thought ugly; the moment when Beatrice Zucker, another new member, opened up and began pouring out her bitterness and her regrets and afterwards laughed at herself— *that* moment, which each of us in the group had experienced.

All this helped me learn two important things about learning. I learned how to use story-telling as a way of transmitting experienced ideas—and in return, heard many good stories from the other persons in the group. I also began to learn the proper use of silence.

I ended up doing so much writing in the group that they ceased to feel in any way intimidated by it. It was taken for granted: they spoke, I wrote, poems got born. Working with formulas, however, still had the power to intimidate. Hilda would speak lines that were tremendously awake with life when she was spontaneously uttering the poem: it was she who had spoken of sitting among her dead, filled with that strange feeling of grief and joy that always comes when we think of dead people who were once truly alive, and we are suddenly flooded with the realization that "I am the only alive person here." Unlike many of the classics that Hilda had read in high school in the 1920s, the words that she spoke, when she was in touch with her vital experience, were "classic": they belonged to a distinct order of experience, which she spoke of with vigor and authority, and what she had to say then "teaches me the words I need for soliloquy and conversation."[5]

Hilda, who was so exciting when left to her own devices, would get all blocked up when we were working with a poem-device. Her authentic speech was blotted out by the one great thought that filled her head: "Now I am a poet, I am dictating the words of a poem and I must talk like a poet. Ozymandias, where are you now that I need you? And where are you, Longfellow lines of yesteryear? Oh Milton, oh Shakespeare, oh Poe, oh Thoreau! Oh where are you, Drayton, now that I need you!" She remembered having been told that Milton woke up every morning and dictated fifty lines of *Paradise Lost*. The great poets, then, worked as she was working: they, too, thought big thoughts (in big words!) and had scriveners. They were the standard she was trying to live up to.

[5] Judah Goldin's definition of a classic in his "Introduction" to Agnon's *Days of Awe*, New York: Schocken Books, 1948.

Nothing could be more clear from the bardological postures she assumed when she was "composing." She leaned back, put her fingertips to her brow, wrinkled it, drew her head up, to receive the great Light that was dove-like about to descend into her, opened her mouth, took a deep breath—and spoke garbage. Her oracular utterances composed a manual of bad poetry, which, as a matter of editorial and personal tact, I did not copy and present to her.

What I learned from Hilda, who was still carrying the scars of the vicious treatment that poetry usually gets in the hands of American educators, was that I had better steer clear of anything that would provide the group with an opportunity for pomp and circumstance. Hilda had come to the poetry group under a great misapprehension. She had genuinely enjoyed poetry as a girl, and she had expected to find Longfellow all over again. Well, she did find some of the "old favorites," the big hits of the seventeenth century. And I found, in working with her, that it was by no means necessary to avoid the "classics"—the poetry that had deadened us all to poetry. And I also learned from her, more than from anyone else, the limitations of working with formulas.

It was not long before I stopped using workshop-formulas in the Thursday Poetry Group. Certainly I wanted the poems we made to have a descernible shape, and the parallel structure of the formulas provided a simple and liberating form. But the poems arrived at by a concentration of thought and feeling, going in their own direction, were just as shapely and far more interesting. The "spontaneous utterance poems" of an individual and the "conversation poems" of the group were, certainly, free-form, but they allowed room for the play of voices and tones and textures which made up their riches. Their shapeliness came from their directness with respect to reality. They were the thing itself—experience stripped of excuses, elaborations, pretenses, false rhetorical postures, the true voice of the speaker, coming through at last.

The group developed by the making of poems, and the poems developed by the making of the group. It all happened by way of organized spontaneity. There was the flowing, and also the containing. There was the reaching out, and also the limiting. Beatrice, on her first day in the group, did not want any part of the theme which Bella proposed after we studied Milton's "When I

consider how my light is spent"—the theme of "accepting my fate."
Beatrice wasn't interested in accepting her fate, she was interested
in bitching about it. But she did not know the group well enough
to start her bitching, so she just wanted to avoid the whole subject.
She wanted to maintain the high moral tone with which she had
walked into the room. She didn't want the group to know that she
was eaten up inside by the thought of her poverty—she wasn't all
that poor, as we later found out—and by her intense jealousy of
people who had more money than she did. No one in the group
pushed Beatrice to accept her fate. The other women accepted her
refusal to do so, and this prepared the ground for all the wonderful
spleen that came out of her later. And once she had allowed herself to be her splenetic, bitchy self, she produced what are probably the most powerful and poignant "spontaneous utterance
poems" that came out of the group.

Each person in the group set her own limits, and the group as a
whole created the limits which it wished to observe. It had a sense
of its own distinct identity which, at first, exceeded formulation,
but it was something that was experienced by every member of the
group. Each one, in the course of our working together, offered
her own definition of the group, and each one defined it in a way
significant to her.

When Bella sought to explain the value of the group, she spoke
of its "Jewishness." Vera said it was a place to release tensions,
and reminded her of therapy. Hilda saw it as her poetry class. Lilly
was interested in what the group had in common with a workshop,
the making of poems. Beatrice, although she never said as much,
saw it as a place to perform. She performed the poems that she
had written in the past, she paraded her "superiority," and she
never let up long enough to get the respect she ardently craved—
and warranted.

Beatrice was, truly, a woman of large gifts, but a lifetime of
working in factories, and a bad marriage, had hopelessly damaged
her. Beneath her contempt, her vanity, and her quick indignation
there was a great and terrible hurt. What was so terribly sad was
to see her put the other women off, and prevent herself from getting the recognition which her giftedness would have otherwise
won for her. She was so brittle and bull-headed that she made it
extremely difficult to give her the help that she needed.

There was one session where she got some of the recognition that she coveted. She brought in a sheaf of poems, each one an exquisite piece of calligraphy, each one a savagely intelligent piece of wit, the earliest dated 1915, the latest dated 1954. The group received Beatrice's poems as a thing of wonder. The women passed around the black leather scrapbook in which the poems were bound as if it were a precious object. They handled it with terrific care. It was as though they were afraid to actually touch it—the yellowed pages seemed in real danger of disintegrating on contact. They marvelled at her penmanship, they were more than a little impressed with her dexterity in handling quatrains and densely patterned stanzaic forms, they asked for—and got—a lengthy reading of her poems. The accent of the reader, an old Jewish seamstress from Brooklyn, turned distinctly British, and carried vague intimations of great times, now gone, and of Edwardian lawn parties and familiar acquaintance with great lords and ladies.

Beatrice was not the only one who provided poems. The women in the group quickly began to take some responsibility for selecting the poems we worked with. I encouraged them to tell me what they wished to read and study, and said that, unless I positively couldn't stand the poem, we would use it. The only poem I ever vetoed was "Hiawatha," which Hilda suggested. But we read sonnets by Milton and Shakespeare at her request. Bella proposed *Psalms* and *Ecclesiastes,* and we read passages from both. Hilda's Milton and Bella's *Psalms* were, for each of them, special texts— they were the sacred texts of their youths and carried rich and happy associations. The *Psalms,* generally celebrated for their curative power, had had a steady and increasing importance in Bella's life. "When my husband died and by me the world stopped, this helped bring me back. It is the greatest poetry. I keep it always next to my bed and every day I read a little of it—this is what my husband used to read to me, and now when I read it alone, I feel he is always with me."

On the day that we studied Milton, Hilda clearly felt the pride of a hostess who had succeeded in serving us a beautiful poem. She said of *her* Milton sonnet: "It's food for thought."

Lilly Palace was wild about Whitman. "My father gave me *Leaves of Grass* for my birthday and inscribed it with the most beautiful words, this was in 1945, and I always keep this book

near me, I always loved Whitman, my father was a man just like
Whitman, down to earth, and wise, he appreciated the beauty of
nature, I follow in his footsteps. To me there is nothing more
beautiful than when my husband and I go away to the country, we
spend a whole afternoon wandering in the woods, talking and
looking at the wild life, we lose all track of time."

We read a great deal of Whitman. One day I brought in "Hours
Continuing Long, Sore and Heavy-Hearted," and after we had
read and discussed it for a while, Vera asked, "I don't understand
one thing. Is this his friend or his lover? It's hard to tell."

"It's both his friend and his lover. But it's hard to tell whether
this person is a man or a woman, isn't it?"

That was Vera's real question.

"Does the poem give you any clues?"

Vera read the following passage aloud:

> Sullen and suffering hours! (I am ashamed—
>   but it is useless—I am what I am);
> Hours of my torment—I wonder if other men
>   have the like, out of the like feelings?
> Is there even one other like me—distracted—
>   his friend, his lover, lost to him?

Silence, complete silence.

I said that there was little doubt in my mind that Whitman was
gay, even though some scholars disputed this. The lines seemed to
be speaking of homosexual longing and of the revulsion that this
aroused in him. "Whitman himself can't accept the fact that he's
gay, it must have been even harder in those days. But how do you
feel about this?" It was O.K. with Vera. If Whitman was gay, so
were a lot of other people, and it was just one of the many ways
that people were. That was an eye-opener. But what really made
me wake up was Bella's response. I expected that because she
came from the old country and was fiercely attached to Jewish traditions, she would disapprove of Whitman, the poem, and homo-
sexuality. What she said was: "Everybody is boss over his own
body and can do whatever he feels like." The old women were not
shocked. I was. I had been walking around with considerable prejudice as to the nature of their prejudices, and I was delighted to
find out I was wrong. I was particularly delighted by Bella's re-

sponse. I had always been fond of Bella. Now I began to think she was wonderful.

Sometimes she wasn't so wonderful. Her need for love, for a great deal of love from me, moved me deeply. I quickly became very close with her, but I also found that she could be a terrible *nudge*.[6] Because of her "old country" quality, because of her emotional generosity and the intensity of her passions, she reminded me of my grandmothers, and I was especially open to her, so that each time she came running to me, in one of her black moods, in her moments of dejection and rage, it would tear at me. Her love was a jealous love, and a demanding one. She was all too quick to feel rejected when I could not or would not give her the total attention she wanted. She had to become more independent of me, and I had to separate myself in a proper way from her. This took "hours continuing long, sore and heavy-hearted."

Whitman's poem gave the group a lot to work with. I said that the poem was a self-portrait that was making a strong point: it said clearly and forcefully that a person's torment comes from his own inability to accept what he is. Something clicked in Vera. She began speaking the words of the "self-portrait" poem. She said, "If I had become a school teacher, I would never have married a man like my husband." More than that she would not, at present, say. But she opened up a subject that had been, if anything, more difficult for the women to talk about than death. She had begun to speak "of the woe that is in marriage," and we would return to this later on and find that it was a subject of some importance to others in the group.

Whitman's poem also provided the occasion for one of Bella's most moving "arias." I suggested that we make up a poem called "Hours," and that the word "hours" act as the starting-point for each line or stanza. Here is what Bella said:

> The hour of my first day in Jerusalem, over there
>   is the Yad V'Shem, all the remainings of
>   the ovens, it's on the highest mountain in
>   Jerusalem, it's King David's tomb.
> And an Arab soldier was walking back and forth.

[6] *nudge:* nag, pain in the ass.

And the first thing that struck me
   a bar of soap, wrapped in the traditional colors, and
   printed on it was *Reine Judenfetz.*[7]
The most terrible thing I saw was the sacks of
   ashes, and the little children's shoes
   all bloody.
The horror is finished, I want to say what I
   lived through that moment.
I lost my group and met an old Jew who told me:
   "Genug, tachter kind, kum ariose."[8]
Then our guide was running up the mountain and
   when he found me, he said: *"Boruch Hashem,*[9]
   I found you alive. If the Arab saw you
   alone, you would be shot."
I broke out with a cry, it was a cry
   from bitterness and pain, the pain of 2000 years
   and of all the people lived through
   —fire and torture.
It took a long time till that cry stopped in me.

Lilly Palace was deeply responsive to Bella's *cri de coeur.* She said, "You never let go enough. It's a sore inside you when you went through what Bella went through."

Beatrice was not impressed. She was not about to sit back and let the title of Chief Sufferer be handed to anyone else. "I lived through it too, here in America. I worked in a factory with Polish and Italian. Haters! Haters! I lived through it too!"

Beatrice was, herself, full of hatred—the hatred of having lived an unfulfilled life. From this, much venom.

Bella stood up for herself. She was capable of yielding her right of way, at many turns of the conversation, but anyone who challenged her right to feel as she did about her "Jewish experience" was headed for a collision. "It's hard to understand it unless you've been through it—the way they tore out my uncle's beard." (Her father had died fighting the Nazis in the sewers of Warsaw.)

---

[7] *Reine Judenfetz:* Pure Jewfat.
[8] "Enough, my child, come out."
[9] *Boruch Hashem:* "Blessed Name," thank God.

MARC KAMINSKY   223

Beatrice sneered: "Is that all *you* can remember about anti-Semitism?"

Bella: "I could write a book." She was enraged.

Lilly, always willing to sympathize with Bella, was also quick to check excesses. "Bella, you have to live in the present. You have to be a one hundred per cent member of the here and now." This phrase, which Lilly used with Bella on more than one occasion, always worked, it was like a charm. As soon as Lilly spoke these words, Bella relaxed. She turned to her "dear friend Lilly," took hold of her hand, and said, "Yeh, Lilly, I shouldn't aggravate myself." She was beaming with love.

Bella had had a heart attack, and whenever she got up in arms, whenever a real or unintended offense brought on an attack of tearful fury, it was enough for Lilly to say, "Bella, this isn't so good for you," and Bella, by degrees, would calm down. It was a remarkable thing to see. Lilly's sure, deft touch would transform Bella, in front of our eyes, from a hurt and enraged old woman to a mellow, warm, even chipper friend. What made the transformation more remarkable was its rapidity. A moment after she had been consumed with wrath, she would be in good spirits again.

Hilda always sat silent and withdrawn when Bella spoke of the suffering she had witnessed and experienced. Warsaw and the Yad V'Shem were alien and incomprehensible places to her. She came alive in praise of her husband. He had provided her with a comfortable life. In doing a formula-poem based on the *Psalms,* Hilda said, "Praise be my husband! I have a toe with a bone projecting, and thanks to him I could afford $90 space shoes." Beatrice couldn't stand to hear about the comfort and security that Hilda had known all her life; Hilda became sullen and defensive when she had to listen to Bella speak of "the cruelties of life"; Lilly became irate when somebody—anybody—would not hear Bella out with sympathy; and Vera seemed to be able to hear and understand everyone.

I had a lot of respect for Vera. She was never one of the principals in the group's round-robin of conflict, but it was not because she avoided conflict. When anyone said something she thought mistaken or inappropriate or distorted, she would state her own thought in the matter—firmly. When Beatrice kept whining about Florida, Vera said, "To me Florida is the last stop, and I want to keep moving." Beatrice complained that Vera, who must have had a nice bank account, could afford to say that; Vera could come and go as she pleased, but she, Beatrice, was stuck. Vera promptly unstuck her, and quite forcefully demonstrated, both to Beatrice and to the group, that if Beatrice's complaints were not entirely a sham, they were also not entirely realistic, and that Beatrice could, in fact, afford "that little one-room in Florida" which she kept talking about. Two months later, as a result of the verbal slap which Vera had administered to her, Beatrice did go off and do what she dreamed of.

Vera had also challenged Bella's intolerance of the "*mishuganeh* hippies." "Here's what I say: 'Kids of today, you're smart, you're making the most of every moment, you do what you want—you have to break with your mothers."

Vera neither poured out her heart nor held things back. She was tactful, and she was blunt. She was reserved, and she was outgoing. She always seemed to know how to keep her balance. When the time came to speak, she spoke—honestly, judiciously. When it was time for silence, she kept silence—and took everything in. If she had a friend in the group, it was Hilda.

There were the "modern" women in the group. They shared a culture in common, a culture different from that of Bella, and different, too, from that of Beatrice, who was off somewhere, living between the Lower East Side and the court of the Rothschilds. Lilly Palace, like Hilda and Vera, was American-born and a high school graduate; but her intense alliance with Bella did not leave her open for friendship with them. If Lilly was particularly receptive to Bella, Vera was particularly receptive to Hilda. Beatrice wasn't particularly receptive to anybody, and the group, by and large, returned the compliment.

Vera often helped create a climate of mutual acceptance. She played a small, but decisive, role in clearing up "the difference" between Hilda and Bella. It became clear that Hilda didn't know what to do with the thought that Bella's mere presence was gradually forcing upon her—the thought that life is unfair. If the other women had accepted this as a fact of life, and had taken up some clear attitude in relation to this unpleasant reality, Hilda had managed to avoid it all her life. She had been sheltered as a girl and as a grown woman. The misfortunes of others were something that had been made all too easy for her to hide from. She could hide no longer: the group exposed her to a range of experience that shook her up. She realized that she had gotten a better deal than Bella, and it made her dislike Bella—and herself. It upset her picture of the world. What was to be made out of this new and disturbing thought?

A poem! Vera provided the way in. She said that no two lives were the same, you couldn't expect them to be the same, and that even someone who was comparatively well off also had his or her troubles.

Hilda began making peace with Bella and the injustice of life in speaking of "the difference."

1.

Each one is different: Bella talks about Zionism and God,
she talks about the cruelties of life.

My life was different: I was brought up with a golden spoon,
my husband was a good provider, I never knew want.

I had an easy time of it until my husband had a stroke.
Until he was 65 we didn't know what a doctor was.

I gave him my all, and he made a 95% recovery.

He's not the same: he lost his enthusiasm. *The New York Times* he had to read through and through, now he has no interest to read it.

From the man that he was he lost all his interest, there is no interest, I am his interest, I am his life.

2.

Hilda always had soft white rolls. Let me tell you about the bread we ate.

In 1915 the Germans came in, this was by the time of Kaiser Wilhelm, he was a good man, he didn't harm the Jews, he tolerated, freedom we had.

They took out all the bread, all the food, and we got back half a pound of food each day.

Such a hunger it was terrible! We had to wait on lines a half a day, five o'clock in the morning we had to go out.

Three or four days the bread had to lie before we could cut it, it was so like clay.

In the bread we found glass, rope, and dirt—mice droppings! From this we got sick, the epidemic broke out, people fell like flies, dysentery and typhoid. What we went through!

We were hungry and sick, but we had freedom, this was by Kaiser Wilhelm in 1915.

—HILDA GLICK & BELLA JACOBSKIND

This poem did not resolve the conflict, but it did bring it out into the open, and give it a name and a shape. It made the conflict acceptable, and, above all, it was Hilda's act of self-affirmation in the face of "the cruelties of life."

In recognizing "the difference," Hilda began to admit to the group that she had troubles of her own. She was no longer ashamed to speak of them. If anything, she felt that life had also given her burdens and responsibilities, and she felt a certain sense of pride in the value that she had for her husband. This was a far cry from Bella's or Vera's sense of their independent value as persons. It was, nonetheless, something. But her wifely pride led straight to the heart of her wifely oppression.

The picture of marital bliss she had painted for us had begun to crack. Her husband's paralysis was the first piece of bad news. Hilda had already heard Vera speak of her dissatisfaction in marriage, so that it wasn't an entirely taboo topic. The week after she told us about her husband's stroke, she came in upset. Her difficulties were far more severe than she had allowed us—and herself—to realize.

"Yes," she said, "I'm well off all right, but I'm like a well-kept slave, with a chain around my neck. I can't even go out for an hour's walk. He won't even let me do that. He lets me come here, to the poetry group, but that's *it*. And even *that* I had to plead for. I sit with him all day and every day and I get restless, I just want to go out for a walk in the park. Sometimes, in the late afternoon, I get so restless, I'm dying for a walk in the park. Is that too much to ask? And he says if I'm not back in an hour, he'll call the cops. What can I do? He keeps me locked up."

Vera nodded and smiled knowingly, but didn't say a word. Bella sat silent. Lilly was distressed. No one wanted to approach the anger and unhappiness of this "happy-go-lucky" woman, and everyone knew all too well what it was all about: the sexual jealousy, the fear masquerading as concern, the outright threats. The strong man of the house had become a sick old man, in a single stroke, and his wife had remained a youthful-looking woman with a beautiful figure. Time had wrecked the whole foundation of their marriage. Old age would never come to the all-American male on the sign across the street, but it came upon living men, and it came as a tragedy. Hilda's husband was a representative American type: a heart-attack victim who had planned on everything but growing old, a man who experienced the coming of age as a loss of status, as a form of failure, a man so used to ruling the roost that when he did not entirely get his way he was all set to call the cops. Not only because he was worried that his wife would get raped, but because he was jealous and scared of her sexuality, scared it might attract a younger and stronger man than himself. So he became a bully, he would call the cops to support his old male dominance. Old age had come into Hilda's life suddenly, and she was not prepared for it. Her husband's stroke had robbed her of a lifetime's adjustment to male supremacy.

What I said, however, was: "We're all in chains, there's a rope around everybody's neck." I got out of my chair and walked to the middle of the room. "Here's my stake, I'm attached to this stake, and we've all got a stake in life. The question I have to ask myself is this: 'How much rope have I got?'" I moved away from the imaginary stake, slowly and carefully. "I've got to find out how much rope I've got and play it for all it's worth. I've got to try things out, maybe I've got enough rope to move freely around this room." I walked slowly around the room, coming next to each person, seeing how far I could go. "My rope doesn't stretch from here to Alaska, but maybe I've got some of the rope I need already. It would be stupid to sit down next to the stake and sulk when I had enough rope to come over and pay you a visit." I went over and sat down next to her. "Hilda, take your walk in the park. If an hour's all the rope you've got right now, use it, use it for all it's worth, use the freedom you do have. Then sit down with your husband and bargain for more."

I told Hilda that I had often felt distressed when I was carrying poems inside me and I had to give birth to them wherever I happened to be, and not under the best conditions, at home, with my sharpened pencils and my typewriter and my erasers and my correction fluid and all my notes and thoughts arranged at my desk; and once they were born, they were naked and hungry and demanded attention and I was frequently called away from them for many hours at a time, sometimes whole days would pass before I could take care of them, and I could hear them speaking to me and there was nothing I could do about it, and sometimes when I came home from work I was too tired for them and I had to neglect them, and I sometimes felt great rage and frustration. I said that it had become necessary for me to learn to make the most of the free time that I did have, that over the years I had found that I had enough time to get done what I wanted to do, but I had had to learn to discipline my time and my passions and to work in patience, and from this great good had come, that I now felt less like a mother guarding her kids from wolves, and that all the things I wanted to do got done—but in due time. Whenever I became impatient, I would tell myself, "You will do it all, but in due time." And wasn't the voice that answered Milton's complaint, in the sonnet she loved, the voice of Patience?

Ah hah! That clinched it.

Starting that week, Hilda began making her own private one-hour freedom marches.

And that was the first time the poetry group helped someone change her life.

PART VI

RALLYING CRIES:
Agendas for Action

A FREE-LANCE AGITATOR CONFRONTS THE ESTABLISHMENT

Tish Sommers

Tish Sommers, co-ordinator of the Committee on Older Women's Rights of the National Organization for Women (NOW), describes herself as a "free-lance agitator on the ageist front." Working out of Oakland, California, she lectures, organizes, writes, leads how-to workshops, testifies on and promotes legislation, and serves on Governor Brown's Commission on Aging. In this dramatic testimony at a hearing held by the Administration on Aging, she scathingly criticizes the "social-service" approach to helping the elderly. "The seniors' problems are the bread and butter of a growing army of social workers, schools of gerontology, bureaucrats, and proposal writers," she notes. "A great many of them mean very well, but with friends like that, who needs enemies?"

Thank you, Commissioner Flemming, for the opportunity to testify here. The notice indicated that you seek a variety of viewpoints and would welcome recommendations. I assume you want dissidence as well as approval. My view, I fear, is sharply critical of the background paper on which we were supposed to comment, because that statement does not address the basic questions. And until we ask the right questions, we shall never find solutions. In fact, we may be adding a great deal to the problems without intending to.

The tone of the background paper would suggest the major problem is a shortage of "qualified" and adequately trained persons who are paid well enough and who receive sufficient benefits to keep them satisfied to stay put in service agencies for the elderly. "The lack of financial resources clearly ranks first on the list of factors preventing a more rapid expansion of services," the paper states. Not a whisper of doubt about the value of those services or a word about why seniors can't provide those services for themselves. But if indeed transportation, home care, legal and other counseling services, and residential repairs are the four national priorities (and I would certainly challenge those), money to buy those services in the hands of seniors themselves is the obvious answer to personnel problems in these areas. Most communities have taxi services, which function twenty-four hours and don't even ask the purpose of the trip. All the other services could easily be made available, if older persons had money to pay for them.

Of course, everyone in the aging field gives lip service to increased social security benefits, and a few even quickly mention guaranteed annual income, but these are too hard to tackle, so they move rapidly on to Band-Aid programs, without asking if these may not be doing a greal deal more harm than good in the long run.

As a feminist I am acutely aware of the selling job by media, unions, and opinion makers which spurred the back-to-the-home movement after World War II, during which women by necessity moved rapidly from dependency to self-sufficiency. Perhaps there is a parallel happening now in regard to older persons. Out of genuine concern, and also self-interest, the helping professions may be overselling the "pitiful plight" of the elderly—selling dependency as women were sold dependency in the postwar period.

There is great appeal in jobs to help other people, especially if accompanied by a good salary and status, and ladders into prestigious administrative employment. To maintain such jobs, and to increase the number of the programs that provide them, an increasing number of helpless and dependent people to serve are needed. The seniors' problems are the bread and butter of a growing army of social workers, schools of gerontology, bureaucrats, and proposal writers. A great many of them mean very well, but with friends like that, who needs enemies? While the selling job may not be as crassly materialistic as it was for the back-to-the-home movement (the joys of split-level living, stoves, refrigerators, etc.), there is in fact subtle pressure on old people to give up and let themselves be cared for, thereby creating jobs for the young in the field of aging. Don't organize and demand a livable income. Relax, we'll take care of you, is the theme. Who, other than seniors, are saying older people should have the right to support themselves if they can?

No one suggests that perhaps we might like to work, ourselves, in these programs for the aging. Even though employment is the most obvious method to make it possible for seniors to pay for services, employment opportunity is not seen as a priority for older persons; in fact it is never once mentioned in the position paper. What is the greatest manpower problem of all in this field? It is institutionalized discrimination against older persons. There would be no labor shortages in the field of aging if older persons had a crack at the jobs there.

Of course that would require a whole new head set about the matter of retirement, and what constitutes "qualified." In fact, some countries are beginning to rethink these questions. Sweden's new pension system allows the worker to retire as early as sixty years of age and work part time, yet receive a partial pension and a wide range of fringe benefits available to full-time workers. Also, a worker can come out of retirement and assume a job. Over sixty-five, workers in part-time jobs can continue to draw a full pension. Instead of a built-in *disincentive* to work, as with our social-security earnings limitation, the older person has an added benefit, making it possible to pay for some of those needed services.

In this country the pressure to keep older people out of the job market is still very strong, and when employment is tight, the pressure increases. But as the economic burden such as social security taxes becomes greater, and the number of non-working persons living primarily on public funding grows, there will be a shift in attitude. It just does not make sense to keep a growing proportion of the population out of jobs, then deplore the burden of caring for them.

Some of the blocks to employment of older people are institutional, and these need to be changed. The social security retirement test is obvious. Why prevent an older person from working and then pay someone else to provide services she or he can't pay for? The age-discrimination-in-employment law is another. At sixty-five, the worker loses all protections against discrimination (such as they are). Mandatory retirement at whatever age is certainly incompatible with the concept of equality, and is becoming economically indefensible. More subtle are the health plans and pension plans that make it more costly for employers to hire anyone fifty-five or over. These could be eliminated easily, with the will to do so.

But even more appallingly ageist are those piddling programs that do exist to employ the elderly poor. For example, everyone loves the Foster Grandparent program. It has been an outstanding success because elderly women and men have given loving help to retarded children and been proven more effective than many professionals in the field. In some cases they have been more permanent than the well-paid social workers who moved on to better jobs. But how are the Foster Grandparents rewarded? Pay is $1.65 an hour, with a limit on hours, yet these great jobs are only available to persons with minimal income and assets. *Who else* has to pass a means test in order to get a job? Certainly not the social workers or the gerontologists, or anyone in the Office on Aging. And how many of those Foster Grandparents were promoted to jobs in the same program when the social worker moved on? Very few, if any, I am sure.

Title IX of the Older Americans Act was supposed to be such a breakthrough for employment of persons fifty-five and up. But it provides only a few hundred "training slots," again only available to those with very low income, mostly women. Many of the persons involved do indeed provide needed outreach services, and become sensitive advocates for the elderly poor. But the pay is minimum wage or little more, hours are limited to twenty, and the greatest benefits accrue to the agency that administers the program. One such director bragged recently that bookkeeping of their multimillion-dollar project was provided by one of these aides at less than three dollars per hour. The bookkeeper was indeed proud of her responsible job. But she was paid sixty dollars per week, and to qualify for the job, had to be below the poverty line.

Another such program recently funded is called Cal Esteem. Under pressure by seniors groups for employment assistance, the California Employment Development Department (EDD) has just hired forty-five persons fifty-five and older to work in twenty-six field offices. These persons must meet federal poverty criteria and be unemployed. They will in turn provide employment assistance for older persons at EDD. They are paid $3.94 an hour, and may not work more than thirty hours a week and 194 days a year, for a maximum of nine months. Funds from the U. S. Dept. of Commerce were funneled through The National Council on the Aging and the California Office on Aging, each of which no doubt took a healthy bite from the funds allocated.

This program is in lieu of the employment program for older persons that used to provide "older workers specialists" in the EDD, which was discontinued in 1969 by then Governor Ronald Reagan as an economy move. The persons recruited by EDD through Cal Esteem may serve older workers well. But if they do, why are they not paid the same as other workers? Why are they means-tested when no other employees of EDD must pass a poverty test? Why will the program end after nine months? If they are not worth at least as much as other EDD employees, then this employment service is just another shuck.

Exploitation of the labor of older persons in programs designed to benefit seniors is rampant. Here is an ad for a cook in a senior nutrition program. The city of Davis, it reads, offers a challenging and rewarding employment experience for a "senior lady." Requirements were cooking experience for large groups, and knowledge of good nutrition and dietary needs for seniors. Pay offered was $2.25 an hour, for nine hours per week, or $20.25 gross pay a week. No fringe benefits of course.

Or take the Area Agencies on Aging, which are supposed to be exemplary programs. How many of them hire older persons, especially non-professionals, except for exploitive, low-paid, part-time work without insurance, pensions, or other benefits? Other government programs are equally discriminatory. CETA has not one person over sixty enrolled in Alameda County, and only a handful over forty-five. The excuse given is that older persons are difficult to place, so with training monies in tight supply, they are better spent on younger persons.

It is not necessarily true that the people running these agencies, especially those related to aging, don't like old people. They like old people in their place—in the rocking chair, and certainly not included in the affirmative-action plan. The background paper has a lot to say about "properly qualified" and appropriately trained personnel. It is rank with educational elitism. By whose standards are courses in gerontology more appropriate to working with elderly persons than life experience? Perhaps a good test case based upon the *Griggs* v. *Duke Power* decision, which challenged employment criteria having a negative impact upon employment of blacks, might be in order. As that Supreme Court decision mandated, let the employer prove that these educational requirements are relevant. The success ratio of Foster Grandparents might show that degrees had little to do with success in that work. Schools of gerontology could provide a great service by tackling the built-in ageism in all our institutions. Rather, they contribute to exclusion and dependency of elders by building another barrier to employment.

Of course, some older people do go back to school, and older women are often attracted to gerontology because it seems to offer possible careers not as closed to them as others. But such persons soon take on the professional stance that views other older persons as potential clients, the inevitable one-upmanship of the "helping" professions. The status difference between client and "helper" reinforces dependency.

In one case I know of, a young person, freshly employed with a gerontology degree, learned the ropes from a knowledgeable senior aide, who in effect trained her to be her supervisor. This brings to mind the secretaries who teach the young management trainees who subsequently become their bosses.

Another parallel with women is the exploitation of older persons as volunteers. RSVP (the Retired Senior Volunteer Program) was the government's answer to the growing need for social services and unwillingness to spend the money. Older people can't work, they have a lot of time on their hands, and have had much experience, was the logic. Why not tap this pool of talent for personal service, hire some "qualified" persons to supervise them, and take care of some of these unmet community needs, thus accomplishing several objectives for the least amount of money and providing a place for seniors to feel useful, too.

If the *option* were available for paid work, that might be valid. RSVP only provides carfare and lunch (and that only if the agency the volunteer works for agrees). If the choice were available for a similar part-time job for pay and if there were not penalties under social security for working, you can be sure that most RSVP volunteers would jump at the chance for pay. Not only do many need supplementary income for a modest standard of living, but in our society reimbursement puts an entirely different value on the work done.

The head set that assumes that older people should work for nothing or for carfare and lunch is cruelly exploitive, even though it may be a preventive health measure for those who participate. A large percentage of older persons do not have the option of paid employment. Just because volunteering beats making macaroni jewelry in a seniors center does not justify that exploitation.

Since criticism without recommendations is insufficient, here are some constructive proposals from the other side of the age and sex tracks.

1. *Transportation services.* Use the funds to subsidize ambulatory seniors to take advantage of existing systems such as taxi companies. In Sweden, seniors receive coupons to use taxis without charge. Only for more handicapped persons are more specialized transportation services needed.

2. *Home repair.* Many older men and women can do minor repairs. Such programs are too small to be a threat to union labor, who have retired personnel also to serve as foremen. There is no reason why these services could not be *paid,* providing part-time jobs for seniors—not as aides, trainees, or volunteers, but as *workers.*

3. *Home health.* Here is an area with great promise for employment of older persons, if this were seen as just as important to the success of the program as the service to the homebound person. Unfortunately, the work is viewed as custodial only, and the pay is exploitive. For example, Alameda County has a unit cost for home health care of $6.50 per day, but pays two dollars per day to the worker who provides the service. Beyond housekeeping, many concerned displaced homemakers could quickly be trained to maximize the autonomy and positive image of the homebound person. This is a new paramedical function which we hope to develop at the Displaced Homemakers Center in Alameda County.

4. *Legal and other counseling services.* A complicated maze of services has been created and such cumbersome bureaucratic jurisdictions developed that one needs a Seeing Eye dog to function. Rather than add another layer of information and referral agencies, new jobs could be created for older persons to become lay advocates, ombudspersons, and mutual-help counselors. The National Paralegal Institute could be induced to train such persons for jobs in legal-aid offices, senior centers, and area agencies on

aging. Yes, the legal profession will balk, but they must be challenged to help (on a volunteer basis of course), rather than set up roadblocks.

The principles underlying these proposals are simple: autonomy and the right to self-sufficiency. A recent study published by the New York Office for the Aging found that the majority of elderly are very independent and prefer to rely on themselves and informal systems of support, rather than turn to formal assistance through the more than fifteen hundred voluntary and governmental agencies providing services to New York's elderly. Fewer than half of the elderly interviewed had turned to a community agency for assistance during the past year, and mostly in regard to *income maintenance,* the report said.

5. *Use your influence to combat means tests.* Desire for autonomy is systematically stripped by programs that reflect a welfare mentality or are hamstrung by welfare rules. A simple information and referral service I was connected with, Jobs for Older Women Action Project, received a $9,900 grant from Title III funds. The county required a signed affadavit of all income, on penalty of perjury, just to receive *information* about possible jobs. The group refused to do so, and was not recommended for refunding. The reason for this outrage is desire to substitute federal aging funds for county welfare money, thus reducing taxes at the expense of the elderly. Individual means tests should be eliminated from all programs dealing with aging, not just because we need our dignity when we're old—so does everyone else—but because means tests strengthen the welfare vise, which punishes the poor.

6. *Stripping away of autonomy* reaches its lowest level in nursing homes, where so many older women end their days. As a *first* step to alleviate their miseries, we recommend upgrading the pay and working conditions of the providers of primary care, the nurse's aides. Legislation heard today in Sacramento sets standards for wages comparable to wages in acute-care hospitals, as well as establishing staffing ratios and required training in such facilities. Similar legislation should be passed in every state.

7. *Job creation for older persons* should be a top priority for the Office on Aging of HEW, especially until there is an office on aging in the Labor Department. Here is a good area for pilot programs and demonstration projects. For example: mutual self-help groups

like Anne Beckman's "Rent-A-Granny" program, which show spunk and imagination, need to be encouraged, not replaced by "professionals." Our Displaced Homemaker Center, funded by passage of a state bill (which we were instrumental both in drafting and passing) is in the process of creating new jobs for older women. The principles of job creation we are pursuing can be effective elsewhere. Passage of full-employment legislation will at least establish the right to a job. But we will need to push further to open up new ideas for employment, using the strengths and taking into account the limitations of older persons.

8. You could also use your influence both as director of the Office on Aging and with the U. S. Commission on Civil Rights to change the bias against older persons in CETA programs. Not just against outright exclusion but also recommending alternative training programs for second or third careers, leading to part-time as well as full-time employment. At present, clerical skills are all that are offered to older women, if any.

9. You could call a conference of the best minds on aging (not to be confused with the highest-paid or most-credentialed) to tackle the economic implications of changing dependency ratios. They should be charged with developing a policy to provide: increased job opportunities for older workers and retired persons through a number of *financial incentives;* steps to institute flexible retirement, at least within government, which would allow a person to postpone retirement or assume part-time work at an earlier age; a plan to vary the retirement age according to occupation, based primarily on the physical demands of the job; etc. Similar proposals were already passed by the Council of Europe's Parliamentary Assembly in 1975.

10. Most certainly you can advocate employment opportunities for older persons in *all* programs related to aging. We must make a breakthrough somewhere. Not that younger persons don't have a great deal to offer (honorary older women have provided much assistance in our own self-help program, for example, but they are working "with," not "for" us. In that connection, seniors in the city of Hanover, Germany, elected their own council. According to the mayor, old people will not be integrated into society until other age groups begin talking *with* the elderly, rather than *about* them.

In general, your office may be limited in terms of its funding and responsibility, but you can challenge, you can raise questions, and you can facilitate opportunities for others on the outside to be heard. Most certainly you can influence people on Capitol Hill and in HEW. That background paper was macaroni jewelry. (Anyone who does not know what that is should visit any senior center, to understand why Maggie Kuhn calls these centers playpens.)

Thank you for listening to me, and by now you realize that listening is not enough. Those of us who are in the adolescence of aging—I'm sixty-one—have a great sense of urgency and feel the need to change a lot of heads around. We plan to grow old rebelliously, and woe be to those who contribute more to the problem than the solution!

TO FIND THE ANSWERS

Robert N. Butler

Robert N. Butler is the leading authority on aging in America. He has worked with the elderly for years as a physician and has written numerous articles and books, including the 1976 Pulitzer Prize-winning *Why Survive? Being Old in America*. He was appointed director of the recently established National Institute on Aging, which is devoted to fundamental or basic research on aging. Here he defines some fundamental problems and questions that need answers. "Our challenge is not to replicate years in which huge numbers of us live on, dependent, frail, ridden with disease, unproductive, unhappy and lonely, in fear of crime, dissatisfied with ourselves, falsely regarded as sexless, and tempted to suicide." In a second selection, from *Why Survive?* he outlines a national policy on aging to meet the real needs of older citizens.

I ask you to look at the United States in the year 2020, the year in which our children—yours and mine—the postwar "baby boom," pass the age of sixty-five.

It will be an older America, a grayer America. The children who greened our land in the 1960s and 1970s will most surely have grayed it.

Successful human and biomedical triumphs over infant and childhood diseases, maternal mortality, especially infections, and in some measure the diseases of the middle and later years have resulted in a steady increase in the absolute numbers and population of older people in this twentieth century.

In 1900 there were some 3 million persons over sixty-five. Today there are over 22 million, and sixteen hundred more pass their sixty-fifth birthday each day. By 2020, there will be about 43 million older Americans, almost twice as many as today. Most will be women, and widows.

There are, as always, some caveats. Changing life styles, including women's increasing participation in the worldly rat race, might shorten their life span and equalize the balance of the sexes in the

older population. But evidence does not favor that possibility. Biomedical research could make progress against cancer and heart
disease, and one in five Americans could be sixty-five or older by
2020.

One in five Americans over sixty-five! What kind of world will
they—your and my children—enjoy? Indeed, will they enjoy it at
all? How will they relate to their children and grandchildren? Will
they live isolated and apart? Will they still be forced to retire in
their mid-sixties? If so, how will they spend their long retirement
years (now about fourteen years, then perhaps as many as twenty-
five)? If not, will there be enough jobs for them—real jobs—and
enough programs to retrain them? Will the colleges and universities open the doors to them as the number of college-age youth
drops?

Will there be sufficient, livable housing for them, and fulfilling
leisure-time activities? Will the generation that fled to the suburbs
in the mid-twentieth century continue to be stranded there in the
twenty-first, without sidewalks to walk on or close neighbors to
talk to? When they are not well, will there be enough hospital and
nursing units for them, or enough specially trained doctors, nurses,
and paraprofessionals to care for them? Will the conflicting pressures as to who should foot their bills—for benefits or for health
care—pit the generations against each other and heighten the tension under which they live?

"Death is not the trouble," said Zorba the Greek. "Life is the
trouble." The challenge confronting officials like you and me today
is to assure that our swelling number of older citizens—one tenth
of our nation now, one fifth by 2020—do more than simply survive. Our challenge is not to replicate years in which huge numbers of us live on, dependent, frail, ridden with disease, unproductive, unhappy and lonely, in fear of crime, dissatisfied with
ourselves, falsely regarded as sexless, and tempted to suicide. Our
challenge is to extend the fruitful middle years, healthy and vigorous years in which we can live creatively, to the best of our ability,
carrying our own weight and paying our own way as productive
contributors to our society.

As a nation, we can enhance our efforts to meet this challenge
in three broad ways. *First,* we can intensify our attempts to improve the economic and social conditions under which older peo-

ple live now and will live in the future. *Second,* we can work to change the negative attitudes toward old age—attitudes that result in labeling older men and women "crocks," "geezers," or "biddies," who are "over the hill" and "fading fast." I have labeled this prejudice "ageism." *Third,* we can acquire new knowledge about the aging process and the diseases—acute and chronic—associated with aging.

The study of aging is not just the study of decline, loss, and decrement—which do indeed accompany aging—and not just the study of disabilities or diseases that may in part be due to social adversities. Rather, it is the study of the normal processes of development that are fundamental to life and about which we know all too little, including creativity, life experience, perspective, and judgment.

As county officials, you are aware of the special social and economic needs of older people; you have started valuable service programs in housing, in transportation, in nutrition, and in recreation, to name only a few. The very fact that as an organization you have turned your attention to the elderly and are holding this series of conferences suggests your willingness to lead in the struggle against the negative attitudes of ageism. Your resolution in convention last March, subscribing to the Older Americans Act, shows your awareness of the great needs of older people.

I wish this morning to talk to you chiefly about the third area, the search for new knowledge. You may ask, why us? We are not research scientists or practicing physicians. What can we, as officials of Cape May, Prince George's, Nassau, or Jefferson counties do to find new knowledge to improve the lot of older men and women? Wouldn't it be more realistic to challenge us to commit ourselves and our resources to immediate social-service ends, rather than to a long-term investment in research?

As a long-time toiler in the community vineyards, I feel very secure in answering: Yes, we must intensify our efforts to deliver badly needed community services, but, also yes, one of our most urgent priorities as a nation now is to find new knowledge about many subjects, including the aging process—the universal biological condition common to us all, in Congress's words—and so new ways of preventing, modifying, or even reversing some of the deleterious aspects of that process.

New knowledge, fundamental understanding through *research,* I submit, *is the ultimate service* and the *ultimate cost containment.* Without new knowledge through research, we will just keep on doing the same old things in the same old ways, at ever-increasing costs.

We will keep on warehousing older people in nursing homes— 1.2 million now, in twenty-three thousand homes (at least half of which cannot pass even basic sanitation and fire-safety inspection), at a cost, in New York State alone, of about fifteen thousand dollars a person per year; $15 billion per year is now the national cost. We will keep on hospitalizing older people and spending two thirds of the billions spent by the federal government on health care for men and women over sixty-five. The total national health-care bill rose from a staggering $117 billion in 1975 to $139 billion in 1976.

But think: Breakthroughs in discovering the causes, and in the effective diagnosis and prompt treatment, of the devastating brain disorders with their horrifying destruction of personality and memory, which are responsible for the majority of institutionalizations in the later years, could reduce the nursing-home population. If we released 10 per cent of admissions, we would cut institutional costs by at least $1 billion.

In the same way, finding how to prevent osteoporosis, that softening of the bones which occurs so often after menopause, could drastically cut the number of painful and expensive fractures that older people (almost always older women) suffer, fractures that can mean the end of an active life.

Adapting the marvelous technology that placed men on the moon and enabled astronauts to fly in space, to new prosthetics could permit elderly people who are severely disabled by stroke, arthritis, or muscular weakness to move about their own homes and lead independent lives. I am referring to cane and hand sensors and activators, remote-control devices, wheelchairs that can climb stairs, and other novel but realistic devices. And finding out more about drugs could prevent unnecessary falls and fractures, or the confused episodes (often misdiagnosed as "senility") that so often result in excessive hospitalization and nursing-home institutionalization. We know our bodies handle drugs and react to them differently as we grow older. The basic tools for developing the pharmokinetics and pharmodynamics of aging—or how drugs are absorbed and distributed in the body and how the body reacts to them—exist. But the classic text on pharmacology does not even list the word "age" in its index. Doctors are usually trained in medical schools without special geriatric courses of any types, including pharmacology, and they have no reliable prescription guidelines for older people.

So an older woman receiving a certain anticoagulant begins to bleed profusely; or a tranquilizer that may calm a vigorous young man creates a dangerous drowsiness in an older one.

Research is the ultimate service, and the ultimate cost container. It is urgent that you consider this concept seriously. For without your understanding and support, and that of similar strategically placed Americans, those of us responsible for devising research plans cannot get very far.

This is true because the value especially of what we call "basic," or fundamental, research has been questioned repeatedly in recent years. Some national policymakers, perhaps naturally in search of quick payoffs and instant cures, have mistrusted the scientists' long years of step-by-step, basic research in biochemistry or cell biology. They have considered this "test-tube" research impractical, without directed goals, and not tied closely enough to human health needs.

But such research can be the most people-oriented, the most practical research of all! Without such research, which, in the past years, has attempted to understand the components of the cell—their organization and basic chemical reactions—we cannot assemble the information we need to start to investigate regulatory mechanisms. Without such research, we cannot develop the base on which to build, and produce the most stunning and practical results—like the polio vaccine, or penicillin, or the discoveries of last year's Nobel Prize winners in medicine, Dr. Baruch Blumberg and Dr. Carleton Gajdusek.

Dr. Blumberg, formerly of NIH, found a strange protein he called Australia Antigen while investigating genetic variation in the disease susceptibility of different people; now it is used routinely to fight hepatitis. From NIH scientist Dr. Gajdusek's work on kuru, the laughing disease that was destroying an obscure people in the remote hinterlands of New Guinea, came the fundamental discovery of a new type of slow-acting virus that can produce brain degeneration. It may be involved in multiple sclerosis and in the brain diseases of old age, as well as in other major neurological diseases.

Without research, we might still be relying on leeches and the purge, and we might be resigned to periodic outbursts of devastating plagues. But at budget time in the past we have had to reply on "anecdotal evidence": "Look, just forty years ago, most families had four or five members cut down in their prime by lobar pneumonia or tuberculosis." Or "remember the savings made when the polio vaccine replaced iron-lung machines—in dollars as well as human suffering."

Intriguing papers published last year now give us more than anecdotal evidence of the value of basic research. Writing for himself and the late Dr. Robert Dripps, Dr. Julius Comroe has reported on their years of study of how research is accomplished. What had to be learned, they asked, to permit the cardiac surgeon routinely and successfully to open the thorax, stop the heart, open the heart, restart the heart, and care for the patient to ensure full and speedy recovery? That was the clinical advance chosen in a poll of cardiac- and pulmonary-medicine physicians and surgeons as the most important direct benefit to patients since 1945.

To find the answer, Comroe and Dripps examined four thousand scientific articles and picked 529 as "key articles," essential to clinical advance. Forty-one per cent were not clinically or disease-oriented at the time of publication; more than 60 per cent described studies of how living organisms function, or drugs act—or, in other words, basic research. Dr. Comroe concludes the heart surgeon hardly took a giant leap up the pinnacle of open-heart surgery. Rather, he climbed slowly, drawing on twenty-five different bodies of knowledge—including transfusion, intravenous feeding, anesthesia, and chemotherapy. He climbed on steps laboriously chiseled out of the cliff by thousands of workers in many branches of science, over the years—well over a century, in fact.

In the same way, we at the new National Institute on Aging must continue our efforts—sometimes slow—to understand the age-related changes in connective tissues that cause so many to suffer severe arthritis, and thus perhaps to prevent, even to reverse, these changes. We must understand why there is a decline in immunological competence with aging—why it is harder for us to fight off disease as we grow older, and how we can prevent, even reverse, this dangerous state.

We must, in short, study the basic biological mechanisms of aging, at the molecular and cellular levels. This does not mean we should not also pursue other sorts of research; I only stress basic research because it is so necessary, yet often difficult to understand. In addition, we need to pursue "applied," or clinical, research—investigative medicine that will show us, for example, why there are so many more sleep disturbances in old age, or why our bodies' tolerance of sugar changes.

What's more, we need to employ the social and psychological sciences to understand why we fear aging and deal with it so poorly, and how we might age more successfully. How can you and I improve and maintain memory as we grow older? How can we move more smoothly from middle age to old age? How do we adjust to inevitable life-cycle crises: retirement, widowhood, death? What are the advantages and disadvantages of flexible retirement policies? Can't we devise retirement test batteries— scientifically sound standards that society can use to measure whether a person does or does not have the capacity to continue working? Why involuntary retirement, the lazy way out, when there are so many older persons who have so much to contribute and have the capacity, desire, and need to do so? Why make people unnecessarily dependent?

As we seek answers to such fundamental questions, we will collaborate with the other established National Institutes of Health. We will join the Institute of Neurological and Communicative Disorders and Stroke in an assault on that dreadful disease senile dementia, and the Arthritis, Metabolism and Digestive Diseases Institute in trying to alleviate the crippling effects of osteoporosis. The Heart and Lung Institute's well-known Framingham study offers us a valuable resource, for the subjects who participated in the development of the highly useful coronary profile—through which physicians can identify those susceptible to heart disease—are now older people, appropriately subject to NIA's studies.

We ask your understanding and support as we work to maximize and enhance the quality of life; to assure that more of us—

more black and Spanish-speaking people, and more of an unusual minority, men—reach old age; and to extend the productive middle years.

American industry spends 3.2 per cent of net sales on research and development, but the federal government invests less than two tenths of 1 per cent of its $17 billion annual health-services-to-the-elderly expenditure on aging research.

One requirement of the Research on Aging Act of 1974, which created the National Institute on Aging, was the development of an HEW-wide research plan for aging. This plan has been completed through the efforts and generosity of the American community of scientists who have worked in aging, the National Advisory Council of our Institute, and the NIA staff. I have named this plan "Our Future Selves," in order to bring attention to one of the major problems of aging, particularly in this country: the denial of the realities of aging as something that will inevitably happen to oneself and to one's family.

In turn, let me assure you, we expect you to demand that we in science and medicine actively serve the public interest. You should rightfully demand that we try better to organize and co-ordinate our efforts in attaining short- and long-term goals.

In these efforts, we must move quickly, but wisely. We must approach our scientific goals rationally, with respect to the investment of dollars and the transfer of knowledge. At times we must guard carefully against moving too fast. This may surprise you, after talk about the painstaking pace of basic research. But, in his studies, Dr. Comroe found that, if anything, our society may be too quick in transferring the fruits of research from bench to bedside. Wilhelm Konrad Roentgen discovered X rays in November 1895. Within six weeks, the news was out, and within a year a new professional society had been formed, a new journal established, and a thousand papers published, all about X rays. That, Comroe concludes, was probably too fast, because we did not understand X rays well enough, or realize harm could come from them. It could, and did: people developed ulcers and lost skin from overexposure. Some even lost the tips of their fingers.

Among older people, I have often seen the unhappy results of using discoveries too swiftly, before they are properly tested and evaluated. One of the most terrifying is a condition called tardive dyskinesia. Imagine yourself with no control over your own mouth, your face twisted, your tongue reaching out as though trying to catch a fly. Now consider that this condition is extremely hard to treat, and that we see it all too commonly in elderly women who have been on certain tranquilizers over long periods of time. Less dramatically, but no less sad, the casual overuse of psychoactive drugs, or drugs that act on the brain, has left many patients confused, and others anxious, even agitated. And evidence now suggests that the routine long-term prescription of estrogen for postmenopausal women has left victims of cancer.

We need the establishment of a unit of government whose job is to evaluate new scientific discoveries before they are funneled to doctors for use on you and me and on our children and our parents. This does not have to be a new agency. It could be an existing agency, or part of one. The National Institutes of Health and the National Institute on Aging will co-operate with the evaluators in every possible way. But NIH and NIA must pursue their main goal, of acquiring new knowledge. If NIA were called upon to test drug discoveries or regulate nursing homes, we would have time or money for little else.

Our nation has slipped into an informal collegial bench-to-bedside non-system of knowledge and technology transfer, a non-system that permits highly potent technologies to be used in the practice of medicine after remarkably uneven evaluation: papers are published in scientific journals, a "consensus" is reached at an academic medical center, a clinical trial is run—sometimes. Even if practicing physicians had the time to read all the papers and attend all the scientific meetings in Atlantic City, they would still have a difficult time evaluating new knowledge. I am sure that as we move toward more co-ordinated, effective health care, we will find a way to remedy this serious defect in governance and still permit the National Institutes of Health to concentrate on its research job.

In asking your appreciation and support for intensified and efficiently organized research, I realize the pressures upon each of you in your own community. I want research to help you as you go about your work. As you apply the latest research along with the resources of a humane society in behalf of older people, remember that every tax dollar spent on aging research will return to them—and to your children—a thousand times.

TOWARD A NATIONAL POLICY ON AGING
Robert N. Butler

The 1960s and '70s saw a crisis of awareness in the United States, increasing the recognition of the inequities based upon race, sex, class and, to a lesser extent, age. Nineteen seventy-six marks the two hundredth anniversary of the United States. It also marks another campaign for the presidency. Thus 1976 is an appropriate occasion to press once again the needs of the elderly.

I would like to see a citizens' committee of inquiry—with open-ended membership—that would convene a special conference on the elderly in Washington, D.C., in June of 1976 for: (1) a post-mortem audit of the administration's and the Congress's implementation of the 1971 White House Conference on Aging recommendations; (2) a revision of those recommendations toward the fundamental resolution of the problems of old age; (3) a review of the 1976 and 1977 federal fiscal budgets to obtain a picture of the incumbent Republican administration's commitment to the old; and (4) the presentation of programs on behalf of the elderly by all 1976 presidential aspirants of all parties.

I have briefly summarized here the major, immediate goals to be included in a national policy on aging:

GOAL 1. REORDERING OF PRIORITIES
At the risk of emphasizing the obvious, it remains necessary to state the importance of reordering national priorities toward human needs, including appropriate provision for all high-risk groups—children, the disabled, the sick and the elderly. In a more dramatic way, Senator Church has said, "We could abolish poverty among the elderly for what it costs to run the war in Southeast Asia for just three months."

GOAL 2. CREATION OF A WHITE HOUSE OFFICE ON AGING
To represent the case of the elderly and to build and implement a national policy on aging effectively, a White House Office on Aging is required. Governmental programs for the old are too

diffuse and too low in priority to gain access to the President and his staff. The President's Task Force on Aging in 1970 and the Senate Advisory Committee of 1971 both called for such an office. Senator Church introduced an Action Office on Aging Act in 1973 which would have established a White House-level office, directed by a Presidential Assistant on Aging. An alternative is a Secretary of Aging heading a separate cabinet department. The post of Assistant Secretary of Aging should be established in the Cabinet departments having concern with human resources, such as HEW, HUD, DOT and Labor.* In addition, there should be cooperation between the new Committee on Aging in the House and its Senate counterpart.

At the state level, governmental bodies created to deal with the elderly (commissions, advisory committees, and the like) should be given authority similar to that of the federal Administration on Aging. Creation of offices of Secretary of Aging in state government cabinets would keep the needs of the elderly before the governors.

GOAL 3. ELIMINATION OF MALNUTRITION AND POVERTY AMONG THE ELDERLY

In order for older Americans to live somewhere near the average American standard of living, poverty must be redefined in realistic terms, more nearly like the deprivation index proposed by economist Leon Keyserling. The federal floor on income for the elderly should be elevated to that of the highest of the budgets for elderly couples, prepared by the Bureau of Labor Statistics.

Financing of Social Security through the payroll plan now falls most heavily upon the low-income groups. This may soon incur a counter-reaction of workers against the elderly, which ultimately means against their future selves. Payroll taxes are the fastest-growing taxes, contributing 4 per cent of the revenue dollar in 1949 but 23 per cent in 1971. Instead, a compulsory national Social Security system financed through general revenues, utilizing a graduated income tax, could become one component of a three-part retirement system which would also include private pension

* The American Academy of Pediatrics (AAP) has called for an HEW deputy assistant secretary for children and youth. Thus the idea of different age groups having their special advocates is not confined to the elderly.

plans and voluntary pension plans. Such a national Social Security system should have two built-in escalators—one related to the cost of living, which now exists; and the second tied to the general economic productivity.

There should be a supplementary, voluntary, national Personal Security System that is individually financed but subject to federal standards and protection of its investments. This would be similar to the present self-employed individuals' retirement plan under the Keogh Act and the "Individual Retirement Accounts" (IRAs) created by the 1974 Pension Reform Act.

The 1974 private pension reform law should be vastly improved. Thus both collective and individual providence could characterize income provision in old age.

Blacks and other minority groups have higher mortality rates and therefore often do not live long enough to receive Social Security benefits. Computational arrangements must be made so that these groups can be assured of Social Security benefits in accordance with their life expectancies and greater degrees of disability.

GOAL 4. PROVISION OF CHOICE IN HOUSING

Six million older Americans need better shelter, and varieties of living arrangements should be created to provide options for them. Such choices should be facilitated by adequate income maintenance and, as necessary, through the interim steps of housing vouchers or allowances.

Property taxes need to be drastically reduced to make home ownership possible. Federally collected general revenue funds rather than local property taxes would better enable states to support quality education. (President Nixon called for federal relief for elderly home owners at the 1971 White House Conference and during his 1972 campaign.)

Zoning laws on the local level need revision in accordance with human needs.

There should be a refund of that part of rent payments which is allotted to property taxes, to provide relief for elderly renters.

GOAL 5. THE RIGHT TO WORK

Arbitrary retirement and age discrimination in public and private employment at all ages must be ended. The Social Security penalty

that forces older persons to lie about their income and discourages
them from working must be eliminated. A public policy of full employment with the government as the employer of first resort
rather than last resort is necessary for the old.

GOAL 6. THE RIGHT TO SOCIAL ROLES

A wide range of roles of substance and purpose should be available for those elderly who choose to retire. Part of this could be accomplished through a National Senior Service Corps, encompass-
ing Foster Grandparent and other programs, and a national service
program that matches skills and needs for persons of all ages.

Greater flexibility could be encouraged through reallocating
work, education and leisure thoughout the life cycle so that people
of all ages have more choices.

GOAL 7. PROVISION OF CONTINUING AND LIFE
CYCLE EDUCATION

Public and private schools and universities should extend their responsibility beyond youth to provide both continuing education
and education concerning the nature of the life cycle. Provision
could be made for periodical sabbaticals for all workers, with opportunities to advance and to switch jobs and careers and thus reduce unnecessary human obsolescence.

There are two aspects of lifetime education: continuing education throughout life to maintain and/or build new skills and to
support flexible choice, and education that is tailored to fit the
changing characteristics of the life cycle. Such life-cycle education
would deal with childhood, courtship and marriage, career, leisure,
grief, death—all the major occasions and processes of life.

GOAL 8. FREEDOM OF MOBILITY

There should be a balanced mass-transit system. Transportation
systems must be redesigned to fit the needs of the elderly, ill,
handicapped, pregnant women, and children, with elimination of
architectural barriers. These systems must be public utilities with
control of fares.

GOAL 9. PROTECTION FROM CRIME

Protection from crime is essential. Old people are disproportionately vulnerable to violent crime, such as robbery and assault; to fraud, shady land deals, quick remedies and other schemes. Old people should learn protective skills. In addition, protective services, public guardianship, legal assistance as well as police protection and service should be available. There should also be specific emergency funds to help crime victims meet their daily needs when these have been jeopardized.

GOAL 10. SUPPLY OF COMPREHENSIVE SERVICES

Old people do not have time to wait. Appropriate services must be made rapidly available to help them remain in their own homes when they wish to do so, through expansion of such manpower services as case aides, homemakers and home health aides, and visiting nurses. A National Personal Care Corps would overcome jurisdictional disputes among the different vocations and help provide comprehensive care. A fully established national nutrition program should include meals on wheels for the homebound, as well as group dining. While every effort should be made to help maintain older people in the community, if institutionalization becomes necessary it must be skillfully arranged, beginning with a careful transition from home.

Services *must* be categorical at first, targeted directly to the needs of the elderly group until such time as older people are no longer placed at the bottom of the barrel in the allocation of personnel and monies. Services should be available without humiliating means tests and special stigmatizing arrangements. Ideally they should be offered in the form of noncommercial social utilities. Financing of services could come through a national human-services plan, of which national health care would be one major component.

GOAL 11. CREATION OF DECENT HEALTH AND SOCIAL CARE

Structural reform of the health-delivery system is required as well as changes in its financing. A comprehensive social-care program in the nation would include health, social and other services. Particular attention must be given to chronic illness. Geriatric medicine must be developed within medical schools, and special training in the field of aging should be given to allied health professionals, social workers, nurses. Pending adoption of a major reform in the structure and financing of national health care, revision in Medicare is mandatory. Deductibles, co-payments and other features that *deduct* from the care of the patient need to be eliminated. Outpatient medications should be provided for, home health services must be expanded. Prevention of illness must become a major focus.

GOAL 12. SUPPORT OF SOCIAL UTILITIES IN PLACE OF COMMERCIAL NURSING HOMES

The nursing-home industry is already a subsidized rather than a free-enterprise industry. Monies provided by the federal government in such subsidization, in both construction and patient care, should be diverted to nonprofit organizations which would establish care programs that emphasize home care and outpatient care as well as institutional care. Nonprofit social utilities should be created that would control profits and maintain standards.

GOAL 13. THE RIGHT TO MENTAL-HEALTH CARE

The mental-health specialties, including psychiatry, must assume their responsibilities in research and the provision of service for the emotional and mental disorders of late life. Community mental-health centers, hospitals and other facilities must provide a network of quality programs for the diagnosis, treatment and care of both acute and long-term emotionally and mentally ill patients. Medicare revision and ultimately a national social and health-care program should finance such services. Class-action legal cases must be undertaken to reinforce the right to treatment of emotional problems and mental illnesses. If the psychiatric, social-work, psychological and other mental-health professions do not appropriately meet the mental-health needs of the elderly, a new profession should be supported. In order to set national policy with respect to the mental-health care of the elderly, a Commission on Mental Illness of the Elderly should be established by Congress. The National Institute of Mental Health should have a center on aging and a network of training, research and other programs throughout the nation.

GOAL 14. BASIC AND APPLIED RESEARCH

A National Institute on Aging has been established to plan and co-ordinate studies in the biomedical, social and the behavioral aspects of the aging process and to conduct and support education and training in both research and service in the field of aging. HEW has been dragging its feet in getting the Institute started and "moving." Studies should be as concerned with the quality of life as with the extension of it.

There are three major focuses in the politics of building an appropriate and dignified old age for Americans: first, a positive change in cultural sensibility toward the needs of the old; second, the allocation of national resources in this direction; and third, the creation of effective political representation and activist outlets for the old and their supporters.

NOURISHING THE MINDS OF THE AGING

Jack Ossofsky

"The 1960s were the time of civil rights [for minorities]. The 1970s emphasized women's rights. I think the 1980s will be the time for the rights of the aged," says Jack Ossofsky, executive director, The National Council on the Aging.

Here he calls for the fullest possible opportunities for older people to keep their minds and hearts alive through intellectual, cultural, and artistic experiences and contributions.

In 1780, John Adams wrote to Abigail, "I must study politics and war that my sons may have liberty to study mathematics and philosophy. My sons ought to study mathematics and philosophy, geography, natural history, naval architecture, navigation, commerce and agriculture in order to give their children a right to study painting, poetry, music, architecture, statuary, tapestry and porcelain."

We are the inheritors of that dream and we are more than that. We are the generation that can make it come true.

We still study war more than philosophy and commerce more than poetry, but more than ever before we know the difference and we can finally, as a nation, move toward new goals. Indeed there are among us those already able to live them, both young and old.

In the two centuries since Adams set forth his hopes, we have filled the continent with states and peopled them. We have reached across oceans to plant our flag and our influence, our commerce and our culture. We have populated, integrated, urbanized, mechanized, automated, and outdated just about all that Adams could, in his most expansive dreams, have foreseen.

In John Adams' day the average life expectancy at birth was about thirty-five years. We were a young country and a young people. We have in these two hundred years more than doubled the average life span. And in spite of a recently declining growth rate and a diminished birth rate, we are the beneficiaries of a longer period of life that can be spent in the pursuit of happiness. Not just happiness as we use it in common parlance today but as it was expressed so clearly by Adams. Jefferson, too, would have agreed that happiness as he understood it encompassed the pursuit of intellectual stimulation, development, and growth.

I do not mean to suggest that we have established an adequate economic base for those in retirement to plunge into cultural, artistic, and intellectual activity without a care for who pays. I do believe that we have made considerable progress in this direction, that there are today already a great many economically secure older people and that their numbers and proportion will continue to increase.

Great masses continue to perch precariously on a tightrope between a shrinking savings account and a lengthening longevity while buffeted by inflation. They, however, can find some solutions to their problems and create others for the rest of society through using or becoming the intellectual resources of our society. It was, after all, the poor who gave us jazz and bluegrass. Many of the French impressionists starved while they painted. Many in Appalachia are hungry now while their TV antennas can bring them educational public television along with "Mary Hartman—Mary Hartman." And busloads from our poorest communities can bring senior citizens to concerts, to the theater and museums while home economists from our land-grant colleges can visit their homes to teach them how to prepare nutritious meals bought on food stamps.

While this paper is not supposed to deal with such issues as income maintenance, home health services, transportation and supportive services, we all know that for a significant minority of older Americans, how these issues are dealt with will determine how they contribute to our intellectual growth, what use they make of our facilities, and who pays the tab. For how we react to issues of life and death will give us a key to how we as a nation can fund or find answers to the enhancement of the quality of life we have prolonged into retirement.

Thomas Jefferson's views about retirement and government expressed to the Republican citizens of Washington County, Maryland, in 1809 are, I believe, pertinent here:

> If in my retirement to the humble station of a private citizen, I am accompanied with esteem and approbation of my fellow citizens,

trophies obtained by the blood-stained steel or the tattered flags of the tented field, will never be envied. The care of human life and happiness, and not their destruction, is the first and only legitimate object of good government.

Jefferson could never have anticipated that our land would have over 30 million people retired or quickly approaching it, each of whom, too, wishes for the esteem and approbation of her or his fellows, each of whom seeks as well a federal policy that effectuates the purpose of government laid down by Jefferson and strives to care for human life and happiness and not their destruction.

If Thomas Jefferson had read the Administration's new proposals for Social Security, Medicare and Medicaid, and the Defense Budget, he would understand the concerns that grip the hearts of the nation's elderly, and those yet to be old, as they seek in vain a remnant spark in today's national leadership of the torch lit by Jefferson, the brightness of which comes from giving priority to human life, not its destruction.

If we cannot feel secure in the government's goals to protect and expand Medicare and Social Security, what hope can we have that its funding of the arts and humanities will ever exceed tokenism or that the elderly will ever gain adequate access and involvement in cultural services so that we gain from their being not just beneficiaries but contributors to those areas of the nation's life.

As New York City grappled with its budget, it sought to find a solution through early retirement of its civil servants. Move the old out of the way. Let the pension fund pay them rather than the city. Never mind individual choice or capacity and desire to work. When that gambit failed, the program cutters came along and, high on the list of cuts, were the senior centers, the public libraries, the cultural services, the special education programs. Where does any school system in the country cut first when the budget squeeze is on? The music and arts program or the physical education program?

What are our priorities for intellectual services?

The involvement of the increasing number of older Americans in intellectual pursuits requires that the services and resources be there to accept them. The lack of facilities and their inaccessibility remain obstacles to the participation of many older people.

The National Council on the Aging last year published the results of an extensive study of America's attitudes about aging and the aged. That study, *The Myth and Reality of Aging in America,* prepared for NCOA by Louis Harris & Associates, asked a cross section of older and younger Americans about their use of cultural, recreational, and intellectual resources and facilities. In all cases the elderly made significantly less use of such facilities or programs than did the young or the middle-aged. Past education and income status affected the response, but so did convenience and accessibility and program content.

One of the questions asked was whether or not the respondent had been to the facility in the past year or so. Here are some of the replies of college graduates, who had higher attendance than others:

A movie:

86% of those 18–54

63% of those 55–64

46% of those 65 plus

A park:

80% of those 18–54

58% of those 55–64

44% of those 65 plus

A library:

87% of those 18–54

78% of those 55–64

63% of those 65 plus

Live theater, dance, or concert:

75% of those 18–54

57% of those 55–64

45% of those 65 plus.

Even among the most affluent, we found that increasingly age is reflected in decreased attendance at movies. For example, of those reporting an annual income of fifteen thousand dollars or more, 81% of those 18–54 had been to a film in the past year;

62% of those 55–64;

39% of those 65 plus.

Of all the elderly, that is, those over sixty-five,

> only 22% had gone to a movie;
> 22% to a library;
> 17% to a concert;
> 18% to a museum;
> 17% to a community or senior center.

While more older people, particularly older poor people, indicated that these facilities were not conveniently situated for them, it is true that convenience is determined by more than physical location, but includes mobility of the individual, time when open, fear of crime, and indeed interest in going and overcoming the inconvenience. The program has to appeal, has to be pertinent, has to have relevance, for the elderly to participate.

It is interesting to note that the role of senior centers and clubs has grown markedly over the years. While 13 per cent of the public fifty-five and over have been to a senior center in the past year or so, another 19 per cent said they would like to attend one. That's another 7 million potential clients for centers. NCOA's just-completed study of the senior-center movement underscores its role as a vehicle for intellectual activity and involvement and as a bridge to other facilities and programs.

Only four hundred thousand, or 2 per cent, of those over sixty-five were found by the NCOA-Harris study to be enrolled in an educational institution or taking courses. Similarly, only 5 per cent of those fifty-five to sixty-four and 5 per cent of those forty to fifty-four were so enrolled. While these younger groups, too, have only a modest enrollment, they are still more than double that of the older group. Only 37 per cent of those now over sixty-five have graduated from high school. Seventy-four per cent of those eighteen to sixty-four are high school graduates. Since past educational experience is a factor in participating in education in the later years, there is in these figures signs of a significantly growing market among future retirees. However, more could be enrolled now if more were done to reach the potential students, to make the experience more acceptable, and to offer programs of interest to them.

Of the four hundred thousand presently taking courses (and most of these are not in academic institutions), 76 per cent are enrolled to expand their knowledge; 39 per cent to make better use of their time; 28 per cent to be with other people; 6 per cent to acquire job skills; and 2 per cent for other reasons.

The 98 per cent who say they are not enrolled in courses give the following reasons:

> Not enough time: 13%
> Not interested: 45%
> Too expensive: 2%
> Poor health: 22%
> None available: 3%
> Don't have any courses for me: 4%
> I'm too old: 27%
> Other: 7%

In spite of the apparent progress being made by community colleges and others to draw retired students in, clearly few have yet been attracted. NCOA's own experience in organizing a nation-wide consortium of educational facilities in Colorado underscores the need for much more outreach to the elderly, involving them in developing programs and restructuring the delivery mechanisms.

The Academy for Educational Development, in its publication "Never Too Old to Learn," suggests some options that are appropriate for adult educators and for other kinds of facilities as well:

Courses on a campus or residential basis
Courses in off-campus locales
Peer-group instruction in which there are older people capable of teaching the courses
Comprehensive programs in areas where elderly are concentrated
Educational vacations on campus
Mass-media instruction
Providing transportation and other supportive services
Using consortiums to maximize resources of several institutions.

Most of all, it is appropriate to underscore that the elderly are a varied lot. The programs developed on their behalf and the content need to be adapted to their interests and especially their need for survival and intellectual growth and for strengthening their impaired self-image.

Let us not minimize the fact that many of those who develop

programs for the aged accept the stereotype accepted by the 27 per cent of the aged themselves who said they are too old to take courses.

The aged are not too old to learn, nor are they unable to compete successfully with younger students, especially if they are reasonably well.

The question returns again and again: toward what purpose education for the aging? There are few jobs for them to compete for. Few new careers will last long. Is the investment in the old worthwhile? Will it pay off?

Perhaps these thoughts will cause us to sharpen the original question. Not, what is the purpose of education for the aging but, what is the purpose of education? Better yet, what is the purpose of life?

In the controversial (and therefore useful) book *The Coming of Age,* Simone de Beauvoir castigates our society for condemning the majority of men and women to a meaningless life in old age. She writes:

> Old age exposes the failure of an entire civilization. There is only one solution if old age is not to be an absurd parody of our former life, and that is to go on pursuing ends that give our existence a meaning—devotion to individuals, to groups or to causes, social and political, and to intellectual or creative work.

The social, economic, and intellectual opportunities available to any group in our society depend not only on their own resources, capabilities, and aspirations but to a great degree on the resources, capabilities, and aspirations that the public at large attribute to them. Older Americans are no exception. The potential contributions that older persons can make to this country depend not only on their own self-confidence and belief in their own abilities and desire to remain active and useful members of society but also on the confidence that the public at large and the gatekeepers of opportunity, in particular, place in them as contributing, vital human beings.

Ah, there's the rub! The NCOA-Harris poll documented the fact that most older people in this country have the desire and the potential to be productive, contributing members of our society and that they do not want to be "put on the shelf" and excluded from social, economic, and intellectual activities. But the public at large viewed most older people as warm, friendly, and experienced but sedentary, inactive, and inflexible, limited in their ability to learn new skills. Sadder is the fact that the public sixty-five and older themselves have also bought the stereotypes of their peers, though they deny them as a description of themselves.

We who are leaders in our communities and on behalf of the aging have a long history of knocking down physical barriers that impede the dignity of old age and of building new paths and new systems, of researching the implications of social obstacles and of exposing them to view and to action, now have a new challenge and a clearer target. Lack of transportation, inadequacies of SSI, substandard housing—these are enemies we are familiar with and are arduously fighting to conquer. But what of attitudes? What of negative, false attitudes toward the aged and aging, the unconscious, often intangible, barrier woven into policies and institutions that shape their lives and ours? And after all, if we survive, their lot and their obstacles *are* ours.

We now have the opportunity, the new imperative, of challenging the educational and cultural institutions, the molders of opinion, the shapers of our society's norms, the dispensers of knowledge, to re-examine their assumptions and therefore their programs as they affect the aging. They need to deal accurately and justly with the aged as well as the young, for it is through the institutions of intellectual activity that man strives for a higher degree of purpose, and we may offer no less an opportunity for that pursuit to the aged.

Let our intellectual resources accept the admonishment of Yehudi Menuhin, who wrote in *An Inventory of Hope,*

> Let men play the violin, play chess, fence, go to the moon, play ping pong, and write poetry—but let them not degenerate into dumb automatons, robots of the nation-state, manipulated physically, spiritually, and morally by the abuse of all their gifts and by the debasement of all their faculties.

As advocates for the aging, let us vie with each other to find and cultivate new outlets for the experiential wisdom and creative abilities of older Americans. As advocates for intellectual resources, let us bend our thinking to including the aging in our audience, staff, performers, artists, and volunteers, for they and our institutions will both be richer from the symbiosis that will result.

For then we can sing with John Logan,

> Oh could I fly, I'd fly with thee!
> We'd make with joyful wing
> Our annual visit to the globe
> Companions of the Spring.

Let us be aware, too, that our deliberations cannot last forever and that action is needed now—both so that it happens in the lifetime of today's aged and so that it is ready for tomorrow's.

Tomorrow's old men (and women) will be better educated, more articulate, with higher expectations and more easily expressed demands than their predecessors. They will be healthier and live longer. Perhaps, if Bernice Neugarten is right, they will retire even earlier and have twenty-five to twenty-eight years of retirement ahead of them. This coming generation of the aged will not be the turn-of-the-last-century young but the turn-of-the-next-century old. Their connotations of Chicago will be less a fire and more a rock band and a political confrontation, in which some of them will have participated. Detroit will mean less Model T and more Motown and Burn Baby Burn. They will have known the limits and the frustration of mass action as well as its positive results. They will have learned to demand.

The earliest signs of an involved and demanding senior citizenry, outgrowth of the development of the labor movement, the church, and fraternal movements, are to be found in the emerging senior-power movement. They are behind the changes in the political structure and party balances in the four counties of southeastern Florida and elsewhere.

They want a voice in their destiny, first economic and political but soon social and cultural. There is a vitality there, a demand not to be overlooked. There is a gold mine of creativity, that remains largely untouched, for social progress for our whole society and for our cultural enrichment.

The young of this generation have walked gingerly on the moon. The old of this generation are experimenting with a new freedom from labor on earth. They are indeed the emerging leisure class. How that leisure is spent will shape how ours is spent. Let us light their road, provide it with opportunity, and sustain them in the newest exploration of man: not what he will be when he grows up but what he is as a grownup.

This conference can set the stage for that newest exploration. Through educational, cultural, artistic, and humanistic endeavor, we can provide more options to the varied needs and aspirations of the aged, we can involve the participator and respect the spectator. We can crumble false stereotypes and strengthen the notion that one must not be too old to create, to build, to give, to love, to change, and to demand. One must not be too old to be.

GROWING OLD IN AMERICA

Margaret Mead, interviewed by Grace Hechinger

During her seventy-fifth year, Margaret Mead was interviewed by Grace Hechinger for *Family Circle* magazine, in the office she has worked in for fifty years, atop a Victorian turret of New York City's American Museum of Natural History. "Dr. Mead's energy and unflagging interest in life pervade her own unique and inspiring perspective on old age in America," wrote the interviewer.

FAMILY CIRCLE: America has a bad reputation for our treatment of the elderly. Do you think it is warranted?

DR. MEAD: America is pretty negligent in this respect. As a nation of immigrants, we have always put a tremendous premium on youth. The young people, the first generation born here, understood American life better than their parents, who had come from other countries. In the more uprooted families, grandparents became a source of embarrassment. Though children whose grandparents were not English-speaking might learn to understand their grandparents' language, they would refuse to speak it.

But at least older people used to stay in the family. Homes were big, and there was room for extra aunts and grandparents. Families lived close together in communities. Today we have many more old people than in the past. And we have changed our whole life-style. The flight to the suburbs in the last 25 years has done a great deal of harm. In these age-segregated, class-segregated communities, there is no place for old people to live near the young people they care about. So the poor ones are stacked away in nursing homes, which are sometimes called "warehouses for the old." The more affluent ones move into golden ghettos or go to Florida, but they too are segregated and lonely.

FC: How were the elderly treated in some of the primitive cultures you have studied?

DR. MEAD: You don't find many early or primitive societies that treat old people as badly as the civilized societies do. The very earliest civilizations, of course, had to let their older people die, very often because they weren't strong enough to walk the necessary distance to find food. But as soon as there were ways of storing food, older people were looked after.

FC: Do you see any parallel in the way America treats its older people and the way we treat our children?

DR. MEAD: Our treatment of both reflects the value we place on independence and autonomy. We do our best to make our children independent from birth. We leave them all alone in rooms with the lights out and tell them, "Go to sleep by yourselves." And the old people we respect most are the ones who will fight for their independence, who would sooner starve to death than ask for help.

We in America have very little sense of interdependence. The real issue is whether a society keeps its older people close to children and young people. If old people are separated from family life, there is real tragedy both for them *and* the young.

FC: How could we structure our society to help bring older people back into the lives of their families?

DR. MEAD: It is primarily a question of replanning, of building communities where older people are welcome—not necessarily your own grandmother, but somebody's grandmother. Older people need to live within walking distance of shops and friends and family. They need younger people to help with the heavy chores, to shovel the snow and cut the grass so they can continue to live on their own.

FC: What do you think about the way we approach retirement?

DR. MEAD: The practice of early retirement is terribly wasteful. We are wasting millions of good years of good people by forcing them into retirement. The men especially suffer. Whether or not women work, they've always had to do the housekeeping and the shopping and the planning. So when they retire, they still have some continuity in their lives. But the men are admirals without a fleet. They don't know what else to do but die.

FC: What can we do to keep older people active in community life?

DR. MEAD: We can do many things. Some universities are building alumnae housing on campuses so that graduates will be able to move back near the universities. Some can teach, and all can enjoy the lectures, the intellectual stimulation and being near young people.

We shouldn't drop people from the PTA when their last child leaves school. We should have a grandparents' association that works for the local schools. At present, older people vote against school bond issues for schools their children once attended. They get selfish because they're no longer involved.

FC: It has been a fond American myth that in the good old days —whenever those were—we treated old people much better. Did the elderly really have fewer problems?

DR. MEAD: For one thing, there weren't a great many older people, and the ones that lived long lives were very, very tough.

Older people are more frail today. Many are the kind who would have died during infancy in earlier times and have had uncertain health all their lives. I had never seen an older person lying around like a vegetable, taking up the energy of doctors and nurses, until I was 28 years old. Every old person I knew as a child was somebody I could admire and listen to and enjoy.

When we're involved with old people whose hearing and eyesight go and who have to be cared for, we don't treat them like people, and that is frightening to old and young alike.

FC: When you were a child, grandparents had a much more active role in child-rearing than they do today. Do you believe that grandparents can educate their grandchildren?

DR. MEAD: If only today's grandparents would realize that they have seen more social change than any other generation in the history of the world! There is so much they could pass on!

In the small towns of earlier times, one good grandmother went a long way with her stories, her store of old-fashioned songs and her skills in the vanishing arts. From her, children absorbed a sense of the past and learned to measure time in meaningful biological terms—when grandmother was young, when mother was young, when I was young. Dates became real instead of mere numbers in a history book.

When my grandmother died in 1928 at the age of 82, she had seen the entire development of the horseless carriage, the flying machine, the telephone, the telegraph and Atlantic cables, radio and silent films.

Today, telephoning has largely replaced the family correspondence of two generations ago. I still treasure a letter that ends: "You are always in the thoughts of your grandmother by the sea. P.S. 'Apartment' is spelled with one 'P.' "

FC: Was your grandmother very important to you when you were growing up?

DR. MEAD: One of my grandmothers, who always lived with us, was the most decisive influence on my life. She sat at the center of our household. Her room was the place we immediately went when we came home from school. We did our lessons on the cherry-wood table with which she had started housekeeping. Later it was my dining room table for 25 years.

I think my grandmother was the one who gave me my ease in being a woman. I had my father's mind, which he had inherited from her. Without my grandmother's presence—small, dainty and pretty—I might have thought having my father's mind would make me masculine. Though she was wholly without feminist leanings, she taught me that the mind is not sex-typed.

You know, one reason grandparents and grandchildren get along so well is that they can help each other out. First-person accounts of the parents when *they* were children reduces parental fury over disorders and fads of "the younger generation" and does away with such pronouncements as: "My father would never have permitted me to. . . ."

In small-town schools, there used to be teachers who taught two generations of children and mellowed in the process. They were there to remind the children that their parents had once been young, played hooky and passed forbidden notes in school. They were also able to moderate the zeal and balance the inexperience of young teachers.

FC: It is a popular belief that the way people were treated as children influences the way they treat older people. Do you agree?

DR. MEAD: There is a story that I like about a father bird who was carrying a little bird in its beak over the river. The little bird was completely in the power of the father bird. The older bird said, "My son, when I am old, will you care for me?"

The little bird said, "No, father, but I will care for my children the way you have cared for me."

The story shows something of the way affection is passed down through the generations. But it also reveals a fear of aging. In this country, some people start being miserable about growing old while they are still young, not even middle-aged. They buy cosmetics and clothes that promise them a young look.

A concomitance to the fear of aging is a fear of the aged. There are far too many children in America who are badly afraid of older people because they never see any. Old people are not a regular part of their everyday lives. Also, children are aware that their middle-aged parents cling to youth.

FC: It's true. We Americans are obsessed with staying young. There are not enough models like you, Dr. Mead, to show younger people goals to grow toward.

DR. MEAD: We have always had a good number of lively old people—it is just the proportions that are changing. We had Bernie Baruch sitting on his park bench, advising one President after another. We have many physicians who go on practicing late in life. Writers, too, and justices of the Supreme Court.

FC: How can middle-aged and young people lessen the fear of growing old?

DR. MEAD: It's very important to prepare yourself. One useful thing is to change all your doctors, opticians and dentists when you reach 50. You start out when you are young with everybody who looks after you older than you are. When you get to be 50, most of these people are 65 or older. Change them all and get young ones. Then, as you grow older, you'll have people who are still alive and active taking care of you. You won't be desolate because every one of your doctors is dead.

Another thing is to consider what you want to do later in life while you are still young. If you think of your whole life-span and what you are going to do at one stage and then at another, and incorporate these plans in your life picture, you can look forward confidently to old age. If you associate enough with older people who do enjoy their lives, who are not stored away in any golden ghettos, you will gain a sense of continuity and of the possibilities for a full life.

FC: How did you plan for your life when you were young?

DR. MEAD: I went to work at the Museum of Natural History as a young girl, and of course I had no idea how long I'd stay. You don't when you are 24. Then I saw a doddering old man walking around the corridors, and I asked, "What is he doing here?" I was told, "He is working on a book. He retired 20 years ago." I discovered that at the Museum they keep you until you die. And so I decided to stay right there.

FC: How do you think people can learn to appreciate the past?

DR. MEAD: I frequently have my students interview older people. For the Bicentennial, we developed a model book called *How to Interview Your Grandfather*. It is the reverse of a baby book. The students made up the questions simply by thinking of what they wanted to know about the past. The older people adore being asked. They stop complaining that nobody is interested in them or that "nobody listens to me anymore. . . ." And the young people find that what they have to say is fascinating.

FC: It's so important for children to sense the treasure of memory, both personal and national.

DR. MEAD: Another thing we are doing with students is to tell them to write an autobiography for their as-yet-unborn grandchildren. What would you like your grandson or granddaughter to know about you? Thinking like this gives young people a new perspective about the future: They begin to realize that someday they themselves will be old.

My mother was very fond of Robert Browning. She used to quote these lines from *Rabbi Ben Ezra*. They are favorites of mine:

> *Grow old along with me!*
> *The best is yet to be,*
> *The last of life, for which*
>   *the first was made:*
> *Our times are in His hand*
> *Who saith 'A whole I planned,*
> *Youth shows but half; trust God:*
>   *see all, nor be afraid!'*

THE SENIOR CITIZENS' DECLARATION OF INDEPENDENCE

Lou Cottin

Lou Cottin's regular column on activism for the aged appears in *Newsday* and is syndicated in newspapers around the country. If your local paper doesn't carry his always stimulating words, a letter to the editor—or a dozen of them—might be in order.

When in the course of human events it becomes necessary for the elderly to assume among the People of the nation the equal station to which the Laws of Nature and Nature's God entitle them, a decent respect for the opinions of Mankind requires that they should declare the causes which impel them to state their case.

We hold these Truths to be self-evident, that old men and women are the equals of the young and middle-aged, that they are endowed by their Creator with certain unalienable Rights, that among these rights are Respect, Comfort, and the Pursuit of Happiness.

That whenever society or Government becomes destructive to these ends it is the duty of elderly People to institute new concepts of their worth, organizing their powers in such form as to them shall seem most likely to affect their Happiness.

Prudence, indeed, will dictate that Myths long established about the aged should not be changed for light or transient causes; and accordingly all experience hath shown that the Aged are more disposed to suffer while evils are sufferable. But when a long train of abuses and insults evince a design to reduce them to lower-class citizens it is their Right, it is their Duty, to join all action which may alter their condition for the better.

The History of the present Government and the younger Population is a history of repeated injury to the self-esteem of Older Americans, having the direct object of establishing a low status for us who are over sixty years old. To prove this, let facts be submitted to a candid World.

They have refused to recognize our contributions to the country's peace, prosperity, and pride, presently enjoyed by all but the poor and the old.

They have failed to pass Laws of immediate and pressing importance to our health, well-being, and welfare. Indeed they have sentenced the very old and very ill among us to a living death in profit-making nursing homes where we are ill-treated by unqualified personnel; insufficiently cared for in our persons and unprotected by laws that require frequent and thorough inspection; with the result that we are dehumanized during the final years of our lives.

They have foisted upon us, in some communities, inept, ill-trained, and politically appointed leaders to direct State and Local Departments of Aging and the social and recreational activities of our senior citizens clubs, to the end that we have been isolated and separated from the mainstream of American Society and with the result that our growth and perspectives have been limited and depressing.

They have failed to raise our Social Security income so that we can fully enjoy a good life similar to that which our labor when we were young assured to those who are now young.

They have shut us off from earning extra income by reducing Social Security payments to Any who earn more than three thousand dollars a year by honest labor. Yet, they permit extra income in any amount to rich old people whose extra income is unearned, coming from stocks, bonds, or Savings Interest.

They have dealt unfairly with elderly wives, denigrating their status as American Workers and citizens, by accepting Social Security Taxes from them while they have failed to return this money to them in Social Security payments which are independent of those received by their Husbands.

They have erected an ugly edifice of local, County, Village, State, and Federal tax regulations against our properties, our purchases, and our Persons, which threaten the continued ownership of our homes and our right to a life of comfort and security within our homes.

They have established a medical program for the aged hedged about with restrictions and unallowable medical expenses. Thus, in our Country, the Fear of extended illness contributes largely to tensions and to the dissipation of our meager savings.

They have been deaf to our appeals for redress and blind to the sight of our suffering. We must therefore acquiesce in the necessity which affirms our rights to a full life and hold them as we hold the rest of Mankind as Antagonists when they demean us, Friends when they help us.

WE, THEREFORE, the THOUGHTFUL SENIOR CITIZENS of the United States of America, appealing to the Supreme Judge of the World for the rectitude of our intentions, do in the name of our contemporaries solemnly publish and declare that we are, and of Right ought to be, respected for past contributions to our country, our Children, and our Communities; and be permitted to participate as we can in the task of enriching life in this Nation during our remaining years.

And for the support of this Declaration, with a firm reliance on the guidance of Divine Providence, we mutually pledge to each other and to the Nation, the rest of our lives, our aging strength, and our Sacred Honor.

ISSUE ANALYSIS: PROBLEMS
OF THE AGING

National Council of Senior Citizens

The National Council of Senior Citizens is an activist group representing the needs and concerns of older Americans.

BACKGROUND INFORMATION

There are now 22.4 million men and women aged sixty-five or over in the United States, 15.2 per cent of the voting-age population.

Another 19.8 million people are aged fifty-five to sixty-four, many of them already retired or close to retirement. People fifty-five or over make up 28.6 per cent of the voters.

The well-being of this large segment of the population is not only an important socioeconomic consideration for America but should be of major concern to all candidates for public office.

Increasingly, older people are becoming aware of their political strength and are responding at the polls to issues that vitally concern them. The first evidence was as early as 1964, when Goldwater's threat to their Social Security program proved an important factor in his overwhelming defeat. Enactment of Medicare, in 1965, marked the end of their long fight for this essential protection. While senior citizens were joined in this struggle by organized labor and other groups of non-seniors, their essential role was recognized by the late President Lyndon B. Johnson when he said, "Without the National Council of Senior Citizens there would have been no Medicare."

For a variety of reasons, more and more older men and women are joining senior-citizen organizations. It has been estimated that one of every two Americans sixty-five and over belongs to some kind of senior-citizen group.

National groups of the elderly have clubs or individual members in all Congressional districts. They have their own highly developed channels of communication and an organizational structure that serves national, state-wide, and area-council policies.

Senior citizens and their spokesmen, who saw significant progress and promise in meeting the problems of the elderly during the Kennedy-Johnson era, were utterly dismayed by the actions of the Nixon-Ford administration over the past years in turning back the clock on programs for older Americans. Time and time again, they have had to appeal to a Democratic Congress simply to maintain their hard-fought gains. Improvements in Social Security benefits were bitterly opposed by a Republican administration that would then try to take credit for them.

They have seen the promising recommendations of the 1971 White House Conference on Aging gather dust in the national archives because of Republican-administration neglect. They felt betrayed by the Nixon election propaganda barrage that followed that conference. And President Ford did not even attempt to pay lip service to these recommendations.

It is important that Democratic office seekers not be misled by the commonly held belief that older people are overly conservative on social issues. On most issues of vital concern to them—Social Security benefits, Medicare, services to the elderly, transportation and housing, opportunities for meaningful retirement including part-time job opportunities, to name a few—older Americans respond with enthusiasm to a candidate who clearly highlights these issues in a positive way.

This is not to say that most elderly people want these improvements only for themselves. They also want to improve the quality of life for their children and grandchildren. They want the protection they have under Medicare to be strengthened and extended to the total population. They recognize that gains in Social Security benefits not only help them and younger beneficiaries now but assure future retirees of a more secure old age. They want Congress —and the next Democratic administration—to help solve their problems in harmony with the national interest. In the years ahead, as we recover from the "stagflation" brought on by the past Republican administration, a nation as wealthy as ours can afford to do more for its older people without decreasing its efforts for the younger generation.

The candidate who wants to help older Americans will be interested to learn that, on the average, 65 per cent of Americans fifty-five and over exercise their right to vote. For those under forty-five, the figure is considerably less. People sixty-five and older make up 14.8 per cent of the voting-age population but cast 17 per cent of all votes.

In most Congressional districts, the support of older voters is important to assure a candidate's success; in marginal districts, it is essential.

No less important is the role senior citizens can play in helping with the campaign. Their leisure and wisdom are valuable resources that should be fully utilized. When organized and motivated, seniors can mean the difference between victory and defeat through their efforts in registering voters, organizing rallies, manning telephones, and getting out the vote on election day.

THE PROBLEM OF INCOME

Despite significant progress in recent years—thanks to the ability of a Democratic Congress to override administration resistance to improvements—this nation is still far short of its income goal for the elderly. Every older person in America should have sufficient income to assure a standard of living no lower than the intermediate level set by the Bureau of Labor Statistics—a modest level adequate to maintain health and enable the individual to be self-sufficient.

In 1974, this modest level of income would have required $6,041 for elderly couples and $4,229 for single persons. Nearly 40 per cent of aged families and 70 per cent of aged individuals had incomes below this level.

A total of 3.3 million elderly are still living in poverty. Countless others have incomes below the poverty level but are uncounted among the nation's poor because they live in households with income above the poverty level. To rise above the poverty level would require an income of $247 per month for an elderly individual and $352 for a couple. Yet the maximum payment under the federal program of Supplemental Security Income (SSI) is only $157.70 for an individual and $236.60 for a couple. Any additional supplementation varies widely from state to state. As a result, nearly all levels of SSI total payments fail to meet the lowest, poverty-level, budget of the Bureau of Labor Statistics.

For most elderly people, Social Security benefits are the mainstay of their income. When last surveyed, 14 per cent of all elderly couples and 32 per cent of the individuals had no significant income other than the Social Security benefit. In August 1975, the average Social Security benefit was $205.59 for a retired worker, $104.54 for the wife of a retired worker, and $193.43 for an aged widow. These amounts are obviously significantly below the level needed to maintain any decent standard of living. While most older people have sources of income in addition to Social Security benefits, those with the lowest benefits are likely to have little supplementary income.

Not surprisingly, then, only about one in five persons aged sixty-five and older has sufficient taxable income from all sources to have paid any federal income tax in the past taxable year.

The low income position of our older population makes programs of food stamps, Medicare, tax relief, housing assistance, and social services—in support of our basic Social Security program—absolutely essential to their daily existence.

THE PROBLEM OF HEALTH CARE

The problem of health care for the aged is multifaceted: costs are heavy, because they include more disability than do health-care costs for the general population—especially chronic and long-term disability—and because of the emphasis in our present health-care system on use of expensive hospitals and nursing homes.

Compared to people under sixty-five, those sixty-five and over are more than twice as likely to be hospitalized during a given year, and once hospitalized, they stay twice as long. The aged have 50 per cent more physicians' visits than the younger population.

Total personal health-care expenditures for the population sixty-five and over were $26.7 billion in fiscal year 1974, an average of $1,218 per aged person, in comparison to $420 for those aged 19–64.

Medicare provides valuable protection for the aged, especially those who are hospitalized, but it covers less than two dollars out of every five dollars of their health costs. As a result of skyrocketing medical charges, the elderly are now paying much more out of pocket than their total health costs in the year before Medicare.

More than one million people currently live in long-term-care institutions—nursing homes and homes for the aged. About one person out of five is likely to spend some part of his life in such an institution.

The threat of institutionalization haunts most older people, especially the very old. The younger population shares this concern, dreading the day when a parent may have to be put in a nursing home simply because there are no services available to permit independent living.

THE PROBLEM OF HOUSING

A majority of the elderly live in metropolitan areas, a large proportion of them in central cities—too often in ghetto areas—where the cost of housing is higher and the quality is poorer. Soaring property-tax rates and heavier costs of maintenance have placed an intolerable burden on the aged homeowner, whose home is frequently her only significant asset. Rents that rise periodically (and it is almost certain that one of the increases will be timed to, and more than offset, any increase in Social Security benefits) pose a serious problem for the renter. And his problem has been compounded in recent years by the trend in converting older, low-rental apartments into condominiums far beyond the financial reach of the aged.

OTHER NEEDS OF THE ELDERLY

Singled out above for special attention are the major and all-prevailing issues of income, health care, and housing.

Also of great importance is the improved availability of adequate transportation, either mass transit in our cities or special arrangements in more rural areas. It is useless to provide special services for the elderly if lack of transportation places these services beyond their reach.

Adequate income alone is not enough to assure that older people eat nutritious meals. Also needed are special hot-meal programs in group settings—so important, too, in providing social contact for the lonely—and home-delivered meals to the housebound.

Opportunities for part-time employment in community service, such as the highly successful Senior AIDES programs, under Title IX of the Older Americans Act, must be expanded to provide meaningful jobs for older persons who cannot—or do not wish to—compete in the regular labor market but who need the financial and psychological benefits of paid employment.

A GENERATION OF BLACK PEOPLE

National Caucus on the Black Aged

The critical issues facing the Black elderly are income, housing, and health services. The caucus lobbies to overcome discriminatory practices against blacks and provides technical support and consultant services.

Well over a decade ago, strong men and women with just cause came together to right the wrongs of more than a century. Their names are legion and their accomplishments have changed the face of American society for all time. Some live on to insure the freedom for which they fought. Others, with full knowledge of the risks they were taking, have fallen to fight no more.

They engaged in a combat against oppression. Their victories will insure greater opportunity and a better life for future generations. However, millions of Black Americans will carry, now and in years to come, the scars of past injustices and discrimination.

The tyranny of discrimination, the poverty of opportunity, and the mental and physical disease generated by oppression cannot be cured retroactively. Black Americans exist among us who bore the burdens of that existence and generations of Black Americans to come will carry its vestiges.

There exists in America today a generation of Black people who are too old to work, too undereducated to qualify for work and who, during their productive years, were relegated to menial and low paying work. This gives them, in their twilight years, the lowest of the low income-related retirement incomes and benefits.

Their incomes are substandard. Their housing is substandard. Health services available to them are far less adequate than those available to Whites. Worse yet, the burdens they have carried throughout their lifetime have reduced their potential life-span to an average of six years less than that of their White brethren.

The problem will not die with that generation. Even today, seven of every eight Black males between the ages of 55 and 64 have less than a high school education. One out of three Black families has an income below the federally set poverty level. The median income of Black families headed by persons between 45 and 64, with both parents working, is less than two-thirds that of similar White families. The translation is simple. Less savings. Less home ownership. Less wage-related retirement income in years to come.

And so the problems of the Black aged grow as their numbers grow. As inflation and unemployment grow, the resources potentially available to meet their problems shrink.

In 1970, a number of experts in the field of aging, recognizing the unique problems of the Black aged and the need for programs specifically tailored to them, formed the National Caucus on the Black Aged (NCBA). The primary problems targeted by the caucus then and now are income, housing, and health services—three areas in which there exists a clear discrepancy between the treatment of Blacks and Whites.

The older Black American benefits least from the most common form of retirement income, Social Security. Benefit payments are wage-related and the Black man or woman, due to a lifetime of job discrimination, has a much lower lifetime wage record than his or her White counterpart. In the case of Black males the system is particularly discriminatory in that, statistically, they will not live long enough to collect old-age benefits. Even in cases where such retirement income can be supplemented by public assistance, Black Americans are, numerically, concentrated in the states that pay the lowest public assistance benefits.

The caucus is actively working to combat this injustice by lobbying for increases in minimum Social Security payments and supplemental income and assistance programs. It also carries out education and information activities to increase the ability of aged Blacks to seek out and receive benefits and services to which they are entitled.

According to government statistics, seven out of ten aged Black Americans live in poverty areas. Only one out of four Whites must endure this atmosphere. It can be assumed that this is due, in part, to the fact that White older Americans draw higher Social Security benefits. Many also have far greater income from investments and have purchased desirable housing prior to retirement. Government figures also show that one out of every four housing units occupied by "non-Whites" is "substandard" and nearly one out of every five Black homes lacks some or all "desirable" plumbing. Many of these homes are occupied by Black aged.

To help correct this imbalance, the National Caucus on the Black Aged is working with the elderly Black population and with public and private groups qualified to build and manage low-cost housing to make available more adequate housing facilities. For the aged themselves, the caucus is developing materials on entitlement and application for low-income housing for the elderly. For public groups, nonprofit organizations and churches, the caucus provides technical support and consultant services to help fund, plan, and build low-cost housing for the Black aged.

The high mortality rate of American Blacks between the ages of 60 and 69 years and the significantly shorter life expectancy of Blacks compared to Whites is the product of several factors. Many are not correctable by the time a person reaches his later years. The only meaningful answer to the problem is comprehensive health care for all Americans of all ages, a goal which the caucus strongly supports. In the meantime, NCBA is working with other concerned groups to increase the use of available medical services by the Black aged, to expand the coverage of such programs as Medicare, and to promote the expansion of health services and health service facilities in areas containing high concentrations of aged Blacks.

Early in its existence, the leadership of the caucus realized that to carry out its work effectively, a vehicle was needed to coordinate activities, communicate new information, and provide consultant services to those working to meet the goals of the caucus. That vehicle, the National Center on Black Aged, was established in 1973. The center has conducted research in areas vital to the caucus, trained personnel in service delivery systems for the Black aged, provided technical and consultant services, and acted as a clearinghouse for information on and for aged Blacks. It also works to develop needed curricula, workshop, and conference material for decision makers and policy planners and serves as expert support to both government and nongovernment groups with interests similar to those of NCBA.

HELP FOR THE MINORITY AGED

National Urban League

"Advocacy: In Support of Minority Aged" is an action, research, and demonstration program of the National Urban League. It serves the low-income aged Blacks and aged members of other minority groups through counseling and acting as a clearinghouse for information about projects.

In 1971, after careful assessment of the critical needs of low-income, aged Blacks and other minority groups, and the lack of effective advocates on their behalf, the National Urban League implemented an action research and demonstration program to reduce the multiple jeopardy of this group. The program is called Advocacy: In Support of Minority Aged.

The program is based on the premise that a multitude of social, health, and welfare services can be utilized through documenting needs of low-income aged Blacks and aged members of other minority groups; involving aged Blacks in understanding their rights and obtaining entitlements; and engaging social service agencies in a process whereby they will be more responsive to the needs of the elderly.

When the National Urban League Advocacy project began, two conditions were evident. First, the people the project sought to serve seemed resigned to their unequal "second class status," and were distrustful of any offer of help. Second, there seemed little prospect of penetrating the diffused, vague, and fragmented system of community service. Earlier efforts had been made to alert the country to the inequities confronting aged Blacks and to obtain needed services, but these services (e.g., Social Security, Railroad Retirement, Veterans Benefits, Old Age Assistance) were not substantial nor did they ease ongoing daily economic pressures.

Until the early 1950s, domestic servants and agricultural workers weren't covered by Social Security. Aged Black and other minority persons, many of whom fell into those two job categories and who are now 65 and over, have not worked long enough since the early 1950s to achieve adequate Social Security income. As a result, many of these persons must rely on welfare, relief and/or other federal and state programs to supplement their incomes, such as Medicare, Medicaid, and the food stamp program.

In tackling the problem, certain facts surfaced—core problems that grew from ignorance of the many needs of aged Blacks and other minorities, such as lack of sensitivity in understanding their lifestyles, and the past effects of racism and discrimination.

To initiate the program, offices were established in three Urban League affiliate cities—Chicago, San Diego, and Columbia, S.C. Advocacy announced its presence and began building credibility in the "aging establishment," and in Black, Brown, and White low-income communities. Advocacy staff surveyed the social, health, and welfare agencies to determine what services could be tailored specifically to the Black elderly.

Then Advocacy located and interviewed over 300 aged Black, Brown, and White citizens to identify their needs on the basis of their own reports. The interviews not only provided insight about the lifestyles and opinions of the minority aged as a group, but also about the individual, the crucial target of the effort.

Working in the multifaceted service system, Advocacy staff became at times not only advocate, but lawyer, sleuth, and broker between those who had the services and those who needed them. Some senior citizens wanted to seek welfare or other benefits, but were either afraid or didn't know how to apply for needed assistance. Others had no transportation to take them where they needed to go. In many instances, senior citizens who were unable to walk through the maze of bureaucratic red tape were virtually led by the hand by Advocacy staff. Many were in serious financial straits but did not know they were eligible for Social Security.

The Advocacy staff first concentrated on counseling aged Blacks and other minorities on their rights and opportunities in seeking services in their communities, and on interpreting the sophisticated and often elusive "small print" in agency service requirements vis-à-vis qualifications and eligibility.

Then Advocacy staff served to monitor state and local agency policies, encouraged the uniform assurance of the rights of aged minorities, acted as a clearinghouse for comprehensive information relating to other relevant projects, and helped to secure basic priority needs.

When the Advocacy project began, it sought only to eliminate the disengagement between needy, aged Blacks and their community service resources. As the project progressed and staff became more knowledgeable, however, it became clear that this was only one aspect of the job at hand, a job which demands the cooperation of the entire community.

Advocacy recognizes that nothing less than intensive involvement by minority groups in the work of planning, developing programs, and monitoring the network of service agencies will help the long-range interests of the Black and other minority aged poor.

A century of inequities in the American service delivery system will not be eliminated overnight, but Advocacy has taken major strides forward. It has succeeded in helping many who needed help. It has touched on a vast store of potential ancillary benefits which will prove helpful to the unprecedented "new thrust" in the field of the aging: inclusion of Black and minority aged curriculum in gerontology in social work schools; expertise on methods of outreach to aged Blacks and other minorities; counseling; proven new research techniques that are technically oriented and calculated to destroy misconceptions promulgated by pseudo social scientists; training interested Black senior citizens to become their own spokesmen, and to participate on local and state boards of those groups speaking for the elderly in general.

IT'S NOT ALL DOWNHILL!

Merrell M. Clark

Merrell Clark believes that the plight of old people in our society has been greatly exaggerated. But his contention has not made for complacence: he has encouraged and supported significant innovative programs, first as vice-president of the Edna McConnell Clark Foundation and currently as senior vice-president of the Academy for Educational Development. Here he demurs from the dire analysis that dominates in this book and explains where he thinks the real challenge of serving the aged lies.

In an environment of fear and guilt about aging, it is no wonder that the swelling of the older population to 22 million today and the projection of 30 million in two decades are accompanied by the wringing of hands. The population explosion of the old is used frequently to add urgency to arguments that something more must be done about the problems of older Americans.

It is not my intent to disprove that old people (or young people) have problems, nor to diminish their claims to various corrective or supportive resources. What I want to stress is that the news about aging in America is not all bad: it isn't all nursing home scandals, Social Security suffering, and meaningless routine. Indeed, to begin with, the very fact that so many of us now live to be old is good news. Today's old are the first generation whose lives have been lived within the most affluent culture in human history. They have benefited from radical changes in medical knowledge and expansion of health care. They have benefited from a shorter work week, improved transportation, home appliances, and many other advances. The touting of numbers alone as an argument to increase concern about the old seems perverse. Even though India and the Soviet Union are much larger nations than the United States, we have more citizens who have lived to old age than either of those countries.

Second, although the data are sketchy, it may be true that the proportion of people in the older population who have severe problems is steadily declining. Less than 5 per cent of people 65 and older are institutionalized. Ninety-five per cent live in the community with all the rest of us. Four out of five older people have no limitation on their mobility. The overwhelming majority of old people in America are well—not sick—and it looks as if the improvements in education, income, and insurance of recent years will steadily increase the proportion of the well old.

Third, the massive and diversified education system in the United States has produced an unprecedented population of educated elders. The notion that old people are primarily useful for passing on cultural traditions is obsolete in an age when large numbers of educated old people are inventing the patterns of the future. True, today's older Americans, on the average, lag slightly behind the education level of the younger people whose educations they financed. But not that much: the gap between older Americans' median grade level of greater than eight years and a median of more than twelfth-grade level for all adults is closing rapidly. At the end of the next decade there will be no significant gap, with proportionately as many professionals, college and high school graduates among the old as among the young.

Fourth, one does not need to search the mountains and valleys of South America or Asia to find people who have discovered the secret of longevity. Recent unsubstantiated articles have misled many into believing that today's fountain of youth could be found in primitive mountain-top life-styles in distant lands. Yet the media have neglected the prosaic cities and towns and farms of our homeland where there are some 14,000 Americans over 100 and nearly a million over 90, thousands of whom are still actively employed or participating in community services or pursuing academic interests.

Fifth, those who bemoan the American retirement system and idolize foreign leaders who remained active in government in their later years, such as Winston Churchill, Konrad Adenauer, Charles de Gaulle, Golda Meir, and others, might do well to cast their view over the current American scene where leadership in virtually every field of endeavor is shared, if not dominated, by elders. The list of older mayors, senators, judges, labor leaders, artists, sculptors, business owners and chiefs, musicians, actors, comedians, publishers, scientists, attorneys, clergy, writers, inventors, and even athletes is so long and well known that it will suffice to mention just a few: Daley, Meany, Calder, Hope, Fuller, Rubenstein, Hepburn, Sanders, and so on.

Sixth, and finally, we must gain perspective on the question of inflation versus fixed incomes. The high inflation rate is a problem of all Americans, although less so for Americans than for citizens of virtually all other countries, and is erroneous to regard old people as disproportionately victimized by this syndrome. The problem is serious but far more widely distributed. Of course old people on limited incomes are hit hard. So are young people on limited incomes and young people whose family expenses are growing faster than their cost-of-living increases. Despite the worst year of inflation in 40 years, only 15 per cent of older Americans told a Louis Harris survey team that they had "very serious money problems" in the summer of 1974. While from a larger view, this is 15 per cent too many, 18 per cent of people 18 to 64 years old had the same complaint. And in what other country do 80 per cent of the people, young and old, feel they do so well?

Among the urgent needs of Americans is the need to curtail the infernal, self-destructive bad news about American aging.

If one accepts the facts presented here, then one faces a new kind of problem. Smothered by a preoccupation with bad news, we have been slow as a people to recognize the new reality of able old people in large numbers. Now that our good fortune has yielded this new world of talent, we need to discover how to stop its insane waste. We need to redeploy our life-experienced, skilled, largely self-financed, and motivated elders where they can have the greatest impact on the unfinished agendas of our nation. But unless the image of aging in America is brought up to date, no one will expect older persons to do anything significant with their lives, and dangerous tensions between different age groups will become characteristic of our society. As long as only 29 per cent of Americans believe older persons are "good at getting things done," it is unlikely that olders will be acceptable to younger Americans as coworkers and equals. The fact is that older Americans are generally very good at getting things done, and we must adapt our expectations accordingly.

Too frequently the efforts of community agencies to keep old people involved and active are limited because they provide entertaining but largely inconsequential activity, if measured by the unmet needs of the community, and because they fail to attract many really able retirees who have no need for additional social contact or activity, and so they segregate the most dependent or depressed from the influence of much more active and optimistic peers.

It is not older Americans but our major institutions that most need to increase productivity, offset the costs of inflation, deliver better services, and restore public confidence. Old people can be powerful resources in achieving these ends. Indeed, there are some such efforts under way. Public education, higher education, hospitals, government agencies, courts, employment services, and many other institutions have only begun to explore the use of older experts or older skilled workers on an unpaid or part-time job basis. Early results are most encouraging on all counts with benefits to the clients of these institutions, benefits to the institutions and their active employees, and benefits to retirees who can see their efforts make an important difference. Hundreds of significant examples could be cited. This new phenomenon will grow in the years ahead as more major institutions learn to find and deploy able elders to help solve their problems. And while many elders are at work to solve major problems in the United States, others in growing numbers will be sought by businesses and governments in developing countries to transfer their know-how there.

There may be no more exciting venture in the decades ahead than the discovery of new and important roles for able, educated older Americans in this new, new world. Not a burden to themselves or others, these people—talented, available, and largely self-financed—may be the most important man- and woman-power resource we have to solve our problems as a nation and to help other nations solve theirs. Those who worry needlessly about exploiting older Americans (who will say no if uninterested) do not understand how grateful and proud many elders are to be able to pay back some measure of benefit to the society that gave them their good fortune and to the society and world which they helped to build.

GERONTOLOGY COMES OF AGE

Beverly T. Watkins

"The study of aging has come of age," says Ruth B. Weg, assistant dean of students for the Leonard Davis School of Gerontology, at the University of Southern California. Colleges and universities across the country are offering programs for practitioners serving the elderly, whose demands for more and better services grow as their numbers increase.

Gerontology, which hardly existed as an academic field ten years ago, has become one of higher education's fastest-growing disciplines.

The changing age structure of American society has brought gerontology out of the research laboratory and into the classroom. The growing numbers of elderly people are demanding more and better services, and they are turning to higher education to provide some of them.

Colleges and universities, with increasing support from the federal government, have responded to the rising consumerism of the aged with about thirteen hundred different programs in gerontology, and uncounted seminars, workshops, and training institutes. Even so, they cannot meet the need for qualified practitioners, and the unrelenting demand for them, in the opinion of some scholars, is a threat to the entire field of gerontology.

Many at the annual meeting here of the Association for Gerontology in Higher Education expressed concern about the new consumer orientation. They questioned the uneven quality of college programs and the value of short-term training that produces "instant" gerontologists.

Some advocated establishing standards for the profession as quickly as possible. Others, afraid that the field is outpacing their ability to control it, favored efforts to curtail expansion.

"PHENOMENAL GROWTH"

"The study of aging has come of age," says Ruth B. Weg, assistant dean of students for the Leonard Davis School of Gerontology, at the University of Southern California. "Gerontology has been around a long time as a research effort but not as an organized area in academia. Today it is having a phenomenal growth from an educational point of view. The very nature of society is changing. Society is growing older. There are 22.8 million people today over the age of 65, out of a total population of 215 million. We expect 33 million by the year 2000."

Ms. Weg says "the desires of older persons in the community" have prompted colleges and universities to establish programs and multidisciplinary centers in gerontology.

"In 1967, gerontology had only incipient programs across the country," she says. As of July 1976, however, a national directory published by the association listed 1,275 different educational programs.

"Ten years ago there were five gerontology centers," Ms. Weg says. "Today there are at least fifteen."

A multidisciplinary center, such as the Ethel Percy Andrus Gerontology Center, at the University of Southern California, provides research, education, and community programs. The center's gerontology research institute, which for ten years has served as a model for other universities that were developing centers, has facilities for research on the biological, behavioral, and social mechanisms of aging. It grants the doctorate.

The center's school of gerontology, the first in the country, develops practitioners, administrators, and educators at the certificate, bachelor's, and master's-degree levels to work in community agencies that provide services for the elderly.

TYPICAL CURRICULUM

A typical gerontology curriculum is a multidisciplinary combination of biology, psychology, sociology, social work, and architecture and urban planning. Gerontology courses are often taught by faculty members with an appointment in another discipline but an interest in gerontology.

Other colleges and universities are "making efforts to 'gerontologize' the areas of higher education, including the humanities," says Martha Storandt, associate professor of psychology at Washington University.

She says, "Almost all disciplines have something to offer the aged."

The goal of many colleges and universities is to have "one faculty member who addresses issues of aging in every under-represented discipline."

Institutions of higher education have received support from the federal government in their efforts to help the aging. The Older Americans Act of 1965, which created an Administration on Aging, provided "a stimulus and a source of funding" for education, Ms. Weg says.

The Comprehensive Older Americans Act Amendments, passed in 1973, authorized multidisciplinary centers and required that, among other things, they "conduct basic and applied research on . . . education of older people." The amendments also authorized the inclusion of research on aging in the education programs administered by the Department of Health, Education, and Welfare. Reports on the legislation in both the House of Representatives and the Senate endorsed grants to help colleges assist the elderly.

Today there is an agency in every state that administers funds under the Older Americans Act to finance individual programs for the aging.

Robert N. Butler, the first director of the National Institute on Aging, indicated in testimony before the Senate's Special Committee on Aging, in the fall of 1976, that the institute would be concerned with academic gerontology as well as with research. In a survey of practicing physicians, he reported, 75 per cent answered Yes to the question "Do M.D.'s need special training in geriatrics?"

"It is imperative that the special perspective of 'geriatric medicine' be introduced into the curricula of our 114 medical schools, into our intern and residency training, and into our program of continuing education," Mr. Butler says.

"ENCOURAGED" BY CARTER BUDGET

William Oriol, staff director of the Senate Special Committee on Aging, is optimistic that the government will continue to support higher education's efforts in gerontology.

"I find reason to be encouraged by the Carter budget," says Mr. Oriol, noting that the President added $3.8 million for multidisciplinary centers and $20 million for senior centers in his proposed amendments to the Ford administration budget, which had included neither of those items.

President Carter retained Mr. Ford's request for training and research money but cut funds for the Administration on Aging.

In spite of higher education's efforts and the government's support, there is still a shortage of professionals with a knowledge of gerontology. Some academic gerontologists are beginning to see an element of danger in producing more practitioners.

"Right now is a period of growth in gerontology, but volume is not quality," Ms. Storandt says.

"I value social justice, but I value a knowledge base, too. Before we develop practitioners, we must develop research clinicians. How can a practitioner practice if he doesn't have anything to practice with? Each program on aging should have one person expert in gerontological-research methodology to make sure all our new and wonderful programs are wonderful, not just new."

However, Warner Schaie, director of the Andrus Center's research institute, doesn't see any conflict between research and consumer-oriented gerontology.

"The question is, What are we training for?" Mr. Schaie says. "The center is training service providers. Service providers must be research consumers. They must read research articles, but it will not increase their knowledge base if we train them to do research. The answer is to keep research at the doctoral level."

Attempts to train enough professionals to satisfy the job market have produced uneven academic programs, according to Walter Beattie, professor of social work and gerontology at Syracuse University.

"If fifty per cent of the curricular offerings in gerontology within the formal structure of higher education met any strict academic criteria, that would be a lot," Mr. Beattie says.

PLAYING "CATCH-UP"

"Playing frantic catch-up" has also produced gerontologists with dubious qualifications, says Wayne Vasey, visiting professor of gerontology at the University of South Florida.

Mr. Vasey says gerontology and its professionals need to establish standards "to provide a minimum level of competence."

"If we have to provide *post hoc* instruction," he says, "we should insure accountability by putting faculty members who will conform to educational standards in charge of the courses and seeing that institutions retain final approval. A growing number of people are concentrating in gerontology. Are they responding to the need, or did they just hear about the gold strike? Gerontologists must control access to the field. We have to keep out the quacks."

NEW LIFE FOR THE ELDERLY:
LIBERATION FROM "AGEISM"

Maggie Kuhn

Activism on behalf of the aged took a giant step forward one day in June 1970 when Maggie Kuhn and five of her friends began meeting to discuss their problems as retirees. The Gray Panthers struck a new note in the field: broad-based social conscience expressed in opposition to the Vietnam War; wide-ranging liaison and coalition with other activist groups, particularly of young people; and a spirited style, exemplified in Kuhn's rallying cry: "Get off your asses!"

I'm one of twenty million Americans who've had a sixty-fifth birthday and I rejoice. I'm glad to have achieved my seniority in this new age of liberation. I recognize, however, that there are many ways of looking at this age and the new life styles it requires. Some view accelerating change with fear and distaste. Some reject it with a passion, declaring to all how good and beautiful life was in the old days; yet they don't have the remotest thought of turning off their TV sets or electric blankets. Many are apathetic, escaping into little private worlds, uninvolved and disengaged. But neither critics nor escapees have caught onto the most striking characteristic of the new age: the world-wide struggle for freedom and humanness.

Liberation movements are everywhere. Focused on people rather than technology and things, they sharply challenge every institution, system, and political structure. The old-order, acquisitive society, which values property more than people, is under attack. Leading the battle are the young dissenters and other powerless ones—including certain militant elderly.

Into this new age of people power comes the budding revolution of old people. Like blacks and Mexican-Americans, Puerto Ricans, and Indians who have revolted against racism, the liberation of older adults seeks the end of ageism.

RACISM AND AGEISM

There are analogies between racism and ageism in their effects upon persons:

1. Both are built-in responses of our society to persons and groups considered to be inferior.

2. Both deprive certain persons and groups of status and the right to control their own destinies and to have access to power, with the end result of powerlessness.

3. Both result in social and economic discrimination and deprivation.

4. Both deprive American society of the contributions and of many competent and creative persons who are needed to deal with our vast and complex problems. This is a great social loss.

5. Both result in individual alienation, despair, and hostility.

6. To be eliminated, both will require mobilization and commitment of the national political processes, and public and private institutions.

Ageism permeates our Western culture and institutions. It infects us, the aging and the aged, when we reject ourselves and despise our powerlessness, wrinkled skin, and physical limitations. It's revealed when we succumb to apathy and complacent acceptance of the things that society does to diminish us. Thus a symptom of our sickness is that we feel complimented when others tell us we do not look or act our age.

Ageism dictates the policies of most places of employment with fixed and arbitrary retirement rules. It's an old complaint that employers discriminate against older workers. "Denture breath" and "irregularity" are frequent excuses for keeping us out of job markets.

Ageism has also afflicted many of the institutions serving older persons with a deep, insidious paternalism. Those who live in rest homes and retirement communities have little or no voice in the governance or programs of such places. Members of golden-age clubs are lucky if they are permitted to plan their own fun and games.

In nursing homes probably the ultimate indignity is to be given a bedpan by a perfect stranger who calls you by your first name.

Too often, institutional managers, along with staff, regard and treat the residents as children, incapable of making sound judgments or managing their lives. So successful is this benevolence that retired residents soon become children or vegetables.

The fact that American society *tolerates* old people and assumes that they will generously step aside to make way for the young is in itself another form of rejection.

All the problems that beset older white people are compounded when we consider the plight of our non-white peers. Elderly blacks, Chicanos, Puerto Ricans, and Indians live in triple jeopardy not only because of age but also because they are non-white and, in most instances, poor. The majority of aged blacks and members of other minorities depend upon Social Security and/or public assistance for their primary source of income. Few elderly non-whites have private pensions, annuities, or savings. Their Social Security benefits are pitifully small, because the jobs in which they have been employed were only recently covered by Social Security benefits.

Our black and Puerto Rican peers frequently have to live in unsafe housing, usually in the least safe of the unsafe streets; they live in constant fear of mugging, robbery, and rape. In large cities some low-cost public housing is available to non-whites, but the backlog of need is tremendous.

IDENTITY CRISIS

In the process of aging, most of us experience some sort of identity crisis. Our image of ourselves reflects the image society has of us. Our self-image is affected by a society that considers old people superfluous because they are not productive and useful.

Consider what happens to millions of older adults when they retire. Overnight their status changes. One day they are persons of purpose and productiveness. The next they are the forgotten ones. In our society our identity as persons is determined by our jobs. When jobs are gone, selfhood also is threatened. We have no place —we have no power. Some retirees from long-active careers in business or industry go into shock. Many who have lived only for their jobs never recover; they become ill and die or retreat into senility. The survivors face a bleak and lonely future. Greatly reduced income and inflation add financial privation to emotional stress. Our throwaway society with its matching throwaway mentality scrap-piles people as it does old automobiles.

Modern science and medical research have enabled many more people to add ten, twenty, thirty, or more years to their life span. Medical technology grows more sophisticated by the hour with such marvels as pacemakers implanted in the chests of cardiac patients. However, few advances have been made in understanding or dealing with the psychological-emotional aspects of age. Little help has been given to relieve the terrible anxieties and frustrations of age. Such understanding and corresponding efforts of our own to give longevity some meaning and purpose are needed. Otherwise, life-extending measures are but more evidences of ageism: cruel experimentations with elderly guinea pigs.

Deep-seated feelings of loss of worth, of friends, and of loved ones, as well as strange new fears of disability and nothingness, are real. They will not go away. They have to be countered by new thinking, new self-images, and new life styles.

A probing analysis of what old people can contribute to the world around us is highly important. What we have to offer is suggested in the following assessment of our potential.

RATIONALE FOR REVOLUTION

1. Older persons in our society constitute a great national resource, which has been largely unrecognized, undervalued, and unused. The experience, wisdom, and competence of older persons are greatly needed in every sector of society. Creative, innovative ways must be found to enable older people to make their contribution to a new age of liberation.

2. Older persons have freedom: freedom to think, reflect, and act. We are free to be involved in large issues and controversies. We are free to fight against the forces that suppress us and also the forces that oppress other minorities deprived of freedom and selfhood. We have nothing to lose and nothing to fear by being so involved. Our pensions and Social Security checks cannot be taken away. Our jobs and families cannot be put in jeopardy by our actions. Only the young and the old have such freedom today. Both groups are gaining in self-awareness and corporate strength. As a result, the beginnings of a coalition of the young and the old are just being glimpsed.

3. Older persons have demonstrated their ability to "cope." They have dealt with the setbacks and tragedies of life, interacting with others in the process. We never reach old age by our own individual endeavors. Longevity depends upon the combined efforts of the individual and society. The high "survival quotients" of those who have lived threescore years and more may be more important in this new age than "intelligence quotients" have been.

4. We oldsters have to make basic changes in our thinking about ourselves and our peers. We will have to "reprogram" ourselves and adopt new personal and group life styles. This will be hard for some, easier for others. We need to help one another, and gladly accept the help of allies.

NEW LIFE STYLES

The new life styles proposed here are at once deeply personal and broadly social. All are related and interdependent. The listing is by no means complete. These and other life styles are needed to build sturdy, shockproof self-esteem. All are needed to heal and humanize our ruthless, wasteful society.

Living-with-grace Life Style I: Accepting Ourselves and Our Accumulated Years with Grace and Authentic Maturity of Spirit and Emotion

This life style requires a new and positive self-awareness, including an appreciation of our years and the social value of our experience and knowledge. Instead of denying our age, we begin to celebrate it as part of life's fullness. The term "authentic maturity" is appropriate here. It is an all-embracing, basis-for-being term, including the emotional, psychological, and physiological aspects of life. It's based on self-knowledge and self-acceptance.

To adopt this basic life style means learning to live with ourselves: our wrinkles, gray hair, stiffening joints, fears, and bifocals. It also means availing ourselves of health knowledge and measures at hand to prevent degenerative and crippling illnesses. With new discoveries about nutrition, exercise, and intellectual stimulation we are able to maintain our physical and mental vigor throughout life.

Society makes a fetish of being young and keeping up youthful appearances. The mythology of perennial youth is kept alive by lies, subterfuge, and self-deception. Silly, sometimes exhausting, and always expensive efforts to maintain the youth cult should be unnecessary. Age has its own attributes. We shall have come a long way toward authentic maturity when we no longer feel complimented on being told how "youthful" we look.

Authentic maturity also involves the facing of the fears of the aging, the fear of being alone, of becoming useless, of becoming helpless and senile. Our fear of death makes that subject taboo also, even in the Christian community. We seldom speak of it except in euphemisms and we employ morticians to pretty up the corpse.

Authentic maturity is not usually a goal of the standard-brand golden-age clubs, organized chiefly to amuse and entertain. Some of us consider them little more than glorified playpens. They're designed to keep people in their second childhood safe and out of the way of mainstream living. Tea and organized games do not equip us to make the most of our experience and competence or to live with the *angst* of age. Yet we know some well-meaning congregations who consider sponsorship of a golden-age club as their only senior-citizens ministry.

Life Style II: Continuing to Work for Love or Money, or Continuing to Do Useful Work

We emphasize *work* because large numbers of older persons need more income. Our government has been miserly about Social Security benefits, which are the sole source of income for millions. They are supplemented by pensions for only 18 per cent of adults sixty-five and older. Social Security payments have increased over the years, but they are not linked to the cost of living or adequate to keep retirees out of near poverty.

LIFE-CYCLE EDUCATION

Along with work and community involvement we need "life-cycle education"—a womb-to-tomb activity covering the human life span. As envisioned by psychiatrist Robert Butler of the Washington, D.C., School of Psychiatry, it means basic cultural transformation. All persons are provided an opportunity to review and re-create themselves at each period of life. Dr. Butler sees education, work, and retirement interwoven and integrated.

Arbitrary policies for retirement at sixty-five or seventy make no provision for individual differences, capacities, and needs. They deny personhood, particularly for the people who want to keep on working. They also represent an enormous social loss that nobody has ever computed.

Our ageist society usually lumps all old people into one great, gray mass without differentiating them. Yet there are several subgroups that should be taken into account. They have an important bearing on a life style of continuing work and community involvement.

1.   Preretirement from forty-five to sixty-five years. Preparation for retirement from one job and possible movement into another career.

2.   Immediate postretirement from sixty-five to seventy years (young elderly) in which steps are taken to enable people to pursue special interests—do what they want to do.

3.   Middle-aged elderly from seventy to eighty-five years.

4.   Aged elderly eighty-five to one hundred years.

These subgroups make up what is now seen by sociologists as a subculture. It will enlarge as the proportion of older persons increases (from 10 to 17 per cent) in the United States population.

At present, pending the changes that must be made about old people, society views them *avocationally*—not productively. It is generally assumed that they will automatically develop leisure interests. The only social outlets really open to them are for play and relaxation. Thus the "leisure worlds" now springing up around the country may trap the affluent elderly. However, such bread-and-circus efforts are not going to be socially or economically useful, because they are not in the mainstream of life.

To live significantly (and above the poverty line), to establish a new image of ourselves, we must find work and community activities that society considers worthwhile.

"RESTING" IS DEADLY

Second, third, and fourth careers are envisioned in the new life style. This explodes the myth that the more you rest and recreate, the better it is for the body. We retire from one job to move on to other fields, perhaps quite different fields of interest. We may weave in several careers in volunteer service as well as paid employment. We act on the discovery of gerontologists that the harder and longer we work, the more likely we are to stay well and alive. But we also work because we have skills and experience that are needed. Some rest is, of course, essential, but "resting" as a way of life is deadly. Many look forward to retirement after working hard, happy in the thought that total rest and recreation will improve their health, enabling them to live longer. But just the opposite is true. Total rest is almost a sure way to bring on physical and mental degeneration. It's new activities and new goals that add life to the years.

In *The Second Forty Years* Stieglitz wrote, "Abrupt or obligatory retirement of [persons] still in the prime of life, their [chronological] age notwithstanding, is often tantamount to signing their death warrant." He adds that the retiree should not wallow in inactivity but find some work in which his energy and abilities can be put to advantage. The mind and the body must be kept going to preserve not only life but self-reliance and selfhood.

Older persons should press for liberalizing the present restrictions on earnings without loss of Social Security benefits. They should also seek the opening of more part-time jobs.

The services of older workers even on a part-time basis should be welcomed by public schools, planning and housing authorities, and hospitals. Or work teams of two to four retirees could provide the number of working hours equivalent to full-time assignments. Banks and department stores have found such arrangements highly satisfactory for securing experienced, competent workers. Churches and judicatories should do likewise and urge other private employers to take on older workers. Research has shown that increasing age does not always lessen reasoning or productive abilities.

MOBILIZATION FOR AGING

Dr. Theodore D. Ernst (associate dean and associate professor in the School of Social Welfare, State University of New York at Buffalo) has proposed a nationwide "Mobilization for Aging." It would parallel Mobilization for Youth, the program that provides jobs and education for disadvantaged young people.

"Mobilization for Aging" could bring together church bodies, private foundations, business, industry, labor, and government agencies. Present efforts of these groups are scattered, unrelated, and scanty. Dr. Ernst sees the need for totally new services in the larger public interest performed by old persons in their communities.

He calls for second-career counseling and new testing programs. These would uncover and demonstrate the great variety of skills and experiences of older adults.

A new group of militant old people sees the need for mobilizing cadres of retirees to aid Ralph Nader. They would expose ways in which consumers and users of services are bilked and short-changed. Older people are free for investigating nursing homes, rest homes, and clinics. They could report and protest poor services, mistreatment, and fraud. They would also evaluate and report good services and consumer satisfaction.

"VALUE IMPACT FORECASTERS"

New products are field-tested and subjected to extensive market research to be sure they will sell. But, as Alvin Toffler points out in *Future Shock,* little attention has been given to post-test the effects of those products on human beings or the environment. Little thought is given to how they affect or change human values.

Old people in retirement communities and in their own homes could band together in "enclaves of the future" to set up living experiments. They would pretest samples of houses, environmental family styles, and the human side effects of products. Thus, Toffler sees a new profession emerging: "value impact forecasters"; men and women trained to appraise the value implications of proposed technology. Old people open to new ideas would be naturals for this. Church boards could initiate such experiments.

In addition, "mature-temp" job placement is now available in some metropolitan areas. Such service should be extended to smaller communities, with older persons as placement officers.

Also, *for every retirement home organized by church groups there should be efforts to get retirees into work assignments in the church and community, even for a few hours a week.*

Our nation is moving from producing goods to the production of services. In this process Toffler sees evidence that our economic system is becoming more responsive to social and psychological pressures. Churches should be generating some of this pressure.

Life Style III: *Maintaining Interest in Sex*

The need to affirm and express our sexuality is fundamental in persons of all ages. We believe sexual interest and activity is needed in the life style of older adults. It provides a basis for self-esteem and an energizing force that invigorates body and mind.

What we are saying is that there is no age limit to sexual responsiveness. Free relationships can and should flourish as long as we live. We have freedom from the hang-ups and conflicts of youth and the experience and time to enjoy these relationships. If we are anxious or uncertain about the physiological or psychological aspects of sexual relations, there are books and counseling services to help us. Too long have we accepted the myth that physical intimacy is restricted to the earlier years of life.

A NEW LIFE AT EIGHTY-TWO

The following incident illustrates the power of the sexual drive in old age and the appropriateness of it.

For a number of years the grandmother of a colleague of the author's had been living in the home of one of her sons. For at least five years she had been in bed for days at a time.

One day she received a letter from a man whom she had not seen for years. A week or so later she received a phone call from him. Shortly after the call, she appeared downstairs fully dressed and ready to travel. To the astonished son and daughter-in-law she announced she was leaving and going to be married as soon as possible. She asked only that she have help taking her suitcase to the cab that she had called.

She thanked them for their faithful care, gave them her love and a forwarding address, and left for a new life at the age of eighty-two. She then lived happily with her second husband until she died, at ninety!

It was fortunate for her and her future well-being and happiness that her children did not oppose her plan. They rejoiced with her that life could go on anew.

Companionship is important at any age but crucial in the lives of older persons in countering loneliness. Medical science has helped to lengthen the life span and enable many persons over sixty-five to remain physically and mentally vigorous.

Masters and Johnson, researchers in sexual relationships, offer a great deal of hope and encouragement to us to develop this life style of sexual interest. They state, "There is no reason why . . . menopause [or the male climacteric] should [blunt] the sexual capacity, performance, or drive" of older persons. "Regularity of sexual expression coupled with adequate physical well-being and healthy mental orientation to the aging process will combine to provide a sexually stimulative climate within a marriage [extending] to and beyond the eighty-year age level." They conclude that "sexual interaction between older marital partners can be established easily, warmly, and with dignity."

On the plight of the older woman these researchers say, "The trend of our population toward an aging society of women without men must be considered. Roughly 10 per cent of women never marry. In addition, the gift of longevity has not been divided equally between the sexes." Much more should be known about women who live alone. Also, creative ministries need to be developed now on the basis of what is known.

Social isolation of the elderly is worsened by present Social Security laws. Widows and widowers who remarry cannot receive benefits from both spouses; they receive Social Security payments only through the marriage that provides the higher benefits. While this may not seem inequitable, we observe that under private pension and insurance plans, a remarried person retains full benefits from both spouses.

GERIATRIC COMMUNES

The "Report on Sexuality and the Human Community," received by the 182nd General Assembly for study in the churches, affirms that "the church has at least the obligation to explore the possibilities of both celibate and noncelibate communal living arrangements as ethically acceptable and personally fulfilling alternatives for unmarried persons."

Alvin Toffler, in *Future Shock,* forecasts the shattering of the modern nuclear family and its coming together in unexpected ways. He predicts the emergence of "geriatric communes"; that is, group marriage of elderly persons drawn together in a common search for companionship and assistance.

Disengaged from the productive economy that makes mobility necessary, they will settle in a single place. Banding together and pooling funds, they will collectively hire domestic or nursing help and proceed to have the time of their lives.

Life Style IV: Democratizing and Humanizing Institutions Serving the Aged

Churches have responded to the needs of older persons in compassionate but quite traditional ways. They've established retirement and convalescent homes, most of which are run *by* church-related committees *for* the aged. The resident users of such services are given no voice or share in the planning, managing, or operation of these institutions. Residents are usually treated like children, forced to live by rigid rules and regulations. They are denied any part in decision-making.

Although many church-related homes and hospitals have declared an open-occupancy policy, few retirement institutions—except county homes or poor farms—make any effort to serve non-whites. Church boards and boards of homes assume that older persons will not adjust to multiracial living and do not press the implementation of an open-occupancy policy.

Many of us feel that such paternalism, however well-meaning and benign, can be tolerated no longer. The above new life style requires revolution from within the institutions by the residents. This would be supported by revolutionary change outside the institution, sparked by the sponsoring groups.

It means that we as old persons petition and band together to challenge sponsoring groups to change the governance of such institutions. Having advisory councils of older persons is not enough. What we want is full board membership and even shared ownership. Co-operatives and condominiums would give residents some tax advantages.

This institutional life style will provide for the democratically elected representation of residents on governing boards and program councils. It will mean full participation of "users of services" in the decisions that affect their lives. If we believe in a free and humane society, the life style and governance of our institutions should be based on such belief.

Many retirement homes and communities include persons who have had wide experience in management and program development. It is a foolish waste of human resources not to make use of their competence.

COMMUNITY SERVICE HOMES

We suggest that a variety of living styles should be included in retirement communities, with a mixture of age, ethnic, and cultural groups. Let the homes change their white Anglo-Saxon Protestant mind-set and become multipurpose, multiracial centers of a great variety of community services.

They will then *radiate out to serve many instead of turning in to serve a few*. They'll provide such services as legal and financial counseling, credit unions, health clinics, and rehabilitative therapy. They'll offer psychiatric counseling, "meals-on-wheels," home crafts, and continuing educational services.

The homes will be lively, inviting places where community groups and older residents gather to pursue creative interests. They'll contain libraries; book and record shops; and employment, placement, and counseling centers. Day-care centers, and drama and choral groups will function in them, providing interaction with groups of all ages.

In some quarters things are already changing. Some perceptive directors of homes, and churchmen on church boards, working with older adults, are initiating policy changes. They are calling for the same degree of self-determination and democratic participation that all groups seek for liberation. A few institutions have changed bylaws and constitutions to provide for democratic governance. Others are moving in this direction but need encouragement and some pushing. Much, much more experimentation in this for this new age is needed.

There is also the need to experiment with new styles of flexible organization. This means avoiding the large, bureaucratic structures that are so expensive to maintain and often so hard to change.

Life Style V: The Capacity to Be Outraged About the State of Misery, Powerlessness, and Poverty in the World

Massive and dramatic efforts have to be made to overcome the terrible weight of our own apathy. Collective action is the only way to involve isolated and alienated old people. We will encourage and minister to one another in the process.

A growing number of us are challenging the state of marginal or actual poverty and powerlessness in which most are forced to live. Too long we have endured loss of status and decline in income in the so-called "golden years."

Our outrage is properly directed against agencies that purport to serve our needs: nursing homes without nurses, Medicare without a dollar for *prevention* of illness, retirement homes with admission fees of ten thousand dollars minimum and no say about how our life's savings will be spent. But outrage must not be directed solely against our powerlessness. More than our own interests are at stake.

Too long our nation has been indifferent to the hunger and deprivation of little children. Too long has it neglected the terrible misery of the slums and their captive residents. Also often ignored are students who want to eradicate poverty and pollution and reform the system of American higher education. The mounting despair and disengagement of these students across the country could be even more ominous for the future than student violence.

This life style of outrage means that many of us will become radicalized and militant rather than "mellow." We will take risks and responsibility for:

organizing ourselves for corporate action;

becoming advocates for other powerless groups, especially children and young people;

forming coalitions with the young and with others seeking liberation.

GRAY PANTHERS ON THE PROWL

Carol Mackenzie

Grass-roots action is the hallmark of the Gray Panthers. Carol Mackenzie, of the national headquarters, in Philadelphia, vividly evokes the kinds of local activities devised by members around the country.

Gray Panthers have been on the prowl nationwide for over six years. As they prey on the various existing forms of ageism, they deftly uncover issues of trenchant public interest: health care, housing, income security, utilities, crime. The following portray Gray Pantherism at its sharpest in the United States today.

Not many physicians are aware that in 1973 there were two American Medical Association conventions, both in New York City. On June 23, 1973, Maggie Kuhn convened Gray Panthers health colleagues in an AMA Alternative Convention entitled "Do We Need a National Health Service?" Physicians, nurses, health planners, union representatives, social workers, and community organizers addressed the politics of health care and strategies for change. Participants listened enthusiastically to what Gray Panthers want in a National Health Service and helped themselves to a free health lunch. This year, while the AMA congratulates itself on a cavalier motion in support of National Health Insurance, the Gray Panthers have already joined the forces of their Health Service allies in Washington, D.C. Health care for people not for profit may well be one of the biggest battles yet on Capitol Hill.

Consumers face formidable barriers when they attempt to find out information about doctors. In late 1974 the New York Gray Panthers organized a mass survey of doctors on Manhattan's West Side, an area that has a high concentration of older people. Yellow pages in hand, the inquirers manned twenty-five telephones at a local television station and began calling. Does the doctor: take Medicaid? make house calls? charge more than Medicare will reimburse? have after-hour coverage? As the survey progressed, it was confronted with the limitations of publishing even a concise directory, for a small part of Manhattan, that would be out of date in a matter of months. In the spring of 1976 it was decided to produce instead a report that would summarize and interpret the data and extrapolate its significance in terms of the over-all unavailability of doctors. Since then the Gray Panthers have joined several groups to initiate legislative challenges to the no-advertising laws enacted by the medical profession, which restrict consumer access to information about doctors. Someday consumers may really be able to find out whether "the doctor is in."

Pharmacists came under similar scrutiny by the Portland, Oregon, Gray Panthers, who determined to assess the effectiveness of the year-old generic drug law passed by the 1976 Oregon state legislature. More than two thirds of the nearly one hundred area pharmacists contacted in the Gray Panthers telephone survey volunteered no information when asked whether there is a lower-priced, generic equivalent to three brand-name drugs. The Gray Panthers drug-secrecy demolitionists now plan to press their state legislature to require pharmacists to inform consumers verbally.

The Portland Gray Panthers will not be guilty of discriminating against pharmacists. The Oregon "watchcats" launched a stringent campaign in August 1976 on Portland-area nursing homes. Teams of Gray Panthers make unannounced inspections of the facilities, checking for odors, quality of food, isolation of patients, physical restraints, sedation, and availability of staff. The Portland Gray Panthers will review the reports, make public any problems, and confer with the state health department. The Oregon Gray Panther partnership is headed by youthful law graduate Ron Wyden and octogenarian Ruth Haefner, co-conveners of the Portland Gray Panthers. This is what the Gray Panthers like to call age and youth in action.

There is in this country a still disenfranchised minority called pension losers: workers who lose pensions by leaving a job before age fifty-five or who are denied pensions from new employers because they are over fifty-five. The Springfield, Massachusetts, Gray Panthers Pension Reform Committee has initiated its own plan for dealing with the present "caviar to cat food" system of so-called retirement security. The group has circulated petitions calling attention to the fact that the Employee Retirement Income Security Act (ERISA) of 1974, also known as the Pension Reform Act, leaves thousands of workers who lost pensions before 1974 with no legal recourse. The Gray Panther pension reformers continue to make themselves heard at ERISA hearings and through successive revisions of their handy pension-rights booklet. They have also established a connection with the newly formed Pension Rights Center, in Washington, D.C. The Springfield Gray Panthers will keep fanning the flames of corporate conscience in hopes of obtaining full pension rights soon.

Heat or eat? The people of Kansas City, Missouri, were in no mood for mere technical explanations of their high utilities bills last winter. Frustrated by utility consumer channels, the Kansas City Gray Panthers convened a meeting on February 16, 1977, of some five hundred bristling consumers who took turns at the podium to unload two hours' worth of their complaints on the utilities commissioners. The meeting received considerable press and provided a highly charged challenge to utility companies' profits in every city.

"Who is the mugger?" New York Gray Panthers joined with other senior groups on February 24, 1977, to ask this question in a first-of-its-kind program held at the New York Ethical Culture Society. Participants pursued several "dark alleys" for seniors in American society, seeking out the "mugger" in such areas as health, housing, utilities, employment, income, and crime. Afternoon workshops dealt with crime itself as a community problem, including ways in which senior citizens and young people can cooperate to combat crime. The New York Gray Panthers plan to continue such effective public programs to arm consumers in confronting the "mugger."

How do local Gray Panthers get started? In March 1977 St. Louis, Missouri, Gray Panthers Jan McGillick and Helen Hunnicutt decided they would have to do more than call a meeting. Instead they mustered a full-fledged array of supporters, skits, and even a state senator. Participants were roused with the Gray Panthers' song and a swift agenda of happenings. Speakers asserted the need for educated activism and for improved health-care delivery. These topics were then dramatized by unabashed local Gray Panther talent in *The Rats Are Eating Grandma* and *The Senile Shuffle*. The entire extravaganza took place in just two hours and attracted plenty of public attention and new members for the out-going Gray Panthers of St. Louis.

"Where do you expect us to live—in tents?" This query of Gray Panther Anne McDougall to Mayor Tom Bradley set in motion a spectacular demonstration with hundreds of people and tents strategically pitched in the heart of downtown Los Angeles on June 28, 1977. The Gray Panthers' "Tent City" became a colorful dramatization of the need for affordable housing, especially for senior citizens, in the city of Los Angeles. Delegations from dozens of senior citizens' groups, tenant organizations, and groups from black, Chicano, and Asian communities participated in the rally, led by megaphone-wielding Rose Marshall, chairperson of the Gray Panthers' Housing Coalition. The mayor, city council, and board of supervisors could hardly ignore the repeated demands of the "canvas coalition": quality low-cost housing, rent regulation, housing rehabilitation, and the right to housing in the area of one's choice. Tenting, anyone?

"Keep on, keeping on" would be an apt theme for the un-flinching consciousness raisers of the East Bay, California, Gray Panthers. The group has been meeting twice monthly since March 1976 to dig into the gritty aspects of aging that can wear even Gray Panthers down a bit. Dauntless discussions have followed such topics as: loss of spouse, sex and sociability, physical impairments, senility among one's peers, and the perils of volunteerism. Personal experiences are freely aired and challenged. The goal of the Gray Panther rap sessions is to generate greater personal energy among the participants and other Gray Panthers to "keep on."

PART VII

THE STRUGGLE OVER RETIREMENT

"THE COMPANY TELLS ME I'M TOO OLD"

James A. McCracken

Soon to be "put out to pasture," the author contemplates the possible virtues of stamp collecting, woodworking, and chasing the blue jays. James McCracken was a magazine editor for twenty-six years.

I was a young man, once. Now I'm not. Now I'm an old man. Leastwise, the company I work for tells me I'm old. I'm almost sixty-five. In a couple of months they're going to retire me. Put me out to pasture.

What's old? Folks sixty-five don't think sixty-five's old. It's the young people who think sixty-five's creaking age. Once I thought anybody sixty-five was ready for the grim reaper. Now? Well, now I'm hoping I've got a few years left, anyway. I find that life doesn't become less precious as you get older. I keep jumping out of the way of cars just as keenly as I did twenty, thirty years ago. And when lightning's flashing around in the sky, I don't go outside looking at it, thinking, *Well, if it hits me, it hits.*

There was a time, a long time ago, when I used to watch my old man when he was sixty-five or so. He'd sit in his chair just thinking about getting up. He'd run his hands up the arms of the chair a little way, brace, and push. And he'd stand up. Well, he was up. He'd stand for a moment, put his hands on the back of his hips. He'd still be bent over a little bit. But then he'd straighten up and be off about his business. Maybe his business was going to the bathroom or into the kitchen to ask my mother what was for supper. My old man had a belly. And jowls. They hung down from his cheeks like his face was made of soft wax that was beginning to melt and run down.

I can remember. Maybe I'd be sitting in a chair, too. I'd watch my old man get himself started. Then I'd get up. Quick. No creaks or grunts. I was young. I had a young man's body. My hair was dark and thick. Plenty of it. I tried to picture myself old, like my old man. No way. I wasn't *ever* going to look like that. No soft belly for me. I was good-looking. I knew I'd always be good-looking. Even when I was old. No wrinkles. No soft white wax running down to my collar. Maybe my hair would turn white. But I wouldn't go bald. I wouldn't sag. I wouldn't groan when I sat down. Or when I got up. I'd do it quick. Sit down. Get up.

I always thought it was my old man's fault for getting old. He could have run a mile or two every day. He could have lifted weights or played tennis or worked out at a gym.

I look back now. My old man's gone, of course. And in a sense I'm him. I wake up in the morning. I lie there. Well, I haven't got a headache. My toes work. My fingers move. So I didn't have a stroke or nothing during the night. Friend of mine, my age, he woke up one morning. Felt same as usual. Only his left leg didn't work. He didn't know it didn't work. He didn't find out until he got out of bed. Left leg didn't work. Left arm didn't work, either. He wondered, *What the hell*. Tried to call his wife. Mouth didn't work. Well, in the hospital they told him he'd had a stroke. Right there in bed. While he was sleeping. It just crept up on him.

Now I get up from a chair like my old man did. And then I stand there. Got a little crick in my back. Just a little one. So. There's some grass to cut. And I ought to fix that venetian blind. My wife's been after me for two weeks to fix it. Aw, I've been cutting grass and fixing things all my life, it seems. Something's always got to be fixed or moved or trimmed or hauled. That's what keeps you young, they say. That doesn't keep you young. Always doing things. That gets you old. I stand and think about things like that. My wife's in the kitchen, clattering around. I hear the pots and pans banging. I go in. "What's for supper?" I say. Just like my old man used to.

Now, though, I'm going to get retired. It's like I've been in a corral, fenced in with all the other working horses. Along comes a man and he slips a halter over my head. He takes ahold of the halter and he leads me out of the corral toward a long white fence. I've seen that fence many a time. I've glanced over there at a couple of old horses off there in the pasture. They move slow. They raise their heads slow, then lower them and go back to grazing. Old horses. Old folks' home. A condo in Florida, maybe St. Petersburg. Sit on a green bench in the sunshine. So the man leads me over to the white fence. He opens the gate and pats me on the rump. "It's green pastures for you, old fella," he says. He takes the halter off, walks back to the gate. Closes it. And there I am.

That's what my company says. They hold a little party. Not much. I'm not a big shot. All the younger ones, they say, "Boy, are you lucky. No more getting up early to rush to work. Play golf, work at hobbies. Don't do nothing if you don't want to." They laugh and clap me on the back. They sort of look at me. Yeah. It would be nice to have some time off, all right. But they sure wouldn't want to be old. What can you do when you're old? Striving's gone, ambition's gone. Competition's gone. Challenge's gone. This old man here, his road's all downhill now. Down and out.

So I'm a Golden Ager now. The golden years, they say. Maybe they mistake rust for gold. The hinges get rusty. The bones creak, but there isn't any oil that's going to fix them. Do I mind? Well, it'd be nice to move around quick again. It'd be nice to shed this fat and these jowls. And grow a little more hair. I don't much like being bald. I got a few hairs left on top. So I massage them and comb them around a little bit. There aren't many, but they're all I got. And do I hate to sort of creak and groan a little? Well, I guess so. But you know something? As long as my joints creak, they're still moving. It's when they stop that I'll have me some problems.

I been reading some about how you should prepare for old age. For retirement. Prepare for the golden years. Develop hobbies. Take up woodworking or arts and crafts. Get yourself a little corner of the house where you can set yourself up a shop and do something. Well, what? I collected postage stamps when I was a kid. I collected them for about six months.

I didn't have enough money to buy an album, so I kept the stamps in an old shoe box. Well, one day I was home from school, sick. My old man was at work and my mother had to go down the street to buy some groceries. I didn't have anything to do but be sick, so I was looking at my stamps. They weren't doing any good lying around in the shoe box. I wanted to display them. We had a big sort of picture window. I got busy and mixed up some paste—flour-and-water paste. My mother was proud of that picture window. It looked out on a little garden she kept. I figured I'd pretty things up even more.

I guess I had three, maybe four hundred stamps. I pasted up the back of every one of those stamps one at a time, and one at a time, I stuck them onto that picture window. It was some sight. You couldn't see anything but postage stamps. I got the whole job done before my mother came home. I knew it would surprise her, but I didn't know it would surprise her so much.

I rushed off to bed and was lying there, sick, when she came home. Downstairs. I was upstairs. I could hear her humming around the kitchen while she put things away. The window was in the parlor (we didn't call them living rooms in those days). I heard her walking from the kitchen into the hall. First the footsteps stopped. Then the humming. There was silence. I was chuckling and laughing to myself, lying there in bed.

Suddenly there was a scream, then a sort of yelp. Then my name came up. *"James!"* (I was usually "Jimmy" around the place, but when somebody became angry, I became *"James!"*) *"James!"* my mother hollered. I stopped laughing and giggling. She wasn't happy with what I had done? Where she got the hairbrush so fast I'll never know, but she did. First she got it, then I got it.

I spent the next month scraping stamps and paste off that window. I never collected stamps again.

I tried woodworking. I bought a long pine board and cut it down to about four foot long. Foot or fourteen inches wide. I shaped it by planing and sanding. It was going to be a nice table for before the fireplace. And I made legs. I had me quite a time fitting them into the board, but I finally did it. Then I sanded everything until I thought I had a pretty nice table. Then I stained it. And I varnished it. Then I set it up. And you know what? The legs weren't even. I thought I'd got them even, but I hadn't. So I sawed a mite off one leg. It still wobbled. I guess I'd sawed a mite too much. I sawed another one off a touch. That didn't do it, either. That table was about a foot and a half high when I started. I got her down to about six inches, and she *still* wasn't even. Well, she got to look sort of funny. This table, about four foot long, a little over a foot wide. And six inches high. And still not even. My wife snickered a good bit about it. I was half mad and the other half determined. But sometimes I could see that it did look sort of odd. Finally those legs got down to little nubbins. Like about an inch and a half high. She just barely cleared the carpet. *And she still wobbled.*

We ended up with a nice big fire in the fireplace one night. The stain and the varnish sort of smelled up the house for a while. But I got that table down to even. When she was all burned out and down to ashes, I spread them out on the hearth. Spread them out all nice and smooth. Now she lay level. She didn't wobble anymore. I never tried woodworking anymore, either.

So now I been sort of practicing up for retirement. I sit around the house on weekends, pretending I'm retired. What'll I do this morning? Well, now. There's grass to be cut. Hell, there's *always* grass to be cut. Something new is what I want. A project. My wife says, "Well, then, how about washing the windows?" I've *washed* those windows. My wife's washed those windows. That glass started out years ago being about a quarter of an inch thick. It's been washed so many times, one more washing and you're likely to be washing air. No more glass.

One Wednesday morning we had a hard snowstorm. I couldn't get to work. Maybe twenty years ago I could have. But back then I was racing. I was competing. But I'm not now. The race is run. I didn't win. I didn't lose, either. Just came out sort of even, I guess. Anyhow, toward noon the snow began to melt, and my wife, she says, "How about taking me shopping? I got shopping to do." That'd be a project. She's always telling me about seeing other old fellows down to the supermarket with their wives. So we got into the car, spun the wheels around for a while, and drove down to the village. We got a cart and went shopping. I looked around. Because of the snowstorm, there weren't many people in the store. Just some old wives and their old men. I looked at the old men. Not so old. Maybe like me. The old men, they generally shoved the cart around while their wives studied the shelves. They'd pick up a can of soup, study the label, and either put the can back or put it in the cart. The old men, they'd follow their wives with their eyes. They'd stand and stare. Like tired old horses. Their eyes sort of looked blank. Like there wasn't much going on inside. The wheels had almost stopped turning.

We wheeled around a corner. My wife was going to attack a new aisle. I looked over to one side. There was an old man with his cart. But he was bent way over the handle. He was standing on the ground but his head was darn near in the food. I looked at him and I thought, *Thank God I'm not him.* That old man—he wasn't much older than me—he had arthritis of the back so bad he was bent double. That shopping trip hadn't been much up to that point, but now it was important. It made me mighty thankful. I might be pretty old but I could still stand up straight. The old man swiveled his head out of the food. His eye caught mine. I sort of shook my head in sympathy. You sure got a bad break, friend, I seemed to say. All of a sudden he got embarrassed. And he straightened up! He straightened right up. As straight as I was standing. You know something? There wasn't a thing wrong with him. He was just so bored and fed up he couldn't think of any-thing else to do but lean over something. That's what that old man was doing. I got hold of my wife and we finished up that shopping trip in a hurry, checked out, and I haven't been back shopping since.

So what am I going to do in retirement? Well, like I said, the Golden Age advisers, they say plan ahead. I'm not going to do woodworking, that's for sure. And I won't collect stamps. I can cut grass. Maybe I could cut fancy patterns and designs in it. Just for something to do. The neighbors might not like it, the front lawn looking sort of funny with pictures and things sculpted in it. I don't know yet. I could polish and wax the car. I haven't done that much. The old bus could stand some cleaning. I could work on the engine. But if I did that, I'd sure fix it so she'd never run right again. I'm just not mechanical inclined.

Speaking of mechanical. Once a friend of mine thought he'd teach me how to do my own engine work. My wife and I didn't have much money and we sure had an old car. Always something busting in it. So, to begin, my friend took a carburetor apart. With me watching, of course. And he put it back together again. With me still watching every move. It was the carburetor out of my car. So I learned how to do that. He put the thing back in the car, hooked her up, and she ran perfect. I didn't want to lose my new talent, so the next Saturday, I took the carburetor apart myself. I had a little trouble, of course. That was only natural. But not too much. But then I started to put it back together. That was sure one bad mistake. I should have left it apart. I worked all Saturday morning and well into the afternoon. I'd get her together and have three parts left over. I'd take her down, put her together, and have five parts left. And not the same parts as the first time. I could have made *two* carburetors with all the things I had lying around. Finally, I sort of stuffed everything inside the case and shoved it all together. Something sort of gave. I left it all lying there on the bench and hustled to the telephone to call my friend.

His telephone rang. My friend's daughter answered. She was about eighteen. She was nice and sweet as she could be. "Mommy and Daddy," she said, "have gone away for a week's vacation." I started to cuss out my friend for abandoning me. The girl started to cry. I had to take that carburetor down to a garage on Monday morning for them to fix it. I had to *walk* down, about two miles, because the car sure couldn't run. A smart-aleck mechanic asked me what fool kid had been playing with the auto engine. I told him it was my wife. I missed a day's work and a day's pay. I had to bum a ride the next day while the mechanic came up to the house and put the carburetor back in the car. My wife missed shopping and a bridge game. Neither of us was speaking happy for a couple of days. And it cost me nine bucks! Mechanical inclined? Not me. I never let my friend touch the engine in my car again. I never touched it again, either.

You know how I look at planning for retirement? I look at it, forget it! I didn't plan my career when I was working my way through life. It just happened, and I went along with it. I figure, things come up. You got to cut the grass. It always grew while I was working. It's not going to stop now. Things bust. Maybe I can learn to fix them. Maybe not. I have to be careful about that, though. In retirement I'm sure not going to be able to afford a group of auto mechanics and plumbers and carpenters falling over each other fixing what I mess up. But I'll try. Like fixing a leaking faucet. Trouble is, my wife always could fix leaking faucets better than I could. Well, I'll watch her and sort of supervise. If it isn't right, I'll make her fix it over again. That'll kill some time.

And blue jays! I'll chase blue jays. We got a bird feeder, and those big, blustery birds are always chasing the little ones away so they can glutton themselves on our sunflower seeds. And I'll throw rocks at the neighbor's dog. He always comes over onto our lawn to do his morning business. He does it while I'm at work. Now I'll be home. That dog's going to find some other lawn. Like his own, maybe.

My wife says she'll find things for me to do. She says she's *got* to. She says it sort of franticlike. She says if she doesn't—well, she's got a cousin in California she hasn't seen in years. She never did like that cousin, but she says maybe she's just misjudged her. She says she'll go visit her cousin for a couple of years. She'll get to like that cousin, maybe even learn to love her—that's what my wife says—even if it kills her. My wife's kidding, of course. She wouldn't do that. But if she does, she's got a surprise coming. I'm going with her. It's a man's place to protect his wife. Whether she needs protecting or not.

AGEISM IN EMPLOYMENT MUST BE ABOLISHED

Harriet Miller

The dynamic executive director of the American Association of Retired Persons (AARP) makes a powerful case that "Forcing a person to retire solely because he or she has reached an arbitrary age is no different from denying a person a job solely because of race, religion, or sex."

The American Association of Retired Persons, the National Retired Teachers Association, and Action for Independent Maturity, which I represent, now have more than 10 million members. Retirement age and policies affecting retirement are of great interest to many of our members, as is age discrimination in employment, a subject that must be included in any discussion of retirement.

Let me state at the outset that our associations are not opposed to retirement. We are in favor of *voluntary* retirement, with freedom of choice for all who prefer to remain employed and are capable of working, regardless of age.

Today millions of older people in the United States are victims of age discrimination in employment. Mandatory retirement practices help to put the stamp of respectability on age discrimination. These practices, together with common acceptance of false beliefs about older workers, have created an employment climate that denies equality of opportunity to able and willing men and women not only in their sixties and seventies but often in their fifties and increasingly in their forties. Where racism and sexism no longer can be practiced openly to deny people jobs, ageism flourishes.

Ageism in employment must be abolished not only because it is economically unsound for this nation but because, in a society professing commitment to equality of opportunity, it is wrong.

Ageism in employment includes mandatory retirement and the abuses committed in its name. Forcing a person to retire solely because he or she has reached an arbitrary age is no different from denying a person a job solely because of race, religion, or sex. Forced retirement, by any name, is denial of employment.

National surveys tell us that there are 4 million people over sixty-five, who are unemployed or retired, who want to work. These people have no protection under the Age Discrimination in Employment Act. Most have no hope of ever finding a job.

There are many more under sixty-five who have been forced to accept early retirement as the only alternative to unemployment. These days, we hear a great deal about trends toward earlier retirement, usually in the glowing context of increased leisure for the increasingly young elderly. We rarely hear about the growing number of people who are unwilling participants in that life of leisure (and reduced income) which has been forced upon them by employers eager to push them out.

Recently the *News Bulletins* of our associations carried a column inviting members to send us examples of personal experiences with age discrimination. Thousands of letters have resulted. The great majority deal with mandatory retirement and unfair treatment by employers and unions. Let me quote from just one letter at this time:

"In January of 1975 Chrysler Corporation's top officials made a decision to try and get their executives and salaried personnel, age fifty-five and over, to retire. . . . This was to be a 'voluntary' retirement and 'a once-in-a-lifetime deal' for those involved. . . .

"We (in personnel) were told that each person was to be approached carefully so as not to make it look like we were forcing the person to retire. He was to be given a letter, very cleverly written by corporate lawyers, which the person was to sign, saying he voluntarily retired. In the letter the person was told that due to financial conditions there might have to be many more layoffs and that his job could not be guaranteed. This special retirement would never be offered again. . . .

"Little did I know that it applied to me. Suddenly I was called into my superior's office and told that immediately I no longer had anyone reporting to me. I was told that my position had been eliminated and I was given a clerk's job. When I said I couldn't type, I was told to handwrite all the paperwork. After being a supervisor for many years in this department, this was very embarrassing to me. . . . I might add that I had a top rating in the management development rating system and was at the top of my salary grade, making $25,000 a year.

"To accept the . . . demotion with its loss in retirement benefits, insurance, etc. or to retire with my present insurance and special retirement rate were my two choices. To avoid affecting my Social Security future payments, I chose to retire at age fifty-six although I could not afford it. . . . My house is not paid for and you know what is happening to the cost of living. . . .

"I am only one of hundreds of executives, supervisors, and salaried personnel who were forced out in this manner. . . ."

This member identified his employer as the Chrysler Corporation. We have no wish to single out one employer, so I am attaching a list of others who thus far have been identified by our members: Mobil, Western Electric, McDonnell Douglas, Sears, Seagram Distilleries, a number of banks, and many other employers—including the federal government.

This example is intended to illustrate the abuses that regularly flow from employer-controlled "retirement." In reality, such "retirement practices" constitute nothing other than selective firing of older workers.

Often when involuntary retirement is discussed, there are ageist overtones based on the mythology that older workers really are not as able as younger workers, and if they are to be utilized, they need special treatment.

The letter of invitation to appear at this hearing refers to "efforts to match job to age of worker, where applicable, use of flexi-time, job sharing, and other personnel practices to better meet the needs of workers."

We would agree that these are laudable goals and ought to be pursued, but our position is that they ought to be pursued for the good of the total population, for everyone who would benefit, regardless of age, and not just for older workers.

To be sure, some older workers have disabilities. So do some younger workers. But there is research to prove that older workers on the whole are just as able as younger workers; have as good, if not better, attendance records; are just as productive; and have very positive attitudes toward their work (1972 survey conducted by New York State Commission on Human Rights). That is to say, able older workers need and want no special privileges. What they want is equality of opportunity and a fair chance to compete.

Let us indeed seek to insure employment opportunities for workers of all ages who are less able, but let us not be distracted from concentrating on achieving equity for able workers regardless of age.

In our society, special arrangements may be a long time coming. Rigidity of thought and inflexibility based on habit often constitute major barriers to change. We have become accustomed to educational tracks and career ladders and mandatory retirement—all of which are conveniences for institutions, not for the individual. Such inflexible practices restrict individual options and opportunities at any age, and they become increasingly intolerable for the older person who seeks to remain a contributing member of society.

Unfortunately, the planners and managers seem incapable of fully exploiting such inventions as the electric light and the computer to free people from obsolete patterns of education, work, and leisure. As a result, the working wife whose dishwasher needs service cannot get a repairman to call her home on evenings or weekends; the assembly-line worker who yearns to tend his garden is put on overtime during the growing season; the student soon to become too old for graduate school is forced to keep on with full-time education although she desperately needs a year to work and earn money; and the involuntarily retired engineer looks in vain for some kind of work that will get him away from mowing the lawn and help pay his property taxes.

Yes, many older people would benefit from more flexible arrangements. So would the whole of society. Among other things, the distribution of work among available and willing people could become more equitable, as well as more efficient.

Whenever mandatory retirement is discussed, the matter of job distribution always surfaces. There are still those who believe in the folklore that says old people must step aside to make room for the young, and when jobs are scarce, age must be used to allocate jobs.

If age is to be used as a basis for distributing jobs to workers, then I would suggest that we establish a lottery and draw numbers. This year, if thirty-eight is the age drawn, everyone aged thirty-eight will be thrown out of work. Next year, perhaps it will be twenty-nine, or fifty-two. Such a lottery would be precisely as equitable as firing people who are, say, sixty-five or refusing to hire them at, say, fifty-five.

There will be those who argue that the 38-year-olds have dependents, mortgages, and other obligations. Today we must recognize that many older people have similar responsibilities, and their numbers are growing. Not only do some older people have children to educate, a good many have mortgages to pay, and an increasing number are concerned with the problems of aging parents. With trends toward greater longevity and life-extending technologies, we can expect to see many more families with two generations of retirees.

It was only recently that the prophets of the postindustrial society were anxiously wondering how Americans would cope with the *leisure* that was soon to replace work, as machines and automation took over. Today, thoughtful people must question the wisdom, if not the practicality, of moving at such a headlong pace from a labor-intensive system to an energy-intensive system. While few people really want to bring back the good old days, it is becoming a little less absurd to inquire whether there are some areas where people power might make at least as much sense as automation, if not more. If we must insist on calling individuals "human resources," it seems the least we could do would be to re-evaluate all of the resources available to us in the context of the total needs of our society, and consider whether and where it could be advantageous to have people do the work of machines.

There is no question that the great majority of Americans are opposed to the mandatory retirement of people who want to continue working and are able to do so. Polls by the Louis Harris organization and others provide ample data. The time is ripe for action to correct the abuses and inequities that mandatory retirement has brought about.

In conclusion, I would like to summarize the chief effects of mandatory retirement:

1.   It arbitrarily redistributes jobs, taking work from some and giving it to others solely on the basis of chronological age, thus wrongly depriving willing and able older people of equality of opportunity;

2.   It serves as a convenient substitute for performance evaluation, enabling employers to dismiss without cause a class of employees erroneously regarded as less able;

3.   It provides employers with opportunities to cut costs by substituting cheaper labor for higher-paid, experienced workers (though the apparent savings may be offset by hidden costs of training new workers);

4.   It provides employers with a device for increasing pressures for earlier and earlier "retirement," often cutting short the productive careers of people in their fifties;

5.   It often transfers able and willing workers from payrolls to public support.

Clearly, this list is not dictated by the best interests of older people. With continuing inflation, few people finding themselves involuntarily retired today can enjoy a prospect of financial security. It is little wonder that growing numbers are challenging the laws and practices they find harmful and unjust. The future, we believe, will see many more such challenges.

Mandatory retirement and other forms of age discrimination in employment must go. Freedom to continue working must not be curtailed at an arbitrary age. Able people, irrespective of age, who prefer work to retirement must be free to compete for jobs on the basis of ability. Therefore we recommend:

> That the inclusion of a mandatory retirement age in any employment agreement, contract, or benefit plan be prohibited by law;
>
> That the statutory upper age limit of sixty-five in the Age Discrimination in Employment Act of 1967 be abolished; and
>
> That age be added as a protected category under Title VII of the Civil Rights Act.

THE WILLY LOMAN COMPLEX

Albert Rosenfeld

"Retirement syndrome" blues can be fatal if you allow them to be, explains ace science reporter Albert Rosenfeld.

Jacob Jensen (a fictitious name, invented by his psychiatrist) was, by almost anyone's standards, a happy and successful man. He was the second-highest-paid executive in the company where he had started as a stock boy, right there in the same town, some thirty-seven years ago. He had a lovely wife, lovely children and grandchildren, plenty of money, and excellent health, and he was a respected figure in his community. Now, suddenly, as he approached sixty, his board chairman had given him a stark choice: early retirement or transfer to South America.

Jensen had never given a thought to retirement. There had always seemed plenty of time to get ready for that distant event. The quiet confrontation with the chairman of the board had so unnerved him, however, that he soon found himself in the office of Dr. Herbert Klemme, at the Menninger Foundation, for psychiatric counseling. Klemme, recognizing that Jensen was in serious emotional trouble, advised his employers that either of the alternatives they were proposing would be psychologically disastrous. The company relented and gave Jensen a lesser—though still important —job, and two years to prepare for retirement.

Even under these revised circumstances the patient got worse instead of better. Nine months later, writing Jensen's case history, Dr. Klemme summarized: "Mr. Jensen is . . . agitatedly seeking release from the pain he is experiencing. Because of the severity of his distress, I referred him to the very competent psychiatric facilities available in his local community. He is severely depressed and at this writing suicide is a definite possibility. . . . In my opinion he is also a prime candidate for a severe debilitating physical illness: stroke, acute coronary heart disease, cancer. . . ."

Do many people, in real life, commit suicide for such reasons— as the fictional Willy Loman did, under somewhat similar circumstances, in *Death of a Salesman?* Yes, they unfortunately do. A decade ago Dr. Sidney Cobb, of the University of Michigan (now at Brown), kept track, for two years, of 100 automobile workers who had been laid off from their jobs. Their suicide rate was thirty times the rate that would normally be expected. They were, moreover, afflicted with a considerably higher-than-average incidence of nearly all the major diseases. These were younger men than Jensen, and their unemployment was only temporary—though it may have seemed like forever to them, and the emotional effects were equally profound.

Case histories such as Jensen's are all too common.

But it should be emphasized that they are not *typical.* Nor are they as common as was once believed. Dr. Robert N. Butler, director of the new National Institute on Aging, says in his Pulitzer Prize-winning book, *Why Survive? Being Old in America,* "There is much mythology built into the notion of an emotional and physical condition known as the 'retirement syndrome,' characterized by anxiety and depression. People who retire do not automatically develop declining mental and physical health. What social-science studies we have indicate such generalizations to be a fallacy." An intensive study made in 1957—at McGill University by James S. Tyhurst, Lee Salk, and Miriam Kennedy—of several hundred pensioners of the Bell Telephone Company of Canada revealed that most retirees actually were able to make satisfactory adjustments. And, according to Dr. Bernice L. Neugarten, of the University of Chicago, writing fourteen years later, "Three-fourths of the persons questioned in a recent national sample reported that they were satisfied or very satisfied with their lives since retirement."

Many people, in fact, seem to become happier, even healthier, after retirement than before—especially those who didn't care all that much about their jobs anyway and who have other interests they had always wanted more time to pursue. A retiree often has more opportunity to take care of himself, to eat and exercise properly, to get enough rest, to enjoy play and leisure without guilt, and still derive much satisfaction from continuing to work fruitfully—though, preferably, not too competitively. Most long-lived people *do* continue to work at something; it can be physical, mental, or both. Some people find themselves working even harder after retirement than before. Their attitude toward what they do is all-important. Mark Twain used to insist that he never worked, only played. Challenged by friends who knew how many hours he spent writing, he would reply that writing was *not* work.

Even though the human organism does deteriorate with age, many people in their later years take up sports and other vigorous activities they never tried before, developing new skills, new muscular strength and physical endurance, new powers of coordination. Even sexual powers, though gradually diminishing, are still present and employable essentially throughout life. In many cultures, says Dr. Jean Houston, director of the Foundation for Mind Research, old age is *expected* to be the most satisfying stage of life—as with Browning's Rabbi Ben Ezra: "Grow old along with me!/The best is yet to be,/The last of life, for which the first was made."

New powers of mind may also be developed late in life—the ability to concentrate, to meditate, to turn off unwanted thoughts, to expand awareness and consciousness. In our society, says Dr. Butler, "we rarely find anyone paying . . . attention to the growth of wisdom in the individual" with age. Though people are slower to learn as they age, their intellects are generally unimpaired, and they are perfectly capable of new learning of every variety. Many of the brain's cells do die as we age. Even so, it's a cliché that we never use more than a fraction of our potential brain power. Most people in our culture have been trained mainly to use the left side of the brain—the hemisphere that deals with rational thought, logic, verbal skills, and the kind of mathematics computers can do, too—while neglecting the right hemisphere, which governs visual, spatial, integrative, creative functions and the kind of information processing that no known computer can yet simulate. (See "Left-Brain, Right-Brain," by Roger W. Sperry, *SR*, August 9, 1975.) While some of the brain's capacities may atrophy through disuse or never be developed at all through lack of stimulation, what remains may still provide new abilities, new insights, new aesthetic appreciation. Pianist Artur Rubinstein is still playing brilliantly at eighty-nine—some critics believe with greater depth and sensitivity than ever. Grandma Moses didn't start painting until she was seventy-four, and gained increasing worldwide fame for her creative efforts until her death, at the age of 101.

It should not be surprising that, in the absence of any chronic organic disease, a positive outlook on life can have a positive effect on both our physical and mental functioning. Nor, in view of what we now know of the intimate interrelations between "mind" and "body," should it surprise us that the opposite is also true—that many retirees, like Jacob Jensen, do not successfully make the transition.

After studying long-lived people in a diversity of cultures, Dr. David Gutmann, of the University of Michigan, concluded that "active mastery . . . is the ego state most clearly associated with longevity." Not power over others—but a sense of being master of one's own life and circumstances. In another study of longevity, covering 2,000 subjects over a period of nineteen years, Dr. Robert Samp, of the University of Wisconsin Medical School, noted that an important ingredient was a continuing interest in the future.

When these two factors are missing, their opposites—helplessness and hopelessness—tend to take over. Thus the well-known "giving up" syndrome, with its serious physiological consequences. There exist many anthropological accounts of primitive tribes whose members go off and die simply because a powerful shaman has told them they will die, or because they have been cursed by a witch (Elspeth Huxley tells such a story of one of her father's Kikuyu garden boys in Kenya), or because they have learned, in the words of Dr. Jerome D. Frank, of Johns Hopkins, "that they have inadvertently broken a taboo," which causes "a state of panic and excitement leading to death in a few hours." There are also stories of American prisoners of war in Japan, Korea, and Vietnam who gave up in similar fashion. Dr. Barbara B. Brown, in *New Mind, New Body,* tells the story of a convict who was appearing before the parole board, which recommended his immediate release from prison:

> A moment after release was ordered, a court deputy read a summons from another state ordering the prisoner to be transferred to another prison to serve an additional ten years. As the order was read, the prisoner collapsed, dying. My friend, in the next building, arrived within minutes. Resuscitation procedures were instituted immediately, but it took all the resources of experienced medical treatment to recover the patient. There was no heart attack, no asthma

attack, no cerebral stroke; there was, in fact, no physical reason that could be detected in thorough examination to account for the imminent death. The prisoner admitted that he could not face further imprisonment and had simply decided to die.

A classic experiment was done in 1957 by Dr. Curt Richter, of Johns Hopkins. A rat was thrown into a tank of warm water; it swam valiantly for sixty hours before succumbing to total exhaustion. Richter held a second rat in his hand; though it struggled mightily, it could not break his grip and finally stopped trying. At that point Richter dropped the rat into the water. It splashed half-heartedly, rather than swam, for a few minutes, then went down. In Richter's view, he had taught the rat held in his hand to be helpless. And it died, in the water, of sheer helplessness.

What happens, physiologically, to bring about such startling effects?

Back in prehistory, especially before our ancestors learned to fashion weapons, the human individual lived a life fraught with danger at every turn. In order to survive, he had to react instantly to any threat. There was no time to think about what the danger represented or to reason out his alternatives in dealing with it. As a rule, with an attack imminent from either an enemy or a wild beast, he had only two alternatives—to defend himself or to run away: the famous "fight or flight" situation. There had to be built-in biological systems that would alert and energize the body's resources to act with the necessary swiftness. We are the inheritors of the biological systems that still perform today much as they did then—though we can seldom fight or flee. Animals can often get rid of their frustrations by engaging in "displacement activity." A herring gull, for instance, if put in a threatening situation in which it can neither fight nor flee, will start pulling up grass with great energy. We may, of course, take out our frustrations on some innocent third party—but more usually we take them out on ourselves. If it happens frequently or continuously, the result can be any of a whole range of psychosomatic or psychogenic ailments, some of them serious and life-threatening.

Jacob Jensen, faced by his board chairman, probably reacted very much as one of his Pleistocene ancestors might have in the presence of a saber-toothed tiger. The alert signal went instantly from his cerebral cortex to his hypothalamus, the more primitive brain center that controls the autonomic nervous system—with its complex networks of sympathetic and parasympathetic nerves—which also encompasses the endocrine system with all its hormone-secreting glands. His pituitary triggered a whole series of hormone releases—especially the adrenal hormones—affecting almost every organ system in his body. Sugar and stored fats were mustered for the instant use of nerves and muscles. His blood pressure and pulse rate went up. His circulatory and respiratory systems were accelerated. Red blood cells multiplied to supply more oxygen to his cells and carry off the excess of carbon-dioxide wastes. In case of wounds from the expected attack, his healing apparatus and coagulatory chemistry would have to be mobilized. The digestive processes would come to a halt, being postponable in such an emergency. All this and more happened, quickly and spontaneously. Jensen probably tensed up and grew pale. His Pleistocene ancestors would probably have grimaced visibly, even growled. But civilized men in offices cannot behave in that manner.

Another way of describing the fight-or-flight reaction would be to call it a stress reaction. We do not think of it as stress, however, if we discharge it immediately. Besides, as Montreal's Dr. Hans Selye, the world's leading authority on stress, has repeatedly emphasized, a certain amount of stress is necessary to life and health. When it keeps happening, however, and when we cannot cope with it adequately, that is when we *perceive* it as stress. And that is when it begins to do its physiological damage.

Jacob Jensen obviously perceived himself to be in a stressful situation—the permanent loss of his job—that he was helpless to cope with. It meant constantly elevated blood pressure, elevated cholesterol levels (another consequence of stress), a harder-working heart and lungs, overactive glands; in a word, his body was in an abnormal state of constant emergency from which he could find no relief.

In instances such as the sudden death of prisoners and primitive tribesmen, it's been theorized that the passive, giving-up-the-struggle mood activates a parasympathetic reaction—little understood—that slows down a number of body functions, including the heartbeat. That the heartbeat can be slowed to a lethal level can be demonstrated by Dr. Richter's autopsy on one of his drowned rats: the rat's heart was still full of blood that it couldn't pump out fast enough; it had probably suffered heart failure through helplessness, thus was dying anyway before it drowned.

We can begin to see now some of the ways in which mind and body are related and why attitude and mood can have such far-ranging physiological consequences, both positive and negative. "Keep up your spirits," advised Ben Franklin at eighty, "and that will keep up your bodies."

But spirits can be hard to keep up under some circumstances, particularly under the often anxious and troublesome conditions of retirement and aging. If the attitude and mood of older people have a lot to do with their state of health, those attitudes are frequently the result of negative attitudes toward *them* by the rest of society. It's well known that our self-esteem often depends on how we are perceived—or think we are—by others. Most older people are not so fortunate as Jacob Jensen—who had family, friends, money, and other kinds of support to fall back on. Many have only themselves, and very little money or outside support. Dr. Leo E. Hollister, of the Veterans Administration Hospital in Palo Alto, Calif., believes that "unrecognized depression may be a more important problem in old age than organic brain conditions. . . . Poverty, isolation, and some drugs used in treating physical conditions may impair the mental capacity of the aged. Such reversible impairment often is thought to be permanent senility."

Depression, like stress (depression *is,* of course, a form of stress), has a striking effect on brain chemistry. Indispensable to the proper functioning of brain and mind are the substances known as neurotransmitters—those chemicals (notably the catecholamines) that are responsible for transmitting electrical signals across the synaptic gap from one neuron to another. (See "It's Not All in Your Head," by Seymour S. Kety, *SR,* February 21, 1976.) Lowered levels of some of the catecholamines—such as serotonin and noradrenaline—can, in fact, *cause* depression biochemically. Dr. Jay Weiss, of Rockefeller University, has made a special study of the effects of lowered norepinephrine levels in rats. Stress does lower norepinephrine levels to the point where the animal then is simply not able to organize itself to act protectively in a threatening situation; the chemicals necessary to transmit the messages across the nerve synapses are just not there—at least not in sufficient quantities to do the job. The same kind of deprivation could be taking place in those afflicted with the retirement syndrome.

Dr. Frank writes in *Persuasion and Healing* of a northern Australian tribe known as the Murngin. Among the Murngin, "when the theft of a man's soul becomes general knowledge, he and his tribe collaborate in hastening his demise. Having lost his soul, he is already 'half dead.'" Other tribe members perform mourning ceremonies and make clear what they expect. The victim's efforts, under the circumstances, are not to live, but to die.

Before we put down the Murngin as "barbarians," we should look to ourselves. When we force a still-vigorous individual to retire, do we not, in a sense, steal his soul? The more fool he, of course, for permitting his employment to *become* his soul, to be so easily stolen.

MANDATORY RETIREMENT IS DEATH TO PERSONALITY

Hope Bagger

The Gray Panthers' New York stalwart Hope Bagger here challenges an editorial broadcast over the CBS network.

. . . As you know, the age chosen by Bismarck about a hundred years ago was injurious to no one nor to the society of that time, because hardly anyone ever lived to the age of sixty-five anyway.

Today, with the advances in medical technology, the situation is far different. The age chosen in 1976 for the retirement of today's workers would have to be something above one hundred to be equally appropriate and "reasonable."

. . . I simply do not understand your tender concern for the employing group, your assumption that "businesses and other institutions" need to have compulsory retirement so they can use it as a crutch to enable them to "deal with the inevitable decline of aging workers."

Do you know many employers, have you watched them operate? I have had many years of experience in the employment field, both as placement manager and as personnel worker, and I have observed that one of the prime requirements for a successful employer is that he must know of effective and seemingly reasonable ways of getting rid of unwanted workers at any time, at any age, and even when the employee is supposed to be protected by law, unless he has a strong organization to confront the employer and keep him in line. . . .

Another incentive for firing a worker . . . is likely to be purely financial. Since older workers, especially skilled ones, usually become more expensive with years of experience, and as a pension may be imminent, it is likely to be more profitable to dismiss the older person. . . .

BRANDED WITH STIGMA

At age eighty-five, I work constantly with old people. I know how they feel and what happens to them when they are made to feel branded with the stigma of "no longer acceptable to normal society and its affairs. From now on you live on the fringes of the productive world," even though they know themselves to be as valuable as producers at age sixty-six as they were at age sixty-four and earlier. . . .

People who are discriminated against in employment because of age go through many stages: fear of loneliness . . . loss of confidence in oneself and one's society, which can behave so callously; self-doubt—could it be that "they" are right? . . .

There is the loss of dignity . . . loss of status. There is a hatred of feeling useless, a fear of being unwanted, a dread of becoming a burden on others instead of a support. . . .

Where social involvement of any kind remains, life then becomes a struggle to avoid sources of further humiliation. At first one may report for jury duty as ordered by the court. But one soon learns that the rights of citizenship in this area are closed to him after he reaches the age of seventy.

Or suppose an aged person (as the government designates those over sixty-five) applies for credit at a bank, or a credit card. His credentials will not even be examined to see if he is eligible. His age is enough to prove to the bank his incompetence to handle money—unless he is rich enough already that he does not need money or credit. . . .

GAMES, GAMES

And so the more fortunate of the newly deprived and recently impoverished . . . take refuge in the centers set up for them. There they can find companionship of others similarly deprived and uncompensated; often meals which help out in the budget department, whether essential or not; perhaps arts and crafts; and meaningless games, games, games, which serve principally to kill the no longer wanted time. . . .

Of course, these fates do not happen to all of the retirees. Many of them find satisfaction in hobbies or in voluntary work. Thirty per cent find other jobs after retirement, where they are usually exploited and seldom receive the compensation that would be due to the worth of their labors if it could be sold on the open market without legislative interference. . . .

The rich, of course, manage nicely, as they always have. . . . The poor, the poorest, and the nearly poor are in the vast majority of the enforced retirees.

These are the most unfortunate, destitute poor, scrounging around for food and protection against the elements—or doing without—and the almost destitute poor, kept going by welfare. . . . Then there are those who just made do when they had incomes from work but are plunged into poverty when that possibility is withdrawn or reduced. Even Social Security is not adjusted properly for these people. Because their wages were never high enough to permit them to set aside a source of supplementary income for their old age, they are rewarded (?) by being allowed (of course as they deserve!) the most inadequate of the always inadequate Social Security benefits.

And so, what the pro-mandatory-retirement-at-age-65-or-70 advocates are recommending is actually the death not of a person but of a personality: the core and the worth of a human being.

During this past decade a rapidly growing number of these devastated personalities have been revived, and hope is spreading for the salvation of all. . . . The unwilling retirees are no longer accepting the fate of their personalities; they are using their leisure to unite, to organize, to study and think, and to become active for social change.

These recycled, reconstituted old people no longer believe it when they are told that it is their duty to make way for the young —they can see for themselves that this system does not take care of the young any better than it cares for the old. Regaining their self-respect, their courage, and their momentum, they are preparing for battle against the unseen but powerful forces that require so many sacrifices from them.

PART VIII

MOVING TOWARD A BETTER FUTURE:
Promising Programs and Projects

THE AGING ARE DOING BETTER

David Hapgood

Social critic David Hapgood, author of *The Screwing of the Average Man,* finds that older Americans are becoming better organized and winning more political clout.

They are not the best years of our lives. Few among us, past sixty-five or before, view the years after that watershed as "The best . . . , for which the first was made"; most feel that by then the best years are encapsuled in our memories. Our bleak attitudes toward the state of being old, darkened by fear of aging as well as fear of death itself, make this a subject that cannot be discussed in the bread-and-butter terms of, say, the price of eyeglasses. Most of us, in fact, would prefer not to discuss it at all; with the dissolution of the extended family, we have tried to make of ourselves, as elderly, a problem that government is to take care of for us through Social Security, Medicare, and nursing homes, our role being limited to writing the checks. The result of bureaucratized aging is that growing old is no longer a gradual, lifelong process but an overnight transformation that occurs, usually, with forced retirement at age sixty-five.

That solution, if we can so call it, is coming apart under pressures that are just beginning to be felt. America is aging. The ratio is changing between those who are now working and those whom they support through government-financed retirement. Today each person drawing Social Security is backed by more than three people at work paying the payroll tax—fewer than in the past but more than there will be in the future. The fall in the birth rate, plus, at least in the short run, a government-encouraged state of chronic unemployment, means that the number at work will not expand in years to come, while the number beyond working age, as now defined, will continue to increase. The process is well under way; Social Security is already our fastest-growing tax. Assuming, as most do nowadays, that our economy is not going to grow at anything like yesterday's pace, it seems unlikely that working people will accept the cut in their standard of living that will be required if they are to support each retiree at anything above a dog-food diet. (Working people are also screwed by the way the payroll tax is imposed; here, however, we are concerned with the total burden rather than how it is collected.)

If we are not going to shove ourselves out on the ice with our gold watches, then we'll have to try another way—and that means demolishing the watershed of forced retirement at sixty-five and, indeed, rewriting the entire work and retirement rule book. Here economic and humane motives intersect, for breaking the sixty-five barrier is what some people have been advocating for a quite different set of reasons. Dr. Robert N. Butler, whose 1975 book *Why Survive?* is an angry and compelling indictment of how we treat the old, argues that when the old are incompetent, it is usually because society has told them they are; that most cases of senility are reversible; that the old could contribute a lot more to society if we would only let them. Death is inevitable, Butler is saying, but much of the emptiness and futility and misery of age are not. And in fact, society is beginning to improve how it treats the elderly. There is, as we shall see later in this chapter, a growing effort to keep the elderly in the community: not just to bring better and more humane services to those we now neglect—the people in nursing homes, for example—but to gear those services to maintaining a person's social life as well as physical existence.

An important force in breaking the sixty-five barrier will be that growing number of people who are coming to be known as the "young-old." These are people of about fifty-five to seventy-five (though they are not defined by age alone), who straddle the stereotypes of active-middle-aged worker and idle-old retiree. You've seen them in the ads for certain patent medicines and retirement communities: past middle life, they are in good health; fairly well off; free of family responsibilities; some are working, some not; most important, they are active in everything that younger people do. Bernice L. Neugarten, of the University of Chicago, who has written extensively about the young-old, believes this age group will by its own example lead the way in creating what she calls "the age-irrelevant society," in which growing old will no longer be a cause for automatic exile from the larger world. Already the young-old are 15 per cent of the population and the main power behind the growing political clout of the aging.

That clout has been made manifest in the past decade. Although the picture on the tube of old people living in hunger, and often in terror as well, is all too shamefully accurate, it is far from a full portrait of being old in America. In some ways, many of the elderly have done remarkably well. Thanks mainly to raises totaling 52 per cent in 1970–72, Social Security payments have risen faster than the pace of inflation. This makes the aging the only non-rich group in society to have gained ground during our current hard times; the real income of those on Social Security rose while that of the working class and the poor was falling. Money available for services to the elderly under successive versions of the Older Americans Act has steadily increased. The aging succeeded in getting Social Security tied to the cost-of-living index starting in 1975, and in 1974 a minimum income was provided for all the elderly, including those who did not qualify for Social Security, by SSI (Supplemental Security Income), the only kind of welfare reform to see the light of day. Twice in 1975 the aging defeated the administration: once when it tried to cut the scheduled Social Security increase from 8 to 5 per cent and again when it tried to cut back on the food stamps that are essential to the food budgets of many older people. Both victories were lopsided. In perhaps the sincerest of political tributes, the 1976 presidential contender who advocated cutting $90 billion out of the federal budget was careful not to aim his ax anywhere near money earmarked for the aging.

The aging are winning these battles because they are the best organized of the nation's out people: better organized by far than the poor, the black, the female; better than the working class except for some unions in monopoly industries. Though it hardly fits our stereotype of the old—which seems able to withstand any amount of factual contradiction—you have to go to someone with a gun—the weapons contractors or the National Rifle Association—to find lobbying skills equal to those of the organizations that represent the elderly. Even the American Medical Association, with much more financial firepower, lost to the aging in the Medicare struggle of 1965. The successful organizing of the elderly is fairly new. Francis Townsend, a retired doctor, flashed across the 1930s preaching two hundred dollars a month for the old, but the Town-sendites soon dispersed, and scholars solemnly concluded that the aging were incapable of getting it together in any continuing way. Expert opinion to the contrary, the aging have in fact learned to fight back. To determine the ends for which they are fighting, we shall examine two of their organizations. The American Association of Retired Persons is the biggest, richest, and strongest—it even has its own zip code, 20049—and impeccably straight in style. The much smaller Gray Panthers are calculated to lay to rest our remaining stereotypes about old people in America.

The AARP, with its sister organization, the National Retired Teachers Association, claimed in 1976 a membership of close to 9 million that was growing by one hundred thousand a month. Membership is open to those fifty-five or over and dues are two dollars a year. It is by far the largest organization of the elderly; number two is the National Council of Senior Citizens, largely drawn from union members, which has two thousand local affiliates with 3 million members. The AARP has its origins in the insurance business. The National Retired Teachers Association, which dates from 1947, had gotten into selling life insurance to its members through an agent named Leonard Davis. So many non-teachers wanted the insurance, that the AARP was founded, in 1958, primarily to meet that demand. Leonard Davis became a multimillionaire through his Colonial Penn insurance, and AARP has been growing ever since. It is a solid financial success. AARP depends on dues for less than half its income, the rest coming from the various services it sells its members: insurance, of course, but also low-cost drugs and travel. Tying those services to membership solves the free-rider problem, which plagues voluntary associations: AARP will fight for a Social Security increase that you'll get even without being a member; but if you want the services you have to join. Although its origins may show in its style—AARP occasionally comes on like an insurance man lunging across your kitchen table —it has in fact branched far from its roots both in the services it offers and the causes it espouses. Nowadays, indeed, we find the AARP doing battle, often with great efficacy, against some of the major institutions that screw the average man of all ages.

The AARP's mail-order pharmacy has drawn the organization

into conflict with elements of the health industry. Drugs are important to older people. They account for one quarter of all prescription sales, and largely because drugs are not covered by Medicare, they pay close to 90 per cent of the bill. The burden is heavy on those who are poor as well as old: AARP found by sampling its members that they spend an average of 10 per cent of their incomes on drugs, and some spend close to half. With these needs in mind, AARP began selling drugs, both prescription and over-the-counter, by mail at prices that it claims average 40 per cent below the general market level. Money is not the only value. Invalids and those who live far from a pharmacy find it easier to buy by mail, and AARP sells to its members on credit (with, they say, only "infinitesimal" losses). Only members can use the mail-order service, but AARP runs seven cut-rate pharmacies—the first is in Washington, the most recent in Portland, Oregon—where anyone can trade. By 1975 AARP was the largest private mail-order pharmacy in the nation, filling 4 million prescriptions a year. It was forcing the competition to respond. Here, for example, is what a Vermont pharmacy felt compelled to say in a newspaper ad:

> HERE WE GO AGAIN
> AARP Prescription Prices are 20% to 40%
> Below Conventional Pharmacy Prices
> NOW for our own Vermont Senior Citizens
> we will MEET THOSE LOW, LOW PRICES
> No need to send out of State
> No 7 to 10 day delay
> Just present Proof of Purchase Sales Slip
> from AARP, Name and Quantity of
> Medication.

No one can try to sell drugs at low cost without becoming enmeshed in the politics of guilds and especially the brand-name hustle. AARP soon found itself crusading for the right to substitute generic drugs for expensive brand-name equivalents. Members were sent charts showing which cheap generic equals which high-priced brand-name drug, and when members ordered the brand-name, the shipment was accompanied by a slip identifying the generic equivalent. This led to many complaints from the doctors who write the brand-name prescriptions. It also led to drug-industry efforts in several states to ban mail-order operations; all these efforts failed, an outcome that substantiates the belief that many guilds are able to maintain their monopolies only because no one with any clout takes them on. The drug issue converted AARP into a major lobbyist in all the fifty states for freeing the drug business from guild control and price restrictions. By 1975 the industry was on the defensive, and AARP was a major force in the efforts to allow generic substitution and price advertising of drugs.

The AARP provides a range of advocacy services through which members can get help in their struggles against one or another institution. In two cases government is the antagonist. AARP recruits and trains volunteers to give free tax advice to their elderly peers. The elderly cannot understand the deliberate complexities of the tax code any better than anyone else; and most cannot afford to pay for expert help; so about half the elderly tax-payers overpay the IRS. The AARP's forty-five hundred volunteers in 1975 helped two hundred thousand people with their returns, at a saving of at least fifteen dollars each—the minimum cost of hiring help—plus an unknown amount in overpayments that were avoided. For those who get caught in the paper gears of government programs, there is Teresa Napoli. Napoli, who used to be known on Capitol Hill as a particularly formidable caseworker for former Congressman Albert Thomas of Texas, now exercises her considerable talents as an ombudsperson for AARP. Her office gets 300–350 letters a week from people entangled in Social Security, food stamps, or Medicare. As Napoli says, neither the elderly client nor the local bureaucrat knows the intricate rules that govern those programs, and therefore many lose benefits to which they are entitled. Napoli does know the rules, and her day is spent calling agency heads to reverse injustices inflicted at lower levels; whether the agencies will behave better in other cases because of her intervention is impossible to say. For members who have been stung in the marketplace, AARP's Washington headquarters runs a consumer assistance center, which in 1974 handled more than four thousand cases and recouped more than fifty-seven thousand dollars for its members. Failure to deliver on mail orders, presumably not including the AARP pharmacy mail service, was by far the biggest source of complaints. When the AARP disbanded its local consumer-assistance centers, two of them were absorbed by local governments, and one, in Hyannis, Massachusetts, kept on the elderly staff recruited by AARP. Here is another sampling of what AARP does: its national office and its local chapters turn out publications, give courses, and offer services on just about any subject that might cross your mind.

Service to the members is the bedrock of AARP, but it is also a powerful lobby, in the states as well as in Washington. Any organization with close to 9 million members commands respect in Washington, and AARP has a particularly responsive constituency: the aging vote more than the rest of the population, they show up to buttonhole their representatives, and forests are felled when they undertake letter-writing campaigns. The constituency is not the average elderly person. As its critics are quick to point out, AARP draws mainly on an articulate, white-collar, better-off-than-most population. The underclass of the old, those living in fear and hunger in the slums, remain isolated from this and all other organizations. AARP is happy to trumpet its more-than-average nature when it is trying to sell something. In a 1975 letter seeking a discount from the Chrysler Corporation, for example, AARP bragged that its members have an average family income of $7,776, compared to an average of $5,868 for those over sixty-five. AARP acknowledged in passing that the two figures "are not directly comparable," which is a considerable understatement: since AARP membership starts at age fifty-five, it includes many who are still working and earning more than they will after sixty-five, when they'll drag down the average. The pitch of AARP's letter to Chrysler emerged after another five yards of statistics, all designed to show that the membership has loose cash in its pockets that it might well spend on cars: ". . . any discount available to our members could result in an even greater propensity to spend than for the older population as a whole and might contribute significantly to sales by a particular dealer where the availability of the lower rate is made known."

A family income of $7,776, the best the AARP salesman could muster, hardly makes the organization a brotherhood of the affluent. So AARP is usually found fighting for the interests of the average person who is neither poor nor rich; it tends to neglect the worst-off of the elderly. Predictably, many of its causes are the special interests of the old: It has been campaigning to ban credit discrimination against the elderly, and of course it is always around when Social Security and Medicare are on the agenda. When, as it sometimes does, AARP advocates the plugging of tax loopholes, a few lines down the page it can be found plugging for *our* loopholes: property-tax exemptions for the elderly and an even more permissive estate tax. But many issues cannot be contained within the age bracket of fifty-five plus. AARP cannot credibly lobby for generic drugs and for price competition in pharmacies and eyeglasses for the elderly alone, and the same is true of no-fault insurance, another major AARP cause. Controlling funeral costs, an issue on which AARP mail set records, is important to survivors of any age. When it attacks such issues, it sometimes seems that AARP is the most effective of lobbies for the average man. The logic of its membership's needs drives the organization to positions far removed from its business origins. Here is the AARP during the 1975 tax and budget debate: ". . . an even greater deficit would be preferable this year if it meant a more rapid return to a full-employment economy." While acknowledging that the steps it supported would probably result in further inflation, . . . AARP asserted that "excessive concentration of market power is a far more significant cause of inflation and should be dealt with." Going around asserting about "concentration of market power," a topic studiously neglected by the two-party monopoly, is a long way from selling life insurance and in vivid contrast to the sanctimony of those who trot out the "elderly living on fixed incomes" as a reason for preferring unemployment to inflation. If the most affluent of the organizations representing the aging talks that way, how can we retain the stereotype that the old are more conservative than their juniors?

Then there are Maggie Kuhn and the Gray Panthers. When this one-time Presbyterian Church official comes on the tube, asks permission to give the Panther rallying cry, and calls out, "Off your asses!" you know that you are no longer in the land of the AARP. Their name sounds like something an archaeologist dug up from the 1960s, but the Grays have survived, while Black Panthers are seldom heard from these days, and the forgotten White Panthers were no more than a media event that expired after two press releases. The Gray Panthers' statement of their origins tells us what they are all about:

> We did not select our name; the name selected us. It describes who we are: 1) we are older persons in retirement; 2) we are aware of the revolutionary nature of our time; 3) although we differ with the strategy and tactics of some militant groups in our society, we share with them many of the goals of human freedom, dignity, and self-development; and 4) we have a sense of humor.

Compared to the millions of the AARP, Gray Panthers are as scarce as their jungle counterparts. They keep no membership, collect no dues, and claim a mailing list of only eight thousand for their publication, *Network* (whose logo, by the way, looks more like a kitten than a predator). Unlike the other organizations of the aging, the Panthers are not limited to the gray-haired. They call themselves "Age and Youth in Action," and in a re-creation of the traditional conspiratorial alliance between grandparents and grandchildren, their participants seem to be over sixty and under thirty, with few in between.

The Panthers use their attention-getting style, much of which is Maggie Kuhn herself, to deride the intangible barriers that fence off the old. They urge their contemporaries not to accept exile from society, not to accept the stereotypes of age. When Maggie Kuhn and five others, all on the edge of retirement, founded the Panthers, in 1970, they were seeking not specific benefits for their age group but a chance to remain active in the world, and that remains their primary goal. Maggie herself plans to quit work "when I die." Much of their concern is with images of the old; the Panthers' Media Watch stalks the networks in an effort to blot out the presentation of old age as "disease or naptime" and extracted from CBS at least a promise to do better. Panthers often use tactics we associate with the young. Their approach to nursing-home reform, for example, was to stage a street play at the AMA Convention in Atlantic City in which a doctor sold patients to the Kill 'Em Quick Nursing Home; doctors' wives were reported to have glared in disapproval at what the old folks were doing. Still, the

Panthers do not scorn the less-cosmic issues affecting the old. In Long Beach, California, and Washington, D.C., Panthers have succeeded in getting free checking accounts for the elderly, and in Rhode Island it was free public transportation during off hours. These victories are not world-shaking, and one senses that the Panthers' main concern is elsewhere: they want to remake the world, beginning with themselves.

Like most felines, the Gray Panthers are not strong on organization: they have none of the business-based bureaucratic immortality of the AARP. Just as the Townsendites scattered after the founder's death, the Panthers are not likely to long survive the eventual loss of Maggie Kuhn's charismatic presence. While they are with us, the Panthers can help undermine a few stereotypes, arouse their contemporaries to have some fun, and remind us all of an important lesson: we don't have to die till we die.

The goal of keeping the elderly in the community begins, though it does not end, with providing them a chance to do something productive, but any attempt to do so runs into the twin blocs of forced retirement and discrimination against job seekers in their fifties and sixties (sometimes in their forties). Although something like half of us work at jobs subject to mandatory retirement, typically at age sixty-five, it makes little sense and is opposed by most of the public. There is no reason to suppose that the person capable of working full time at age sixty-four becomes totally incompetent on his sixty-fifth birthday, and even the AMA, usually no friend to the aging, has testified that "Medicine sees in mandatory retirement a direct threat to the health and life expectancy of the persons affected" and that it is "detrimental to the best interest of society" as well. The Louis Harris opinion study on "The Myth and Reality of Aging in America" found that close to half of retired people had not wanted to quit work and that they missed not just the money but the people and even the work itself. Harris found that an overwhelming majority, 86 per cent, of the public at large opposed mandatory retirement and that, even among those responsible for hiring and firing, four fifths believed those willing and able should be allowed to go on working.

Both mandatory retirement and job discrimination based on age are strongly entrenched for reasons that do not surface in answer to a pollster's questions. If you retire, your fellow employees all have a shot at promotion, and the union may legitimately feel that compulsory retirement is the only alternative to forced labor past sixty-five. From the boss's point of view, the retiree goes out at the top of the salary scale, his young replacement comes in on the first rung. Private pension plans have proved to be a reason for job discrimination. The employer doesn't want to hire that older worker who'll stay just about long enough to collect a pension; he prefers the young applicant who'll either leave without qualifying or stay forty years. The personnel department finds that mandatory retirement makes their lives easier because they don't have to make an individual judgment on whether an employee is still capable of doing his job. (Similarly, at the other end of the tunnel, Personnel likes to sort young applicants by diplomas, again avoiding the need to evaluate the individual.) For all these reasons, mandatory retirement will not give way easily. Eventually, as suggested earlier, the sixty-five barrier may become too expensive to maintain as more of us live for more years past that age. Some countries have begun to break the barrier: that other aging superpower, the Soviet Union, has shifted its incentives to encourage people to keep working past retirement age, and Sweden in 1976 instituted gradual retirement between the ages of sixty and seventy. Already, in this country, forced retirement is under attack both in the law and by those seeking to provide more job opportunities for the elderly.

The attack on mandatory retirement has yet to score a conclusive success. Congress and a number of states have adopted laws theoretically banning discrimination by age, but many of the laws are vaguely worded and most limit the prohibition to ages forty to sixty-five, leaving the employer free to discriminate both after and before those ages. The Supreme Court, whose members are not subject to mandatory retirement, has not seen fit in the cases brought before it to extend that right to the rest of the population. The federal government speaks with two voices: while the Labor Department brings court actions against mandatory retirement, Internal Revenue imposes a punitive tax on the earnings of those over sixty-five who collect Social Security.

In the absence of government action, private efforts have succeeded in breaking the sixty-five barrier, but only on a small scale.

Some firms specialize in hiring those over sixty-five, with excellent results. The Texas Refinery Corporation, which makes roofing materials, has more than three hundred salesmen over sixty; their average age is seventy and some are in their eighties and still selling. The company considers its elderly sales force to be good business. "This isn't a charitable thing we're trying to do," Adlai Pate, Jr., the firm's president, said, and he added: "I'm grateful for what I consider the shortsighted policies of firms that enforce mandatory retirement on their employees. Every time they let one go because of age, I have another potential salesperson. Good salespeople, like good wines, get better with age." In South Norwalk, Connecticut, Fertl, Inc., which makes plant food, has a work force that averages sixty-eight years old. Hoyt Catlin, who founded the company, in 1956, when he himself was sixty-five, said the firm has less absenteeism and employee turnover than comparable companies. An important factor at both Texas Refinery and Fertl is that older employees are allowed to work part time; one salesman in his seventies finds himself as productive as ever for four hours a day, but after that he runs out of gas.

Here and there, agencies have specialized in placing the elderly in jobs. In Albuquerque, New Mexico, Anna Beckman, herself a great-grandmother, has been running a placement service for the AARP since 1962. By 1975 she was getting three hundred job orders a month; some were for babysitting, but she had also placed older people in full-time jobs paying over twenty thousand dollars. In Chevy Chase, Maryland, the Over-60 Counseling and Employment Service has been doing the same thing for about as long as Anna Beckman. The average age of the people they place is in the late sixties: many are victims of mandatory retirement and some seek work because inflation ate up their savings. Some have trouble finding work below their level of skills. As the director of the service, Gladys Sprinkle, said: "For the most part, the public doesn't want the commodity we are marketing. It's not that these people are too old, we are told, it's that they are overqualified." Still, they place about eight hundred a year, with full-time pay averaging ten to fifteen thousand dollars. In one case, a company's forcibly retired workers fought back in an unusual forum. The company was a utility, and when it applied for a rate increase, its opponents included a committee of resentful ex-employees: their opposition delayed the rate increase and generated unfavorable publicity for the utility and its mandatory retirement. All these examples, however, are only minor exceptions to the rule of age discrimination; doubtless major change will not occur until enough people make the connection between mandatory retirement and the rising burden of the payroll tax.

Housing is essential to keeping older people in their community —and out of an institution. Although the Harris study found that three quarters of people past sixty-five would like to live among people of varied ages, the goal is not easy to achieve even for the relatively affluent. Those attracted to the fast-sprouting retirement communities in the sun find no young people there, not necessarily because they wanted it that way but because the developer promised the local planning board he wasn't going to bring in any school-age children to make taxes go up. For the retired person whose health is better than his bank balance, the central problem is how to meet the payments. Some states have made this somewhat easier. Most states provide property-tax reductions for elderly homeowners, and a handful provide a similar benefit for renters; Massachusetts pioneered in allowing the elderly homeowner to postpone part of the taxes till his death, when it is paid by his estate out of his equity in the home. The same idea is the basis for what is called "split equity": making it possible for the homeowner to sell his equity in his house, to be delivered to the buyer, presumably a bank, at his death, in return for an annuity that would increase his current income. Split equity hasn't been implemented at this writing, but if it is, it has considerable potential: homeowners over sixty-five hold an estimated $80 billion in housing equity, which will buy a lot of annuities. Elderly renters, on the other hand, face a worsening squeeze as costs and rents go up. They've gotten far less help than homeowners, but in Washington, D.C., the Gray Panther housing group joined in successful campaigns for rent control (though later it was watered down) and a temporary ban on the conversions that were turning cheap rental housing into high-priced condominiums.

As the years stretch out past sixty-five, a growing number of people can no longer manage completely on their own, yet do not need the costly and constant care of an institution, usually a nursing home, where many of them are in fact found for lack of an alternative. In recent years, some efforts, all modest in scale, have been made to supply that alternative. They go by such names as assisted residential housing, congregate housing, or community living, and are usually run by non-profit agencies. Here are some examples.

The Share-a-Home Association began in Winter Park, Florida, in 1969 and now includes ten homes, each housing an average of fifteen people ranging in age from seventy to ninety-five. Each home has a resident manager and family, who are responsible for preparing meals and supplying all the residents' other needs. The cost, for everything except medical care, averages $325 a month per person: too much for someone who has only Social Security, though far less than the cost of a nursing home. In practice the residents tend to be middle-class people with a pension in addition to Social Security, but local church groups have subsidized some who could not pay the bill. The first home was set up by Jim Gillies, a 47-year-old one-time food salesman, in a building that had been a nursing home, with Gillies and his family providing the management. The eighteen residents hold title to the house, with the mortgage financed out of their monthly payments, and in theory can hire and fire the manager. Because the homes are small, the largest having only twenty members, they can remain self-governing and free of institutional rigidity. The elected head of the Winter Park home said: "Some of the members of the family are forgetful sometimes, but here we don't think of it as senility, as they do in nursing homes. We really don't have difficulties with things like that. Everyone forgets something sometimes, but we don't mind." The family atmosphere is fostered; everyone is called "aunt" or "uncle" by the manager's kids and by each other. The Winter Park family even made their self-definition stick in court. Charged with violation of the zoning code, they said they were in fact what the code called a family—"one or more persons occupying a dwelling and living as a single housekeeping unit." After visiting the home, the judge ruled in their favor and called it "a happy, well-run family . . . a superb idea."

A similar project was undertaken in a city environment by the Philadelphia Geriatric Center. The Center bought nine 1-family houses in a residential neighborhood and remodeled them so that each included three small apartments, each with its own kitchenette, and a living room shared by all. The residents were supplied one main meal daily, delivered frozen, weekly housekeeping and linen service, and the recreation and social services of the nearby Geriatric Center. The residents, who had been living before in isolation and fear, were said to be happy with what they got.

These small projects, and several others like them around the country, have shown that it is possible to keep older people who cannot make it on their own in the larger community, but they will not reach any large number of people until government reverses its present bias in favor of institutions. Medicaid is happy to pay the bill for keeping people in nursing homes; it will not pay any part of the much lower cost of keeping them out. From the point of view of the family, the government rewards the person who puts a relative in an institution and penalizes him for keeping the relative at home. In Wisconsin, one program for keeping them out has punched a hole in Medicaid's nursing-home policy.

It was the idea of Martin E. Schreiber, who has been doing for lieutenant-governors what Herbert Denenberg did for insurance commissioners, and it grew out of Schreiber's experience as the state's nursing-home ombudsman. Schreiber had observed that many people now in nursing homes don't need to be there—national estimates start at 20–40 per cent—and could be kept out with enough supporting services, many of which now exist in fragmented state, and enough money to pay the bills. In La Crosse County, the Wisconsin Community Organization began in early 1976 delivering those services to some fifteen hundred elderly and disabled people. Some services are strictly medical; some, such as delivering hot meals and shoveling snow, are not, though they are in fact health services by any rational definition. Most already existed in some form but needed to be pulled together and paid for.

What makes the Wisconsin program different from those described earlier is that Schreiber got Medicaid to agree to pay for it. If the basic premise is proved, that it costs less this way, the Wisconsin experiment will lend muscle to the efforts to change Medicaid rules to allow payment for services that will keep people healthy enough to stay out of the institution. The sponsor of one such proposal, Congressman Edward I. Koch of New York, estimated that keeping a person on home care would cost $2,000 to

$6,500 a year instead of $15,000 to $20,000 in a nursing home. (Senator James Buckley of New York proposed a benefit for families that keep an elderly relative at home, but, by making the benefit a federal income-tax deduction, Buckley insured that those who benefit most would need it least.) Schreiber himself figures that home care will cost half the nursing-home bill. Daphne Krause, executive director of the Minneapolis Age and Opportunity Center, one of the best-known and most extensive keep-them-out operations, makes the point in a more dramatic way. Krause said that if the Minneapolis Center were to receive the money Medicaid saves on keeping 126 people out of the nursing home, it could pay for all these services to those 126—and provide some services to another eight thousand people besides. With Congress in its present, budget-cutting mood, it is probable that home care instead of the nursing home, like measures to reduce government financing of unnecessary surgery and hospitalization, will get more favorable attention than it has heretofore. Doubtless the elderly person who is thereby saved from the institution will not quibble over the fact that those who did it were just trying to save some money.

Services of various kinds for the elderly have been created here and there around the country, most of them with the stimulus of federal money from the Older Americans Act. They are usually small in scale, "tokens," in Maggie Kuhn's view, and when fed by short-term federal grants, are likely to die off when the money runs out. Still, it's more than existed yesterday, and it indicates the directions in which a larger commitment might eventually flow. The largest undertaking is the national nutrition program, which, according to HEW statistics, was in 1975 providing a quarter million meals a day to older people at forty-two hundred senior day centers. Public transportation for the elderly, free or at cut rate, can be found in, for example, Sullivan County, New York, and Hawaii; the AARP and the Gray Panthers have both observed that the rest of the population is equally handicapped by the absence of any way of getting around except by private automobile. Although most of the money for such services is either federal or charitable, Brookline, Massachusetts, where 30 per cent of the population is over sixty, decided to continue at its own expense an array of services originally started under a grant from Washington. Recognition of the particular legal needs of the elderly, who are more embroiled than the average person with the bureaucracies of government and the health and pension industries, has resulted in the creation of a variety of legal-aid programs specifically for the elderly; California is training paralegal aides, some of whom are themselves elderly, to act as advocates for older people. But the total reached by any new legal service is minuscule. It should also be noted that supplying the legal needs of the elderly, as viewed by government, does not include doing anything about their status as the prime victims of crimes of violence.

Anything that helps the elderly cope with their environment is part of the effort to keep them in the community and out of the institution. The time comes when that is not enough. If, let us say, one third of those in nursing homes don't belong there, liberating them will do nothing for the other two thirds, and that's two thirds of a million people. Public attention to the nursing homes has increased considerably since the 1974 publication of Mary Adelaide Mendelson's *Tender Loving Greed,* which provided the first detailed description of how the industry was swindling the public as well as abusing the people in its custody. One of the nursing-home owners she wrote about was Bernard Bergman, whose primary base was in New York State. In 1974–75, John L. Hess, of the New York *Times* carried on the Bergman story in a series of exposés that made it obvious that Bergman and other nursing-home operators were so well entrenched in the state's political structure as to be immune from any need to account for the government money they were receiving in increasing amounts, much less what they did to the patients. Nelson A. Rockefeller, when he was governor, had guaranteed this immunity by the simple expedient of preventing the state from hiring more auditors, in the face of evidence that each day an auditor worked enabled the state to recoup twenty-five hundred dollars in overpayments to nursing homes. The industry itself was still trying, as a headline in one of its trade publications put it, to "Project a Positive Image"! Senator Frank Moss, chairman of the Senate Subcommittee on Long-Term Care, complained that critics like Mrs. Mendelson were blaming a whole industry for the behavior of a few bad apples, but this defense lost whatever validity it had when the special prosecutor in New York reported that every one of the first seventy nursing homes he audited was overcharging the government.

The accumulating evidence eventually proved impossible to ignore, investigations started, and by 1976 twenty figures in the industry and state politics had been indicted, including Bernard
Bergman, four had pleaded guilty, and some sixty nursing homes
had been closed. It was the most vigorous investigation the nursing-home industry had ever known, and yet there was profound
pessimism about how much had been or could be accomplished. In
one sense this was a recognition of the familiar principle that regu-
lated industries, no matter how shaken up they may be today, will
tomorrow regain their hold on the levers of power. But those investigating the industry, and some of the regulators themselves,
were also saying that government by its nature was incapable of
playing its assigned role as substitute for the family in the care of
people in nursing homes.

Mary Adelaide Mendelson, who had reached the same conclusion, believed that the only lasting hope for improving nursing
homes lay in the patients' relatives. Only the relatives know the
details of nursing-home abuses and can be counted on to have a
continuing interest in what happens behind the institutions' closed
doors, Mrs. Mendelson argued, and only organized relatives can
provide a counterweight to the industry in the lobbies of government. Her position was confirmed by Martin Schreiber's experience since 1972 as Wisconsin's nursing-home ombudsman: Of the
first thousand complaints his office received, almost half (46 per
cent) came from relatives, only 11 per cent from patients, who are
typically fearful of retribution. (The second-largest source of complaints, by the way, was nursing-home employees. All regulatory
agencies together provided a grand total of 2 per cent.) Accordingly, Mrs. Mendelson set out to help form an organization of relatives. Her first goal was to organize relatives in Cuyahoga County,
Ohio, which includes the city of Cleveland, and ninety-three nursing homes. In early 1976 Mrs. Mendelson put together enough
financing to start a non-profit organization called the Nursing
Home Advisory and Research Council, headquartered in Cleveland Heights, where she lives. She canvassed the social-service
workers in hospitals, who place people in nursing homes, and voluntary and religious agencies, which deal with their relatives, and
drew an enthusiastic initial response. Mrs. Mendelson believed
that if enough relatives joined in a continuing organization, both

nursing homes and regulatory agencies would have to pay attention to their demands. And if it worked in Cuyahoga County, it could be emulated elsewhere.

The organizing of nursing-home relatives is based on the recognition that government regulation as we now know it has failed hopelessly to protect the public interest. The alternative is an organization made up exclusively of those who have a direct interest in the subject.

"I AM STILL LEARNING"

Ronald Gross

Courses and programs for older people are burgeoning throughout the country. Here is an overview with glimpses into several exemplary programs such as the Institute for Retired Professionals and the Institute of Study for Older Adults.

At age 80, Goya inscribed these words under a sketch of an ancient man stooped with age and propped on two sticks. The artist was mocking his own notorious infatuation with novelty, of course —but he was also celebrating the simple truth that an active mind is relatively impervious to age. This truth, spiked with Goya's bracing irony, might be the motto of a new movement in higher education to meet the needs of older people.

One out of every five colleges and universities is currently moving in this direction, according to a recently published study by the Academy for Educational Development (AED). The urge to serve this new constituency is spurred by declining enrollments on the one hand and by federal grants on the other. But it may have a larger import for the campus. These new programs for students in what the French call "the third age" are not constrained by the pressures of testing, grading, and credentialing. In these classrooms one finds something rare in American education above the primary grades: learning for its own sake.

"Older people don't just want to be shuffled off to a retirement home," says Alvin Eurich, president of the Academy for Educational Development. "They're not played out and unteachable, though many are reduced to that state by neglect. What they need are new outlets for their many skills and interests, activities where they are wanted and needed, chances to be of use. Colleges can respond to these needs with new kinds of offerings, and find good use for their special resources, facilities, and expertise. We believe the field is worth a hard look by every faculty and administration."

A few full-fledged programs already exist and give a glimpse of the prospects. The forerunner was the Institute for Retired Professionals (IRP) at the New School for Social Research in New York City. It started over a decade ago with a unique do-it-yourself approach not unlike the young students' "free universities" of the late sixties.

Frankly fashioned for an elite clientele, the institute consists of 600 former doctors, schoolteachers and professors, executives and businessmen who create their own educational and social community. Each pays $200 a year for the opportunity to teach and learn (all courses are conducted by members; there are no paid teachers), as well as to take free courses in the New School's brimming adult program. Many spend a good part of every weekday at the school's attractive building off lower Fifth Avenue just north of Greenwich Village.

Recent courses ranged from French to Creative Dramatics, Music to Biomedical Developments. In one morning I sat in on a fiction writing workshop taught by a former editor, a lecture on language by a fast-talking 72-year-old polylingual spellbinder, and a seminar on comparative cultures. Sociability was clearly the dominant value rather than intellectual rigor. But the discussions were not without flashes of insight, shards of wit, and occasional erudition.

Of course, the institute is no answer for most retired people. But it works well for those who already have the most—intellectually, financially, and socially. The drop-out rate is only 10 per cent annually, and the idea is spreading to other cities: Boston, Philadelphia, Cleveland, San Francisco, and San Diego have centers inspired by the IRP.

The AED survey, sponsored by the Edna McConnell Clark Foundation, disclosed that nationwide the responses of most colleges and universities have been more modest and conventional. Free or reduced tuition in regular courses is the most widespread practice. Some institutions are experimenting with innovations such as courses at off-campus locations convenient for older people, preretirement planning, educational vacations, provision of health, transportation, or counseling services, residential programs, and even retraining and new careers programs.

At North Hennepin Community College in Brooklyn Park, a suburb of Minneapolis, several hundred students over 55 years of age are enrolled. The college began its experimental tuition-free noncredit courses especially for the elderly three years ago, largely in response to community pressure from older people themselves. Federal funds have aided the enterprise.

The program started with practical courses, such as Budgeting on a Fixed Income, Lip Reading, Psychology of Change, The Urban Environment, Public Speaking, and preparation for passing high school equivalency exams. But subsequently the course offerings have become bolder, including Organizing for Power and Sex over 65. Moreover, many of the students have moved on into credit courses and degree programs as well as into campus life through joining social activities and the musical and dramatic groups.

The older students usually hold their own in regular classes; in fact, the chief resistance has come from young students who complain that the older ones, who take only one or two courses and have more time to study, end up "raising the curve and leaving a lot of kids in the dust," as one of the youngsters plaintively put it.

Even more ambitious is a program called The Institute of Study for Older Adults, run by New York City Community College. Rather than inviting the old people onto the campus, the institute goes to where they are: some 60 locations throughout the five boroughs, from the elegant Jewish Guild for the Blind in mid-town Manhattan to dingy retirement homes and "senior centers" in the farthest reaches of the Bronx.

The program started only three years ago, when members of a Brooklyn "Friendship Club," many of them foreign-born, asked for a course in English "so we can talk to our grandchildren." This year 5,000 people, many over 80 and averaging 70, enrolled in 160 courses ranging from home nursing and health needs to American Cultural Origins and video workshops.

Supported by $100,000 a year from the State Office of the Aging and $35,000 from the City University of New York, the program operates through the city's eight public community colleges. (The cost works out to $32 a year per student.) Courses are proposed or selected by groups in each of the centers where the students meet. The most popular offerings are in Basic Psychology, followed by Basic English, Sociology, Current Events, and Spanish. Last year Joseph Schoenberger, a 100-year-old retired diamond setter, took a particularly heavy schedule. After finishing

China Today he took two nine-week courses simultaneously: Aging in Other Societies and Current Issues: Watergate. He received certificates of accomplishment based on his record of attendance at a "commencement" ceremony that is held at every center at the end of each nine-week term. "I feel like 75," says Mr. Schoenberger. Another student, Sarah Schottland, 94, proclaims that "my studies have made a new woman out of me."

The student body and the curriculum vary tremendously. "While there are former lawyers and teachers among the participants, most have less than a high school education," reports Director Peter Oppenheimer. "Many have not completed grade school. Some are illiterate. Moreover, in dealing with an age range from 55 to 100, teachers find themselves confronting a span of one and a half generations—which makes it difficult to provide one fare or approach for everyone, to say the least."

Personal tragedy has often shattered these people's lives. "If it wasn't for looking forward to this class every week—and my sick husband who needs me to care for him—I'd end my life tomorrow," one student told her teacher. Several classes are at facilities for elderly people who are blind, mostly as the result of recent illness. This is education conducted on the edge of despair—many of these people are understandably full of an inexpressible rage, which they and their teachers must learn to deal with together. Some are too defeated to respond at all: Recent attempts to initiate courses at a large city hospital and a welfare hotel faltered because the environments were too chaotic or depressing to be readily redeemed by instruction—though even here there were individuals who benefited.

But most of the students respond gratifyingly. One group finished a course on the problems of older adults, came to the conviction that their findings should be shared with others, and promoted themselves a monthly program on a local radio station. Many students have joined the United Senior Centers and even more activist groups.

Sometimes this tension between academic study and activism erupts into open confrontation. A young bearded teacher found his course America, Where Are You Going? derailed by a "gray panther" in the class who demanded that the group eschew abstract theorizing about the national malaise and march down the street to solve the problem of three old people being evicted from a welfare hotel. "She couldn't do those people any good," the radical professor insists. "All she did was undermine what could have been a beautiful class." Says the panther: "Education doesn't mean anything if it doesn't lead to helping individuals in the community." Other members of the class were torn between the two poles, some sympathizing with the activist student, some afraid to oppose her vehemence, still others quite keen on getting into general sociological issues and "learning something."

The larger question of what these students really want or need sparked sharp discussion at one of the regular seminars for teachers. Longtime teacher Bob Disch observed that "the lack of structure, examinations, grades, and credit coupled with the lack of any compulsion in bringing students to class results in a true learning experience that comes closer to the ideals of Ivan Illich than anything I've ever seen." To which another teacher responded sharply that in her experience, what these old people wanted was the experience of going to school again, and this should not be taken away from them by having "too little structure."

Most of the programs for older people around the country are, like these two, run by community colleges. Hawkeye Institute of Technology, for example, enrolls over 6,000 people in a large rural area around Waterloo, Iowa. Miami-Dade Community College conducts courses in community centers, large housing complexes, churches, schools, and nursing homes. Snead State Junior College in Boaz, Alabama, goes a step further through its participation in the VISTA-sponsored Retired Senior Volunteer Program. Here, older people can volunteer their services and thereby learn through activities in the community.

But four-year colleges and universities are increasingly getting into the act. At Fairhaven College in Bellingham, Washington, 31 older people live on campus as part of an experimental multigenerational program bringing together preschool children, middle-aged adults, and senior citizens living in converted dorms. In Syracuse, the 400 residents of on-campus public housing for the elderly have access to the university's offerings.

Programs for older people will likely loom larger on the higher education scene over the next decade as the elderly population and its needs grow, and the supply of younger students continues to decline. "We see this as one of the frontiers of service for many institutions," says Samuel Gould, chairman of the Council for the Progress of Non-Traditional Study. "There are literally millions of older people who are ready and eager to become involved in programs on and off the campus. But so far, relatively few colleges have seized the opportunity. I wonder whether some institutions that have been doing the same thing for 60, 70 years aren't the ones that are a little slow to learn."

SENIOR LOBBY: A MODEL FOR SENIOR/STUDENT ACTION

Arthur M. Hanhardt, Jr., and Ron Wyden

A funny thing happened to Professor Arthur Hanhardt's class on "The Politics of Aging" at the University of Oregon. It bumped up against a practical question: why are seniors not more politically active on their own behalf? "What began as a highly academic approach to the theories and facts of aging and politics gradually focused on [this] question," the authors report. The commendable response was to gear the class into statewide and local efforts to influence the legislative process in favor of bills designed to help seniors. Here's what happened.

When political activism, senior advocacy and academia merge in a manner that is of mutual benefit to all concerned these days, it is something of a rarity. The elderly's memories tend to turn to the turbulent late sixties and early seventies; academics and students are not prone to get involved in politics for the elderly, and the intergenerational problems inherent in student-senior relations become all the more difficult.

But student generations come in four-year cycles, and change has occurred on the campus; older people are beginning to realize they have to fight for their rights, and sometimes it all comes together just right. What follows here is a report on how the efforts of seniors and students, working together after a nudge in the right direction, furthered the interests of the former and contributed to the latter's education.

When the Oregon Center for Gerontology was established in 1967 at the University of Oregon in Eugene, a series of core courses was designed to give the gerontology trainees a broad, multidisciplinary framework for their future work with the elderly. One, the "Cultural, Economic and Political Factors of Aging," was jointly offered by the university's School of Business and Department of Political Science. Eventually, the political and economic aspects of aging settled into separate courses, "The Economic Aspects of Aging" and "The Politics of Aging."

In its evolution as a course, the politics of aging class has undergone many changes. What began as a highly academic approach to the theories and facts of aging and politics gradually focused on the question: "Why are seniors not more politically active on their own behalf?" While other minority groups were militantly asserting their interests, seniors appeared to be relying on others to act for them (especially on the state and local levels away from the well-organized national lobbies headquartered in Washington, D.C.).

By the 1973 session of the Oregon State Legislature, the politics of aging class was geared into statewide and local efforts to influence the legislative process in favor of bills designed to help seniors. On the local level, students from the class and the Legislative Action Committee of the Emerald Empire Council on Aging, the county advisory body, met weekly to decide on legislative priorities and what action to undertake.

STUDENTS DID LEGWORK

The students did a good deal of the research and legwork; the seniors consulted with their retirement organizations to coordinate letter-writing campaigns and send individuals to the legislature to testify before committees. With the aid of a third-year law student on a gerontology grant, the class and the council made suggestions for redrafting bills.

At the state level, the class experienced at first hand the frustrations involved in concerting the actions of the elderly, who often tend to be isolated (socially and geographically), poor, relatively immobile and apart from the political process. Class participation in a "Senior Advocacy Day" at the state legislature, which included visits of students and seniors to their representatives, brought home their differing perceptions of politics.

Students interacted much more easily with the legislators than did the elderly, and the elderly seemed to equate youthful appearance with political radicalism: Long hair, jeans and peace symbols meant far-out politics. Inevitably, tensions between young and old surfaced occasionally, but most of the stereotypes soon broke down as the relationships stabilized.

In 1974, efforts were made to take advantage of a year in which the legislature did not meet to educate students and seniors about legislative politics, local programs for the elderly and what might be done during the 1976 legislative session. The class met at the Celeste Campbell Senior Center with a broad range of elderly. Video tape-recording equipment was introduced experimentally as a means to bridge the gap between the isolated seniors and their representatives. Students majoring in speech produced a television program, and a systematic effort to communicate with as many seniors as possible was made.

Two underlying problems of continuity limited the course's effectiveness. The first was a lack of consistency in participation of both groups—but especially that of the seniors. The seniors were outnumbered by students; those of the former who did participate were already serving on many community committees and commissions, leaving them relatively little time to contribute to the joint effort of the course. The rhythm of the academic year and the need for continuous senior activity, no matter what the political or academic season, caused a second serious discontinuity.

At this point, Ronald Wyden, a young local attorney and graduate of the university's law school, organized the Senior Lobby. He had become involved with seniors earlier when he organized the Senior Law Service, a free legal service for the elderly poor. With the new group, Wyden quickly realized that the problems faced by the elderly were not exclusively legal but to an important extent involved politics.

USES MASS MEDIA AS TOOL

The Senior Lobby solved the continuity problems that the politics of aging class and the organized senior groups could not effectively address. Its format of weekly meetings, broad senior participation and active programs of political and community involvement ushered in a new era of senior politics in the area.

Wyden, recognizing that seniors often tend to be homebound, decided to use the media as the most effective way to reach the elderly with political news. Thereafter, the Senior Lobby either held press conferences or issued news releases every week during its early stages of development. Radio and television covered lobby activities extensively, especially after a reminder that broadcast hours devoted to seniors would count toward the public service time each broadcast station must show at the time of license renewal.

The lobby selected political issues designed to appeal to the widest possible spectrum of seniors. One priority was state legislation to permit pharmacists' substitution of an inexpensive generic drug for an expensive brand name prescription. The bill's advocates demonstrated that its passage would save Oregon consumers $800,000 to $1 million annually in drug costs, and lobby members repeatedly pointed out that those over 65 average $300 per year on prescription medicine.

After the bill's passage, a number of legislators singled out the lobby as the major reason Oregon's generic drug legislation became law. Other medical legislation, including a bill for home health care for the elderly as an alternative to institutionalization, was also supported because of the broad interest of virtually all seniors in quality medical care at reasonable prices.

Community action projects, nonlegislative in nature, were initiated during the legislative session—producing quick, tangible accomplishments to impress those seniors who asked, "Well, what has the lobby really done for us?"

SUCCESSES INCREASE MEMBERSHIP

The lobby worked for and won: Reduced newspaper rates for low-income seniors; a paid senior advocacy position on a congressman's staff to be filled by a senior on a rotating basis, and a free hearing-aid program. Because of these local successes, many seniors came to the weekly lobby meeting out of simple curiosity—and were sufficiently impressed to stay and become legislative advocates for the senior cause.

The goal of each weekly lobby meeting was to spread the work of political organizing fairly around the group. Too often, past senior meetings had been monthly affairs that ended with one or two individuals appointed to a "legislative committee." Invariably, the "committee" would soon realize that they could accomplish little by themselves, usually spending their tenure bemoaning being appointed in the first place.

But the lobby divided up the chores of political advocacy: Whether telephoning, research, petition drafting and passing, fund-raising, publicity, transportation or letter writing, each member's assignment was consistent with his/her skills and interests.

Media presentations, community action projects and legislative lobbying require central direction and supervision; here the continuity provided by Wyden's role as the lobby's executive director was crucial. Missing in earlier senior political efforts was a person who could serve as a knowledgeable advisor, to ramrod projects on a virtually full-time basis.

CLASS, LOBBY JOIN FORCES

Student participation was welcomed. In 1975, the politics of aging class met with the lobby, jointly developing programs to maximize intergenerational cooperation. For example, a senior and a student were assigned to each member of the Joint Legislative Committee on Aging to help the legislator monitor and understand the many senior issues. Students video-taped senior testimony and lobby meetings and transported them to the state capitol, enabling legislators to receive senior input on extremely short notice from the older people, often physically unable to drive there.

Students also opened several "Neighborhood Senior Lobby Offices" in their homes, where area seniors could drop in and pick up copies of senior legislation and other pertinent political news. As often as possible, the young and old also socialized together, relieving residual tensions. Once the lobby held a fund-raiser (dubbed the "Senior Boogie") with students inviting the seniors as their dates.

In retrospect, much progress has been made in intergenerational cooperation, though we realize some conflicts are inherent in the personality/structure setup. Some of our previous conflicts emerged when students presented research findings, such as on the generic drug legislation; seniors bridled at being "lectured" by students young enough to be their grandchildren or suspected them of pursuing political ends of their own. But, overall, it was a successful exchange.

Now gearing up for our winter class, that success is evidenced in our enrollment: There will be 40 to 60 students involved and a like number of seniors. We believe the example could be duplicated or even improved on anywhere in the U.S. if the elderly and their advocates would:

Meet weekly and divide up *equally* the work of political organization, with members reinforcing each other

Use the media to reach the elderly and to dramatize the likelihood of success through political organizing

Use a mix of community action and legislative projects to produce some quick, tangible victories for the group while more lengthy legislative processes are evolving

Work closely with students and other young advocates to help bring out the best advocacy skills each member has to offer

Have a politically skilled coordinator available and active on a nearly full-time basis

Through such techniques, senior groups may be able to turn yesterday's "Senior Power" rhetoric into tomorrow's political reality.

SENIOR PERSONNEL PLACEMENT

Lawrence Hochheimer

Norwalk, Connecticut, boasts a Senior Personnel Placement Bureau, which interviews and finds employment for seniors. Hochheimer, the president, eighty-one, believes chronological age "is no reason ever—unless physically unable—for a person to stop doing what he wants to do."

It's no news to most that the elderly find it difficult to obtain employment. Too often, commercial agencies seem to feel they cannot profitably spend time on them when the demand is mostly for younger persons; even governmental offices fail to make special efforts, apparently trusting Social Security checks to carry them through. On their own, the elderly tend to lose heart after rejection, dropping out of the labor market.

In late 1965, a small group of elderly people in Norwalk, Connecticut—a lawyer, a social worker, a retired corporation executive, a retired bank president and a retired manufacturer—decided to organize a project to help the elderly help themselves. All had had experience in community projects, such as United Way, Senior Foundation, YMCA, boy and girl scouts; all shared an objective, not only to keep older people in their own homes, given the benefits of an augmented income, but to bolster their morale—to let them know, in a seemingly uncaring world, that they were still wanted, needed and useful.

COC GIVES SUPPORT

The result, Senior Personnel Placement Bureau, Inc., the first of its kind in the state, was welcomed by the Norwalk Chamber of Commerce with open arms: Experienced, efficient labor was scarce, and here was an untapped lode.

For the bureau's first eight months of operation, the chamber supplied—without charge—an office, telephone and clerical help. By then, the fledgling bureau had become such a busy place that it interfered with the chamber's functions, besides becoming identified in the public's mind as an adjunct of the chamber. So the bureau moved to a three-room office in an old, well-located and maintained building, quarters it still occupies.

Contributions (tax-deductible) paid for the rent, telephone service, postage and the salary of the one employee, a secretary, it became necessary to hire for the sake of day-to-day continuity. (Our present secretary, in her seventies, has not been absent or late even once in the more than five years of her employment. How many younger employees can match that record?)

RECEIVE STATE GRANT

In 1966, we applied to the Connecticut Commission on Aging for a three-year grant of $5,200 per annum and received it—the first project to be so funded by the commission. Though the state grant has long since expired, we are managing: Of the bureau's $7,000 annual budget, United Way contributes $2,000, and the balance comes from membership dues ($10 minimum, though many give more). Membership entitles the individual or company to absolutely nothing but the right to attend and vote at the annual meeting, a privilege seldom exercised; large contributors receive no more attention than nonmembers who give nothing.

Two volunteer interviewers are on duty daily from 9 a.m. to 1, with all 20 volunteers serving one day a week. The interviewers, of course, are an all-important factor, as the success of the project rests mostly with them. They must be chosen with care; mere willingness to serve is not enough, nor is efficiency. Those who come to us looking for jobs must leave feeling better than when they came in, reinforcing our original objective of letting them know they're cared about, whether or not a job is available.

IMPROVES WITH AGE

Obviously, positions have not been found for all applicants, though more than 1,500 have been placed. Figures have ranged from placements of 120 to 174 annually in the 10 years of our existence, with 1975, though the figures have not yet been tallied, promising to be the best year yet. The reason for the upsurge is not that jobs are more plentiful now (they aren't) but that the interviewers over the years have developed an expertise which greatly enhances the chances of placement, saving a great deal of wasted motion by both interviewer and client. One morning each month, all 20 interviewers meet to bring up special problems that have arisen and to consider ways of improving the operation.

Discounting any job the bureau may secure for the client, the idea that someone cares and takes the time to talk the job problem out promotes an increased feeling of contentment and security. In effect, the men and women interviewers also serve as counselors.

JOB TYPES VARY

Most placements have been in the $2.50 to $3.50 hourly rate range; however, a considerable number have been in jobs paying more than $10,000 per annum. For instance, there's the architect in his seventies who wanted to practice his profession without being tied to a desk; we found him a job as consultant to the City of Norwalk. Every blueprint of any city construction work must have his approval, and he also sees to it that the materials called for in the project are actually used. He has saved the city many times his salary.

Another client, an attractive metallurgist of high standing in her profession, found little need for her abilities in our area until she came to us. We found her a job with a large electronics concern, where she is charged with conducting visiting scientific groups through the plant as well as practicing metallurgy. She and the firm are both delighted.

THEY DO THE TALKING

We find it highly advisable to let the client do most of the talking, with the interviewer asking general questions in the hope that the client will disclose, sometimes unwittingly, some of the interests he/she may have thought too insignificant to mention in other job hunts. For instance, there was the man who had been in the field of textile manufacturing before he moved to our area, where there is none. In the course of conversation, the interviewer found that he is an omnivorous (though undiscriminating) reader. His good appearance and pleasant manner helped in his placement in a bookstore, where he is a most happy man.

Then there was the man who had been in the restaurant business in New York City for his total working life, had retired to Norwalk and extreme boredom with idleness. He needed extra income as well as the work itself but only knew how to run a restaurant. We found him one, whose owner wanted more time for other pursuits. It worked out perfectly well until the restaurant was sold to make room for a housing development.

Instead of going back to boredom, our client moved to Columbus, Ohio, where he created his own senior personnel placement bureau! Which, incidentally, now operates very efficiently, on a much larger scale than ours.

MANY JOBS MENIAL

The preceding cases were for unusually well-paying jobs. For the most part, the openings we have are for companions, factory workers, clerks, custodians, babysitters, yard workers and home repairmen. Before sending anyone to a home job, we screen the applicant carefully, as there have been some unfortunate experiences. One job for which we have constant requests, and often cannot fill, is that of a round-the-clock "companion," in reality amounting to practical nursing. The going rate for this work is so high that those who need the service usually cannot afford it.

We labor under one great disadvantage—the withholding of Social Security payments above earnings of $2,760 annually. Few of our clients are willing to forego these monthly checks; cash in hand is what they want, and no arithmetic can convince them otherwise. Many employers, as well, hesitate to hire a person they know will quit when the magic figure is reached, perhaps at a time when the employee is vitally needed. Something must be done to correct this situation!

FREE PUBLICITY LAVISH

Publicity is of great importance to maintain our function, and we have been extremely fortunate in that respect. The Norwalk "Hour," a newspaper with a huge proportionate circulation that is read by just about everyone, gives us frequent coverage with articles and every Tuesday lists four of our job openings and the job skills of four of our applicants who need jobs, with a box to fill out and mail to us for an appointment. The local radio station, WNLK, frequently broadcasts information about our operation, and we make tapes that it broadcasts as often as is feasible. Also,

Radio Station WMMM, in nearby Westport, is equally generous. We are never charged for any of these services.

Our own promotional work is handled by a retiree with many years of experience in the personnel department of a large New York corporation, who also freely donates her services. Once or twice a year, one or two of our interviewers visit the personnel managers of area business concerns to make sure they don't forget us.

Not long ago, we received a telephone call for an appointment from a voice that sounded very young. It developed that she was in the high school graduating class. We told her regretfully that ours was not quite that kind of "senior" enterprise, suggesting she call us again in about 50 years.

We'll be around.

AN ALTERNATIVE TO INSTITUTIONAL CARE IN KANSAS

Elbert C. Cole

The Shepherd's Center is being imitated all over the country. It is a unique, innovative co-operative of churches that offers an extensive range of services to, for, and by the elderly in the community. Dr. Cole is pastor of Central Church, Kansas City, and has had a major role in creating the five-year-old program.

With 21 million people over age 65 in the American scene, the political world has been discovering older people since the White House Conference on Aging in 1971. In the last few years, thousands of community groups and single services have developed for older people.

This is the story of one church leading an ecumenical cluster of 22 churches in designing a new style of ministry with older people.

The Shepherd's Center is a concept rather than a piece of real estate. The Center uses existing agencies of the community, existing facilities and older people themselves in a comprehensive program that is as broad as the capabilities of the people. It is directed to meeting a wide variety of needs of the people.

ALTERNATIVES TO INSTITUTIONAL CARE

The Center was created in the summer of 1972, offering "Alternatives to Institutional Care." Now after more than two years of operation, working with more than 2,000 different people, it is clear that the leaders of The Shepherd's Center really have been inventing a new institution. That is, by systematically providing *home* services which in part have helped older people stay in their own homes. For many older people, the Center-sponsored activities have given them a new lease on life through useful service or meaningful programs.

The Kansas City story began with a long distance telephone call to the Rev. Al Murdock with the United Methodist Board of Health and Welfare Ministries staff. We requested his assistance in giving direction to a local group of eight United Methodist leaders from five churches who had formed an *ad hoc* committee to build a United Methodist retirement home facility.

Housing and care are generally so greatly needed by older people that the committee assumed that this was the only answer to the question of how our church can help older people. We soon learned from a professional study made for us by Neil L. Gaynes & Associates that there were other answers to that question.

The study recommended that we give top priority to creating a community service group capable of helping people remain in their own homes. Mr. Gaynes and Mr. Murdock pressed the facts.

Building a multimillion-dollar facility for 300 people was defensible, but how do you respond to the figure that only 5 per cent of the persons over the age of 65 take up residence in institutions, while 95 per cent remain in the community? They also pointed out that developing a retirement facility is very complex and that it is no place for amateurs to dabble.

Working in the community would provide experience. Their argument made good sense, even though at the time it seemed less dramatic and even a detour in planning.

MANY CHURCHES INVOLVED

Churches or clusters of churches all over America are in a unique position to help older people remain in the community and assist them in achieving their life goals. Idle weekday facilities, a reservoir of volunteers and limited dollars can be put to work in pioneering ways to turn older years into a time of enrichment.

The Shepherd's Center was created and the name selected with its image of caring being spawned from a place, forming a supporting network capable of sustaining people on a short-term or a long-term basis.

Although the specifics came from leaders of Central Church, the *ad hoc* committee of other United Methodists supported the dream. It was immediately apparent that to serve all the people in a specific section of the city, the job needed to be shared with all of the churches and synagogues in that area. Therefore, a corporation was formed on the basis of a simple commitment by each church for cooperation and participation.

The target area has a population of 53,000 people with 11,603 over the age of 65. Our first goal was to design services needed for survival, using older persons themselves as planners and volunteers.

Each service was launched and evaluated as functioning effectively before the next service was initiated. Recipients had to live in the target area (or nearby), and be unable to perform the specific service for themselves. It did not seem wise to do things for people which were already being done by someone else or by themselves.

Keeping people independent does mean a careful watch on dependency ties. Using older people themselves as volunteers, it really does not take complicated screening systems to avoid misuse of the services.

The Shepherd's Center has developed seven *home* services with new services added as the need surfaces.

Last year 189 different persons received a hot noon meal produced by the Swope Ridge Health Care Center, but delivered by volunteer men from The Shepherd's Center. This program uses only male volunteers in an effort to encourage men. Retired men have a harder time than women in putting life together after retirement. Teams of six to eight men are used each day to deliver the meals.

The Shoppers are younger housewives who take about 18 persons shopping each week or go shopping for them.

The Transportation volunteers use their own cars to take 20 to 30 people to keep doctors' appointments or to take medical treatment.

The Visitation Program assigns volunteers from the Soroptimist Club who keep in touch with a select list of about 20 persons who are identified as isolated.

The Handyman Project utilizes the skills of 12 to 18 retired craftsmen who are kept busy making minor repairs at a very modest cost for 100 residents of the area each month.

One of the newest services is the Crime Assistance Program. Trained aides who themselves are over 65 work with elderly victims of crime in the area. They deal with questions of resolving anxiety, prevention measures, safety instruction and other means of helping older people. The Shepherd's Center is developing a community model for the Midwest Research Institute in Kansas

City where a two-year study of crimes against elderly persons was recently completed. We are hopeful that this plan may be used elsewhere.

The Night Team has limited use, but is a team of volunteers related to a 24-hour answering service, responding to emergencies involving older people in the target area.

These *home* services do help people remain in their own homes. "If it weren't for The Shepherd's Center, I couldn't stay in my own home." Unresolved is the question of how one helps persons make the decision to take up residence in an adult facility, especially when the person strongly opposes the move.

REFLECTS WESLEYAN CONCERN

Some people might argue what is the church doing in the social service business, but that implied criticism sounds irrelevant in the unfolding drama of people simply trying to make it in life. Physical needs become so intimately related to the pointed questions, "What is life about? What does it mean to grow old and have so difficult a time managing life?" We reflect the concern of John Wesley all over in a new age with new problems but life's same struggle.

However, The Shepherd's Center is not only *home services*. For a different group, sometimes called the young elderly, there are all kinds of things offered. Again a very small percentage of older people really are homebound.

The nursing home stereotype, resisted and resented by older people, fails to understand that people over 65 have a great deal to give. They can be a "swinging" bunch. After all, persons who have spent a lifetime developing their own individuality and uniqueness just won't fit into one slot—"Those old people."

Adventures in Learning is their kind of program. Patterned after a similar program at St. Luke's Church in Oklahoma City, Okla., nearly 800 persons are registered each quarter for a full day of adventure.

Currently, 36 classes and activities are offered, starting at 9 a.m., with painful choices having to be made each hour on "which class to attend this hour."

The most popular Adventures in Learning events are the travelogs, foreign affairs lectures and money matter courses. Equally helpful are yoga, Bible study, French, personal growth, gardening, basic education such as speed reading, knitting or history subjects. About 65 volunteers each are required.

The Forum at noon presents an outstanding person or cause as well as a hot meal and plenty of conversation. All the faculty are volunteers and largely drawn from older people who are having a great time themselves sharing their skill or hobby.

Adventures in Learning has become the showcase of The Shepherd's Center, with much happening besides classes. Volunteers man a desk of "privileges, services and discounts." They offer public library cards, transportation passes, magazine exchange and a table full of things.

Friday is also a great day for recruiting volunteers, not only for the many services of The Shepherd's Center, but also for an endless number of causes and groups in the community. The Forum is a much sought-after platform for service agencies to tell their stories, public leaders to find support and just interesting people doing exciting things. Governor Christopher Bond launched his year's program for older people in Missouri from the Forum program. And Senator Thomas Eagleton and Representative Richard Bolling make regular reports from Washington.

MAIN CONCERN IS HEALTH

Older people are futuristic. They are eager to keep informed and up-to-date about new developments in the city or hear a scholar explore some knotty problem in society or in personal health.

Like young adults, older people are "now" people. They are not much interested in idle talk or suggestions that violate common sense.

As personal health is listed by older people as their number one concern, The Shepherd's Center holds an annual Health Fair exclusively for those over 60. The Fair has exhibits by 35 or 40 health agencies who are eager to get their message to older people.

Screening tests are offered as well as medical lectures for general information. Each year dozens of persons are turned up who are encouraged to see their private physicians.

In the works now is a regular weekly health screening program for older people.

The annual Pre-Retirement Seminars of six sessions are directed to a younger group in their 50s to 60s.

The Shepherd's Center plays an advocacy role too, never missing a chance to interpret to the community or to political leaders some of the basic needs and concerns of older people. Leaders of the Center have tried to be helpful to others working in their neighborhoods so that better things can happen for older people.

The Center conceives of itself as a conduit to the older people of the target area, helping other agencies from the larger metropolitan area to be more effective by serving the people of the neighborhood.

The Life Enrichment Center is another new program with great potential. Its purpose is to bring together a limited number of older people who need additional support, love and understanding. It is for those whose physical, emotional and spiritual resources have been depleted, but who, in association with one another and under professional leadership, might find new life and hope. In its present form it meets twice each week and the enrollment is limited to 24.

The Life Enrichment Center is a "slashaway" from medical problems suggesting the great number of older people who find more need for attention regarding their "dis-ease" than they do disease.

So there is the Kansas City story. It all began with a telephone call. Put it all together and it is called The Shepherd's Center, projecting the image that someone cares.

Central and the other churches have special programs for their own people, but The Shepherd's Center gives impetus to all of them. As the work of The Shepherd's Center has matured, there is increased awareness of a whole new field that needs attention by church leaders. If God created life and called it "good," as the Genesis story tells it, can the older years realistically be called good?

If the apple helps us know the difference between God and man, then when this difference is accepted, we might turn from notions of pursuing youth with the thought that we will live forever, to accepting those years we have from age 65 to 100 to live a useful life of fulfillment.

Others will have to sort out the impact of The Shepherd's Center on Central Church, the most involved of all the 22 churches. Perhaps the words of a visitor will be sufficient for the present. "This must be some different kind of church."

SENIOR ACTUALIZATION AND GROWTH EXPLORATIONS (SAGE)

Suzanne Fields

Gay Luce, a Berkeley psychologist well known for her book *Body Time,* became intrigued several years ago with the Tibetan attitude toward old age. Among Tibetans, it is considered the ideal time for inner growth and contemplation. Her inquiries and experimentation resulted in SAGE—a fresh and promising approach toward mental health for old people.

It is probably not surprising that SAGE began in California, which some skeptics see as the psychotherapy fad capital of the country. But don't let that seduce you into automatic belief or disbelief. People from all parts of the country have expressed interest in watching videotapes of the program; there are increasing requests for SAGE training workshops from professionals and paraprofessionals working in the field of gerontology, and parts of the SAGE programs are being evaluated in a research and demonstration project funded by the National Institute of Mental Health.

Harold Wise, M.D., director of the Family Center at Montefiore Hospital and Medical Center in New York, and an observer of the program, attests to its "sound medical and psychological foundation." He writes that at SAGE "there exists a programmatic approach to realize the positive aspects of the definition of health where health is regarded not just as the absence of disease. . . . The meditative practices are sound both for relaxation and for assisting this group to take stock of their lives and to face the prospect of death in a growthful way."

To find out how the human potential movement has spilled over into programs for the elderly, with the audacious philosophy that the elderly have human potential too, relax with an open mind, breathe in, and read on.

CREATING A NEW IMAGE OF AGE

Says a SAGE staff member: "We're not just talking about techniques that make older people feel better, though that's part of what we're doing. We're talking and doing something about changing attitudes toward older people, creating a new image of age."

SAGE began as the brain/feeling child of Gay Gaer Luce, Ph.D., science writer, psychologist, and a forceful advocate of the notion that there can be life after middle age, even in America. She was encouraged to help older people draw on her knowledge of meditation, relaxation, and biofeedback techniques when she saw how these techniques helped her mother, 71, feel better physically and mentally. She believes that depression among older people is often a direct result of cultural attitudes that "discard the elderly while idolizing the youthful." This country, she says, encourages a sense of uselessness and loneliness, "a negative self-image among older persons that results in a general resignation to a continued decline."

She acknowledges that her theories and methods appear unorthodox to those people working in more conventional ways with the elderly, but she points out that many exercises used in SAGE programs are taken from ancient cultural traditions that "not only recognize the usefulness of the elderly, but are more successful at integrating older people within society."

In Eastern societies, where meditation is highly valued, she says, "Old age is looked at developmentally as a time to look inward, to examine oneself and one's relationship to the universe. Insomnia, for example, which we label a disease, is looked upon as natural, not something to erase with a pill. People wake up early for meditations and think about spiritual matters. Old people are valued for their wisdom."

For people working in the fields of humanistic and transpersonal psychology, there is nothing new in what Luce is saying. However, she is one of the first persons to apply these ideas in a practical way in a program specifically for the elderly.

PROGRAMS TO "GROW" ON

In 1972 she began to look for a program she would wish for herself when she reaches her 60s. She attended gerontological conferences and workshops, and surveyed the gerontological literature, but she couldn't find any mental health programs that perceived old age as a time for growth, a time for opening new possibilities, a time for heightening awareness of body and mind.

With the help of Eugenia Gerrard, a therapist who also special-
izes in breathing and dance techniques, Luce started a pilot project
based on the theory that "people could grow as much at 75 as at
25, if given the same conditions that inspire growth in the young—
nurturance, support, challenge, freedom, and continued activity."

It was not difficult to find 12 relatively healthy volunteers in
their late 60s and 70s who were willing to participate in an experimental program. The major criterion was a willingness, and an
ability, to perform the exercises, and to promise to practice what
they had learned. Each person also had to receive permission from
his or her own physician to participate in the program.

Nine women and three men, all over 65, formed what came to
be called Core Group 1—there have been several core groups since
then—in what could sound to an outsider like a mini-Esalen for the
aging. For two months each participant had two private sessions of
one-and-a-half hours each, during which he or she was taught
techniques of relaxation. For six more months, in church base-
ments and living rooms, they met weekly as a group with several
group leaders (private sessions were optional) doing everything
from staring into each other's eyes to discussing their own fears
about death.

"Eight months sounded like a long time to sign up for in the beginning," says one Core Group 1 member. "We didn't know then
that we'd be begging to continue when it was over." It was not
until last summer, two years later, that the group voted to meet
only once a month, and then without a leader.

"We started with biofeedback in the private sessions as the initial instrument for teaching relaxation," says Luce, "because it was
an impersonal technique, and there was a built-in cultural respect
for the machine. It helped people open doors into themselves without feeling threatened.

"Biofeedback equipment is expensive, but it is not difficult to
train staff to use biofeedback machines," she says, "and of all our
techniques, it's the hardest to fake results." A meter indicating degrees of tension tells the trainer how much a person is relaxing so
that he can help the participant overcome blocks in the process.

John Jameson, 68 (his name is a pseudonym but his age is
real), volunteered because he was tense, depressed, aching from arthritis, and a psychiatrist had not helped him. He had been an ac-

tive business administrator before his retirement and had always been able to relieve work stress through sports. He also liked to build furniture. At 68 he had trouble accepting his physical limitations. Interests, beyond a concern for his ailing body, had disappeared. Through biofeedback and deep breathing exercises John learned to relax. He discovered that when the sensors were attached to his head and he thought about pleasant things the machine clicks would stop.

Gradually the feelings associated with the clicks could be controlled with deep breathing. John became better able to accept his body through yoga movement and massage. Even his arthritic pain seemed to subside. His temperament improved. He gave up smoking. "You can't smoke and deep breathe at the same time," he says. By the time he joined in group meetings he wanted to talk about his dreams. His wife was so impressed with his positive changes that she volunteered to join the next group.

John now speaks frankly about what troubled him. "I had begun to worry about eventually becoming a burden in old age," he says. "The worst part of being old is having to have someone else take care of you, of being dependent." He had thought his pain would be crippling. He now does exercises that seem to relieve it and he has the feeling that he can take responsibility for himself, that he is more in control. He also feels that he has a network of friends he has made through the group with whom he can share problems. "Beats chess or checkers at the senior center," he says.

Old people experience loss all the time. Close friends and relatives die. Funerals become a common social event. Fear lurks in the shadows of the mind. Group consciousness becomes a powerful tool for rebuilding simple emotions of trust, for sharing common concerns about life and death.

"Death itself has taken on a new meaning," says one core group member. "It seems less frightening. The group exercises gave me time to think thoughts I had spent a lot of time denying. The yoga and meditation especially allowed me to contemplate spiritual matters. I never expected that to happen, but I have to admit that I feel better because of it."

The SAGE techniques are offered as aids to growth. No one is forced to do anything he or she doesn't feel comfortable with.

Most of the exercises are conducted with eyes closed so that there is no competition about who can do what.

"Deep breathing is a simple device for creating more energy," says a woman in her late 70s from Core Group 2. "Now when someone talks I not only listen, I breathe. I have a natural resource I can always tap."

Exercises from Tai Chi were initiated when one core group member mentioned her fear of falling and a longing for a surer sense of balance. "Soon people who had been unbalanced were able to stand on one foot, and Tai Chi became an esthetic and contemplative form for centering and quieting the mind," says Luce. "We used well over a thousand different exercises, repeating some of them many times, discarding others as useless."

"Core groups are not for everybody," Luce says. "The people in them have to be willing to be self-aware. We are not offering therapy. Each person comes in to *grow* in a different way, to find new possibilities for himself. Meditation is a good way to pay attention to what one is doing. Core Group 1 was an experiment in preventive medicine, in revitalization, and there is no doubt in our minds or those of our observers that the process succeeded."

For each person breakthroughs have been different. One woman, who celebrated her 75th birthday just before leaving the group, arrived at the first meeting describing herself as "a candidate for a heart attack." She was having severe marital problems. The relief of tensions and the supportiveness of the group gave her the courage to get a divorce and move to Florida to live with her sister.

For another, the affection and nurturance of the group helped her to create a new image of her future. She had arrived despairing and believing that she "belonged nowhere." A year and a half later she was teaching SAGE exercises in a senior center and negotiating with a tourist line to lead elderly people in SAGE exercises on a cruise to South America.

"It would be hard to demonstrate that our participants have actually reduced the amount of medical care they would otherwise need," says Luce. However, many of them state they have been able to rid themselves of aches, pains, and migraines that have bothered them all their lives. One woman, says Luce, brought her blood pressure down from 160/100 to 140/80 after learning Autogenic Training and how to use a sphygmomanometer.

"The most convincing aspect of the program," according to Luce, "is not the verification that relaxation methods and improved mental outlook can eradicate symptoms of illness, but that it can extend methods of preventive medicine and help the individual accept responsibility for his own well-being.

"None of our techniques work across the board," she continues, "and they take time and commitment. What's exciting is that once people begin to see that they can change their lives, unlock themselves, they want to share their experience with others. Today many people from the core groups are taking our training courses so they can teach others what we have taught them."

THE SMELL OF URINE AND APATHY

Twice a week two SAGE staff people and their trainees lead group work in three institutions for the aging—a rest home, a nursing home, and a convalescent hospital. Nothing so fancy or esoteric as Tai Chi goes on here, but the leaders help the older people open up about their feelings and begin to learn the simplest of the deep breathing exercises.

"By their structure and purpose, institutions serving the aged encourage their clients to 'rest' or 'convalesce,' engendering feelings of uselessness," says Eugenia Gerrard, co-founder and co-director of SAGE, and a group leader in a rest home. "There are few opportunities for residents to explore their potential for growth and change, to experience the depth of their feelings, or to talk about their concerns."

What SAGE is doing in these homes is fighting what Luce calls "the smell of urine and apathy." Group leaders feel they are offering healthy alternatives, a sense of group cohesiveness, ideally, a sense of community.

In some group discussions the older people talk about their resentments for having been "abandoned" by their children, their increasing fear of crime on the "outside," current events, their memories of work and child raising. In Crosby's Rest Home, one elderly woman told a SAGE leader, "Other people bring us religion, music, entertainment. You're the only people who let us talk."

Says group leader and SAGE co-director Kenneth Dychtwald:

"I have to keep reminding myself that these people don't get in their cars and drive home. They will probably stay here until they die. I'm shocked with their vast unused energy of wisdom and love."

Jim Cummings, an intern leading a group of about 20 women in their 70s and 80s in Claremont Convalescent Hospital, spoke about his 29th birthday, which he was celebrating that day. He asked each woman what they remembered about their 29th year. Some of them understood him to mean 1929, but in almost every instance they warmed to the task of relating a specific memory. To integrate some physical exercise into the discussion, he asked them to animate some of the anecdotes—rock a baby in their arms, clap their hands with enthusiasm at a salary increase, stir the batter of a birthday cake.

There was rich applause after certain recitations. A feeling of camaraderie was infectious. Responding to the affection everyone was clearly feeling towards him, Jim went around to every woman for a birthday kiss. Even those women prone to falling asleep because of their drugs rose to the occasion. For just one moment, as if by a sorcerer's magic, each of them became a vivacious young woman with a gentleman caller. A real visitor of any kind is a special event.

Each group meeting in a nursing home or convalescent hospital takes a different form. "Professionals say you can't get a group process going in this kind of institutional situation," says Sarah Newbern, a group leader at the convalescent hospital, "but we meet in a group and there is a group process operating. The old people respond to each other's memories and participate with enthusiasm, anger, sadness, and laughter."

On one election day, for example, a leader asked all the participants in one group how they would feel if they were president. Out of this question developed a spirited discussion by all the participants about their own feelings, not of being president, but of power*less*ness. The topic struck a chord in these elderly people, and group process played upon it.

EVALUATION AND TRAINING

SAGE staff would like to set up an evaluation process for their institutional work as they have done for their core program, with the help of a research and development grant from the National Institute of Mental Health. They want to see if they can have a long range influence on altering certain negative effects of institutional living. For the moment, however, they depend on small grants, donations, and income from their training program to finance their group work, and their budgets don't always make the payroll. There is no money for evaluation research.

"It is likely," says Luce, "that our impact on the nursing homes will be largely attributable to training aides and directors in alternative attitudes toward the last phase of life, offering them guidelines for activities that do not trivialize these precious weeks, days, hours. We hope we can convince them of the value of expanding consciousness instead of obliterating it, and can offer the dying an undrugged transition in heightened awareness, using the individual's own symbology."

SAGE staff would like to expand their training programs to people working inside institutions for the aging. The bulk of the courses has been made up of social workers, nurses, core participants, and college students. The training is designed to develop skills and does not result in any kind of job credential, but credentials aren't in special favor among SAGE staff, anyway. Some of them have doctoral degrees, others have master's or undergraduate degrees, but experience in the program is usually the value which is stressed. Those more experienced supervise the less experienced. Criteria for group leaders are sensitivity, caring for older people, patience, and an ability to be self-aware and to work on oneself, too.

"I'm concerned with getting people to use what's already there," Eugenia says. "Without us, these older people have less. In the institutions, many of them are simply 'killing time.' What we've got to do is build on our strengths, discover ways to offer them more. We're not making sensational claims. We need to learn from every experience. But you wouldn't believe some of the changes we've seen. People look forward to meeting with us and talking about themselves, people who otherwise sleep most of the day."

"The only demand we make on each other," says group leader Gene Kunitomi, "is that we remain honest and open. That's why we are constantly meeting with each other and discussing our own process. We want to be sure that what we are doing with the older people is what the older people want. We have to examine and reexamine our choices and preferences. We are not therapists who create a dependence. We are facilitators reaching out to each person's humanity."

There is an enthusiasm and dedication about SAGE staffers that is reminiscent of the passions of many college students in the 1960s who were more concerned with being *involved with* than *studying about* a subject. An observer doesn't need an elaborate methodology, SAGE people say, to measure a bright-eyed smile on an old person's face.

But there are always complex financial problems for this kind of program. If SAGE is going to get people to pay for their programs, it must show that what it is doing can be replicated with results. SAGE hopes an NIMH grant will do this. There are always some people who will benefit more from these exercises than from medication. But who are these people? What discrimination should be made? What kinds of funding besides grants and private monies can support SAGE programs? What kinds of incentives can there be for nursing home operators to contract SAGE services or send staff to train with them? Time, experience, and present research will suggest some future direction.

SAGE intends to publish a how-to-do-it manual of its techniques. Until then, SAGE people rest their case on their experience with the volunteer participants, men and women in their late 60s through their 80s, who often heard of the program through the gerontological grapevine: "There's this crazy group in Berkeley that's turning old people on. . . ."

LIVING TO THE END: THE HOSPICE EXPERIMENT

John Knoble

The hospice movement is a new approach to terminal care. Imported from England, it promises to provide environments "which can humanize the process of dying—by consecrating death as a part of life."

Some Connecticut Yankees have imported from England a revolutionary medical concept that promises liberation from one of humanity's oldest fears—the drug-deadened, death-in-life long considered inevitable for the patient with a chronic degenerative disease. Known as the hospice movement, it makes the thought of euthanasia unnecessary.

The hospice movement (the word "hospice" means a community of sojourners along the way) says the time has come for medical science to apply its wisdom to the task of helping people who can't get well die comfortably and meaningfully. It seeks to do this by establishing specialized terminal-care facilities where patients may live until they die. Over 50 groups have been formed in the U.S.A.

Interest in the concept was sparked in 1969 when the Rev. Edward F. Dobihal, Jr., director of the Department of Religious Ministries at Yale-New Haven Hospital, spent several months as visiting chaplain at St. Christopher's Hospice in northeast London, founded in 1949 by Dr. Cicely Saunders.

Chaplain Dobihal had seen countless people go through the dying process in the hectic atmosphere of a general hospital and he was impressed with the difference at St. Christopher's. He began to talk with his Yale Medical School and School of Nursing associates. A group visited St. Christopher's and was impressed.

A young expert in pain control, Dr. Sylvia Lack, came to New Haven in 1973 to initiate the Home Care Program. She had worked for two years in a joint appointment at St. Joseph's Hospice and St. Christopher's. In her work she uses combinations of drugs instead of just one, with excellent results, and stresses that "non-narcotic drugs can be used for a long time effectively when psychological factors affecting the patient are positive."

Financed by the National Cancer Institute, Hospice, Inc., has completed the second full year of its Home Care Program. Now, foundations and individuals have contributed to the goal of building a $3.1 million, 44-bed inpatient facility in Branford, Conn. A $1.5 million Federal appropriation was approved by the House Subcommittee on Labor and Health, Education and Welfare in May 1977. A National Advisory Council headed by Elisabeth Kübler-Ross (author of the best-selling *On Death and Dying*) includes more than 50 physicians and nurses, all recognized across the country for their expertise in terminal care.

The Branford inpatient facility was inspired by what has been done in hospices in England. It is designed by a group of New Haven concerned citizens, including doctors and nurses, as a model for American hospices. The group has already shown how well the concept works in the Home Care Program. Money for the facility is being sought from small as well as large contributors; it is for everyone.

Only a score of American general hospitals now have terminal-care departments that provide medical resources for comfort beyond the scope of nursing homes or convalescent hospitals.

To date, the Home Care Program has served some several hundred terminal patients and their families. In one recent 12-month period, 50 out of 170 patients died; of these, 17–23 per cent more than the national average percentage—died at home. Although the numbers are too few to make a statistical point, hospice people consider this a direct experience confirmation of similar percentages over the years in English hospices. And the figures provide grounds for their own confidence that hospice-type home care will enable many more people to have this universal wish granted.

Drugs are administered orally before the onset of pain. The procedures are used that have been found effective in England. "No one ever has to cry out for relief," Chaplain Dobihal promises.

A hospice report also showed that those who did die in a hospital had been able to stay home an average of approximately two weeks longer before entering.

The daughter of one patient wrote: "My mother, ill with can-

398   THE HOSPICE EXPERIMENT

cer, wished to stay at home with her family. I needed help. Her physician recommended hospice. It was very reassuring to know that we could get help at any time, day or night. They always came to the house daily. In fact, they offered to come and stay with mother all night so I could get some sleep. At the time of her death they were here with us. It's been two months since her death, and they are still in touch with us."

By means of a sophisticated combination of anti-emetics, individual formulas are found for each patient for control of nausea, so that patients have an appetite for eating. "A simple meal is a powerful symbol of life," Nurse Charlotte Gray of the Yale School of Nursing says.

Hospice people do not like the term often applied to hospices— "a beautiful place to die." The focus, they insist, is on life. "Most patients will be able to engage in meaningful conversation right up to the day of taking leave," is a familiar prediction by hospice enthusiasts. In the new building, children will be welcome visitors.

Not long ago, my wife and I decided to see St. Christopher's for ourselves. We found a building more like a vacation lodge than a hospital. "Ministering to the whole person is so important in pain control," Dr. Saunders says. "And that has many facets. It starts with the morale of the staff and the volunteers who go into the community. It includes relations with the patient's primary physician." She mentions how spiritual well-being is furthered by the help of clergy, psychologists, and other professionals, as well as by the constant evidence that those who surround the patient *care*.

Nurse Barbara McNulty of St. Christopher's told us: "Six patients who recently came into residence have been released to their homes. We have actually found that there is a good chance in many cases that our methods may prolong life."

The Branford Hospice will copy St. Christopher's provision for a nursery for children of staff members, "so they won't have to worry about their youngsters, and so the sound of children's feet and voices will witness to life."

Dr. Saunders, however, insists that St. Christopher's should not be thought of as a model for Branford's Hospice. "You in America have your own distinctive genius," she says.

Lo-Yi Chan, the architect of Branford's Hospice, talks about the facility: "Color, furnishings, and space will convey the impression that this is a pleasant place to be. Whether in a wheelchair or a bed, the patient will be mobile. In good weather, patients' beds can be moved into a garden."

While technical support systems will be at a minimum as compared to a general hospital, palliative X-ray, pharmacy, diagnostic radiology, oxygen, and suction systems will still be used as needed, with a back-up arrangement for quick transportation to a general hospital if other supports are prescribed.

"The Hospice will look like a part of life," Chan says. "Windows make it possible for a world outside to come inside. The setting must invite a nurse to sit on a bed with a patient, maybe hold a hand or shed a sympathetic tear. There will be places for serenity, for when one comes to visit one's father he may find something to say if the room is designed so they are truly alone."

The cost of care in the residential facility will be more than most nursing homes, but considerably less than in a general hospital; it is estimated at 50 per cent less. The fact that the Hospice Program of Home Care reduces the number of days necessary for hospitalization makes for additional saving.

As the hospice movement grows, more and more beds will be freed in acute-disease hospitals throughout the country for care of patients who can possibly recover.

Chaplain Dobihal says: "In the hospice program, patients, family and staff share in the care-giving process. Patients provide other patients with inspiration and encouragement, giving them a sense of service when they might otherwise feel they are of no further use to anyone.

"They enable us to surmount the denial of death we have been taught—denial that has allowed us to tolerate the inhuman vegetation that is the hallmark of superfluousness among the terminally ill in America. But there are no superfluous people, and the extent to which we can humanize the process of dying—*by consecrating death as a part of life*—is a measure of our ability to humanize the process of living."

RETIREMENT PLANNING CLASSES IN LOS ANGELES

Marion Marshall

Older adults can be strengthened to face and enjoy the challenge of retirement living. The final quarter of one's life can be filled with satisfying learning, gratifying service to others, fresh friendships, even a totally new life style. This experimental program is one of many probing this frontier of education.

Since 1948, the Los Angeles Unified School District has offered such a program for older adults. One class began that year; today some 200 year-long classes are offered throughout the district, and almost 50 short-term classes last from four to ten weeks each year. Almost all activities and classes are held during daytime hours, making it easier for older adults to get to class locations. Since the schools are filled with children during these hours, classes go out "to where the older people are," in Senior Citizen Centers, recreation centers, parks, churches and synagogues, retirement and convalescent homes.

No tuition is charged to any student in gerontology classes, nor is there a charge to anyone 60 years of age or over in *any* adult school class. A voluntary student identification card, at 25 cents, is good for a full semester.

CONCENTRATE ON ONE COMPANY

One of the Los Angeles schools' most important and fastest growing classes is retirement planning. Skilled teachers specialize in this area, working with the people most concerned with preretirement planning in one company or organization to make the course meaningful to the students. A teacher may start preparing the curriculum several weeks before class begins, talking with retirement personnel, lining up speakers on the particular retirement benefits involved, finding guest lecturers for areas outside the teacher's particular competence. A typical program will include such subjects as the following:

Changing life styles: The loss of the work role; the "empty nest"; loss of income; the beginning impairment of hearing and sight; changing family relationships and responsibilities, changes in friendships and similar changes that affect one's life style.

Wills and Estates: Why a will is important; how to make a will; defining and distributing one's estate; what is involved in probate.

Health: Why mental health is important in retirement; physical health and how to take care of oneself; emotional stability with the advance of old age; nutrition and exercise needs.

Leisure time: How to use the rest of those free hours after one has done the promised reading and fishing and travel. Developing satisfying hobbies, belonging to organizations, creating new friendships and social contacts.

New careers: We speak today of paid or unpaid "careers," hoping retirees will offer their services to nonprofit public and private agencies often needing volunteers to continue operation.

'DOVES' WORK WITH CHILDREN

Nearly 1,000 older volunteers work in the Los Angeles City Schools extension program, DOVES (Dedicated Older Volunteers in Educational Services). Retired people with time to give are asked to volunteer in elementary, secondary or adult education. Some prefer tutoring; others work in offices, libraries, lunchrooms or playgrounds. One 73-year-old woman coached water ballet in a high school. An 83-year-old man helps teach woodcraft to elementary children. A man with very little education helps ghetto children learn better reading and writing. Still another, an immigrant, helps youngsters with spelling and arithmetic.

The children also look forward to "grandma or grandpa" helping with arithmetic, woodwork or softball. Many just want a "grandparent" to talk with, someone who will listen sympathetically. Stories of "when I was young" capture children's attention and imagination, thus becoming a source of oral history.

New, paying careers can be developed from hobbies, or entirely new interests may be discovered. Retirement planning courses explore means to these ends.

Pension plans: Here again, the teacher works with the organization's personnel towards the best possible presentations. Only someone within the organization can have all the information employees will need in order to calculate their retirement benefits.

Social Security: Experts from the Social Security office in the area where the class is held discuss Medicare and Social Security benefits. This is of particular interest to both participant and spouse; with or without another pension plan, Social Security benefits make up the entire income of many Americans after retirement.

Taxes: Benefits offered to older adults, including income tax, property tax and rental rebates, are explained to participants. Exemptions can make quite a difference in income level.

Agencies and organizations involved with retired people tell of their services: Where to get help; how to apply; where to find special programs, including recreation and education. Books in large print, nutrition programs and housing help are included.

Problems: Housing after retirement, transportation needs, fraud schemes and consumer protection are explored.

A school in the south-central, predominantly black area of Los Angeles was the first to ask for a course in retirement planning. Only a small group attended, but the benefits to those who did take the course were quite obvious. Some of the participants, classified employees of the Board of Education, took the idea to one of their associations, with the result that the next class met in the boardroom at the main office. Almost 100 attended that class, were enthusiastic about the learning experience and recommended that the class be offered at least once each year.

COURSE POPULARITY GROWS

Several years passed before the certificated employees asked for a preretirement planning course. A separate series was established, but soon the two groups were combined and the course continued to grow. Now given twice a year, it is attended by some 400 employees. The only separate sessions are the ones on pensions; the two groups of employees belong to different retirement plans.

Research has shown that the more thoroughly one plans for the retirement years, the more likely it is that these years will be successful. Life satisfactions are much higher in those who look forward to retirement, who have plans to retire *to* something and are not just retiring *from* a job.

"Fishing is a great sport, but after eating all the fish you like and giving gifts of fish to friends, what will you do then?" asks Alva Nealy, a well-known teacher of preretirement planning. She goes on to point out that though travel is stimulating and educational, for most people it is economically possible only for that one big trip one has been promising oneself.

To paraphrase Eric Hoffer, a former labor leader and more recently a philosopher, a tree must have roots to continue to grow. An older person must continue to grow in order to keep his roots established; what better way to grow than through study? "Retirement," says Mr. Hoffer, "should be spent in good books, conversation with friends and leisurely study."

ADVOCATES LIFETIME LEARNING

Karl Kunze, retired personnel director for Lockheed of California, has said that good counseling should point out the educational needs "K through K: Kindergarten through Kaput." In practice, this would involve counseling for all phases of life, suggesting that people *do* live after the age of 25 or 30, which is where many studies seem to end. Too often counselors are willing to help a person understand what will be needed in the conventional school years and may even assist into first employment, but seldom do they go any further. "The education we don't get is education for our later years, and that often is when we need it most," Mr. Kunze says.

Many companies and unions, although otherwise concerned with their members' well-being, fail to offer any form of retirement planning. Now that more union members are in the age of retirement, the unions must begin to consider seriously the needs of these retirees. Some unions have offered occasional courses, trips or special events; some have organized retiree clubs, such as the highly successful Pioneer Club of the Pacific Telephone Company. Companies such as Lockheed, the Automobile Club of Southern California and TRW offer regular services to their retirees, calling on educational institutions or utilizing their own personnel to give regular retirement counseling.

AGING SHOULD BE TAUGHT

When should such education begin? Gerontologists generally agree that the whole concept of aging needs to be included in elementary and secondary education. By the time retirement occurs, the individual has accepted his age and looks forward to the "golden" one-fourth of life. Surely, everyone should begin serious planning 10 to 15 years before retirement.

It should be remembered that retirement involves the entire family; not only the retiring worker, but the spouse is greatly affected. Margaret Mead is credited with saying, "Retirement is half as much income with twice as much husband." Another time she quipped, "I married him for better or for worse, but not for lunch."

All of which illustrates some real problems for many retirees. Discontent grows when husband and wife, thrown together 24 hours each day, don't know what to do about it. Divorce rates go up; adult children are often plagued by doting grandparents who have nothing else to do but spend their days with their children, who, though delighted to see them, if it occurs too frequently may also resent the additional work involved in having extra people around. Many people approaching retirement are afraid to discuss their fears or the problems they foresee. A skilled teacher can help allay such fears, aiding participants to work out ways to avoid or take care of problems.

RETIRE TO SOMETHING!

What can one retire *to?* That depends largely on personal interests. My husband planned years ahead, beginning a book publishing company now growing in his retirement years. Karl Kunze has become a counselor in retirement planning; Eric Hoffer is a writer and philosopher. Margaret Mead continues her research, speaking and writing.

Retired policemen become teachers in traffic safety or police science. Some friends of mine have taken up traveling as guides and sponsors, satisfying the urge to travel while making it financially possible. And many older people become volunteers, giving of their skills and services wherever needed, as in the Retired Senior Volunteer Program (RSVP) sponsored by ACTION on a national level. Nonprofit public and private agencies also recruit older people to perform work that, satisfying to them, also gives real service. Veterans' hospitals, family welfare agencies, community centers and youth groups are among recipients of such services.

With skills they enjoy using, volunteers can teach formally or informally, make useful items for distribution, answer phones, do preliminary screening of clients, serve as receptionists and perform a myriad of jobs the agency might otherwise not be able to afford. Who benefits? Both the volunteer and the service recipients.

Voluntary ACTION Centers are another source of volunteer opportunities, where volunteers of all ages train together and work side by side. These programs have been so successful that ACTION is now sponsoring others specifically for older adults.

MANY AGENCIES NEED HELP

If none of these organizations are now in your community, invite agency representatives to speak at a retirement planning course, telling of their needs and of the advantages to the volunteer. Also of interest to retirees are the national and local retirement organizations such as the American Association of Retired Persons (AARP), the National Association of Senior Citizens, the National Retired Teachers Association, the Gray Panthers and many others. Churches, community organizations, recreation departments and educational institutions offer clubs and groups in leisure-time activities.

If your community doesn't have a retirement planning program, the adult education department of the local school system is the logical place to begin. Most adult school programs include the concept of "community" and are eager to live up to that commitment. This means that a school district often will help a business, industry or an agency by providing a certificated teacher who will teach his/her own areas of expertise and also act as coordinator for the invited experts. If there is a tuition charge, it is usually very nominal. Adult schools are flexible, meaning that the class can be held at a plant or facility, or the school will find another suitable location. The teacher assigned will have community contacts with speakers and can arrange for hand-out materials as well as for registration and attendance records.

Some businesses offer working time off for those taking such a class. A class scheduled from 4 to 6 p.m. may include one hour of work time plus one hour of personal time. Or the class may be held in the mornings or evenings. When none of these arrangements are practical or when participants have to travel long distances, some have held all-day Saturday seminars. The advantages include the participation of spouses, a more relaxed atmosphere because it is a day off, and the opportunity to include a luncheon, making for sociability.

Disadvantages are a possible reluctance to take a whole day from a coveted weekend and the fact that there is little time to absorb the many facets of retirement. Fatigue sets in about 3 p.m., and almost any information delivery after that may be wasted. Still, the one-day seminar is better than no chance to plan at all. An alternative, if no weekday time is available, is to hold the class on two or three Saturday mornings. Evaluation is important for any educational course, and retirement planning is no exception.

Until at least three or four complete courses have been offered, it is hard to determine the style that best suits the people from a given company. Input from students, teachers, company personnel and impartial observers can all be combined to determine the best approach. Also, many private firms offer preretirement packages. Many are quite good, though expensive. AIM, an AARP branch, has developed a packet and a course that takes a full weekend at a cost of $225 per person. The instructor's kit is $300.

Though the AARP material is good, it still requires a knowledgeable person to lead the discussions and to answer questions. The same goals can be accomplished through your local community adult school at far less cost, with the advantages of having a community person who is both interested and involved in future planning. Another way is that used at TRW in Los Angeles, where selected key personnel were trained by an adult schoolteacher. After three complete seminars, the trainees felt ready to take over. This method may suit certain organizations that can afford to release such persons for this purpose.

HOW DO YOU ORGANIZE?

How do you organize a retirement planning class? Some agencies send personnel letters to employees who will reach retirement age in five to ten years, inviting them to attend (with spouse if one is involved). Others advertise in house organs, opening the class to any interested persons. Churches and synagogues have offered such classes to their congregations, usually inviting other community residents to join them for the course.

Some adult schools list the course in their regular schedules, so local residents can plan to attend. Newspapers, flyers, radio and television announcements all help if a large group is desired. An adult school will usually be able to help an organization with flyers and other printed material needed in the teaching.

The retirement planning class emerges as the one broadly satisfactory means of assisting almost every man and woman approaching retirement. If available times and meeting places aren't completely satisfactory, go ahead and plan the class anyway. Those who attend will tell you what additional information they need and how the class can improve the next time it is given. Some of your students will return to take the class again. You may even come up with a new format that will revolutionize the teaching of retirement planning!

AFTER 65: RESOURCES FOR SELF-RELIANCE

Theodore Irwin

The range of services useful for the elderly is deftly sketched here, including transportation, meals, in-home care, visiting and telephone checkups, senior centers, and legal assistance. Many communities have instituted such services in the past few years, but the absence of one or another of them can provide a fine focus for senior activism. Particularly promising is the day-care option as an alternative to institutionalization.

The capacity of an older person to function at a decent level of health and well-being may depend largely on the community resources open to him. Traditionally, these have been fragmented among family service agencies, public welfare departments, community centers, churches, settlement houses. Currently, resources range from home nursing to mobile meals, telephone calls to the homebound, friendly visitors, and day center facilities.

Such services are designed to supplement rather than substitute for family help. "Expansion of community social and health services," contends Elaine M. Brody, "can strengthen family ties and enable family members to maximize their functioning in meeting responsibilities to the elderly."

The Older Americans Act of 1965 gave considerable impetus to community planning for the elderly by authorizing funds to help establish and strengthen agencies on aging and to develop opportunities for older people. As a consequence, a wide diversity of demonstration projects were set up in such fields as legal aid, libraries, nutrition, transportation, homemaker service, and employment counseling.

These and other programs are tools with which to combat both the withdrawal from society by members of the older generation and their exclusion by our society. Yet these tools are still inadequate in many respects. In some communities, these resources do not exist at all; in others, they meet only a small part of the need.

A large segment of the aging population would pay a fee for needed services but are unable to acquire them for a fee they can afford. And even the reasonably affluent suffer when services are unavailable. But new provisions for the elderly are emerging. . . .

DAY CENTERS FOR THE ELDERLY

After her stroke, seventy-seven-year-old Myra Barrow became a burden to her daughter and son-in-law, whose home in Baltimore she was sharing. Mrs. Barrow could move about to a limited extent, but needed help and rehabilitation. Her family felt she shouldn't be left alone; the constant demands on them were a strain.

Highly sensitive, Mrs. Barrow feared being put in a nursing home, which to her meant "the end," cut off from her beloved family. And her family was more than willing to keep her in their home—if somehow the pressures could be reduced.

The happy solution: day care at a Baltimore geriatric center and hospital. Each weekday morning, Mrs. Barrow and seven other older adults are picked up by a van-type vehicle fitted with a lift to accommodate those who would otherwise find it hard to step into it. At the center's affiliated hospital, she receives treatment from a physical therapist, following a program prescribed by her own doctor. A nurse is there to observe her, carry out the doctor's orders, and give her her medication on time.

During the day, Mrs. Barrow enjoys making afghans in arts and crafts, occasionally watches a movie, attends parties, listens to speakers on current events. She has gained new friends—men and women of her generation—many of whom have heart conditions or other serious physical handicaps. Mrs. Barrow has her special-diet lunch in the common dining room and a late-afternoon meal that further relieves the pressure on her daughter. In the evening, Mrs. Barrow returns home to her familiar bed. A social worker from the center occasionally visits the family.

Her daughter reports that Mrs. Barrow has improved remarkably. More talkative now, she always has something to relate when she comes home. She no longer stays up late at night; at the day's end, she's ready for bed, and she gets up in the morning eager to go to the center. Her daughter expresses deep gratitude for the respite—she is now able to concentrate more on her children. And the idea of placing her mother in a nursing home is no longer mentioned.

Relatively new, day centers for the elderly are a growing trend. More than fifty such facilities already are functioning in twenty states. They are designed to serve the disabled and enfeebled who need constant attention, but not the around-the-clock care furnished by a hospital or a nursing home.

Besides the socializing and therapy, a major merit is that the center is much less costly than other forms of care. Going to a day center eliminates the need for and expense of a nurse-companion or a nursing home, both often more than a family can afford. At the Baltimore center, Mrs. Barrow's family pays only thirteen dollars a day, including transportation. A semiprivate room in a first-class nursing home would cost thirty to fifty dollars for a twenty-four-hour day.

Most day centers are still in a somewhat experimental stage. Generally, they observe criteria of the Department of Health, Education, and Welfare: a pleasant, safe environment; immediate access to skilled medical attention; provision for self-care training, including dressing and grooming; leisure-time activities in groups; supervised administration of required medication; and at least one nutritious meal a day.

The majority of centers are run in conjunction with hospitals or nursing homes supported by public or charitable funds. Increasing interest, however, has been shown by proprietary hospitals and nursing homes.

Unfortunately, Medicare does not cover charges of such centers, and thus far, in most states, neither does Medicaid.

GETTING AROUND

In many parts of the country, lack of transportation constitutes a major handicap for the elderly. If there is no way for them to move around, in or out of a community, healthy and physically mobile persons can be isolated as completely as if they were bedridden. Most older persons do not drive or own cars. Taxis are apt to be too costly, and fares for mass transit—where there are such facilities—keep rising.

For these reasons, many older adults can't enjoy free concerts or visits to parks. Supermarkets are often too far for walking, particularly with heavy packages. Some people, due to physical weakness—or because of fear in certain neighborhoods—need an escort. Without mobility, the elderly often abandon the idea of visiting friends, relatives, and senior centers, or engaging in other social activities.

Al Haven, seventy-two, has high blood pressure and a troubling hip condition. He could use free medical services, but finds traveling to the clinic very difficult. He would also like to go to church on Sundays, but that's three miles from his home. How can he get around?

His son learned that the local Red Cross had set up a transportation clearinghouse for the elderly, to provide door-to-door service when needed. Some community and voluntary organizations sponsor a special bus for needed trips. In Chicago, for example, the YMCA has set up a Senior Citizens Mobile Service. Transportation is free to such places as welfare agencies, and for outings or shopping tours. Many who have taken advantage of the service have said they feel at least ten years younger as a result and enduring friendships have been made during the rides.

In South Providence, Rhode Island, a station wagon bought by the State Division on Aging makes trips to doctors' offices and hospitals, though many people use it to go grocery shopping. Some senior citizen centers provide a bus that runs between members' homes and the centers. A "Dial-a-Bus" system in Menlo Park, California provides transportation for senior center members. The bus is also used for group outings.

As an alternative to regular bus transportation, a "Dial-a-Ride" project in Haddonfield, New Jersey provides door-to-door mobility. One bus is specially equipped for handicapped persons and people in wheelchairs. Wichita, Kansas has a similar system for low-income persons otherwise unable to get to medical facilities.

Elsewhere, particularly in suburban and rural areas, volunteers drive private cars for the elderly. North Carolina conducted a successful demonstration project, "Helping Wheels," in which one hundred volunteer senior drivers provided rides for their peers to club meetings, doctors, and churches.

Because over 40 per cent of all older persons are poor or nearly poor, there is a great need for reduced fares on mass transit. More than fifty cities in fourteen states now offer senior citizens low fares on mass transit during nonrush hours. In San Francisco, senior citizens pay only five cents; New York City and Chicago charge half-fare; in Lorain, Ohio, it's free.

More and better mobility gives the elderly a much needed lift in spirits, too. For people like Al Haven, getting around now has reopened the world.

MEAL SERVICES

"I eat alone, so it's hardly worth bothering to cook much," says Mary Oblonski, a painfully thin seventy-one-year-old. Mealtimes for her are irregular and too often she turns to snacks to satisfy her hunger. Her physician tells her she is undernourished, almost anemic. Mrs. Oblonski only shrugs helplessly.

Loneliness can lead to poor nutrition. Throughout Mrs. Oblonski's life, before her husband died and her children moved away, meals were a social occasion, a pleasant time for family gatherings. Deprived of the social element, meals hold little attraction for her.

For people living in solitude, or unable to market or prepare food satisfactorily for themselves, home-delivered, nutritious meals are available in many communities. Often they consist of a balanced hot noon meal and a cold supper left for the evening meal. This service, commonly known as "Meals on Wheels," may be carried on under the auspices of a religious or civic organization. In some communities, private cars are used to deliver the meals; in others, special vehicles with equipment to keep food hot or cold are used.

Charges vary, often based on ability to pay. Welfare departments may authorize and pay for the service to persons receiving old-age assistance or those with very low incomes. Meals on Wheels may also be purchased with food stamps.

One of the largest programs, in Baltimore, is run almost entirely by volunteers. It has ten separate kitchens, most located in churches, and uses the services of state nutritionists.

Another service is group meals in a social setting, which can be important for the mental well-being of older people. Dining locations are easily accessible, though food may be prepared elsewhere, such as in school cafeterias after the students' lunch hour. In St. Louis, eight to twelve neighborhood residents meet at one another's homes for a noon meal, which is delivered. Thus, old people can get together informally and eat family-style with a minimum of travel time. Denver has SAMS (Serve-A-Meal to Seniors) in five different locations. Rent and utilities are paid by host organizations such us the Salvation Army.

Many group-meal projects add programs featuring speakers on nutrition, health, Social Security, and other subjects of interest to the elderly. A number of senior clubs hold meetings in conjunction with a meal, then offer their recreational facilities. Besides better nutrition, group meals provide the fringe benefits of generating new friendships and a renewed interest in life. For the housebound, home-delivered meals provide a daily link with the outside world, someone to greet every day.

Aimed at aiding the isolated elderly, a $100-million nutritional program has been made available to all states through Title VII of the Older Americans Act. Projects funded under the program will provide hot meals at least five days a week for persons sixty or older. Though income will not be a criterion, priority will be given to low-income and minority people and "those who lack the skills to prepare nourishing meals, have limited mobility, or have feelings of rejection which obliterate the initiative necessary to prepare and eat a meal alone." Recipients may be required to pay all or part of the cost.

IN-HOME CARE

Many elderly persons, even those who are chronically ill, want to remain in familiar surroundings—in their own apartments or homes—but they need regular, continuing assistance in personal care, housekeeping, laundry, or preparing meals. For these people, a homemaker-home health aide can be the difference between having to go into a nursing home or living independently. Even when an older adult does not live alone, this kind of help can lessen the stress on the whole family.

Typically, a homemaker-home health aide is a mature woman who is skilled in home management and who has an understanding of human behavior. She has had some basic training, including personal and household care, but she is not a pinch hitter for a nurse or for a maid. She is supervised by a registered nurse, a social worker, or other professional as part of a health or social service team. When she functions under the supervision of a nurse, she may perform a variety of out-of-hospital services.

In many communities, there are homemaker-home health aide agencies. In others, homemaker-home health aide service is coordinated or operated by a multiservice social agency, a welfare department, or a visiting-nurse association. In all, about two thousand agencies throughout the country provide homemaker-home health aide service, but this is not nearly enough to meet the need.

Licensed practical nurses for skilled practical nursing in the home can be hired through agencies in this field. For people who need a registered nurse, on an occasional or regular basis, 520 nonprofit Visiting Nurse Associations are located in cities and towns all over the country. The fee per visit varies from community to community and covers costs to the association. Nationwide, the median charge is $10.40. In New York City, the charge is $20.00 a visit, but it is adjustable to what the patient can afford. In emergencies, of course, the nearest hospital should be called.

About twenty-three hundred home-health agencies are qualified under the Medicare program. Some provide homemaker-home health aides; others do not, but do offer the services of registered nurses, physiotherapists, or other personnel. Medicare reimburses for home-health services under both Part A and Part B. After a minimum of three days in a hospital or after a discharge from an extended-care facility, Part A pays for up to one hundred hospital-related home-health visits within a twelve-month period. Part B pays the home-care agency for up to one hundred home health-care visits each year when a patient has no prior hospital stay, if such services are provided according to a treatment plan approved by a physician.

Many communities have created other ways to help the elderly care for themselves at home. In Washington State's STEP (Service to Elderly People) program, teenagers do heavy housework, mow lawns, help with other chores. Elder-Care in Jasper, Alabama provides housecleaning, marketing, and house repairs done by older persons employed by the local Community Action Agency.

FRIENDLY VISITORS

Joe Zimmerman, seventy-five, a retired cutter in the garment industry, was often depressed, still grief-stricken after the death of his wife. "I'm just put away on the shelf," he'd say. Recently, his morale was raised by a Friendly Visitor from his trade union, sixty-six-year-old Sam Berger, who had also been a cutter. Mr. Berger came to sit with him one morning, chatted about many things, later arranged for occasional household help, took Mr. Zimmerman for a hearing test and to be fitted for a hearing aid. "I feel like a human being again," says Mr. Zimmerman.

Friendly visiting is organized neighborliness. Once a week, or more often, volunteers or paid workers call on homebound older persons. To those who have few friends or relatives, the visitors bring continuing companionship. They may play cards or chess, lend an arm to lean on during a shopping trip, or write letters for the older person. Or the two may just sit and talk for a while.

In a recent survey of elderly people in Portland, Oregon, home visits to shut-ins and live-alones topped the list of needs—even ahead of the need for higher income. In Portland, "home visits" include some household chores and handyman-type services as well as friendly meetings.

The visitors may be social workers or volunteers. Their major essential qualities: a genuine capacity for friendliness and reliability in sticking to a regular schedule. In one western community, a school bus driver visits several old folk every day between the time he delivers the children and the time he picks them up again. In several cities, high-school students do the visiting, run errands, mostly talk with their "adopted grandparents."

Certain trade unions have launched impressive Friendly Visitor projects for their retired members. Most outstanding is the one conducted by the International Ladies' Garment Workers Union in New York. Of the staff of ninety, over seventy visitors are themselves retired workers aged sixty-four to eighty-four. Besides former operators, cutters, finishers, and office clerks, the ILGWU sometimes hires retired bakers, furriers, and postmen for the program. Each year, they call on twenty-eight thousand retirees. They give information on health and social services; assist in filing for Medicaid, Medicare, public housing; escort people to and from doctors and hospitals. The ILGWU project is considered a national model for such programs.

The elderly find the Friendly Visitors a real boon. Some typical comments: "I look forward to her visits." . . . "It makes me feel like I'm still somebody worth talking to." . . . "It gives me a chance to speak of things in my heart."

TELEPHONE REASSURANCE

Ella Berns, a spry seventy-two-year-old, prefers to live in her own studio apartment. Her one fear is that some day she might fall, "maybe break a hip," or become suddenly ill and be unable to reach her phone to call for help. Recently, she read a news item about a woman who died that way.

For just such contingencies, many communities now have telephone reassurance projects. Calls are made to older persons who have few, if any, outside contacts for long periods of time. The calls come each day at a predetermined time. If there's no answer, a personal check is made immediately, usually through a neighbor, relative, or nearby police or fire station. Such details are decided before the service is started.

Fortunately, Ella Berns took on the service. One day, some months later, her regular caller noticed a slurring in her speech, though Miss Berns had no complaint. When a check of her condition revealed she had suffered a heart spasm, she was rushed to a hospital in time for proper treatment.

Telephone reassurance becomes a lifeline for live-alones. Various organizations and agencies sponsor the services. Callers may be other elderly people, or they may be teenagers. In Florida, daily calls are made by senior center members; in Albuquerque, by a hospital auxiliary and the Business and Professional Women's Club; in Ohio, six churches cooperate as sponsors. Boston's Family Service Association has "Lifeline," through which "captains" call sixty-five elderly persons every day.

Another type of phone service is known as "Dial-a-Listener." The older person is given a number to call if he or she just wants to talk. In Davenport, Iowa, elderly professional people are the listeners. In New York, the Red Cross runs a Telephone Club for homebound and lonely people.

OPEN DOORS TO CULTURE

Libraries and museums are excellent resources for leisure-time activities for older adults. Public library extension services are designed for people who can't conveniently use the regular facilities.

These services may include delivery of books and materials to homebound older persons, either through bookmobiles or personal distribution by aides. Subbranches are often located in senior citizen centers and in residences for older people.

In Milwaukee, all the paid library aides in the city's "Over Sixty" service are themselves sixty-five-plus. And in Vermont, where older persons were hired to amplify their meager incomes by working as temporary senior aides in small libraries, they proved so valuable that a number were retained on a permanent basis.

Some libraries sponsor programs specifically for the aging. Among the exemplary programs, Boston's "Never Too Late Groups" function at the main library and at fourteen branches. Cleveland has sponsored the "Live Long and Like It Library Club," which conducts meetings on such topics as current affairs and biographies. The Wake County Library in Raleigh, North Carolina cosponsors courses on basic living skills and the rights of, and benefits available to, older adults.

Elsewhere, group programs conducted or sponsored by libraries, either at their buildings or at outside locations, include clubs for the elderly, discussion groups, and adult education courses.

Not widely enough known is the fact that many libraries have large-print and talking books for those with failing vision or physical disability. In Baltimore, staff members of the Pratt Library make regular visits to recipients of talking books to demonstrate how to use the equipment and to help select materials.

In addition, a number of libraries have recordings, tapes and cassettes, magnifying equipment, page turners, and projectors. And libraries usually publish lists of local activities at least once a month; so a library card opens many doors.

With funding by the Administration on Aging, the Kennedy Center for the Performing Arts and The National Council on the Aging are involved in a national effort to increase opportunities for older Americans to both enjoy and participate in the performing and visual arts.

Museums are also likely to offer special programs. And the elderly can take advantage of free concerts and film showings—often listed in the local press—as well as adult courses at local high schools or community colleges.

OPPORTUNITIES TO SERVE OR WORK

Gertrude Myers, physically fit and fully alert at sixty-eight, felt restless and useless just sitting home, watching television, playing solitaire. At a neighbor's suggestion, she joined SERVE (Serve and Enrich Retirement by Volunteer Experience), conducted by the Community Service Society in New York City. Her assignment: to work with a mentally retarded boy at the Willowbrook State School.

There, for the past two years, Mrs. Myers has been playing and talking with Timmy, giving him her love. At first, he wouldn't speak, lay all day on his back in bed. Now he not only sits up but goes for rides as Mrs. Myers pushes his wheelchair, and he even walks. Recently, Timmy has begun to play with other children.

In most communities, all kinds of opportunities are available for volunteer and even paid work for those who can get around. Valuable skills and experience need not be wasted; many older people prove to be dependable, capable, willing workers.

Nationally, there are three major service programs predominantly for older adults: the Foster Grandparents Program, Retired Senior Volunteer Program (RSVP), and Service Corps of Retired Executives (SCORE)—all funded by ACTION, a federal agency.

In the landmark Foster Grandparents project, low-income people over sixty work part time with children in infant homes, convalescent facilities, schools for the disturbed or retarded. "Grandparents" do not replace regular staff, but establish a person-to-person relationship with a child. They receive an hourly stipend; and they receive the child's affection and trust.

RSVP offers opportunities for voluntary community service in schools, courts, libraries, museums, hospitals, nursing homes, and programs for the homebound.

Of course, virtually every community has openings for volunteers. There are, for instance, the Green Thumb and Green Light projects, which employ low-income men and women in rural areas to beautify parks, roadside, and other public areas. Some of the most effective volunteer programs have set up talent pools.

For those who want to supplement inadequate incomes, the Senior Worker Action Program (SWAP), under the auspices of the Office of Economic Opportunity, promotes employment—particularly part-time and temporary jobs—among older people. The program is usually housed in a community or neighborhood center. Staff members attempt to find and recruit older workers, interview and counsel applicants, develop new placements. Jobs run the gamut from school aides to babysitters, companions, handymen, homemakers, and seamstresses.

Many older people are being trained in new skills or helped to brush up unused skills, such as typing. In some Model Cities areas, elderly residents are employed in children's day care centers, thus permitting parents to take jobs. The National Council of Senior Citizens employs men and women part time in twenty-one projects from coast to coast, performing services that include low-cost meal preparation and outreach activities.

Schools are recruiting older people to give children educational enrichment. Dade County, Florida public schools, for example, hired people over fifty-five as teacher aides in industrial arts and language arts classes. These aides make it possible for regular teachers to handle twice as many pupils. In Vermont, senior library aides enable public libraries to remain open longer and on more days. Senior citizens in two Michigan counties work as tourist guides at fishing and camping sites.

Private industry, too, is dipping into the older-people reservoir. One company hires former employees to guide visiting salesmen through its plants. Mature Temps, the free employment service of the American Association of Retired Persons, has offices in at least thirteen major cities and places older people in temporary paid jobs. One New York firm hires fifty Mature Temps every month. A group of retirees in Norwalk, Connecticut has organized the Senior Personnel Placement Bureau, and similar groups are springing up elsewhere.

Senior Home Craftsmen in Maryland are men who do minor home repairs such as replacing faucet washers and fixing leaks. At Good Neighbor Family Aides, elderly women who have been homemakers offer aid to other older persons or to families that need help in caring for elderly relatives. These women receive training in home nursing at the local Red Cross chapter and in home economics from a state university extension agent.

SENIOR CENTERS

Unquestionably, the most widespread socializing and recreational resource for older people are the familiar Senior Citizens Centers, which are playing an increasingly central role in the lives of old people. They may go by other names: "Golden Age Club," "Silver Age," "Over Sixty," or "Sixty-five Plus."

Here, elderly persons come together for diverse programs and "fun and games." Activities range from card-playing to professionally directed hobby and group ventures, stimulating lectures, and just chit-chat. Some centers provide counseling and referral services, as well as a job registry. Others act as central umbrella agencies for virtually everything related to the elderly. A number offer hot midday meals, either free or at a nominal charge.

Some centers are run rather informally, while others reflect a highly structured approach in terms of staff and facilities. At one popular hobby-oriented center, men and women are found sewing, painting, working at ceramics and photography, attending exercise classes. Here, outings are arranged each summer, and members go in groups to theaters and museums. An Oklahoma City center gives courses in archeology, creative writing, piano, whatever the members ask for.

Nashville, Tennessee has a highly comprehensive program, boasting a main senior center with twelve satellite centers. They offer special health education programs—glaucoma screenings, classes for diabetics, courses for people with hearing loss.

More than twelve hundred centers are now open throughout the country, and they may be found in every state. Of the main categories, a Multipurpose Center operates in a permanent place and is open year-round at least four hours a day, five days a week, with a professional staff. A Senior Citizens Center may not have a professional staff or a full scope of programs. A Senior Citizen Club usually meets fewer than three days a week, and may not have a permanent location or paid leaders. Many public housing projects reserve space for senior centers. In one Colorado town, a former railroad station has been converted into a senior center.

Membership is usually free, though certain centers charge a small fee, perhaps fifty cents a month; the fee at Golden Age Clubs may be a few dollars a year.

LEGAL ASSISTANCE

In their later years, especially if they have to get along on a low income, people may run into all sorts of legal problems.

John Gordin, seventy-three, was having trouble with his landlord, who refused to make needed repairs. His downstairs neighbor, Simeon Brown, a sixty-five-year-old retired electrician who suffered from arthritis, was inexplicably denied Medicare coverage. Neither knew where to seek advice, and both were reluctant to get involved with anything "legal."

They could have gone to the local office of the Legal Aid Society. Throughout the nation, over 750 legal assistance offices are open to people like John Gordin and Simeon Brown. Services are based on financial eligibility. Typically, there is no fee; where one is charged, it is nominal. In some programs, however, clients are required to help defray actual out-of-pocket filing fees and miscellaneous court costs for certain cases.

The elderly face much the same legal concerns as others in the population, with some extras thrown in: Social Security or pension claims, welfare rights, Medicare and Medicaid benefits, eligibility for special housing; also problems related to probate and estate planning, making a will, taxes, disability insurance, driver's license, apartment leases, credit arrangements, consumer contracts.

In one case, a blind man living solely on Social Security sought assistance from Boston's Council of Elders. With the help of a legal aide, he was certified under Aid to the Blind and received $4,600 in back payments. Another elderly man, a welfare recipient, had been denied a request for false teeth; a legal aide obtained the money for him on the ground that lack of them would harm his health and force him into a nursing home.

Alternatives to the Legal Aid Society are the local bar association or lawyers' reference service.

AN INVENTORY OF INNOVATIVE PROGRAMS

Virginia Fraser and Susan Thornton

This excellent inventory of notable programs around the country was compiled by the University Without Walls, at Loretto Heights College (Denver). The purpose was to provide basic information about programs that should be more widely known and that could be adapted to local needs. "We have sought programs which seem to enhance the quality of life for elders," the authors explain, "or which seem to increase the ability of older persons to direct their own lives."

COMMUNICATIONS

SENIORS' RADIO PROGRAM

An hour-long radio talk show for seniors in San Diego is helping keep elders informed on whatever topics interest them. "Seniors' Rap Session" is moderated by the older volunteer who originated it, Leo Mulcahy.

Each Monday at 9:30 A.M. since 1975, many elders in the area have been tuning their radios to KPBS-FM to hear Mulcahy introduce his special guest—perhaps a state assemblyman or some other official. Two panelists sharing the air are a representative from a senior's group and a retired psychiatric social worker.

Interested seniors telephone in live to ask questions, comment or just generally speak their minds. If the elders need information, Mulcahy may get on another phone to get an answer from experts in the state capitol or elsewhere.

CONTACT:
Leo Mulcahy
KPBS-FM
San Diego State University
San Diego, California 92182
(714) 286-6431

TELEVISED HEARINGS ON AGING

In 1975 elderly people who wished to testify at the Ohio Commission on Aging's public hearings did not have to worry about overcoming distances, fatigue, expense or physical barriers. To make their views known they had to travel no further than their own telephones.

Rather than hold several hearings around the state on the Commission's proposed programs for the elderly, Ohio televised its hearings on 12 educational television stations. Listeners were told to call a toll-free number to ask questions or give their comments. Twenty-one persons appeared before the Commission at the hearing; another 78 called in their comments.

CONTACT:
Joseph Gall
Communication Coordinator
Ohio Commission on Aging
34 North High Street
Columbus, Ohio 43215
(614)466-5500

COMBATING MEDIA STEREOTYPES

Two groups are attempting in rather different ways to eliminate the pervasively negative image of older Americans often presented on television.

The National Council on Aging in Los Angeles believes in raising the consciousness of television producers on a one-to-one basis. The Council's representative makes an appointment with a producer and attempts to convince him or her that since elders are the largest minority in the U.S., changing attitudes about them is vitally important. The representative points out that senior citizens have a spending power of $55 million which wise advertisers will not ignore. If a producer requests information to use in writing a sensitive show—about sexuality in elders, for example—the Council provides it.

Although the Council works with producers at the network level, interested groups could certainly discuss aging stereotypes with producers of local television shows.

In contrast, the Gray Panthers take a more activist approach as they ask interested persons to join their Media Watch. The project

424 AN INVENTORY OF INNOVATIVE PROGRAMS

provides individuals with criteria for observing TV shows and commercials, along with report forms to be filled out. Participants are asked to write letters of complaint and commendation, sending copies along with report forms to the Gray Panthers.

For information about the Council,
CONTACT:
Helyne Landres
National Council on Aging
1040 North Las Palmas Avenue
Los Angeles, California 90038
(213)461-2911

For information about Media Watch,
CONTACT:
Lydia Bragger, Co-ordinator
Gray Panther Media Watch
1841 Broadway, Room 300
New York, New York 10023
(212)368-3761

NEWSPAPERS FOR ELDERS

A number of newspapers have been established to serve the specific needs and interests of older Americans.

One excellent example is Colorado's *Senior Edition,* with its supplement, *Colorado Old Times.* The newspaper looks at legislation, health care plans, Colorado history, and such controversial issues as nursing home scandals. A subscription rate of $2 brings 12 issues each year, free classified advertisements and membership in a discount buying club. Reader contributions are encouraged, with small payments made for articles and items published.

In Eugene, Oregon, *The Phoenix* boasts that it carries "Features for Lively People 55 and Over." Crime prevention seminars, special cultural events and Social Security changes are among the topics covered. Subscription to the monthly paper is $3 a year.

The newspapers have either state or federal fund support, or both.

For information about *Senior Edition,*
CONTACT:
Bob Moses, Editor
Senior Edition
731 East 17th Avenue
Denver, Colorado 80203
(303)861-8873

VIRGINIA FRASER AND SUSAN THORNTON

For information about *The Phoenix,*
CONTACT:
Alan Boye, Editor
The Phoenix
145 Charnelton
Eugene, Oregon 97401
(503)342-7622

GERIATRICS PROGRAM FAIR

A seniors' fair, held annually since 1974 in Norristown, Pennsylvania, has a dual purpose. It not only provides seniors with information about programs and services available to them, but it puts agencies and professionals in the field of aging together on an informal basis to compare programs and exchange ideas.

The first Geriatrics Program Fair was held in 1974 at the Norristown State Hospital, pulling in agencies and seniors from five surrounding counties. Literature displays, movies and slides were set up, as was a visiting nurse who took elders' blood pressures.

The second year the fair was held at a nearby shopping mall. In addition to the displays, county commissioners spoke and the Syncopated Seniors Band provided entertainment. More than 370 seniors attended the second annual event.

Costs of running the free fairs have been very minimal, about $35 per year.

CONTACT:
Sandra Lewis
Norristown State Hospital
Occupational Therapy Department
Norristown, Pennsylvania 19401
(215)631-2909

EDUCATION

SOCIAL WORK TRAINING FOR ELDERS

Nine older Americans in Seattle are training to be social workers so that they can work with other elderly people.

When the seniors' career training program became known in the fall of 1976, hundreds of applicants contacted the University of Washington. The elders eventually selected have an average age of 60, and have had previous experience working with the elderly.

The older students are enrolled in regular bachelors' or masters' degree programs, and are making good academic progress. (An interesting note: The program director reports that the oldest student of the group is also the best student.)

Institutional problems have been the hardest for seniors to overcome. How, for example, can elders get academic references from 40 years ago? How can gradepoints from 40 years ago be compared with grades today? Seniors applying for scholarships were told they couldn't get aid unless they had no assets. In short, most universities are set up to deal with students in their 20s, and attitudes and procedures must be changed when seniors are enrolled.

The older student initially required more counseling than the 20-year-old enrollees. Seniors needed help dealing with their anxieties, and with establishing a course of study that their energy levels permit. But program sponsors say that overall and as an intergenerational experience, the seniors' training program is working well.

CONTACT:
Phyllis J. Myhr
Projects on Aging
School of Social Work
University of Washington
Seattle, Washington 98105
(206)543-9095

INSTITUTE FOR RETIRED PROFESSIONALS

Retired professionals living in New York City can enroll in a program developed by, run by and taught by other retirees.

The Institute for Retired Professionals at the New School for Social Research provides courses in more than 70 subjects, including languages, history, art, politics, science and economics. All courses are member-originated and taught by retired professional volunteers.

Instead of tuition, IRP members pay a fixed annual fee of $225 which allows unlimited access to classes and seminars. Only retired professionals or executives are admitted, but this requirement does not seem to stifle interest in IRP. More than 650 elders ranging in age from 55 to 90 are involved, with several hundred more on waiting lists.

A workshop held by IRP for university administrators in 1976 resulted in similar programs being established in San Francisco and San Diego (at University of California extension centers), and in Philadelphia (at Temple University).

CONTACT:
Dr. Hyman Hirsch, Director
Institute for Retired Professionals
New School for Social Research
66 West 12th Street
New York, New York 10011
(212)741-5682

THE ALLIANCE FOR DISPLACED HOMEMAKERS

Older women who have been out of the job market for some years often find it difficult, if not impossible, to find work. The Alliance for Displaced Homemakers was formed by women who were frustrated in their attempts to find job placements for these older women.

The Alliance is a political advocacy group which is pushing for laws to set up centers in every state to train the displaced homemaker. The Alliance's efforts were successful in 1975, when California funded such a center at Mills College in Oakland. Two classes of 15 interns each have passed through the center. Each woman decided individually what work she wished to do after leaving the center, and a program was set up for her accordingly. Some have become paralegals, working especially with the legal concerns of widows and divorced women. Some have chosen nutritional work in senior centers. Because enrollment in the center must be limited, non-students have been encouraged to attend specific classes which interest them.

A main emphasis of the centers is to give older women self-confidence, and to show them how their years of experience in the home and the community can be useful on the job.

Mills College is preparing guidelines for groups or states wishing to open similar centers. The nation's second center was inaugurated in Baltimore in October, 1976.

The Alliance, which has one paid employee with other jobs done by volunteers, gives workshops about the problems of and solutions for displaced homemakers. Its main effort, however, is directed to passing national legislation setting up the centers in each state.

For information on the California center,
CONTACT:
Milo Smith, Director
Displaced Homemakers Center
Mills College
P. O. Box 9996
Oakland, California 94613
(415)632-3205

For information on the Maryland center,
CONTACT:
Center for Displaced Homemakers
2435 Maryland Avenue
Baltimore, Maryland 21218
(301)243-5000

For legislative information,
CONTACT:
Laurie Shields
Alliance for Displaced Homemakers
3800 Harrison Street
Oakland, California 94611
(415)658-8700

EMOTIONAL HEALTH

AFTER-CARE FOR EMOTIONALLY FRAIL ELDERS

In Houston older persons who are released from psychiatric institutions are not allowed to "fall through the cracks."

The state-run Texas Research Institute of Mental Sciences (TRIMS), with a staff of six caseworkers and 11 paraprofessionals, follows 500 clients each month as they emerge from institutions. If social isolation has led the senior to emotional problems, TRIMS attempts to involve him or her in the community. Caseworkers stay in contact by phone or in person with the newly-released elder, checking to make sure medication regimes are followed, and arranging transportation to a local out-patient mental health clinic for treatment.

Hospital staffs too often feel that when an older person is released into a nursing home, no more follow-up is needed. But the TRIMS workers have found this is not always true. Nursing home personnel are not always trained in mental health after-care, they are not always aware of services available, and too often they don't provide enough individual attention. In addition, seniors are often released from institutions with few clothes, and having lost their dentures. TRIMS attempts to alleviate all these problems.

One advantage of the after-care program is that special attention to treatment and medication has permitted increased numbers of elders to live in foster homes. Some of the agency's clients are even able to live on their own.

CONTACT:
Nancy Wilson
Geriatric Service Section
Texas Research Institute of Mental Sciences
1300 Moursund
Houston, Texas 77030
(713) 797-0490

GRIEF THERAPY GROUPS

To an older American, the death of a spouse, child or special friend can be devastating. Loneliness and depression can set in, perhaps becoming so severe that the senior is no longer able to live independently.

To combat these problems, the Minneapolis Age and Opportunity Center, Inc., a nonprofit organization run by the elderly, has begun grief therapy groups. The first group, which began in 1975, was composed of 12 people who talked about their feelings and problems together in the presence of a counselor. As the elders began to draw strength from each other, they also began to socialize and do volunteer work together, until their need for the counselor waned and finally ended.

So successful was this first attempt that five grief therapy groups are now operating. Each is composed of both men and women in similar stages of grief and need. As the need for a highly-trained counselor ebbs, a counselor of less expertise is gradually worked into the group.

Group members can ask for information programs, including those about probate and wills or about legal help with businesses or taxes. Three attorneys are among the professionals available to meet with the groups on request.

CONTACT:
Daphne H. Krause, President
Minneapolis Age and Opportunity Center, Inc.
1801 Nicollet Avenue South
Minneapolis, Minnesota 55403
(612) 874-5525

IN-HOME MENTAL HEALTH THERAPY

In many communities, elderly people with emotional problems cannot obtain professional help in their homes, but must go to mental health clinics.

A program in Seattle's King County was born when it became obvious that the elders referred to such clinics usually did not go; the clinics in turn rarely sought out the elderly. King County's new program provides that trained social workers—not medical assistants, as in the past—will be primary therapists to the elderly, giving them mental health counseling in their dwellings.

Initially the program, which began in January of 1977, will serve 300 low-income people, despite the estimated 26,000 seniors in the area who could benefit from some kind of emotional support. A state grant funds the project through a nonprofit organization, Community Home Health Care.

CONTACT:
Terry Axelrod
Community Home Health Care
2627 Eastlake Avenue, E.
Seattle, Washington 98102
(206) 322-0930

SAGE

Senior Actualization and Growth Exploration (SAGE) is an innovative program in California which has the philosophy that the years over 60 should be a time of growth, a rich and creative time.

To improve physical health and overcome elders' own negative views of themselves, SAGE uses a wide range of techniques from biofeedback to art and breathing therapy, yoga, massage and meditation.

SAGE works both with relatively active groups of older persons and with institutionalized seniors. A training program for leaders includes introductory and advanced workshops, and several internships.

Many elders exposed to SAGE report feeling almost a complete rejuvenation. They say they have improved mental attitudes and agility, increased mobility and even improved overall health.

SAGE has prepared two excellent videotapes which demonstrate how the SAGE idea works, and which show seniors involved in the varied activities. The tapes can be either rented or purchased.

CONTACT:
SAGE
Claremont Office Park
41 Tunnel Road
Berkeley, California 94705
(415) 841-9858

HOSPICE FOR THE DYING

Too often terminally ill patients in the United States are put into hospitals or nursing homes to spend their last days in a cold, uncaring environment which gives little support to either them or their families. But a hospice concept, patterned on programs in England, is emerging in several parts of America.

The New Haven, Connecticut, Hospice has been operating for three years. Because a multi-million dollar hospice facility for cancer victims has not yet been built, the Hospice is currently providing home care for terminal patients of all ages who want to stay with their families as long as possible.

The Hospice sends professionals and trained volunteers into the home, giving medical and emotional care to both families and patients. Emphasis is placed on pain control so that the dying person will be as comfortable, active and alert as possible until the moment of death. Families are helped to deal with the patient and their own feelings throughout.

The service is free to patients through funding by the National Cancer Institute. On call 24 hours a day are both full- and part-time doctors, nurses, physical therapists, pharmacists and social workers. One financial advantage to the hospice concept is that the cost is less than half that of a hospital.

The hospice effort does not stop with the patient's death; hospice workers follow grieving families as long as they need support.

CONTACT:
Frank Kryza
Director of Public Information
Hospice of New Haven
765 Prospect Street
New Haven, Connecticut 06511
(203)787-5779

SENSITIVITY COURSE ON DYING

In an attempt to spread expertise on working with the dying, the Seattle Hospice has run a brief training course to educate both professionals and volunteers so that they in turn can teach others.

The two-day program consisted of lectures and small discussion groups. The curriculum included an examination of cultural attitudes toward death and dying, and handling personal feelings about these topics. Relationships between patients and workers and patients and their families were explored. The emotional stages of dying and pain management were major topics, as were new counseling approaches and an exploration of community resources available for the terminally ill and those working with them.

CONTACT:
Judith Clegg
Planning Coordinator
Hospice of Seattle
208 Lowman Building
107 Cherry Street
Seattle, Washington 98104
(206)682-2665

EMPLOYMENT

JOB PLACEMENT CENTER RUN BY ELDERS

Experience, Inc., of Palm Springs, California, is a seniors-run organization which attempts to place persons over age 55 in both paid and volunteer jobs.

The nonprofit corporation places advertisements in newspapers and on radio and television stations each day. When a job opening becomes known, the staff contacts one of the group's 500 members. Membership in Experience, Inc., is limited to those over

55 and costs two dollars per year. For ease of operation, the service is located in a senior center.

Most of the elders seeking jobs are blue collar workers who can provide services in hotels and private homes. As many as 40 per cent of the job placements are short-term or one-time opportunities.

CONTACT:
Jack M. Levin
Vice President and Job Placement Officer
Experience, Inc.
550 North Palm Canyon Drive
Palm Springs, California 92262
(714)323-8284

NEW CAREERS FOR RETIRED LAW PROFESSORS

Hastings College in San Francisco has a program for retired law professors which could be adapted by other colleges for other professions.

The University of California law school recruits law professors faced with mandatory retirement from colleges around the country. Hastings began the program when World War II caused shortages in the legal profession. The program was so successful that it has been continued for more than 30 years. A third of the 88-member faculty is between 65 and 70 years of age; the elders, who have formed the "Sixty-Five Club," teach regular bar courses.

CONTACT:
William Riegger
Vice Dean
Hastings College of Law
198 McAllister Street
San Francisco, California 94102
(415)557-1320

UNUSUAL JOB OPPORTUNITIES

Several unusual part-time jobs which seniors can fill are available through the federal government at various locations around the country.

One is with the National Weather Service, which offers both paid and volunteer jobs as cooperative weather observers, and as second order station observers. In the first category, observers record the maximum and minimum temperatures and the amount of rain each day, then fill out a form which is sent each month to a designated address. A compilation of observers' reports is published monthly.

Second order station observers sign a contract and then are trained by the Weather Service, which installs such instruments at their homes as wind and rain gauges.

The federal government also hires persons part-time to be census takers. After a brief training program, workers go to homes in their assigned area and interview residents. The position does involve some weekend and evening work. An hourly wage is paid, as is mileage. Persons receiving government pensions should inquire whether or not they can take the job because of Civil Service regulations.

A third "job" option which seniors might wish to take advantage of is really more like a vacation than work. The U. S. Forest Service has established a Campground Host Program at a dozen National Forests across the United States.

The volunteer Hosts live free for the season in small trailers set up in various campgrounds. The presence of the Hosts tends to discourage such problems as vandalism, but if trouble does arrive the Hosts are told not to take action—simply to call the closest sheriff. Occasionally the Hosts are asked to do some light cleaning or keep bathrooms stocked with paper supplies.

For information on Weather Observers,
CONTACT:
Your nearest Weather Service
Forecast Office, Substation
Network Specialist

For information about Census Takers,
CONTACT:
Your nearest regional Census Bureau office

For information about Campground Hosts,
CONTACT:
U. S. Forest Service
Agriculture South Building
12th and Independence Avenue, S.W.
Washington, D.C. 20250
(202) 655-4000

FOOD AND NUTRITION

GROCERY SHOPPING SERVICE

For many weak or handicapped elderly persons, grocery shopping poses tremendous difficulties. In Sacramento, California, these seniors can now call on the Elderly Nutrition Program to have such shopping done for them.

The program, which began in October of 1976 with a $21,000 grant, employs three shopping aides—themselves age 55 or older—who work five hours a day for minimum wages plus mileage. The seniors, who must be homebound and more than 60 years old, pay 50 cents each time the aides shop for them. Arrangements have been made at area supermarkets for the aides to cash the elders' checks.

In many cases the homebound seniors had been hiring local children or taxi drivers to shop for them—or had been going without food for long periods of time until someone came to their rescue.

One off-shoot of the program is that the shopping aides see shut-in seniors in their homes, can keep an eye on their general condition, and can refer problems to the appropriate local agencies.

CONTACT:
Warren Washington, Coordinator
Sacramento Elderly Nutrition Program
2418 K Street
Sacramento, California 95816
(916)444-9533

MOBILE MINI-MARKET

In San Mateo County, California, a Mobile Mini-Market is bringing a small grocery store direct to 5,000 seniors—and saving them from 30 to 50 per cent on food at the same time.

Food Advisory Service, a nonprofit group operating under a state grant, uses five vans to carry food to church social halls, senior centers and housing projects. Cheese, meat, poultry, produce and eggs, all purchased at wholesale prices from local growers and packing plants, are carried inside to seniors.

The measure helps prevent crime, since many senior housing developments are in undesirable areas and the Mobile Mini-Market brings groceries directly to elderly shoppers.

The project helps promote good nutrition, since seniors select the food they want and prepare hot meals according to their own preferences and at their own convenience. Another unexpected benefit has been the socialization that occurs as seniors gather to shop.

CONTACT:
Sandi Piccini, Director
Food Advisory Service
205 Utah Avenue
South San Francisco, California 94080
(415)588-5275

BROWN BAG FOOD PROGRAMS

Through two "brown bag" operations in California, more than 4,000 seniors are providing themselves with free fruit and vegetables which would otherwise go to waste.

In Monterey County, senior volunteers contact local produce growers, asking them to donate the culls of their crops. Other elderly volunteers sort and bag the produce, and staff distribution centers throughout the area. The county funds only a program director, a nutritionist and two drivers for Operation Brown Bag.

The 3,000 older participants pay one dollar each per year, and in return each week receive the equivalent of five dollars' worth of produce and such other foods as may occasionally be donated. Most of the seniors pick up their own "brown bags" from distribution centers, but home deliveries are made to a limited number of shut-ins.

A seniors' group in Santa Cruz has a slightly different approach. The 1,100 Gray Bears make arrangements to go into the fields and pick crops for which market conditions are not right. This way growers are spared labor costs, and seniors get high-quality food which would otherwise be left to rot. The Gray Bears also receive free frozen food from area processors, which is underweight or slightly damaged.

The city of Santa Cruz funds two employees and two part-time secretaries. As in the Monterey program, the rest of the work is done by the seniors themselves.

For information on Operation Brown Bag,
CONTACT:
John Grisim, Director
Monterey County Senior Programs
15 West Gabilan Street
Salinas, California 93901
(408)758-3381

For information on the Gray Bears,
CONTACT:
Cheryce Wallace
Assistant Director
Gray Bears
1298 Fair Avenue
Santa Cruz, California 95060
(408)427-3000

SPACE AGE MEALS—ON WHEELS OR BY MAIL

An experimental program in central Texas has provided 200 rural elders with meals similar to those eaten by American astronauts. The four-month program, which was run with the aid of National Aeronautics and Space Administration (NASA), delivered seven meals to elderly persons once each week; the seniors had merely to heat a meal a day.

To see if personal contact improved the seniors' reception of the meals, elders were divided into three groups. In the first, persons delivering the weekly food allotment were encouraged to spend time socializing with the seniors. In the second, the worker merely left the food at the homes. The third group of elders received their meals by mail, since the freeze-dried, compressed meals were packaged to fit into a standard rural mail box. Researchers found that elders receiving the meals by mail were as enthusiastic as those who received the food plus socialization time.

The balanced meals cost slightly more than food prepared at congregate settings, but the cost is expected to drop if the space-age foods are distributed more widely. Overall, however, savings resulted because meals were delivered only once each week. Costs were cut even more when the meals were mailed.

Funding from HEW and NASA expired in 1976, but follow-up monies to take the program nationwide are being sought from Congress as of this writing.

CONTACT:
Gary Primeaux (SE6)
Lyndon B. Johnson Space Center
Houston, Texas 77058
(713) 483-4211

HOUSING AND CONVALESCENT CARE

RESPITE CARE

The families of many seniors who can no longer live alone would rather take the elders into the family setting than put them in a nursing home. A problem can arise, however, because the family then has the job of full-time care without a chance for a respite. How can the caring family take a vacation? Or what happens when a family member has to be hospitalized?

In San Francisco, Respite Care is now available for these families who care for a senior. The On Lok Senior Health Services has a respite care center under construction, based on the Holiday Bed plans in England. When the facility is completed, elders can be admitted intermittently as the need arises.

In the meantime, the service has found an apartment that up to two older persons can rent on a short-term basis. A woman living in the building handles cleaning and meals, and sees that the seniors are dressed and cared for until they can be reunited with their families.

CONTACT:
Marie-Louise Ansak
On Lok Senior Health Services
1490 Mason Street
San Francisco, California 94133
(415) 989-2578

DO-IT-YOURSELF ENERGY CONSERVATION

Two unusual energy programs, one in Wyoming and one in Colorado, have the promise of lowering seniors' food costs or heating bills—or both.

The Colorado program began in 1975 when the Domestic Technology Institute, a nonprofit organization, gave several solar energy workshops in the state's rural San Luis Valley. The workshops, which were not limited to elders, attracted 60 people. Among other things, participants learned to build passive solar panels covering 64 square feet. Fans blow the solar-heated air into the house; energy cost savings of up to 50 per cent are claimed by some of the enthusiasts.

Some of the participants also built solar-heated greenhouses which attach to their homes, cutting both their food costs and home heating expenses. As an interesting off-shoot, participants have formed an energy cooperative numbering about 100 people which seeks to lower energy costs for those on fixed incomes.

In Cheyenne the Community Action Agency of Laramie County asked the Institute to give a workshop on building community greenhouses fueled by a methane gas digester. Senior citizens volunteered to build the greenhouses, which would provide food for them as well as income when excess produce is sold to the county's Meals on Wheels program. During the week-long workshop, seniors designed three greenhouses each 30 by 50 feet.

The greenhouses will be under construction in the spring of 1977 with the aid of a grant for $50,000. The low cost requires that many materials, as well as the seniors' labor, must be donated.

The Institute's workshops cost participants from $30 to $250 each, depending on their length and topic. The more expensive workshops are a week long, and persons enrolled actually build several solar systems.

> For workshop information,
> CONTACT:
> Andrea Dunn
> Development Technology Institute
> Box 2043
> Evergreen, Colorado 80439
> (303)674-6826
>
> For greenhouse information,
> CONTACT:
> Al Duran, Executive Director
> Community Action Program
> Suite 400, Bell Building
> Cheyenne, Wyoming 82001
> (307)635-9291

NURSING HOME RESIDENTS' COUNCILS

One problem with many nursing homes is that residents are made to feel that the facilities are run at and for the convenience of the staff—not the patients.

To counter this, organizations like the Gray Panthers urge that residents' councils be established in every nursing home. An outsider may have to convince residents that this is their home and that the employees—from doctors on down—are working for them. Why, the Gray Panthers ask by way of example, should residents have visitors only for two hours in the afternoon when in their own homes they would have company whenever it was most convenient.

One functioning residents' council is at the Post Street Convalescent Hospital in San Francisco. The enlightened staff there decided that patients should have a chance to talk with the administration, and asked the Gray Panthers to help set up the council. Patients meet monthly to hear an information program, such as an eye doctor talking about cataracts and other vision problems, and to voice their complaints to representatives from various hospital departments. Problems which can be rectified are; otherwise the staff attempts to explain why not.

CONTACT:
Mary Godfrey, Activities Director
Post Street Convalescent Hospital
2130 Post Street
San Francisco, California 94115
(415) 563-7300

AN INTERGENERATIONAL HOUSING EFFORT

An unusual approach to helping elders remain in their own homes while giving them contact with younger people has been established in Washington, D.C.

The Ladies of Charity of the U.S., a Roman Catholic organization, encourages senior citizens in the pilot area to take in student roomers. Program sponsors appear at church meetings to explain the program, which includes a thorough screening of rooming applicants by volunteers or parish priests. Workshops and orientation sessions are held for the volunteers, who handle placements and follow up to see how the intergenerational experience is progressing.

The students, many who are foreign and many from medical universities in the area, are pleased to get the low-cost housing. The seniors in turn make a little money and have company in the home.

CONTACT:
Anna May Moynihan
Ladies of Charity of the U.S.
1007 Varnum Street, N.E.
Washington, D.C. 10017
(202)832-1628

HOME REPAIR SERVICES

Inability to make or afford minor home repairs can be both frustrating and dangerous for elderly persons. Deterioration of the home can set in, and such unrepaired safety hazards as a loose board can cause serious accidents.

To combat these problems, New Orleans has established Repairs on Wheels. In two years, 300 elders have taken advantage of the project to have minor repairs made on their homes. The program began in 1975 when the Volunteers of America received a $12,000 grant to purchase two trucks and tools for workmen.

Five skilled carpenters were hired through another grant to repair screens, fences, window panes and stair railings. They have rebuilt porches, made minor plumbing repairs and done minor electrical work.

When seniors request assistance, the carpenters' foreman visits the home. Seniors are told that the labor will be free, and are given an estimate of materials costs. If the senior lives on an extremely low income, the program may provide free materials as well.

Initially, Repairs on Wheels aided even seniors living in rental property. But after a landlord raised the rent following improvements, that stopped. Now repairs are made only on homes which the seniors own.

Another program designed to help seniors with minor repair and maintenance jobs stay safely and comfortably in their homes is the Skills Exchange of Arapahoe County, Colorado.

Initially it was thought that elders with a particular skill could help others, and in turn be aided by seniors with different skills. Though the seniors had to pay only materials costs, the program was only a limited success, according to its founder. Too many elderly persons were not well enough to perform services, or perhaps they lacked transportation. At any rate, while the "exchange" idea failed, the need continued.

So the Arapahoe County Council of Senior Citizens, which sponsors the Skills Exchange, enlisted members of local service clubs to perform most of the minor repair jobs for seniors. The United Way of Arapahoe County provides office space and takes messages. The county pays telephone expenses. More than 200 elders have been helped by the program.

> For information on Repairs on Wheels,
> CONTACT:
> Adrienne Carmena
> Volunteers of America
> 3720 Prytania
> New Orleans, Louisiana 70115
> (504) 891-8808

> For information about Skills Exchange,
> CONTACT:
> Greta Brown
> Skills Exchange
> 300 East Hampden
> Englewood, Colorado 80110
> (303) 761-5904

TAX WORK-OFF PROGRAM

Low-income persons—including the elderly—who live in Hartford, Connecticut, can cut down on their house and motor vehicle tax bills by signing up for the city's tax work-off project.

Participants perform work not normally done by city employees, ranging from unskilled to clerical to such professional jobs as data processing. For each hour participants work, they receive a tax credit of from $2.50 to $4, up to a maximum of $1,000.

The effort was funded at $300,000 by the Hartford City Council in an effort to keep the elderly and other low-income persons in their own homes. Like many core cities, Hartford suffers from both high unemployment and high welfare levels.

The program was originally designed to attract 4,000 people, but participation has been low in the first six months of operation.

Enthusiasm is expected to increase as the tax work-off program becomes more well known.

CONTACT:
Mike Cirullo, Administrator
In-Kind Services Program
Municipal Building, 550 Main Street
Hartford, Connecticut 06103
(203)566-6710

INTERGENERATIONAL APPROACHES

INTERGENERATIONAL CONFERENCES

The Santa Barbara Student Board of Education wanted to get high school students and elders from the community together to discuss common problems and needs. The result, in 1975, was a day-long Youth Conference on Older Americans attended by 50 students and 50 senior citizens.

Students selected the topics, which ranged from the economics of aging to recreation, housing, transportation and family relationships. The exchange of ideas brought students to the realization that most stereotypes of the elderly are inaccurate. And seniors found that high school students could be aware of and sensitive to others' needs.

The National Retired Teachers Association and the American Association of Retired Persons have prepared a brochure to interest students in the conference idea, a guide for conference planners, and a brochure containing quotations from conferences that were held in 1976. All three items are available in quantity.

CONTACT:
Yolanda Berg
Associate Program Specialist
NRTA-AARP
1909 K Street, N.W.
Washington, D.C. 20049
(202)872-4700

INTERGENERATIONAL CULTURAL HERITAGE PROGRAM

Students in numerous high schools across the U.S. are learning about and becoming involved with older people through the Foxfire learning concept.

The Foxfire plan has students interview elders about their youth and learn from them the vanishing crafts and skills of another era. The students then write articles and take pictures to illustrate a quarterly magazine which is sold locally to support the on-going project. Advantages to the students are many. They not only learn journalism, photography skills and the crafts of bygone days, but they develop an interest in history. Gradually they find that the elderly have something important to say to which younger people can relate.

The elders, in turn, are made to feel important, their skills are recognized, and they become more involved with community life as intergenerational friendships blossom.

In Hawaii, the Foxfire concept is being used to help failing students. There the students found only two elders still alive who could build a traditional Hawaiian home. After learning the skill, the students have been given land and are building a home for the community as a kind of museum.

Institutional Development and Economic Affairs Service (IDEAS), a nonprofit organization which teaches the Foxfire concept, provides training workshops for teachers as well as such materials as manuals and movies.

In the East,
CONTACT:
Murray Durst
Executive Vice President, IDEAS
1785 Massachusetts Avenue, N.W.
Washington, D.C. 20036
(202)483-9045

In the West,
CONTACT:
Martha Fritts, IDEAS
Western Regional Representative
Magnolia Star Route
Nederland, Colorado 80466
(303)258-7202

PROJECT ELDERLY PERSON

A group of high school girls in Kearney, Nebraska, decided in 1975 that they wished to work with and understand elders in their community. The girls, all members of the Future Homemakers Association, contacted the area Agency on Aging to locate willing elders. The Agency in turn contacted elders at a senior center, finding that many were very interested in Project Elderly Person.

The 15 girls, each making a two-year commitment to the program, are divided into five teams of three girls each. The team captain's responsibility is to make sure that each girl spends approximately two hours a week with the elder to whom she has been assigned. If a girl is ill or out of town, the captain's duty is to find a replacement for her.

The elder involved decides with the PEP volunteer what they both want to do. The girls may run errands for the seniors, shop, write letters or simply sit and chat while watching television. Both the high school volunteers and the elders are enthusiastic about the program after almost two years.

PEP also serves as an outreach effort, for if the girls see needs which they cannot fill—perhaps minor home repairs or short-term health care—they notify the Agency on Aging.

CONTACT:
Wes McCord, Director
South Central Area Agency on Aging
2022 Avenue A
Kearney, Nebraska 68847
(302) 234-1851

LEGAL AID

LEGAL EDUCATION COURSE FOR CONSUMERS

A 20-hour course called "Consumers and the Law" is being taught in southeastern Pennsylvania to educate older Americans so they will be wise consumers and better able to deal with government agencies.

Since the program began in 1975, more than 360 seniors have learned their legal rights in such consumer issues as: contracts, credit and debt, advertising, fraud, warranties, and landlord-tenant relations. The course furnishes information on age discrimination, nursing homes, Social Security, Medicare and Medicaid and wills and probate.

The courses are taught by three law students, overseen by a coordinator. The free seminars, which are funded by a federal grant through Philadelphia's Temple Law Center, are held at senior centers.

A manual detailing information for the course and including notes to trainers is available.

CONTACT:
Sharon Browning
Project Director
Temple Law Center
1719 North Broad Street
Philadelphia, Pennsylvania 19122
(215)787-8948

MOBILE LEGAL AID FOR SENIORS

More than 1,500 seniors living in both rural and urban parts of Dallas County, Texas, are receiving free legal assistance each year.

Three full- and three part-time attorneys take the Older Americans Legal Action Center van, which is equipped with filing cabinets, desks, typewriter and office supplies, to senior centers and to the homes of isolated elders.

The Center provides help in general civil cases, assisting seniors with such problems as wills and divorces. In this area, many of the simpler cases are referred to volunteering private attorneys who are themselves seniors.

The Center also provides legal protective services for adults who are victims of exploitation, physical abuse or even self-neglect. Lawyers for the Center have found that most exploitation is financial, usually inflicted by the older person's own child or children. Most widowed mothers, they say, will go without food rather than turn in a child who is taking their money or physically abusing them.

When an exploiting child refuses to let legal workers inside for an interview with the parent, the Center has resorted to having a paralegal who is also a nurse enter the home in full uniform with the visiting nurse. The system does fall down when an older person refuses to become a client; then the Center is powerless to aid the victim.

The Center receives funding from the state of Texas, the state Bar Association, and the National Legal Services Corporation.

CONTACT:
Sister Rosemary Redmond
Older Americans Legal Action Center
912 Commerce Street
Dallas, Texas 75202
(214)742-1512

PHYSICAL HEALTH

SELF-HEALTH MEDICAL COURSE

Senior citizens in Arlington, Virginia, are learning when—and when not—to go to the doctor, and how to talk with the doctor when they do seek medical care.

The Health Activation Course, which ended its first 16-week session in January of 1977, was designed to encourage seniors to accept more health care responsibility for themselves. Participants were taught to use some of the equipment in the "black bag," learning to check their own respiration and blood pressure.

A self-health medical guide which outlined simple home procedures during illness was part of the course. In case of a common bladder infection, for example, seniors were taught to increase fluids and get extra rest. But they learned that if certain danger signals exist—in this instance high temperatures or blood in the urine—they must get to a doctor.

The course included an "ask the doctor" list so that patients would be prepared with questions and information when they sought treatment. Participants learned to be realistic about what to expect from a doctor, and were given lessons in "speaking the doctor's language."

An interesting outgrowth of the federally-funded course was the formation by the elderly of their own health clubs. The clubs meet monthly, featuring speeches by medical experts as the seniors continue their quest for self-health care.

CONTACT:
Clair Welling, R.N.
Box 7268
Arlington, Virginia 22207
(703)525-6350

IN-HOME TRAINING FOR BLIND SENIORS

A mobile team in rural northeastern Colorado is teaching legally blind elders in their own homes how to cook, clean and generally manage for themselves.

The program, which began in January of 1975, originally utilized a 27-foot van in which the elders were to be taught. Workers soon found that getting handicapped seniors in and out of the van was too difficult, and the program was taken instead directly into nursing and private homes.

In nursing homes, groups of blind elders are taught how to feed themselves and how to use a cane to get around.

Non-institutionalized seniors receive such training at home as how to clean without being able to see dirt, and how to cook without danger of being burned. The course includes such tips as how to label kitchen cans and even how to set oven temperatures.

Four professional staffers work with the visually impaired; they are aided by a supervisor and one secretarial worker. The program, which receives Rehabilitation Services Administration funding, has 130 active clients. Elders who have undergone training receive follow-up attention every three months.

CONTACT:
Ronald Landwehr, Supervisor
Services for the Older Visually Impaired
2662 C-11th Avenue
Greeley, Colorado 80631
(303)356-9393

A SENIORS-OWNED PHARMACY

The first nonprofit pharmacy owned by elders was opened in December of 1976 in Minneapolis by the Metropolitan Senior Federation, a seniors' organization with 80,000 members.

The Federation Pharmacy is staffed by a paid professional pharmacist and one intern. All other workers are elderly volunteers who work four hour shifts typing labels, answering telephones and mailing prescriptions to those who request that service. MSF members and the handicapped receive a substantial discount on prescriptions; members of the public pay regular rates.

MSF borrowed $10,000 from their own funds to buy an existing pharmacy which was on the verge of bankruptcy; the loan must be repaid in five years. As the pharmacy begins showing a profit, prices to elders will be reduced still further.

CONTACT:
Rev. Peter Wyckoff
Director, Metropolitan Senior Federation
1951 University Avenue
St. Paul, Minnesota 55104
(612)645-3796

SOROPTIMIST CLUB DENTURE EFFORT

Dedicated members of a professional businesswomen's club in Denver have shown what volunteers can do by convincing 130 dentists to donate their services and raising $11,000 to pay for dentures for low-income senior citizens.

The Soroptimist Club asked the Colorado Dental Association to publish an appeal in its monthly newsletter seeking volunteer dentists to treat the elderly without charge. More than 130 dentists across Colorado responded.

One other obstacle remained for the elderly poor—lab fees to make dentures can run as high as $150 a set. So the Soroptimists began holding garage sales, dinners and "anything else legal," according to the project's prime sponsor. In 15 months the women raised $11,000, and 95 senior citizens had new dentures.

Recently a dental lab has approached the group to volunteer to lower their $150 fee to $50; if this offer becomes a reality, the 200 elders on the Soroptimists' waiting list will soon obtain new teeth.

CONTACT:
Mary Duty
1756 Elmira
Aurora, Colorado 80010
(303)364-6953

HEARING PHONE-A-TEST

The Chicago Hearing Society has devised a simple, free telephone hearing test designed to reach citizens, including the elderly, who may not be aware they are suffering a hearing loss.

The recorded Phone-A-Test often receives more than 100 calls daily. The taped screening consists of four warbled tones at different pitches and intensities; if the caller cannot hear all of the tones, he or she is urged to consult the family doctor, a hearing specialist or the Hearing Society.

CONTACT:
Dr. William Plotkin
Executive Director
Chicago Hearing Society
178 West Randolph
Chicago, Illinois 60601
(312)332-6850

PHYSICAL FITNESS FOR ELDERS

The National Association for Human Development has prepared a total program, including instructional booklets and slide shows, for persons wishing to improve the overall health of senior citizens in their communities.

Among materials provided by the NAHD are booklets of basic exercises for elders, costing one dollar each. Four slide shows in which older people demonstrate the exercises are also available. Diet and nutritional information is included as part of a total health-care approach.

In July of 1976 the NAHD began running workshops taught by three doctors for regional aging personnel. Workshops will follow at the state and local level, involving such organizations as community colleges, churches, nursing home staffs and professionals in the field of aging. However, any community or group interested in beginning their own program can simply contact the NAHD and request information and materials.

CONTACT:
Ann Radd
National Association for Human Development
1750 Pennsylvania Avenue, N. W.
Washington, D.C. 20006
(202)833-2323

HOME MEDICAL CARE

Chronically ill elders in Los Angeles County do not have to make wearying, expensive and often painful journeys to a hospital, nor do they have to fear premature hospitalization. The Home Care Program of the University of Southern California Medical Center provides 80 off-duty doctors and residents who make house calls for 500 patients.

Home Care, which is funded by the county for homebound seniors, is available 24 hours a day, seven days a week. Since its beginning 25 years ago the project has been going strong, continuing to save both the county and patients substantial amounts of money. The cost to the county for each doctor's visit is $24; a patient checking into a clinic might be charged as much as $100.

In addition, Home Care workers find that seniors who can remain at home stay in better spirits and make better medical progress than those who are hospitalized or put into nursing homes.

On the average, doctors see patients every two weeks when they enter the program, then perhaps as seldom as every four months. The patient calls his or her assigned doctor when in need of medical attention. Home Care administrators say there has been no need for program personnel to call the seniors.

Most of the patients are elderly women who live alone. If they need simple help like having a dressing changed, a visiting nurse responds. Homemaker care is also provided where necessary.

CONTACT:
Dr. Robert B. Mims
Director, Home Care
Home Care Program, Building 4
L. A. County–U. S. C. Medical Center
1200 North State Street
Los Angeles, California 90033
(213)226-2622

NATIONAL GUARD RURAL HEALTH SCREEN

Seniors in many parts of the U.S. are receiving free health screening, but in rural Idaho volunteers from a medical unit of the National Guard are providing the service.

Several times a year the unit—composed of a doctor, a dentist, and several nurses and medical technicians—goes to a remote Idaho community to examine the elderly without charge. The screening is important because some of the communities are as far as 50 miles from medical help and may not even have a drug store.

The checkup provided is quite basic, including blood pressure and heart checks but no lab work. Dental examinations have found that many of the elderly are wearing dentures which are 25 years old and are no longer comfortable. This results in the older people not eating as well as they could.

One drawback to the program, according to its director, is the lack of medical followup. If the doctor or dentist does refer the senior for medical attention, the referral is often ignored either because of cost, distance or ignorance.

However, the seniors are at least receiving a health screening they would not otherwise get, and without cost to either the elderly or the state.

CONTACT:
Joann Cissel, Director
Nutrition Project
Eastern Idaho Special Services Agency
P. O. Box 1098
Idaho Falls, Idaho 83401
(208)522-5391

SINGLE-ENTRY APPROACH TO SERVICES

An experimental program in Connecticut is eliminating the need for an elder seeking medical aid to shop from agency to agency, wading through eligibility procedures and perhaps ending up with fewer services than are available.

Under the Triage program, a nurse practitioner and social worker go together to the homes of senior citizens, evaluating their needs and arranging for care. The seniors are made aware of all available services, and red tape is quickly overcome. The nurse practitioner and social worker also make periodic follow-up calls, changing treatment as that becomes necessary.

Triage attempts to look at the "whole" needs of each older resident in a seven-town area of central Connecticut. The program, which is funded by Medicare and the National Institute of Health, now serves 1,000 persons and is designed to serve 1,000 more as the project continues.

CONTACT:
Jean Quinn
Triage, Inc.
269 North Washington Street
Plainville, Connecticut 06062
(203)747-2761

PROTECTIVE SERVICES

EARLY ALERT

Hundreds of elderly people in New York City have no family or friends, and literally have no one to turn to when they are sick or in trouble. But a program called Early Alert is changing that.

Mail carriers, who watch the residences of people requesting it, are the heart of Early Alert. The carriers know who is on Social Security and who gets pension checks. If they spot an accumulation of mail, know that checks are late, or see anything out of the ordinary, the carriers notify the city's Office on Aging. An employee from that office is at the home within 30 minutes of the call.

In one incident, an elderly couple were robbed and stuffed into a closet. Noting the accumulation of mail, the carrier alerted officials. When help arrived the elderly man had died, but the old woman was still alive.

The program is relatively simple to set up; anyone who wants to be part of the program simply signs up with the Office on Aging, and a dot is put on the back of their mailbox. This is of tremendous psychological value, according to the program's director, because isolated people finally feel that someone cares what happens to them.

The New York City program operates with only one paid full-time staff person and a few seniors acting as aides. When an older person with a problem is discovered, the appropriate agencies are immediately contacted.

CONTACT:
Alice Brophy
New York City Office on Aging
250 Broadway
New York, New York 10007
(212) 577-0848

CRIME-PREVENTING ESCORT SERVICE

A free escort service, originally composed of Vietnam veterans, is available to 1,000 senior citizens living in a high-crime section of San Francisco.

The service is run by the North of Market Senior Service Center, with six escorts paid by the California employment office. Although veterans were the original escorts, the job has now been opened to other applicants.

The task of the escorts is to get the elderly, some of whom are disabled and need physical assistance, to their destinations and back without being mugged or otherwise attacked. The only cost to older persons is for their own and their escorts' transportation, when transportation is necessary. Funds which originally paid all transportation costs have run out, and the senior center is seeking other monies.

The escorts serve still another function; they have some training in social services, so that they can tell the elderly what rights and privileges are available to them.

CONTACT:
Indio Nirmama
North of Market Senior Service Center
121 Leavenworth, Room 200
San Francisco, California 94102
(415) 885-2290

SEMINARS ON CRIME AND THE ELDERLY

The American Association of Retired Persons has organized four two-hour seminars under its Crime Prevention Program.

The sessions, which can be held in sequence or individually, deal with burglary, fraud, street crime and community-police relations. Participants are given two booklets, "Your Retirement Anti-Crime Guide," and "How to Spot a Con Artist." The seminars are free to groups.

In addition AARP is attempting to educate police officers about the problems of aging. Seminars for law enforcement personnel and police training academies explain the physical and emotional aspects of aging. While police are usually compassionate to seniors, AARP says, they often don't know quite how to deal with older people.

It is expected that soon the police seminars will be greatly expanded. AARP has received a federal grant to formalize the seminars and develop curriculums so that the problems of aging can be taught at police and FBI training academies across the U.S. AARP estimates that the courses will be available to teaching institutions at the end of 1977.

CONTACT:
Crime Prevention Program
American Association of Retired Persons
1909 K Street, N.W.
Washington, D.C. 20049
(202) 872-4912

COMMUNITY EMERGENCY FUND

In some communities, elders who find themselves in crisis without money can literally become desperate. But in Ventura County, California, concerned citizens have established an emergency fund which is available to seniors 24 hours each day of the week.

The Ventura County Council on Aging originally sought $17,500 in emergency funds from the county government. When the request was rejected, workers sought help from church groups and service clubs. In the last three months of 1976, $6,000 was raised, and as publicity has made the fund better-known, seniors from other states have sent in private donations.

Most of the need comes when the elderly poor don't get their Social Security or pension checks on time for some reason. Other cases of necessity have involved people who break their glasses, have no money for new ones, and cannot see without them. Occasionally a low-income senior will be without shoes to wear. In these cases the emergency fund comes to the rescue; some of the seniors eventually repay the money, but others cannot, and no bill is ever sent.

Officials say they were afraid to publicize the program at first, for fear there would be heavy demand for "free money." But, they say, seniors know when they can get by and when they are desperate, so requests for the funds have been few and modest.

CONTACT:
Tony Lamb, Senior Citizen Coordinator
Ventura County Council on Aging
3161 Loma Vista
Ventura, California 93003
(805) 648-6171, Ext. 3678

EMERGENCY EVACUATION FILE

An emergency evacuation file has been established in Mississippi to safeguard elderly and disabled persons in case of a disaster.

The South Mississippi Planning and Development District calls elders and asks if they would go house to house in their own neighborhoods to interview other senior citizens. The volunteer canvassers seek their older neighbors' names, addresses, next of kin and any pertinent medical information.

The resulting information is indexed both alphabetically and by street for quick reference by the fire department and Civil Defense. The index is invaluable in case of a fire in a senior's home, or during a massive emergency like a flood.

Outreach is part of the Emergency Action Evacuation File effort as well. If seniors want a visit from aging agency personnel to discuss services available, they have merely to check a box on the interview form.

CONTACT:
Frances Adkins
South Mississippi Planning and Development District
1020 32nd Avenue
Gulfport, Mississippi 39501
(601) 868-2311

RECREATION

CAMPING TRIPS FOR OLDER CITIZENS

Both hearty and handicapped elders in Denver now are able to spend time each summer camping in the mountains.

One program, run by the Park Avenue Senior Center in the summer of 1976, was called "Summertime in the Rockies" and consisted first of lectures about Colorado history and geography. The lecture series was followed by one-day bus trips to the areas which had been discussed. Local guides were recruited in each area, and seniors were provided with a box lunch.

The final phase of the program was a seven-day tent camping experience into Colorado history, which encompassed a maximum of 16 elders at a time. The senior center purchased full camping equipment for participants from a fund set up to buy building furnishings.

In another, related program, the Denver Parks and Recreation Department (of which Park Avenue Senior Center is a part) each summer leases a camp located on 15 wooded acres in the mountains. There handicapped and nursing home elders can "get away from it all," at least briefly. Up to five nursing homes at a time can book the camp for overnights, which cost the elders $5 each including three meals. Marginally handicapped persons who are not institutionalized can attend the camp for $20 during the week set aside for them.

Other lively elders from the Park Avenue Senior Center go snowshoeing or even river rafting, paying their own way at group rates. All arrangements are made by the senior center.

CONTACT:
Lynn Bradley
Park Avenue Senior Center
1849 Emerson Street
Denver, Colorado 80218
(303)297-3164

VACATION APARTMENT SWAP

For elders living in public housing, the sameness of life can lead to boredom. Because of their low income, such seniors know that vacations are out of the question. But a new program developed by the International Center for Social Gerontology is changing that.

Each year seniors living in public housing in 18 cities swap their apartment homes for a week with seniors in a sister city. A federal grant pays most of the cost of transportation, but the elders involved must pay some of their own expenses, such as travel insurance.

The 698 residents of Denver's six senior housing projects were so enthused that 20 of their members could travel to Minneapolis in 1975 that they raised more than $3,300 to help the travelers from both cities. In addition, they solicited free dinners, tours and gifts worth more than $600 from Denver merchants so that the Minneapolis guests would have a memorable vacation.

CONTACT:
Dr. Wilma T. Donahue
International Center for Social Gerontology
1629 K Street, N.W., #801
Washington, D.C. 20006
(202)393-0347

TRANSPORTATION AND RELATED SERVICES

SENIORS' SHOPPING LOUNGES

In many cities, elders who would like to shop in the downtown business district are frustrated because there are no public toilets or lounges where they can rest when tired. Not so in Washington, D.C., where four senior lounges were opened in January 1976.

The lounges were established in existing, rent-free facilities such as churches or church annexes to keep costs down. Each lounge offers free refreshments, comfortable chairs and telephones. A full-time staffer gives seniors any personal assistance needed, and will provide bus tokens or cab fare when necessary. The lounges are also used as information centers, to tell older people about the services available to them.

Peak demand comes between 10 a.m. and 2 p.m., but the lounges are kept open eight hours daily. Advertising has helped publicize the four lounges' locations, which are each used by approximately 30 seniors a day.

CONTACT:
William H. Whitehurst, Jr.
Associate Director
Department of Human Resources
1350 E Street, N.W.
Washington, D.C. 20004
(202)629-2389

SHARE-A-FARE TAXI PLAN

Oklahoma City is attempting to use taxi cabs to solve the transit problems of its elderly citizens.

Seniors interested in the Share-a-Fare plan can buy two $10 books of transit coupons each month for $5. They phone in their request for a ride a day in advance, and a coordinator attempts to match their home and destination with up to three other seniors. The cab driver accepts coupons in lieu of payment.

The first three months of the program, 102 people took advantage of the service to make 400 trips. The program's target population is more than 6,000 seniors and nearly 8,000 handicapped persons.

Grants from the city, the Central Oklahoma Transit Authority, and the Urban Mass Transportation Administration pay half the seniors' fares and the salary of the project coordinator. The cab company provides the coordinator with free office space.

CONTACT:
Craig Dodd, Planner
Central Oklahoma Area-Wide Aging Agency
P. O. Box 1474
Oklahoma City, Oklahoma 73101
(405)236-2426

RURAL TRANSPORTATION PROJECT

West Virginia, which has public transportation in only 32 of its 55 counties, is attempting to meet the oft-neglected transportation needs of rural elders.

In October of 1976, a Transportation Remuneration Incentive Program (TRIP) went into effect in three parts of the state, with the purchase of buses equipped for wheelchairs and capable of carrying up to 20 passengers. Seniors and handicapped persons can buy ticket books worth eight dollars for only $1.18. The tickets can also be used on 140 commercial carriers across the state, including taxis, Greyhound and Amtrak. An important part of the demonstration project is a subsidy to elderly individuals rather than to transit operators.

By the fall of 1977, West Virginia hopes to have in operation seven special buses driven by mail carriers and equipped to hold both passengers and mail. The program has been slow starting because there were no bids from companies wishing to build the special vans.

CONTACT:
Grace Strain
West Virginia Department of Welfare
1900 Washington Street, E.
Charleston, West Virginia 25305
(304)348-3780

SPECIAL EVENING OF SHOPPING

For three years, approximately 900 elderly and handicapped people have been given free bus transportation to a discount store chain in Colorado for an evening of pre-Christmas shopping.

Target Stores, Inc., contacts all the seniors' living units, nursing homes and agencies in Denver and Colorado Springs to inform the elderly about the special night when the six stores involved will be closed to all other shoppers. Twenty-two chartered buses, some of them specially outfitted for the handicapped, pick up the seniors at their homes and return them following the evening which includes a free meal.

Other stores in the Target chain participate in this annual event across the U.S. But it would seem that other large stores in each community could sponsor their own seniors' night, so that the elderly would have such an evening out more often than once a year.

CONTACT:
Dell DeBore
Target Stores, Inc.
4301 East Virginia Avenue
Denver, Colorado 80222
(303) 399-0890

AND LAST BUT NOT LEAST . . .

MEDICAL AID FOR ELDERS' PETS

A pet is sometimes the only companion left to a lonely older American, and when that pet needs medical care it is a serious problem for a low-income senior.

In Berkeley the East Bay Humane Society is trying to prevent any senior having to give up a pet for financial reasons. Humane Society members donate money to a pet fund which pays the major share of a pet's medical bills, including spaying and neutering. The elders are allowed to pay a portion of the bills so they can retain their pride.

The Humane Society also provides the elderly poor with membership cards which give them a discount on pet foods and supplies sold at the Society's shelter.

CONTACT:
Paul Hurych, Executive Director
East Bay Humane Society
2700 Ninth Street
Berkeley, California 94710
(415)845-7735

PART IX

RESOURCES, INFORMATION, HELP

BOOKS AND MAGAZINES

THE "MUST" READING LIST

BEAUVOIR, SIMONE DE. *The Coming of Age.* New York: Putnam, 1972. 585 pages. HV1451/B413/1972b
Sometimes considered the definitive study of the universal problem of growing old, the book has been criticized for its depressing view of aging. Beauvoir's thesis, that treatment of the aged is "society's secret shame," is, however, well documented by historical and present-day examples in varied societies. The book is enlivened by a wealth of historical and literary anecdotes and reflects the author's intense involvement in the problems of the twentieth century.

BLAU, ZENA SMITH. *Old Age in a Changing Society.* New York: New Viewpoints, 1973.
Looks at the critical problems that emerge when society prolongs human life but fails to provide meaningful productive roles for the aged.

BUTLER, ROBERT N. *Why Survive? Being Old in America.* New York: Harper & Row, 1975. 496 pages. HQ1064/U5/B87
Awarded the 1976 Pulitzer prize for non-fiction, this work is an authoritative examination of "the tragedy of old age in America," with a comprehensive account of what is being done and what can be done to help the elderly. Its emphasis on the psychology of aging is particularly good. Lists goals for a national policy on aging. Includes numerous excellent references in chapter notes and bibliography.

———; and LEWIS, MYRNA I. *Aging and Mental Health: Positive Psychosocial Approaches.* St. Louis: C. V. Mosby, 1973. 306 pages. RC451.4/A5/B87
In a scholarly text written for professional and lay readers, the authors explore the possibilities of an ideal society stripped of the present prejudices of ageism. Part One discusses the nature and problems of old age. Part Two deals with evaluation, treatment, and prevention of mental disorders. After each chapter is a full bibliography, and the appendixes consist of sources of gerontological and geriatric literature, organizations, government programs, grant programs, and staff in-service educational material.

———. *Sex After Sixty; A Guide for Men and Women in their Later Years.* New York: Harper & Row, 1976.
Frank, sensitive, and informative book about the reality of an active and satisfying sex life in later years.

COMFORT, ALEX. *A Good Age.* New York: Crown Publications, 1976. "Old people are people who have lived a certain number of years, and that is all."
An excellently written statement debunking myths of old age. Liberating for all readers.

CURTIN, SHARON R. *Nobody Ever Died of Old Age; In Praise of Old People . . . In Outrage at Their Loneliness.* Boston: Little, Brown, 1972.

A powerful indictment against "us" who fear and abandon the elderly, us who deny their rights and forget. . . .

HARRIS (LOUIS) & ASSOCIATES, INC. *The Myth and Reality of Aging in America.* Washington, D.C.: The National Council on the Aging, Inc., 1975. 245 pages. HQ1061/H241

Verbatim quotations from older persons are interspersed with the statistics and charts in this Harris study. Based on almost five thousand in-person household interviews, the survey sampled opinions of a representative cross section of the American public. Data on attitudes are interspersed. A series of nine monographs based on the study focus on its implications for: society, the mass media, education, federal policy, the black aged, service providers, employment, state policy, women.

TEXTS AND SOURCE BOOKS

AMERICAN MEDICAL ASSOCIATION. *The Quality of Life: The Later Years.* Acton, Mass.: Publishing Sciences Group, 1975. 200 pages. HQ1060/N211/1975

In one volume are compiled the complete papers of the Third Congress on the Quality of Life, 1974, concentrating on social, environmental, and educational aspects of life in later years. Hugh Downs, retired television personality, wrote the prologue, and individual papers by well-known specialists cover four major categories: maximizing human potential in later years, physical health, mental and emotional health, economic and social conditions.

ANDRUS (ETHEL PERCY) GERONTOLOGY CENTER. *Aging: Prospects and Issues* (rev.), Richard H. Davis, ed. Los Angeles: University of Southern California Press, 1976. 209 pages. HQ1061/A5/1976

Part One of this completely revised, third edition of the Andrus Center monograph on aging presents an overview of the field by Dr. Davis, followed by essays from varied perspectives: psychology, psychiatry, sociology, physiology, and nursing. In Part Two the areas of special concern are policymaking, legislation, environment, clinical work, and more specific issues. Includes a selective bibliography.

BINSTOCK, ROBERT H.; and SHANAS, ETHEL (ed.). *Handbook of Aging and the Social Sciences.* Handbook of Aging Series, Vol. I, James E. Birren, editor-in-chief. Florence, Ky.: Van Nostrand-Reinhold, 1976. 684 pages.

James Birren's comprehensive one-volume Handbook of Aging and the Individual (1959) has been completely revised and published as three volumes. This first volume presents views of leading authorities relating to social aspects of aging. Its five sections deal with a study of age-related changes in a variety of social systems, the ways older people affect and are affected by social systems, the ways older people affect and are affected by social phenomena, and how societies attempt to provide resources for helping the aged.

BIRREN, JAMES E.; and SCHAIE, K. *Handbook of the Psychology of Aging.* Handbook of Aging Series, Vol. II, James E. Birren, editor-in-chief. Florence, Ky.: Van Nostrand-Reinhold, 1976. 740 pages.

Volume II of this series covers all important approaches to the psychology of aging—from primary sensory phenomena to personality and behavior deviation. Twenty-nine contributors examine changes in behavior and capabilities that occur with advancing age. The volume considers stress, disease, the physical environment, cross-cultural perspectives, and the impact of social structure on the elderly.

EISDORFER, C.; and LAWTON, M. POWELL. *The Psychology of Adult Development and Aging.* Washington, D.C.: American Psychological Association, 1973. 718 pages. BF724.8/A43

Summarizes the state of psychological knowledge about aging and is a collaborative effort of outstanding leaders in the field. "It may be regarded as a preliminary map of a recently discovered territory, not only surveying what is known, but also outlining the unexplored and underdeveloped regions." Fully indexed, it has a wealth of bibliographical references.

FINCH, CALEB E.; and HAYFLECK, LEONARD (eds.). *Handbook of the Biology of Aging,* Handbook of Aging Series, Vol. VI, James E. Birren, editor-in-chief. Florence, Ky.: Van Nostrand-Reinhold, 1976. 700 pages.

This volume explores the varieties of aging changes shown by humans and other mammalian species. It covers aging from a comparative biological and evolutionary point of view and stresses the relevance of animal models to studies of human aging. Reflecting the enormous increase in biological research of aging, it thoroughly examines age changes at molecular, cellular, physiological, and organismic levels.

KIMMEL, DOUGLAS C. *Adulthood and Aging: An Interdisciplinary, Developmental View.* New York: John Wiley & Sons, 1974.

The author has said that he has tried to write a non-textbook that will introduce the subject as well as inform the reader about the problems of growing old in society. He has used a developmental approach for viewing the adult years, plus an interdisciplinary approach by interacting psychological, social, and physiological aspects and has used six case examples as interludes between the chapters.

NEUGARTEN, BERNICE L. (ed.). *Middle Age and Aging: A Reader in Social Psychology.* Chicago: University of Chicago Press, 1968. 596 pages. BF724.8/N3

Emphasizes social and psychological adaptations required as individuals move from middle age to old age. Nine general topics, selected for their usefulness to graduate students, include articles illustrating a wide range of research methods.

OYER, HERBERT J.; and OYER, E. JANE (eds.). *Aging and Communication.* Baltimore: University Park Press, 1976. 302 pages. HQ1061/A455
Seventeen chapters by twenty specialists (sixteen from Michigan State University) analyze the importance of effective communication (individual, small-group, large-group, and mass-media) in improving the quality of life for the aged. From perspectives in sociology, gerontology, and communications, the authors review progress, predict future trends, and propose further research and action in these important, related fields. Each chapter summarizes the most important findings and cites numerous related studies.

RILEY, MATILDA. *Aging and Society,* 3 vols. New York: Russell Sage Foundation, 1972.
Addressed to general readers or students wanting introductory information about the generation gap as well as to researchers and practitioners in the field of aging. A full bibliography follows each chapter. Volume II is suggested as the most introductory reading, with an excellent first chapter, which discusses aging in a broad context. References in Volume I are often cited as additional reading.

WOODRUFF, DIANA S.; and BIRREN, JAMES E. (eds.). *Aging: Scientific Perspectives and Social Issues.* New York: Van Nostrand-Reinhold, 1975. 421 pages. HQ1061/A45
This introductory text, by twenty-three specialists at Andrus Gerontology Center, begins with a broad overview of gerontology, followed by a history of the field. The focus then narrows from sociological to psychological and biological perspectives. It is excellent on demography, social issues, and public policy. Contains a comprehensive name and subject index as well as bibliographies.

OLD AGE AS IT REALLY IS

THE NATIONAL COUNCIL ON THE AGING. *Facts and Myths About Aging.* Washington, D.C., 1976.
Excellent booklet succinctly clarifying facts from myths. Attractive format and design. Illustrated.

PERCY, CHARLES H. *Growing Old in the Country of the Young.* New York: McGraw-Hill, 1974. 214 pages. HV1461/P47
"In no sense a scientific study," Senator Percy's "impressionistic survey" is intended to "heighten a collective awareness of what it is like to grow old in America." By citing numerous cases of older persons suffering from poverty and indifference, he points up, in a human and readable style, the most pressing needs for assistance of the elderly. Part Two, the "Action Resource Guide," is directed to older persons themselves and answers questions about financial benefits, health care, housing, and employment. Addresses given include state aging commissions as well as many other helpful agencies.

SAUL, SHURA. *Aging: An Album of People Growing Old.* New York: John Wiley & Sons, 1974.

Anthology of vignettes giving insights about the learning and aging processes during senescence. Intended for those in service professions for the aging.

SUCCESSFUL AGING

BÜLBÜL; and PAUL, IRENE. *Everybody's Studying Us—The Ironies of Aging in the Pepsi Generation.* San Francisco: Glide Publications, 1976.

"One of the most sensitive, hard-hitting treatments of the realities of aging in America I have read."
—William R. Hutton, executive director,
National Council of Senior Citizens

"It is a great satire and I hope it will be widely circulated."
—Margaret Kuhn, National Convener, Gray Panthers

COLES, ROBERT. *The Old Ones of New Mexico.* Albuquerque: University of New Mexico Press, 1973.

"If you want to know about children, you must first speak with the old people; what they believe, the child soon believes."

An inspiring text and photographs of old men and women who hold a unique place in their society.

KNOPF, OLGA. *Successful Aging.* New York: Viking Press, 1975. 229 pages. HQ1064/U5/K5

An eighty-seven-year-old practicing psychiatrist with twenty years of experience in adult education, Dr. Knopf writes for the aged "to increase their self-awareness and thus to cushion the sting of the hurt of their new role." She also makes herself "spokesman for the older generation" to bridge the gap with the young. Written in everyday language, the book includes practical advice about adjustment and assistance for older persons.

LEAF, ALEXANDER. *Youth in Old Age.* New York: McGraw-Hill, 1975.

A remarkable book with photographs about very old people in remote areas of the world who lead healthy, active, and productive lives. Analysis of factors that contribute to longevity is included in the discussion.

MCLEISH, JOHN A. B. *The Ulyssean Adult: Creativity in the Middle and Later Years.* Scarborough, Ont., Canada: McGraw-Hill Ryerson, 1976. 309 pages. BF408/M22

Defining a "Ulyssean adult" as one who either (1) begins to live creatively in later years or (2) continues to be creatively productive into the very late years, McLeish documents a perspective on later life that is in direct contrast to nearly all other books on aging. Delightful, inspiring study of creativity, with a last chapter on how to become a Ulyssean; with a valuable select bibliography and a useful index.

SMITH, BERT KRUGER. *Aging in America.* Boston: Beacon Press, 1973.

"Up-to-the-minute glimpse of the legislation, leaders, movement, and institutions trying to reunite the social fabric from which the elderly have almost been torn bodily and cast aside to live or die."

—Joseph Levine, Boston Globe staff

SMITH, JEAN LOUISE. *Portraits of Aging.* Winona, Minn.: St. Mary's College Press, 1972.

Presents portraits of old age through works of great masters of art: Rembrandt, Sargent, Eakins, Picasso, and others. Narrative discusses age as a time for growth.

STONECYPHER, D. D. *Getting Older and Staying Young: A Doctor's Prescription for Continuing Vitality in Later Life.* New York: W. W. Norton, 1974. 352 pages. RC952/S79

Provides both the older person and the younger reader with practical advice on achieving a richer, more rewarding old age. Presents a clear picture of the physical and psychological factors in the aging process.

ABOUT NURSING HOMES

GRIESEL, ELMA; and HORN, LINDA; FOR THE GRAY PANTHERS. *Citizens Action Guide: Nursing Home Reform,* 1975.

Provides information on major problems and issues pertaining to nursing homes for the aged. Recommends action programs needed for reform.

MENDELSON, MARY ADELAIDE. *Tender Loving Greed: How the Incredibly Lucrative Nursing Home "Industry" Is Exploiting America's Old People and Defrauding Us All.* New York: Alfred A. Knopf, 1974.

An exposé of the inner workings of the nursing-home business, presenting a stirring indictment of conditions widely prevalent as well as an examination of the reasons those conditions prevail.

THE NADER REPORT. *Old Age: The Last Segregation;* Clair Townsend, project director. New York: Grossman Publishers, 1971.

Documented study exposing the horrors existing in nursing homes in America. Harsh truth about our indifference to these conditions.

ABOUT CARING FOR THE AGED

FRASER, VIRGINIA; and THORNTON, SUSAN M. *The New Elders, Innovative Programs by, for and about the Elderly.* Denver: Loretto Heights College, 1977.

Description of fifty selected programs drawn from various areas throughout the country. Includes grief-therapy groups and a "self-health" medical course.

GALTON, LAWRENCE. *Don't Give Up on an Aging Parent.* New York: Crown Publishers, 1975.

Explodes commonly held myths about diseases of the aged and provides insights into the need for better medical care for "a greatly abused minority."

POE, WILLIAM D., M.D. *The Old Person in Your Home.* New York: Charles Scribner's Sons, 1969.
Written by a physician who gives advice on meeting specific needs of the elderly who share your home.

SILVERSTONE, BARBARA; and HYMAN, HELEN KANDEL. *You and Your Aging Parent.* New York: Pantheon Books, 1976.
"The Modern Family's Guide to Emotional, Physical, and Financial Problems."

UNITARIAN UNIVERSALIST ASSOCIATION COMMITTEE ON AGING. *Aging and Awareness.* Boston: Unitarian Universalist Association, 1975.
This is the first part of a two-part kit developed for the purposes of increasing awareness and raising consciousness about the processes and problems of aging. Techniques are delineated in detail. Although the material was designed for use within a religious setting, much of it can be adapted for use elsewhere.

ABOUT DEATH AND DYING

JURY, MARK; and JURY, DAN. *Gramp.* New York: Grossman Publishers, 1976.
"They treat death as an intimate family affair, snatching it back from technology, hospitals, and nursing homes."
—Anatole Broyard, New York Times

KÜBLER-ROSS, ELISABETH. *On Death and Dying.* New York: Macmillan, 1969. 289 pages. BF789/D4/K8
An outstanding pioneer work on a previously neglected subject, the book is based on over two hundred interviews with terminally ill patients in the presence of students at the University of Chicago's Billings Hospital. Most useful are the descriptions of five stages in awareness of approaching death. Excerpts from actual interviews are included as well as suggestions for therapy with the terminally ill.

———. *Questions and Answers on Death and Dying.* New York: Macmillan, 1974. 177 pages. BF789/D4/K8q
Frank, sensible, and sensitive discussions of universal concern about dying persons, in question-answer format, based on the "approximately seven hundred" workshops, lectures, and seminars the author has conducted on the subject of death. Useful supplement to previous books by Kübler-Ross.

ABOUT RETIREMENT

ASKWITH, HERBERT. *Your Retirement, How to Plan for It, How to Enjoy It to the Fullest.* New York: Hart Publishing, 1974.

ATCHLEY, ROBERT C. *The Sociology of Retirement.* Cambridge, Mass.: Schenkman, 1976. 158 pages. HQ1062/A8
A sociologist views retirement from a historical perspective and "as a process, as an event, as a social role, or as a phase of life." He summarizes major studies in a generous bibliography and suggests some

forty general areas needing further research; for example, "What are the economic costs and/or benefits of having retired people in the community?" and "What cross-national similarities or differences exist with respect to retirement, and why?"

HUNTER, WOODROW W. *Preparation for Retirement* (3rd Ed.). Institute of Gerontology, University of Michigan. Detroit-Wayne State University, 1976.

Popular book for use with preretirement discussion groups and for consideration of problems during postemployment years.

OLDSTEAD, ALAN H. *Threshold: The First Days of Retirement.* New York: Harper & Row, 1975.

A lovely, sensitive daily journal of the first six months of retirement and yet another beginning. "It is full of summer sun and new spring grass and winter snow and a few worries and a lot of good solutions to them."

TOURNIER, PAUL. *Learn to Grow Old* (translated from the French by Edwin Hudson). New York: Harper & Row, 1972. 248 pages. BF724.8/T6813

Although not a specialist in geriatrics, Dr. Tournier, Swiss physician aged seventy-three, upon request of the publisher has written a book of personal counsel for those who are preparing to retire as well as for the retired. He concentrates on the areas of work and leisure, needs of a more humane society, the condition of the old, second careers, and the aspects of faith. Written in an easily understandable yet inspirational style.

ABOUT SOCIAL ACTION AND AGING

THE INSTITUTE OF GERONTOLOGY. *No Longer Young: The Older Woman in America,* Ann Arbor, Mich.: University of Michigan, 1975.

One of two publications resulting from a conference on women and aging, sponsored by the Institute. Material comprises major papers ranging from status of older women to mechanisms and resources for change. Contributors include Susan Sontag and Mary S. Calderone.

KLEYMAN, PAUL. *Senior Power: Growing Old Rebelliously.* San Francisco: Glide Publications, 1974.

Describes the activities of a group of seniors at San Francisco's Glide Memorial Methodist Church, under the leadership of Rev. Edward I. Peet in 1967, and how it helped form the California Legislative Council for Older Americans—"an organization that has become a model for other such groups across the country."

NATIONAL COUNCIL OF SENIOR CITIZENS. *The Law and Aging Manual.* Washington, D.C.: National Council of Senior Citizens, 1976.

Gives an overview of legal problems facing the elderly and a practical guide for establishing legal representation for them on the state and local levels.

NATIONAL COUNCIL ON THE AGING. *Proceedings of the Ninth National*

Conference of Senior Centers: Senior Centers: Options and Actions, Bella Jacobs (ed.). Washington, D.C., 1975.
Describes the options senior centers hold for the elderly.

NATIONAL COUNCIL ON THE AGING, NATIONAL INSTITUTE OF SENIOR CENTERS. *Social Action for Senior Centers.* Washington, D.C., 1974. *Describes how the senior center can involve the elderly in social action.*

ROMNEY, LEONARD S.; and HOFFMAN, LEE A., JR. *Advocacy Handbook for Senior Citizens.* Rockland Community College, State University of New York, 1976.
This is an excellent guidebook to action for the older adult. It discusses the rights of the elderly and the belief that the quality of life depends upon the capacity of the elderly to improve it.

ROSS, DONALD. *A Public Citizens Action Manual* (Introduction by Ralph Nader). New York: Grossman Publishers, 1973.

STRAUSS, BERT; and STOWE, MARY. *How to Get Things Changed.* Garden City, New York: Doubleday, 1974.

WEISS, JONATHAN A. (ed.). *The Law of the Elderly.* Practicing Law Institute, 810 7th Avenue, New York, N.Y. 10019; 1977.
New York Gray Panthers report that this book is superior to any other in the field. It is recommended highly as a resource book. Written in simple language. The cost is high: $25.

FICTION AND DRAMA

ALBEE, EDWARD	*The American Dream*
ASHTON-WARNER, SYLVIA	*Spinster*
BALZAC, HONORÉ DE	*Père Goriot*
BELLOW, SAUL	*Mr. Sammler's Planet*
HEMINGWAY, ERNEST	*The Old Man and the Sea*
HILTON, JAMES	*Goodbye, Mr. Chips*
MILLER, ARTHUR	*Death of a Salesman*
PEARCE, DON	*Dying in the Sun*
SHAKESPEARE, WILLIAM	*King Lear*
SIMENON, GEORGES	*The Bells of Bicêtre*
SOPHOCLES	*Oedipus at Colonus*
STONE, GENE	*Darling, I Am Growing Old*
UPDIKE, JOHN	*The Poorhouse Fair*
WRIGHT, ROSALIND	*Rocking*

FEDERAL GOVERNMENT PUBLICATIONS

U. S. ADMINISTRATION ON AGING. *Basic Concepts of Aging: A Programmed Manual.* Washington, D.C., 1972. Thomas A. Rich and Alden S. Gilmore (ed.). 148 pages. HQ1061/U58A1/1972
Designed for self-teaching "at a pace determined by the user," this text would be useful for anyone desiring a rapid acquaintance with general facts and ideas in the field of aging.

U. S. CONGRESS. House of Representatives Select Committee on Aging. Washington, D.C.: U. S. Gov't Printing Office, 1975–76. 94th Congress.
Contains hearing before various subcommittees on salient issues pertaining to the aged.

U. S. CONGRESS. Senate Special Committee on Aging. *Developments in Aging,* 1969–76. Issued annually. Washington, D.C.: U. S. Gov't Printing Office, 1968–
These annual reports summarize the actions of Congress and examine the progress of legislation concerning the elderly. Included are accounts of major trends in state policies, reports of surveys, and current statistics on aging. Committee recommendations are noted regarding Medicare, nursing homes, Social Security, and other needs of the aging population. A list is given of all committee hearings and reports that are printed separately, followed by a subject and name index.

U. S. CONGRESS. Senate Special Committee on Aging. *Older Americans Comprehensive Services Amendments of 1973: Explanations of 1973 Amendments and Selected Background Materials.* Washington, D.C.: U. S. Gov't Printing Office, 1973. 93rd Congress, 1st Session.
Contains text of Public Law 93-29, the Older Americans Comprehensive Services Amendments of 1973, a title-by-title summary, the House and Senate reports on the Act, and the text of the Older Americans Act of 1965, as amended, including the 1973 amendments. This is a basic legal document for anyone involved in services to the elderly.

BIBLIOGRAPHIES ABOUT THE AGING

ACADEMY FOR EDUCATIONAL DEVELOPMENT. *Never Too Old to Learn.* New York, 1974.
117-item bibliography describing programs for retirees at colleges and universities.

ANDRUS (ETHEL PERCY) GERONTOLOGY CENTER, UNIVERSITY OF SOUTHERN CALIFORNIA. *Technical Bibliographies on Aging.* Office of Publications and Media Projects, University of Southern California Press, 1975, Richard H. Davis, Ph.D., director.
These bibliographies were selected from over forty-five thousand references pertaining to specific areas of gerontological study during the years 1959–74:

Assessment and Therapy in Aging: A Selected Bibliography. Arthur N. Schwartz (ed.), 1975.

Environmental Planning for the Elderly: A Selected Bibliography. Victor A. Regnier and M. Arch (eds.), 1975.

Etiology of Mental Disorders in Aging: A Selected Bibliography. Arthur N. Schwartz (ed.), 1975.

Intellectual Functioning and Aging: A Selected Bibliography. Compiled by K. Warner Schaie and Elizabeth M. Zelinski, 1975.

Intergenerational Relations and Aging: A Selected Bibliography. Com-

piled by Vern L. Bengston, Kim Edwards, and Gary A. Baffa, 1975.
Psychological Adjustment to Aging: A Selected Bibliography. Arthur N. Schwartz (ed.), 1975.
The Relation of Stress and Age: A Selected Bibliography. James E. Birren and Julie E. Moore (eds.), 1975.
Safety for the Elderly: A Selected Bibliography. Annette Jenkins, Nancy H. Corby, Julie Moore, Arnold M. Small (eds.), 1975.
Sexuality and Aging: A Selected Bibliography. Arthur N. Schwartz (ed.), 1975.

NATIONAL COUNCIL ON THE AGING. *The Aged in Minority Groups: A Bibliography*. Compiled by John B. Balkema. Washington, D.C., 1973.
Includes citations of literature pertaining to Asians, Spanish, American, Indians, Negroes, Jews.

NATIONAL COUNCIL ON THE AGING. Current Literature on the Aging. Washington, D.C., 1976.
Quarterly annotated subject guide to selected publications in aging and related fields.

NATIONAL COUNCIL ON THE AGING. *Housing and Living Arrangements for Older People: A Bibliography*. Compiled by John B. Balkema. Washington, D.C., 1972.
Provides information about housing needs and community services for the elderly.

NATIONAL COUNCIL ON THE AGING. *Publications List. NCOA'76*. Washington, D.C., 1976.
Lists, tapes, films, publications, available for purchase.

NATIONAL COUNCIL ON THE AGING. *Retirement Income: A Selected Bibliography*. Compiled by Elizabeth M. Heidbreder, Washington, D.C., 1972.
Facts, issues, and practical information about financial problems, Social Security benefits, and pensions.

NATIONAL COUNCIL ON THE AGING. *Second Careers: A Selected Bibliography*. Compiled by Carol H. Kellcher. Washington, D.C., 1973.
Presents literature on career change during midlife and postretirement years.

MAJOR NATIONAL PERIODICALS
AGING

The official magazine of the National Clearinghouse on Aging in the U.S. Administration on Aging. Useful for keeping abreast of what the national government is doing, and of changes in federal regulations regarding Social Security and other programs. Each issue also features announcements of new programs, organizations, and conferences, reports of important meetings, summaries of activities in the states, and a few accounts of notable local projects. A calendar of upcoming conferences and courses will be of special interest to activists and professionals in the field.

GRAY PANTHER NETWORK

Activist newsletter published quarterly. Reports events, positions, and actions taken by Gray Panthers locally and nationally. Currently focusing on outlawing mandatory retirement, exposing conditions in nursing homes, and consciousness raising to break down stereotypic thinking about old age. Subscription is $3.00 a year. Free to persons who can't afford it.

PERSPECTIVES ON AGING

Bimonthly periodical published by The National Council on the Aging, spotlighting new and innovative programs for the elderly nationally. Each issue includes a Public Policy Report, activities by the Council, specific and relevant information about benefits, and news of new publications. A must for knowledgeable seniors. Membership fees include subscription.

MODERN MATURITY

Bimonthly popular magazine published by American Association of Retired Persons. Gives general information about a variety of subjects of interest to all ages. Includes travel tips, helpful hints, feature stories, personal-survival column for older adults, etc. Annual membership includes subscription price: $4.00.

AARP NEWS BULLETIN

Best monthly report on pending legislation, governmental action in the states, changes in pension provisions for retired government and military workers, and other bread-and-butter topics. Heavy on news of AARP activities, of course, but many of these are of general interest. Editorials by AARP director Harriet Miller and guest columnists also provide cogent commentary on emerging issues. Annual AARP membership dues of $3.00 include $.50 for annual subscription to the *News Bulletin*.

ORGANIZATIONS, SERVICES, AND NETWORKS

MAJOR NATIONAL ORGANIZATIONS

ADMINISTRATION ON AGING
Office of Human Development
U. S. Department of Health, Education, and Welfare
330 Independence Avenue, S.W.
Washington, D.C. 20201

   AoA is the U. S. Government agency responsible for administration of the Older Americans Act. It performs an advocacy function at various levels of interdepartmental federal planning.

PERIODICAL: *Aging* (10/year)

AMERICAN ASSOCIATION OF RETIRED PERSONS
1909 K Street, N.W.
Washington, D.C. 20049

AARP, which works closely with the National Retired Teachers Association (NRTA) is open to any person fifty-five years of age or older. The purpose is to improve the quality of life for older people. The AARP offers health, life, and auto insurance, and group travel insurance, and sponsors community service programs.

PERIODICALS: *News Bulletin* (monthly)
                Modern Maturity (bimonthly)

GRAY PANTHERS
3700 Chestnut Street
Philadelphia, Pa. 19104

The Gray Panthers is an organization of consciousness-raising activist groups aiming to combat ageism. It seeks major reforms in the areas of national health, nursing homes, the present economic system, and media stereotyping. Fifty-five local chapters.

PERIODICAL: *The Network* (5/year)

NATIONAL COUNCIL OF SENIOR CITIZENS
1511 K Street, N.W.
Washington, D.C. 20005

NCSC is an affiliation of 3,500 local senior-citizen clubs, with a combined membership of over 3 million people, actively working for a better life for all Americans. The National Council's professional staff has the responsibility of developing information for members of Congress and the general public on the best method of solving the various problems facing the elderly. In addition, the National Council makes available to its members specific information on the availability of programs and services at the local, state, and national levels.

PERIODICAL: *Senior Citizens News* (monthly)

NATIONAL COUNCIL ON THE AGING
1828 L Street, N.W.
Washington, D.C. 20036

The National Council on the Aging is a non-profit organization that serves as a central resource providing information, materials, and technical assistance to professionals in the field of aging. The Council works with other organizations to develop concern for older people as well as methods and resources for meeting their needs. Among its programs are the National Institute of Industrial Gerontology, The National Institute of Senior Centers, national voluntary organizations for independent living by the aged, and the National Media Resource Center on Aging, which focuses on elevating the image of older people by educating the public to better understand the potential for service and productive contribution older people can make to society if opportunities are provided. The NCOA has published the results of the Harris poll The Myth and Reality of Aging in America.

PERIODICALS: *Perspectives on Aging* (bimonthly)
Institute on Senior Centers (monthly)
Older Worker Specialist (bimonthly)
Current Literature on Aging (quarterly)
Industrial Gerontology (quarterly)

DIRECTORY OF ORGANIZATIONS INVOLVED IN AGING

ACTION
806 Connecticut Ave., N.W.
Washington, D.C. 20525

ACTION is the federal volunteer agency that administers the Peace Corps, VISTA, SCORE, Foster Grandparent Program, and RSVP.

PERIODICAL: *Interaction* (irregular)

ACTION FOR INDEPENDENT MATURITY
1909 K St., N.W.
Washington, D.C. 20006

AIM is a division of AARP that helps people between fifty and sixty-five plan their retirement.

PERIODICAL: *Dynamic Maturity* (monthly)

ADULT EDUCATION ASSOCIATION OF THE U.S.A.
810 Eighteenth St., N.W.
Washington, D.C. 20006

AEA's general purpose is to further the concept of education as a process continuing throughout life. Organized in 1951, AEA today enjoys the solid support of many of the nation's most prominent educators; civic, industrial, and labor leaders; social workers; religious leaders; and voluntary-association leaders.

PERIODICALS: *Adult Leadership* (monthly, except July and August); *Adult Education* (quarterly); *AEA Dateline* (newsletter, 8/year)

AGING RESEARCH INSTITUTE
342 Madison Ave.
New York, N.Y. 10017

ARI encourages, supports, and performs research studies on physiological aspects of the aging processes and the prevention, diagnosis, and treatment of diseases most common among the aged.

AMERICAN AGING ASSOCIATION
c/o Denham Harman, M.D.
University of Nebraska College of Medicine
Omaha, Nebr. 68105

AGA promotes biomedical aging studies directed toward slowing down the aging process, informs the public of the progress of aging research, and spreads knowledge of gerontology among physicians and other health workers.

AMERICAN ASSOCIATION OF HOMES FOR THE AGING
374 National Press Building
Washington, D.C. 20045

The American Association of Homes for the Aging develops curricula for administrators of homes and conducts institutes and workshops. It has published the Directory of Nonprofit Homes for the Aged.

PERIODICALS: *Washington Report* (biweekly); *Concern* (bimonthly)

AMERICAN GERIATRICS SOCIETY, INC.
10 Columbus Circle, Room 1470
New York, N.Y. 10019

The American Geriatrics Society encourages and promotes research in the fields of aging and clinical geriatrics, publishes a monthly journal to disseminate information regarding diagnosis, treatment, and prevention of acute and chronic disease in the elderly, and conducts a continuing-education program.

PERIODICALS: *Journal of the American Geriatrics Society* and a *Newsletter* (both monthly)

AMERICAN HEALTH CARE ASSOCIATION
1200 Fifteenth St., N.W.
Washington, D.C. 20005

Formerly the American Nursing Home Association, the AHCA is a federation of state associations of nursing homes. It conducts seminars and conferences as continuing education for nursing-home administrators.

PERIODICALS: *Weekly Notes; Modern Nursing Home* (monthly); *Journal of the American Health Care Association* (quarterly)

AMERICAN MEDICAL ASSOCIATION
Committee on Aging
535 North Dearborn St.
Chicago, Ill. 60610

The Committee works (1) to promote positive health care and meaningful lives for all older persons, (2) to encourage the development and maintenance of programs for older persons, emphasizing the importance of self-help and independence, and (3) to provide guidance for policies governing the medical, nursing, and related health services provided in nursing homes and other long-term-care facilities.

AMERICAN PUBLIC WELFARE ASSOCIATION
1155 Sixteenth St., N.W., Suite 201
Washington, D.C. 20036

The APWA is a voluntary membership association serving social welfare agencies and interested individuals. It maintains continuing liaison with agencies and civic leaders through publications, regional and national conferences, seminars, and various membership services. It provides expert testimony and consultation for Congress and federal agencies, and administers specially funded research and technical-assistance projects.

THE AMERICAN SOCIETY FOR GERIATRIC DENTISTRY
431 Oakdale Ave., Room 913
Chicago, Ill. 60657

One of the main purposes of the ASGD is the promotion of post-graduate education of the dental practitioner in gerontology and geriatrics, medical and dental. The Society tries to teach that it is essential to know and understand the elderly person in his vast totality before looking into his mouth. Unfortunately, the subject is hardly mentioned in dental school and there are very few teachers equipped to teach it. The ASGD reaches its members through a quarterly journal, and at regular intervals through study assignments. ASGD's educational material is not for sale; it is sent to members without additional charge.

PERIODICAL: *The Journal of the American Society for Geriatric Dentistry*

AMERICAN SOCIOLOGICAL ASSOCIATION
1722 N St., N.W.
Washington, D.C. 20036

The ASA is the professional organization of sociologists.

ASOCIACIÓN NACIONAL PRO PERSONAS MAYORES
386 Park Ave.
New York, N.Y. 10016

Headquartered in Los Angeles, the Asociación was founded in April 1975 to address the needs of the nation's Spanish-speaking elderly. It also has offices in Miami, Albuquerque, and New York City and a liaison office in Washington, and has plans to open offices in Chicago. Funded by a two-year model-programs grant from the Administration on Aging, the Asociación claims a membership of just over five hundred. It estimates that there are upwards of 15 million persons of Hispanic origin—Cuban, Mexican, Puerto Rican, Central and South American, and Spanish—not being accounted for in present government programs.

ASSOCIATION FOR GERONTOLOGY IN HIGHER EDUCATION
Gerontology Society
Suite 520, One Dupont Circle, N.W.
Washington, D.C. 20036

The purpose of AGHE is to provide a network of communication among educational institutions that provide professional education and training, research, and technical assistance in the field of gerontology. AGHE provides a forum that will enable its membership to exchange ideas and knowledge that will serve to advance the field of gerontology in higher education.

ASSOCIATION FOR THE ADVANCEMENT
OF AGING RESEARCH
309 Hancock Building
University of Southern California
Los Angeles, Calif. 90007

*The Association organizes and supports research efforts on the effects
of aging on the quality of later life.*

BUREAU OF THE CENSUS
U. S. Department of Commerce
Washington, D.C. 20233

*The Bureau collects demographic data on the population of the
United States and publishes* Current Population Reports *and other
material that often pertains to the older American.*

CENTRAL BUREAU FOR THE JEWISH AGED
31 Union Sq. W.
New York, N.Y. 10003

*The Central Bureau serves as co-ordinating group for the New York
Metropolitan Jewish community to study the problem of providing effective care for the aged.*

PERIODICAL: *Aspects of Aging* (irregular)

THE CHURCH OF THE BRETHREN HOMES
AND HOSPITALS ASSOCIATION
c/o The Brethren Home
Box 128
New Oxford, Pa. 17350

*Members are administrators and board members of the Brethren
Homes for the Aged and of one hospital.*

CITIZENS FOR BETTER CARE IN NURSING HOMES,
HOMES FOR THE AGED AND OTHER
AFTER-CARE FACILITIES
960 E. Jefferson Ave.
Detroit, Mich. 48207

*CBC seeks to improve the quality of care in nursing homes and homes
for the aged and investigates issues affecting the health of the elderly.*

PERIODICAL: *Annual Report*

DIVISION OF ADULT DEVELOPMENT AND AGING (DIVISION
20) of the AMERICAN PSYCHOLOGICAL ASSOCIATION
1200 Seventeenth St., N.W.
Washington, D.C. 20036

*Division 20 is the arm that co-ordinates the APA's activities concern-
ing the older person.*

FAMILY SERVICE ASSOCIATION OF AMERICA
44 E. 23rd St.
New York, N.Y. 10010

The FSAA is a federation of local agencies that provide family coun-

seling services and other programs to help families with parent-child, marital, and mental-health problems.

PERIODICALS: *Highlights of FSAA News* (15/year); *Social Casework* (10/year)

FEDERAL COUNCIL ON THE AGING
U. S. Department of Health, Education, and Welfare
Room 4260, HEW North
330 Independence Ave., S.W.
Washington, D.C. 20201

The Federal Council is the citizens advisory body established by the Older Americans Act to advise and assist on federal policies regarding the aging.

FLYING SENIOR CITIZENS OF U.S.A.
96 Tamarack St.
Buffalo, N.Y. 14220

Affiliated with the National Council of Senior Citizens, the Flying Senior Citizens of U.S.A. is interested in petitioning for reduced air fares for senior citizens on domestic airlines.

PERIODICAL: *News Letter* (monthly)

FRIENDS AND RELATIVES OF INSTITUTIONALIZED AGED
129 E. 79th St.
New York, N.Y. 10021

City-wide, non-profit consumer watchdog group serving as advocates for elderly patients and residents in long-term-care institutions.

THE GERONTOLOGICAL SOCIETY
Suite 520, One Dupont Circle, N.W.
Washington, D.C. 20036

The Gerontological Society is a national organization of researchers, educators, and professionals in the field of aging. Its purposes are to promote the scientific study of aging in the biological and social sciences; to stimulate communications between scientific disciplines; to broaden education in aging; to foster application of research to practice; to advance the utilization of research in the development of public policy; and to develop the qualifications of gerontologists by setting high standards of professional ethics, conduct, education, and achievement.

PERIODICALS: *The Gerontologist* and *The Journal of Gerontology* (both bimonthly)

GERONTOLOGY RESEARCH CENTER
National Institute on Aging
Baltimore City Hospitals
Baltimore, Md. 21224

The Gerontology Research Center seeks to develop both practical and basic knowledge about aging that can be used ultimately to help improve the lot and capabilities of the aging population. Research is conducted to describe and interpret age changes in various organisms. Investigations include those dealing with the basic cellular and biological mechanisms of aging, and the behavioral changes that take place in both humans and other animal species as they age.

GOLDEN RING COUNCILS OF SENIOR CITIZENS CLUBS
22 W. 38th St.
New York, N.Y. 10018
The Golden Ring Councils promotes social activities in the clubs, better living conditions, and social action to change legislation.
PERIODICAL: *Senior Citizens Reporter* (quarterly)

INSTITUTE FOR RETIRED PROFESSIONALS
The New School for Social Research
60 W. 12th St.
New York, N.Y. 10011
Pioneering school which led the way to providing intellectual activities for retired professionals.

INSTITUTE OF STUDY FOR OLDER ADULTS
New York City Community College
Division of Continuing Education
300 Jay St.
Brooklyn, N.Y. 11201
A project in continuing education as a lifelong process, highlighting the sense of potential growth throughout life.

INTERNATIONAL ASSOCIATION OF GERONTOLOGY
c/o D. F. Chebotarev
Institute of Gerontology AMS USSR
Vyshgorodskaya 67
252655 Kiev-114, U.S.S.R.
IAG is an organization of national societies of gerontology. It promotes research, training of professional personnel, and co-operation among its members.
PERIODICAL: "IAG News," in *The Gerontologist* (bimonthly, see above)

INTERNATIONAL FEDERATION OF AGING
1909 K St., N.W., Room 615
Washington, D.C. 20006
IFA is a federation of national voluntary organizations that represent the elderly as their advocate and/or provide services to them. Its objectives include advocacy on behalf of the aging at an international level and the exchange of information, on a cross-national level, of developments in aging of primary interest to the practitioners.
PERIODICAL: *Aging International* (quarterly)

INTERNATIONAL SENIOR CITIZENS ASSOCIATION
11753 Wilshire Blvd.
Los Angeles, Calif. 90025
ISCA provides international co-ordination to safeguard interests of

*senior citizens and establishes communication among older citizens
about educational and cultural developments.*

PERIODICAL: *Newsletter* (quarterly)

IT'S ABOUT TIME COLLECTIVE
Brandeis University
Heller School
Waltham, Mass. 02154

*A group seeking "radical perspectives on aging," which publishes a
quarterly newsletter,* It's About Time, *"dedicated to debunking the
stereotypic images of old age to search for strategies for progressive
social change."*

JEWISH ASSOCIATION FOR SERVICES FOR THE AGED
222 Park Ave. S.
New York, N.Y. 10003

*This is a social welfare organization with the aim of keeping the older
adult in the community and providing the services necessary to do so.*

PERIODICALS: *Newsletter, Progress Report* (annual)

LEAGUE OF ELDERLY GENTLEMEN
IN REDUCED CIRCUMSTANCES
1457 Sixteenth Ave.
Honolulu, Hawaii 96816

*Affiliated with the Gray Panthers, the aim of this organization is to
secure financial relief.*

LEGAL SERVICE FOR THE ELDERLY POOR
2095 Broadway
New York, N.Y. 10023

LSEP consists of lawyers who advise the elderly on legal problems.

NATIONAL ASSOCIATION FOR MENTAL HEALTH
1800 N. Kent St.
Rosslyn, Va. 22209

*NAMH is a citizens voluntary organization devoting itself to the
advancement of mental health by supporting research, promoting
the training of personnel, and helping establish community mental
health centers.*

PERIODICALS: *Mental Hygiene* and *Reporter* (both quarterly)

NATIONAL ASSOCIATION OF AREA AGENCIES ON AGING
1828 L St., N.W.
Washington, D.C. 20036

NAAAA is the coalition of area agencies on aging.

NATIONAL ASSOCIATION OF JEWISH HOMES
FOR THE AGED
2525 Centerville Rd.
Dallas, Tex. 75228

*The National Association is the co-ordinating organization for Jew-
ish retirement and nursing homes, geriatric hospitals, and other special facilities for the aged and chronically ill.*

PERIODICALS: *Progress Report* (quarterly); *Directory* (biennial)

NATIONAL ASSOCIATION OF RETIRED FEDERAL EMPLOYEES
1533 New Hampshire Ave., N.W.
Washington, D.C. 20036

NARFE serves federal annuitants under the retirement laws and sponsors and supports legislation.

PERIODICAL: *Retirement Life* (monthly)

NATIONAL ASSOCIATION OF SOCIAL WORKERS
1425 H St., N.W., Suite 600
Washington, D.C. 20005

NASW sets standards for the quality of social work, conducts research, and improves professional education.

PERIODICALS: *NASW News* (monthly); *Social Work* (bimonthly); *Abstracts for Social Workers* (quarterly)

NATIONAL ASSOCIATION OF STATE UNITS ON AGING
1828 L St., N.W.
Washington, D.C. 20036

NASUA is the federation providing co-ordination among state agencies on aging.

NATIONAL CAUCUS/CENTER ON THE BLACK AGED
1730 M St., N.W., Suite 811
Washington, D.C. 20036

The National Caucus on the Black Aged recognizes the unique problems of the black aged and the need for programs tailored specifically to them; it has targeted the areas of income, housing, and health services. The National Center on the Black Aged was established by the Caucus to co-ordinate activities, conduct research, provide annuitant service, train personnel, and develop curricula.

NATIONAL CITIZENS COALITION FOR NURSING HOME REFORM
CONTACT: Ms. Elma Griesel
National Paralegal Institute
2000 P Street, N.W.
Washington, D.C. 20036   (202) 872-0755
OR: Mr. Chuck Chomet
Citizens for Better Care
960 Jefferson Ave., E.
Detroit, Mich. 48207   (313) 963-0513

On June 11, 1975, fifteen consumer organizations from ten states announced the formation of the National Citizens Coalition for Nursing Home Reform. The coalition meeting preceded a two-day conference entitled "Participative Management in Nursing Homes," sponsored by the American Health Care Association and George Washington University. The conference was designed to bring together nursing-home owners, administrators, health-care professionals, consumers, and government representatives to explore solutions to nursing-home problems. The National Gray Panthers had called the advance meeting of the consumer/action groups so that they could get to know one another and join together in developing a reform platform to present to the conference in a united consumer voice. On the opening day of the conference the coalition held a press conference announcing its formation and proposed several recommendations for reform. On the closing day of the conference the coalition presented a summary report to the participants. It is hoped that the coalition can provide the vehicle through which consumer groups can keep informed of current movements for change and, when necessary, present their views in a solid consumer bloc. The coalition can be forceful leverage at the national level to counteract the powerful weight that the industry associations have with government regulatory agencies and elected officials.

NATIONAL COMMITTEE ON ART EDUCATION FOR THE ELDERLY

Culver Stockton College
Canton, Mo. 63435

The purposes of NCAEE are to promote development in art education for the elderly and to expand the role of art education in our society.

PERIODICAL: *Exchange* (semiannual)

NATIONAL COUNCIL ON BLACK AGING

P. O. Box 8522
Durham, N.C. 27707

In addition to publishing Black Aging, *which contains research findings and other news of interest about elderly persons, NCBA also provides consultative services about developing projects for the elderly and research about aged persons, and conducts workshops focused largely upon ways of improving the delivery of services to minority persons.*

PERIODICAL: *Black Aging*

NATIONAL GERIATRICS SOCIETY

212 W. Wisconsin Ave., 3rd fl.
Milwaukee, Wis. 53203

The Society is dedicated to the advancement of techniques of care for aged, infirm, chronically ill, handicapped, and convalescent patients.

PERIODICAL: *Views and News* (monthly)

NATIONAL INSTITUTE OF MENTAL HEALTH

NIMH Center on Aging
5600 Fisher's Lane
Rockville, Md. 20052

The NIMH Center on Aging initiates and supports mental health programs concerning the aged.

NATIONAL INSTITUTE ON AGING
National Institutes of Health
Bethesda, Md. 20014

The National Institute on Aging is responsible for the conduct and support of biomedical, social, and behavioral research and training related to the aging process and the diseases and other special problems and needs of the aged.

NATIONAL INTERFAITH COALITION ON AGING
298 S. Hull St.
Athens, Ga. 30601

The National Interfaith Coalition on Aging, Inc. (NICA) is a non-profit, tax-exempt corporation of national-level representatives from Roman Catholic, Jewish, and Protestant faiths and several associate and reciprocal organizations and agencies concerned about the problems that face our nation's aging population. Now in its sixth year of service, NICA grew out of a conference held in 1972 to make a vital response to the 1971 White House Conference on Aging. Since then, milestone by milestone, NICA has taken significant steps toward the attainment of its objectives.

PRIMARY OBJECTIVES OF THE COALITION ARE:

to identify and give priority to those programs and services for the aging that best may be implemented through the resources of the nation's religious sector;

to vitalize and develop the role of the church and synagogue with respect to their responsibility in improving the quality of life for the aging;

to stimulate co-operative and co-ordinated action between the nation's religious sector and national secular private and public organizations and agencies whose programs and services relate to the welfare and dignity of older persons;

to encourage the aging to continue giving to society from the wealth of their experiences and to remain active participants in community life.

NEWSLETTER: *Inform*

NATIONAL ORGANIZATION FOR WOMEN, TASK FORCE ON THE OLDER WOMAN
3800 Harrison St.
Oakland, Calif. 14611

PERIODICAL: *The Network* (5/year)

NATIONAL SENIOR CITIZENS LAW CENTER
1709 W. 8th St.
Los Angeles, Calif. 90017

The NSCLC promotes research in legislation affecting the older American, has established a network of information on state laws, and acts as an advocate for the senior citizen.

PERIODICAL: *Legislative Newsletter* (weekly), from Washington

Office: 1200 Fifteenth St., N.W., Suite 500, Washington, D.C. 20005

NATIONAL TENANTS ORGANIZATION, INC.
425 Thirteenth St., N.W., Suite 548
Washington, D.C. 20004
Represents old people, among others, in public housing.

NEW LIFE INSTITUTE
I. U. Willets Road
Albertson, N.Y. 11507
The New Life Institute promotes part-time and temporary employment for persons over the age of fifty-five.

NEW YORK JUNIOR LEAGUE
130 E. 80th St.
New York, N.Y. 10021
Senior Summary—quarterly newspaper describing news, activities, and events for senior citizens. Large print.

NEW YORK REGIONAL CENTER FOR LIFELONG LEARNING
City University of New York
101 E. 31st St.
New York, N.Y. 10016
Referral service for adults who seek information on location of courses throughout the city.

NEW YORK STATE ASSOCIATION OF GERONTOLOGICAL EDUCATORS CENTER FOR THE STUDY OF AGING
State University at Buffalo
4248 Ridge Lea Rd.
Amherst, N.Y. 14426
The State Association of Gerontological Educators in New York (SAGE) has been organized for the purpose of providing a forum for college and university educators to exchange information and to stimulate inquiry into issues and concerns in gerontological education. Therefore, one of SAGE's primary aims is to conduct programs and undertake such activities as will meet the needs of its members.
THE GOALS OF THE ASSOCIATION ARE:

to stimulate, to train, and to create understanding among college and university educators with regard to the issues and concerns of gerontology.

to provide a forum for the interchange of information about gerontological education.

to develop and implement programs and curricula for gerontological education. In keeping with the basic objectives of the organization, SAGE sponsors conferences, workshops, and seminars considering the relationship between service needs and curriculum development as well as focusing on the need to differentiate and co-ordinate educational materials at various levels of educational attainment.

OFFICE OF GERONTOLOGICAL STUDIES
Center for Advanced Study on Education
The Graduate School and University Center
The City University of New York
33 W. 42nd St.
New York, N.Y. 10036
NEWSLETTER: *Catching Up on Aging*
This institute will assist faculty and students in research, planning of educational and training programs, and delivery of services to the elderly. The agency will serve as a resource center for The City University of New York.

SENATE SPECIAL COMMITTEE ON AGING
U. S. Senate
Washington, D.C. 20510
The Special Committee handles Senate legislation, holds hearings, and issues reports on the needs of the aging.

SENIOR ADVOCATES INTERNATIONAL
1825 K St., N.W.
Washington, D.C. 20006
SAI provides products and services to the elderly at reduced cost and acts as an advocate in general.
PERIODICAL: *Senior Advocate* (bimonthly)

SENIOR COMPANION PROGRAM
Sponsored by United Neighborhood Houses of New York, Inc.
101 E. 15th St.
New York, N.Y. 10003
Assists isolated homebound adults to remain in their own homes, preventing unnecessary institutionalization.

72 HOUR LEGAL HOTLINE FOR SENIOR CITIZENS
Bronx Community College
120 E. 184th St.
The Bronx, N.Y. 10468
Sponsored by the Bronx Neighborhood Office of the Legal Aid Society and Bronx Community College Boro-Wide Program for Older Adults. Answers questions about wills and consumer problems that require help of an attorney within seventy-two hours.

SEX INFORMATION AND EDUCATION COUNCIL OF
THE UNITED STATES
137 N. Franklin St.
Hempstead, N.Y. 11550
SIECUS acts as a clearinghouse of information on human sexuality for educators, physicians, clergy, and other professionals interested in helping people to understand sexuality.
PERIODICAL: *SIECUS Report* (bimonthly)

TASK FORCE ON PROBLEMS OF AGING PSYCHIATRISTS
Council on Research and Development of the American Psychiatric
Association
1700 Eighteenth St., N.W.
Washington, D.C. 20007

*The task force has been created to study the problems of aging
psychiatrists who are members of the American Psychiatric Association.*

URBAN ELDERLY COALITION
1828 L St., N.W.
Washington, D.C. 20036

*The Urban Elderly Coalition is a federation of the designated offices
with the responsibility for programs in aging in the hundred largest
cities of the United States.*

U. S. HOUSE OF REPRESENTATIVES SELECT COMMITTEE
ON AGING
U. S. House of Representatives
Washington, D.C. 20515

*The Select Committee handles House legislation, holds hearings, and
issues reports on the needs of the aging.*

VACATIONS FOR AGING AND SENIOR CENTERS
ASSOCIATION
225 Park Ave. S.
New York, N.Y. 10003

*Vacations raises funds to subsidize organization camps that serve the
elderly to provide funds for those who can't afford the established
rates.*

VETERANS ADMINISTRATION
810 Vermont Ave., N.W.
Washington, D.C. 20420

*The VA administers all programs concerning veterans, many of
whom are aged.*

WESTERN GERONTOLOGICAL SOCIETY
785 Market St., Room 616
San Francisco, Calif. 94103

*This regional group now has a national attendance at its annual con-
ferences.*

NATIONAL NETWORK ON AGING

A national network on aging has been established by the Administration on Aging. Mandated by Congress in the 1973 amendments to the
Older Americans Act, this network consists of state agencies on aging,
over five hundred area agencies, and another some eight hundred
nutrition-project agencies. The network covers over 80 per cent of
the nation's over-65 population.

The network's purpose is to allow localities, with state approval, to shape their own priorities for services to their elderly citizens. Citizens participate in the policymaking process through public hearings and advisory-council seats. Arthur S. Flemming, commissioner on aging, has described this network as "unquestionably the most significant development that has taken place in the field of aging, aside from the Social Security system on the income side. The best thing about the network is the impact of leadership on the life of a community. There are resources there, both in the private and public sectors, and when they are pulled together to focus on specific goals and objectives, it creates an enthusiasm that produces other resources at the community level."

The key elements in this network are the state offices on aging. These commissions, bureaus, divisions, or offices—as they are variously called —may be headed by an individual called a commissioner, director, executive director, acting director, chairman, etc.

To plug into your local network, write to the appropriate agency listed below, addressing your inquiry to the director.

Alabama Commission on Aging
740 Madison Ave.
Montgomery, Ala. 36104

Office on Aging
Alaska Dept. of Health & Social Services
Pouch H
Juneau, Alaska 99811

Bureau on Aging
Arizona Dept. of Economic Security
543 E. McDowell, Room 217
Phoenix, Ariz. 85007

Arkansas Office on Aging & Adult Services
7th & Gaines
P. O. Box 2179
Little Rock, Ark. 72202

California Office on Aging
Health & Welfare Agency
455 Capitol Mall, Suite 500
Sacramento, Calif. 95814

Colorado Division of Services for Aging
Dept. of Social Services
1575 Sherman St.
Denver, Colo. 80203

Connecticut Dept. on Aging
90 Washington St., Room 312
Hartford, Conn. 06115

Delaware Dept. of Health & Social Services
Delaware State Hospital, Administration Bldg., 3rd fl.
New Castle, Del. 19720

Division of Services to the Aged
Dept. of Human Resources
1329 E St., N.W.
Washington, D.C. 20004

Florida Division of Aging
Dept. of Health & Rehabilitation
1323 Winewood Blvd.
Tallahassee, Fla. 32301

Georgia Office of Aging
Dept. of Human Resources
47 Trinity Ave.
Atlanta, Ga. 30334

Hawaii Commission on Aging
1149 Bethel St., Room 311
Honolulu, Hawaii 96813

Idaho Office on Aging
Statehouse
Boise, Ida. 83720

Illinois Dept. on Aging
2401 W. Jefferson
Springfield, Ill. 62706

Indiana Commission on Aging and Aged
Graphic Arts Bldg.
215 N. Senate Ave.
Indianapolis, Ind. 46202

Iowa Commission on Aging
Jewett Bldg.
415 W. 10th St.
Des Moines, Ia. 50319

Kansas Division, Services for the Aging
Dept. of Social & Rehabilitation Services
State Office Bldg.
Topeka, Kan. 66612

Kentucky Aging Program Unit
Dept. for Human Resources
403 Wapping St.
Frankfort, Ky. 40601

Louisiana Bureau of Aging Services
Division of Human Resources
P. O. Box 44282, Capitol Sta.
Baton Rouge, La. 70804

Maine Office of Maine's Elderly
Community Services Unit
Dept. of Health & Welfare
State House
Augusta, Me. 04330

Maryland Office on Aging
State Office Bldg.
301 W. Preston St.
Baltimore, Md. 21201

Massachusetts Dept. of Elderly Affairs
120 Boylston St.
Boston, Mass. 02116

Michigan Office of Services to the Aging
3500 N. Logan St.
Lansing, Mich. 48913

Minnesota Governor's Citizens Council on Aging
Metro Sq. Bldg., Suite 204
7th & Robert St.
St. Paul, Minn. 55101

Mississippi Council on Aging
P. O. Box 5136, Fondren Sta.
510 George St.
Jackson, Miss. 39216

Missouri Office of Aging
Dept. of Social Services
Broadway State Office Bldg.
P. O. Box 570
Jefferson City, Mo. 65101

Montana Aging Services Bureau
Dept. of Social & Rehabilitation Services
P. O. Box 1723
Helena, Mont. 59601

Nebraska Commission on Aging
State House Sta.
300 S. 17th St.
Lincoln, Neb. 68509

Nevada Division of Aging
Dept. of Human Resources
Nye Bldg.
201 S. Fall St., Room 300
Carson City, Nev. 89701

New Hampshire Council on Aging
P. O. Box 786
14 Depot St.
Concord, N.H. 03301

New Jersey Dept. of Community Affairs
Division on Aging
P. O. Box 2768
363 W. State St.
Trenton, N.J. 08625

New Mexico Commission on Aging
408 Galisteo—Villagra Bldg.
Santa Fe, N.M. 87503

New York State Office for the Aging
855 Central Ave.
Albany, N.Y. 12206

North Carolina Dept. of Human Resources
Governor's Council on Aging
Administration Bldg.
213 Hillsborough St.
Raleigh, N.C. 27603

North Dakota Aging Services
Social Services Board
State Capitol Bldg.
Bismarck, N.D. 58505

Ohio Commission on Aging
34 N. High St.
Columbus, O. 43215

Oklahoma Special Unit on Aging
Dept. of Institutions
P. O. Box 25352, Capitol Sta.
Oklahoma City, Okla. 73125

Oregon Program on Aging
Human Resources Dept.
772 Commercial St., S.E.
Salem, Ore. 97310

Pennsylvania Office for the Aging
Dept. of Public Welfare
Health & Welfare Bldg.
Room 540
7th & Forster Sts.
Harrisburg, Pa. 17120

Rhode Island Division on Aging
Dept. of Community Affairs
150 Washington
Providence, R.I. 02903

South Carolina Commission on Aging
915 Main St.
Columbia, S.C. 29201

South Dakota Office on Aging
Dept. of Social Services
State Office Bldg.
Illinois St.
Pierre, S.D. 57501

Tennessee Commission on Aging
306 Gay St., Room 102
Nashville, Tenn. 37201

Texas Governor's Committee on Aging
Southwest Tower, 8th floor
211 E. 7th St.
Austin, Tex. 78711

Utah Division of Aging
Dept. of Social Services
345 S. 6th E.
Salt Lake City, Utah 84102

Vermont Office on Aging
Agency of Human Services
81 River St.
Montpelier, Vt. 05602

Virginia Office on Aging
830 E. Main St., Suite 950
Richmond, Va. 23219

Washington Office on Aging
Dept. of Social & Health Services
P. O. Box 1788
Olympia, Wash. 98504

Wisconsin Division on Aging
Dept. of Health & Social Services
1 W. Wilson St., Room 686
Madison, Wisc. 53702

Wyoming Aging Services
Dept. of Health & Social Services
New State Office Bldg., West, Room 288
Cheyenne, Wyo. 82002

INDEX

"About the Life and Death of Rae Edith Rose," 166–67
Academy for Educational Development, 262, 364, 365
Action for Independent Maturity, 325
Adams, John, 257–58
Administrations (national), attitudes of, toward elderly, 277–78
Adult homes and Medicaid cutbacks, 12–13
Advocacy, 350, 360–61
  home services and, 385–86
  lobbying and, 373–74
  for minority aged, 284–86
Affronti, Pauline, "On Being Involved," 176–77
After-care for emotionally frail elders, 428–29
Age, sociology of, 63–65
Age discrimination. See Ageism
Age Discrimination in Employment Act of 1967, 56, 326
  sexism and, 125, 130
Age inequalities, 63–64
  See also Ageism
Ageism, 56, 74–148, 296–313
  employment and, 233–36, 325–30, 339–41, 354–55
  Gray Panthers and, 310–13
  racism and, 297–98
  sexism and, 123–36
  sociology of aging and, 63–65
"Ageism in Employment Must Be Abolished," 325–40
Age segregation, 63–64
  See also Ageism
Age stratification, 63
Aging. See specific topics

"Aging: Real and Imaginary," 77–88
"Aging Are Doing Better, The," 345–63
"Aging in the Ghetto," 16–27
Alabama, home-health care program in, 414
Alliance for Displaced Homemakers, 427–28
Altenhof, Jody, "The System Makes It Unhealthy to Be Old," 140–48
"Alternative to Institutional Care in Kansas, An," 381–86
American Association of Retired Persons (AARP), 325, 348–56, 405–6, 443
  Crime Prevention Program of, 454–55
American Medical Association (AMA), 55
  Committee on Aging of, 9, 10
  Committee on Geriatrics of, 147
  organizing of aging and, 347
Apartment swap, 457
Arapahoe County, Colorado, home repair program in, 441–42
Area Agencies on Aging, 235
Ariès, Philippe, 160
Arthritis, Metabolism and Digestive Diseases Institute, 247
Arthur, Bea, 115
Artists in aging, 183–86
Association for Gerontology in Higher Education, 291
"Awakening," 191–93

Bagger, Hope, "Mandatory Retirement Is Death to Personality," 339–41

Baltimore, Maryland, day center in,
    409–10
Barrow, Myra, 409
Beallor, Gerald, 13
Beattie, Walter, 294
Beauvoir, Simone de, 125
Becker, Ernest, 160
Beckman, Anna, 356
Bellingham, Washington, education
    program in, 368
Benny, Jack, 114
Berezin, Martin, 137
Berger, Sam, 415
Bergman, Bernard, 361–62
Berns, Ella, 416
"Best Is Yet to Be, The," 187–90
Bills, utility, Gray Panther forum on,
    312
Biofeedback, 389–90
Blacks, 281–86
    ageism, sexism and, 126, 128–30, 298
    aging in ghetto and, 16–27
    in Harris poll on aging, 97–103
        employment and, 118
        interest in senior citizen centers
            and, 105
        media portrayal of elderly and,
            115
    life expectancy and Social Security
        benefits for, 252
Blind, the, program for, 448
Bliven, Bruce, "Greetings from Bruce
    Bliven," 194–99
Bloomgarden, Zachary T., "The End of
    the Line," 42–44
Blumberg, Baruch, 245
Boutin, Richard, 39
Branford, Connecticut, hospice experi-
    ment in, 397–99
Brody, Elaine M., 408
Brown, Barbara B., 334
Brown, Simeon, 421
Browning, Robert, 53, 190, 272, 333
Bureau of Labor Statistics, 251, 278
Burial, attitudes toward, 152–55
Busse, Edward W., 10
Butler, Robert, 138, 241–59, 293, 301,
    332–33, 346
    "To Find the Answers," 241–49
    "Toward a National Policy on
        Aging," 250–56

Calderone, Mary S., "Sex and the
    Aging," 205–8
Cal Esteem, 234–35
California
    Los Angeles
        activity of Gray Panthers in, 313

Home Care program in, 450–51
National Council on Aging of,
    423–24
retirement planning classes in,
    400–7
programs for elderly in, 234–35,
    435–38
    employment, 427, 432–33
    housing, 438
    mental health, 387–95
    nutrition, 435–37
    retirement planning, 400–7
    transportation, 411
California Employment Development
    Department (EDD), 234–35
California Office on Aging, 235
Camenir, Froim, "How an Eighty-
    three-year-old Man Looks at
    Life," 172–75
Camping, programs in, 456–57
Carter, Jimmy, 293–94
Cath, Stanley, 137
Catlin, Hoyt, 356
Centers
    day, 409–10
    home-services, 381–86
    senior-citizen, 420
        and Harris poll on aging, 105–6
        utilization of, 261
Chamber of Commerce and senior per-
    sonnel placement, 376–77
Chan, Lo-Yi, 398–99
Change, acceptance of, 53, 64–65
Checks, Social Security, and crime, 39
Chernus, J., 182
Chevalier, Maurice, 53
Chicago, Illinois, transportation service
    in, 411
Church, Frank, 250–51
Churches, responses of, to elderly, 307,
    382–86
City University of New York, program
    for elderly at, 366
Civil Rights Act of 1964, 130
Clark, Merrell M., "It's Not All Down-
    hill!" 287–90
Clergy, attitudes of, toward elderly,
    143–44
Cobb, Sidney, 332
Cole, Elbert C., "An Alternative to In-
    stitutional Care in Kansas,"
    381–86
Colorado
    energy conservation program in,
        438–39
    home repair program in, 441–42
    newspapers for elders in, 424
Colorado Old Times (newspaper), 424

Comfort, Alex, 1, 53, 146, 205
  "Aging: Real and Imaginary," 77–88
Commerce, Chamber of, and senior
    personnel placement, 376–77
Committee on Aging of the American
    Medical Association, 9, 10
Committee on Geriatrics of American
    Medical Association, 147
Communes, geriatric, 306–7
Communications, programs for seniors
    in, 422–25
Communities, retirement, 308
Community involvement, 175–77,
    268–69, 347–63, 370–86
  and Harris poll on aging, 104–6, 108
  shortcomings in, 289–90
  young-old and, 48
Community service homes, 308
"Company Tells Me I'm Too Old,
    The," 317–24
"Compounding Impact of Age on Sex,
    The," 123–36
Comroe, Julius, 246, 248
Conklin, Bessie, 14
Connecticut
  hospice experiment in, 397–99, 431
  senior personnel placement in,
    376–80
  tax work-off program in, 442–43
Conservation, energy, program in,
    438–39
Continuing education, 364–75
  home services and, 384–85
  in legal affairs, 445–56
  need for, 301–2, 403–4
  political activity and, 367–68, 370–75
  programs in, 425–28
    retirement planning, 400–7
    utilization of, 261–62
  provision for, 253
Cottin, Lou, "The Senior Citizens'
    Declaration of Independence,"
    273–75
Council for the Progress of Non-Tradi-
    tional Study, 369
Courage and aging in ghetto, 19
Cremation, attitudes toward, 152
Crime
  fear of, 34, 37–41
    and Harris poll on aging, 95,
      100–1
  minority aged and, 298
  protection from, 253–54
    programs on, 312, 383–84, 453–56
  Social Security checks and, 39
Crime Prevention Program, 454–55
Crisis, identity, 298–99
"Crowning Years, The," 178–86

Cultural heritage, intergenerational pro-
    gram in, 443–44
Cummings, Jim, 393
Curtin, Sharon, 9

Davidoff, Donald, 12
Davis, Leonard, 348
Day centers, 409–10
Death, 149–66, 429–32
  fear of, 154–55, 172, 301, 389
    physicians and, 159
  grief therapy group and, 429–30
  health care of elderly and, 147
  hospice experiment and, 159–60,
    396–99, 431–32
  sensitivity course on, 432
"Death as an Acceptable Subject,"
    158–60
Dedicated Older Volunteers in Educa-
    tional Services (DOVES), 401
Democratic administrations (national),
    attitudes toward elderly of,
    277–78
Denenberg, Herbert, 359
Dental care, programs in, 449
Dentists, attitudes of, toward elderly,
    143
Depression and retirement, 337–38
"Destruction of the Old," 7–11
Detroit, Michigan, fear of crime in,
    38–41
Dignity and work, 84–86
Disability and elderly, 9, 10
Disch, Bob, 368
Discrimination, age. See Ageism
Discrimination, racial, 281–83
  ageism and, 297–98
    sexism and, 126, 128–30
  aging in ghetto and, 26–27
Disease
  old age as, 10
  research in, 244–49
Disorientation, stereotype of, 137–39
District of Columbia, housing program
    in, 440–41
Divorce laws and ageism and sexism,
    133–35
Dobihal, Edward F., Jr., 396, 397, 399
Domestic Technology Institute, 438
Double standards and ageism and
    sexism, 125–28
Douglass, Frederick, 122
"Dreams" (poem), 211–12
Dripps, Robert, 246
Drugs
  effect of, on older people, 244–45,
    249
  hospices and, 397–98

mail-order pharmacy program and, 348–51
senior lobbying and, 373
Dychtwald, Kenneth, 392
Dyskinesia, tardive, 248–49

Eadie, John, 14
Early Alert, 453
Ebner, Marion, "About the Life and Death of Rae Edith Rose," 166–67
Ebsen, Buddy, 115
"Economics of Aging, The," 66–73
Edna McConnell Clark Foundation, 90, 365
Education, 101–3, 364–75
  aging in ghetto and, 23–25
  gerontology and, 291–95, 370
  and problems of elderly, 101–2
  and self-image of elderly, 103
  statistics of, for elderly, 51–52, 288
  See also Continuing education
Eisdorfer, Carl, 9
Elderly. See specific topics
Elderly Nutrition Program, 435
Emergency Evacuation File, 456
Employee Retirement Income Security Act of 1974, 311
Employment, 233–39
  ageism and, 233–36, 325–30, 339–41, 354–57
  aging in ghetto and, 21–23
  and Harris poll on aging, 117–19
  programs for, 418–19, 432–34
    for displaced homemakers, 427–28
    proposals for, 237–39, 404–5
    senior personnel placement, 376–80
  See also Work
"End of the Line, The," 42–44
Energy conservation, program in, 438–39
England. See Great Britain
Equal Rights Amendment (ERA), 134
Ernst, Theodore D., 303–4
Escort service for crime prevention, 453–54
Ethel Percy Andrus Gerontology Center, 292
Eurich, Alvin, 364
"Everybody's Studying Us," 120–21
Experience, Inc., 432–33

Fairs, seniors', 425
Family
  attitudes toward, 35
    and Harris poll on aging, 103, 115–16
  changing patterns in, 47–48, 267

and health care of elderly, 144–45
  role of, in improving nursing homes, 362
  sex and aging and, 207–8
Fear
  of crime, 34, 37–41
    and Harris poll on aging, 95, 100–1
    minority aged and, 298
  of death, 154–55, 172, 301, 389
    physicians and, 159
"Fear Stalks the Elderly," 38–41
Federal Contract Compliance, Office of (OFCC), 131
Fields, Suzanne, "Senior Actualization and Growth Explorations (SAGE)," 387–95
Finley, Paul, 124
Fischer, David Hackett, "Putting Our Heads to the 'Problem' of Old Age," 58–62
Fitness, physical, for elders, 450
Florence V. Burden Foundation, 90
Florida, housing program in, 358
Florio, Carol, "Older Americans: Facts and Potential," 50–57
Food Advisory Service, 435
Ford, Gerald, 277, 294
Forest Service, U.S., and part-time work program, 434
"For the Rest of Our Days, Things Can Only Get Worse," 28–37
Foster Grandparent program, 234, 236, 253, 418
Fox, Thomas, "Fear Stalks the Elderly," 38–41
Foxfire plan, 443–44
Foxx, Redd, 115
Francis, Polly, "Awakening," 191–93
Frank, Jerome D., 334, 338
Franklin, Benjamin, 337
Fraser, Virginia, "An Introduction of Innovative Programs," 422–61
Fraud, fear of, 39–40
"Free-Lance Agitator Confronts the Establishment, A," 231–40
Friendly Visitors, 414–15
Fromm, Erich, 181
Fulson, Robert, 138
Funding, government
  of employment programs, 234–35
  of gerontology programs, 293–94
  of health care, 244
  See also Medicaid; Medicare
Funeral costs, 312

Gajdusek, Carleton, 245
Galbraith, John Kenneth, 132
Garfinkel, René, 143

Gaynes, Neil L., 382
"Generation of Black People, A," 281–83
Geriatric communes, 306–8
Geriatrics, 85–86
  medical student interest in, 142
Geriatrics Program Fair, 425
Gerontology, 291–95, 370
"Gerontology Comes of Age," 291–95
Gerontophobia, 60–62
Gerrard, Eugenia, 389, 392, 394
"Getting Older . . . Older . . . Old," 171–72
Ghetto, aging in, 16–27
Gilles, Jim, 358
Glick, Hilda, 212–28
Goldfarb, Alvin, 138
Gordin, John, 421
Gorer, Geoffrey, 158
Gornick, Vivian, "For the Rest of Our Days, Things Can Only Get Worse," 28–37
Gould, Samuel, 369
Government funding
  of employment programs, 234–35
  of gerontology programs, 293–94
  of health care, 244
  See also Medicaid; Medicare
Grandparents
  changing role of, 269–70
  Foster, program, 234, 236, 253, 418
Gray, Charlotte, 398
Gray Bears, 436–37
Gray Panthers, 135, 310–13, 348, 352–54, 405
  housing and, 313, 357
  Media Watch of, 423–24
  nursing home residents' councils and, 440
"Gray Panthers on the Prowl," 310–13
Great Britain, hospices in, 159, 396–99
Green Light, 418
Green Thumb, 418
"Greetings from Bruce Bliven," 194–99
Grief therapy groups, 429–30
Griggs v. Duke Power case, 131, 235
Gross, Ronald, "I Am Still Learning," 364–69
Group for the Advancement of Psychiatry, 137
Groups, senior citizen
  popularity of, 276
  See also specific groups
"Growing Old in America," 267–72
Gutmann, David, 334

Haddonfield, New Jersey, transportation service in, 411
Haefner, Ruth, 311

Hanhardt, Arthur M., "Senior Lobby: A Model for Senior/Student Action," 370–75
Hapgood, David, "The Aging Are Doing Better," 345–63
Harris, Julia, "The Best Is Yet to Be," 187–90
Harris poll on aging, 52–56, 80, 90–119, 260–62, 354
Hartford, Connecticut, tax work-off program in, 442–43
Haven, Al, 411
Havighurst, Robert, 110
Health
  and acceptance of aging, 182, 187
  and Harris poll on aging, 93, 95, 101
  home services and, 385
  professional attitudes toward, of elderly, 137–48
  programs in, 391–92, 447–52
  research in aging and, 244–49
  retirement planning and, 401
  See also Mental health
Health care
  cost of, 244, 279
  creation of decent, 254–55
  day centers and, 409–10
  family and, 144–45
  Gray Panthers and, 310–11
  home, 413–14
    employment of elderly in, 237
    hospices and, 396–99
    mental health therapy and, 430
    programs in, 450–51
  problem of, 279–80
  and stereotypes of elderly, 137–39
Health care system
  dying and, 159–60
  elderly as consumer in, 85
  and treatment of elderly, 140–48
Health Department of New York State
  and Medicaid cutbacks, 12–14
" 'Healthy' Elderly Face Transfer," 12–15
Hearing problems, programs for, 449–50
Heart and Lung Institute, 247
Hechinger, Grace, "Growing Old in America," 267–72
Heim, Herman L., 14–15
"Help for the Minority Aged," 284–86
Heritage, cultural, intergenerational program in, 443–44
Hess, Beth, 143
Hobbies, 187–88
Hochheimer, Lawrence, "Senior Personnel Placement," 376–80
Hoffer, Eric, 403, 404
Hollister, Leo, 337

Home Care Program, 450–51
  hospices and, 396–99
Home-health care, 413–14
  employment of elderly in, 237
  hospices and, 396–99
  mental health therapy and, 430
  program in, 450–51
Homemaking
  employment programs and, 427–28
  and sexism in Social Security regula-
    tions, 132–33
Home repair
  as part-time work for elderly, 237
  programs in, 441–42
Homes
  adult, and Medicaid cutbacks, 12–13
  community service, 308
  See also Nursing homes
Home services, 381–86, 412–16
Hope, Bob, 114
Hosanna, Jacqueline, 8
Hospices, 159–60, 396–99, 431–32
Hospitals
  dying and, 159
  mental, elderly in, 9
Hossack, Margaret, 40
"Hours" (poem), 221–22
Housing, 357–60
  problem of, 280
    black aged and, 283
    Gray Panthers and, 313, 357
  programs in, 438–43
    proposals for, 252
Houston, Jean, 333
Houston, Texas, mental health program
    in, 428–29
"How an Eighty-three-year-old Man
    Looks at Life," 172–75
Humor and aging, 189
Hunnicutt, Helen, 312

"I Am Still Learning," 264–69
Identity crisis, 298–99
"I Hate to Be Called a Senior Citizen,"
    121–22
Illich, Ivan, 368
Illinois, transportation service in, 411
Image of elderly, 120–21
  See also Self-image
Income
  ageism and, 83–84
  of black aged, 281–82
  economics of aging and, 69–73
  and Harris poll on aging, 97–101
  inflation and fixed, 289
  problem of, 278–79
  statistics of, for elderly, 51
  young-old and, 48
  See also Pensions; Social Security

Independence
  aging in ghetto and, 18
  public attitudes toward old age and,
    92–93, 268
  resources for, 408–21
  vs. social services, 231–33, 238
India, number of elderly in, vs. U.S.,
    287
Individual Retirement Accounts (IRA),
    252
Inequalities, age, 63–64
  See also Ageism
In-home mental health therapy, 430
Institute for Retired Professionals,
    364–65, 426–27
Institute of Neurological and Com-
    municative Disorders, 247
Institute of Study for Older Adults,
    366
Institutional Development and Eco-
    nomic Affairs Service (IDEAS),
    444
Institutions, 279–80
  ageism in, 297–98
  alternatives to, 381–86
  church-related, 307
  fear of, 280
  percentage of elderly in, 51, 85, 279
  sex and aging and, 207–8
  as solution to aging, 9, 85
  See also Nursing homes
Intellectual pursuits, 416–17
  involvement of older people in,
    257–66, 333, 364–69
  retirement planning and, 403
  See also Education
Intergenerational programs, 443–45
  in housing, 440–41
International Ladies' Garment Workers
    Union, visitors' program of, 415
Intimacy, need for, 207–8
"Inventory of Innovative Programs,
    An," 422–61
Irwin, Theodore, "Resources for Self-
    Reliance," 408–21
"Issue Analysis: Problems of the
    Aging," 276–80
"It's Not All Downhill!" 287–90
"'I Want to Go Home': A Very Old
    Lady Dies in Style," 161–65

Jacobskind, Bella, 210–26
Jasper, Alabama, home-health care
    program in, 414
Jefferson, Thomas, 258–59
Jobs. See Employment
Jobs for Older Women Action Project,
    238
Johnson, Lyndon B., 276

Johnson, Samuel, 53

Kahana, Eve, 40
Kaminsky, Marc, "What's Inside of You, It Shines Out of You," 209–28
Kansas
    alternative to institutions in, 381–86
    transportation service in, 411
Kansas City, Missouri, activity of Gray Panthers in, 312
Kennedy, Miriam, 332
Keogh Act, 252
Kety, Seymour S., 337
Keyserling, Leon, 251
Klemme, Herbert, 331
Knoble, John, "Living to the End: The Hospice Experiment," 396–99
Koch, Edward I., 359
Komisar, Lucy, 135
Krause, Daphne, 360
Kreps, Juanita, "The Economics of Aging," 66–73
Kübler-Ross, Elizabeth, 150, 158, 397
Kuhn, Maggie, 135, 240, 296–310, 352–54
    "New Life for the Elderly: Liberation from 'Ageism,'" 296–309
Kunitomi, Gene, 394
Kunze, Karl, 403
Kutner, Bernard, 138

Lack, Sylvia, 396
"Lamp at Dusk: Adjusting Puts Peace into Growing Old, A," 200–4
Laufgraben, Frieda, "My Advancing Years," 175–76
Laws and ageism, 86–88, 133–35
Lawton, M. Powell, 142
Legal Aid Society, 421
Legal services, 360–61, 421
    employment of elderly in, 237–38
    programs in, 445–47
Legislation and ageism, 86–88
Leisure, 260–61
    ageism and, 82–84
    attitudes of elderly toward, 107–8
    public attitudes toward old age and, 82–84, 92, 107
    retirement planning and, 401
Liberation from ageism, 296–309
Libow, Leslie, 142
Libraries, programs by, for elderly, 416–17
Liebow, Elliot, 17
Life-course transitions, 64
Life expectancy, 51, 67
    black aged and, 283

Social Security benefits and, 252
Life satisfactions
    and Harris poll on aging, 109–11
    retirement planning and, 402
Life styles
    proposals for new, 300–9
    retirement planning and, 401
"Living to the End: The Hospice Experiment," 396–99
Lobbying, 370–75
Loneliness
    attitudes toward, 31–32
    and Harris poll on aging, 93–95, 100–1, 103–4
    and need for companionship, 306
Los Angeles, California
    activity of Gray Panthers in, 313
    Home Care program in, 450–51
    National Council on Aging of, 423–24
    retirement planning classes in, 400–7
Los Angeles Times (newspaper), 7
Louis Harris & Associates, Inc.
    "Myths and Realities of Life for Older Americans," 90–119
    poll on aging of, 52–56, 80, 90–119, 260–62, 354
Louisiana, home repair program in, 441–42
Lounges, shopping, 458
Love
    and acceptance of aging, 183–84
    attitudes toward, 35
    intimacy and, 207–8
    See also Sex
Luce, Gay, 387–94

McCluskey, Neil G., "The System Makes It Unhealthy to Be Old," 140–48
McCracken, James A., "The Company Tells Me I'm Too Old," 317–24
McDougall, Anne, 313
McGillick, Jan, 312
Mackenzie, Carol, "Gray Panthers on the Prowl," 310–13
McNulty, Barbara, 398
Mail-order pharmacy program, 348–51
Mandatory retirement, 317–41, 354–56
    ageism and, 233, 327–30
    attitudes toward, 317–24, 326–27
    danger of, 303, 331–41
    elimination of, 252–53, 346, 354
    and Harris poll on aging, 111–12
    and health of elderly, 145–46
    sexism and, 126–28
"Mandatory Retirement Is Death to Personality," 339–41
Manhood and aging in ghetto, 19

Marriage, 132–35
  ageism, sexism and, 127, 133–35
  alternatives to, 306–7
  Social Security regulations and, 8,
    132, 306
Marshall, Marion, "Retirement Plan-
    ning Classes in Los Angeles,"
    400–7
Marshall, Rose, 313
Maryland, Baltimore, day centers in,
    409–10
Massachusetts
  activity of Gray Panthers in, 311–12
  housing program in, 357
May, Siegmund, "The Crowning
    Years," 178–86
Mayor's Senior Citizens Commission
    (Detroit), 39–40
Mead, Margaret, "Growing Old in
    America," 267–72
Meals on Wheels, 412
Means tests, elimination of, 238
Media
  portrayal of elderly in, 353
    combating stereotypes in, 423–24
    and Harris poll on aging, 114–15
  programs for elderly in, 422–25
  as tool of senior lobbying, 372–73,
    423
Media Watch of Gray Panthers,
    423–24
Medicaid
  and alternatives to nursing homes,
    359–60
  cutbacks in, 12–15
  day centers and, 410
Medical students, interest of, in geriat-
    rics, 142
Medicare, 279
  attitudes toward, 33
  day centers and, 410
  enactment of, 276
  geriatrics and, 85
  home-health care and, 414
  and organizing of elderly, 347
    mail-order pharmacy and, 349
Meditation, 391
Men
  black, 19–26
  population statistics for, 50–51
  sexism and, 123–36
  sexual interests of, 205
Mendelson, Mary Adelaide, 361–62
Menlo Park, California, transportation
    service in, 411
Menopause
  ageism, sexism and, 126–27
  sex after, 306

Mental health, 9–10, 52–53, 79
  and accepting new life styles, 300–1
  aging and, 178–86, 188–93
  programs for, 387–95, 428–32
  retirement and, 331–41, 404
  right to good care in, 255
  and stereotypes of elderly, 137–39
  treatment in, 142–43
Mental hospitals, elderly in, 9
Menuhin, Yehudi, 264
Michigan, fear of crime in, 38–41
Miller, Harriet, "Ageism in Em-
    ployment Must Be Abolished,"
    325–30
Minneapolis Age and Opportunity Cen-
    ter, 360
Minnesota
  education program in, 365–66
  housing program in, 360
Minority aged, 284–86, 298
  See also Blacks
Missouri, activity of Gray Panthers in,
    312–13
Moberg, David, 143
Mobile Mini-Market, 435–36
Mobility, freedom of, 253
  See also Transportation services
Mobilization for aging, 303–4
Monterey County, California, nutrition
    program in, 436–37
Morse, Dean W., "Aging in the
    Ghetto," 16–27
Moss, Frank, 361
"Most of the Problems of Aging Are
    Not Biological, but Social,"
    63–65
Mueller, Charlotte, 142
Mulcahy, Leo, 422
Munch, Marie, 38
Murdock, Al, 381–82
Murphy, Judith, "Older Americans:
    Facts and Potential," 50–57
Museums, programs by, for elderly,
    417
"My Advancing Years," 175–76
Myers, Gertrude, 418
Myrdal, Gunnar, 124
Myths about aging, 52–55, 77–82
  and Harris poll on aging, 90–119
  and health, 147–48
"Myths and Realities of Life for Older
    Americans," 90–119

Name for older people, 121–22
  and Harris poll on aging, 114
Napoli, Teresa, 350
National Aeronautics and Space Ad-
    ministration (NASA), nutrition
    program of, 437

National Association for Human Development (NAHD), 450

National Association of Senior Citizens, 405

National Caucus on the Black Aged, "A Generation of Black People," 281–83

National Council of Senior Citizens, 419

"Issue Analysis: Problems of the Aging," 276–80

National Council on Aging (Los Angeles), 423–24

National Council on the Aging, The, 52, 90, 234, 260–62

National Guard, rural health screen by, 451–52

National Institute of Mental Health (NIMH), 142, 255, 394

National Institute on Aging (NIA), 246–49, 255, 293

National Institutes of Health (NIH), 247, 249

National Organization of Women (NOW), Task Force on Older Women of, 135

National Paralegal Institute, 237

National policy on aging, proposal for, 250–56

National Retired Teachers Association, 325, 348, 405, 443

National Urban League, "Help for the Minority Aged," 284–86

National Weather Service, part-time work with, 433–34

Nealy, Alva, 403

Neugarten, Bernice L., 265, 332, 346
"The Rise of the Young-Old," 47–49

Newbern, Sarah, 393

New Jersey, transportation service in, 411

"New Life for the Elderly: Liberation from 'Ageism,'" 296–309

New Orleans, Louisiana, home repair program in, 441–42

New School for Social Research, program for elderly at, 364–65, 426–27

Newspapers for elders, 424–25

New York City
activity of Gray Panthers in, 312
City University of, program for elderly at, 366
crime prevention program in, 453
nursing-home scandal in, 361–62

New York State
activity of Gray Panthers in, 312
crime prevention program in, 453
education program in, 366

Medicaid cutbacks in, 12–15
nursing home scandal in, 361–62

Nixon, Richard M., 277

Nobody Ever Died of Old Age, 9

Norristown, Pennsylvania, Geriatrics Program Fair in, 425

North Carolina, transportation service in, 411

North Hennepin Community College, program for elderly at, 365

Norwalk, Connecticut, senior personnel placement in, 376–80

"Nourishing the Minds of the Aging," 257–66

Nursing Home Advisory and Research Council, 362

Nursing homes, 244, 357–63
alternatives to, 357–60, 381–86
day centers as, 409–10
hospices as, 159–60, 396–99
social utilities as, 255
attitudes toward, 32–33, 280
improvement of, 362–63
as institutional solution to aging, 9
Medicaid cutbacks and, 12–15
mental health programs for, 392–93
organizing of elderly in, 353, 440
residents' councils in, 440
scandals in, 361–62

Nutrition
home services and, 383, 412–13
problem of, 280
programs in, 435–38

Oakland, California, employment program in, 427–28

Oberleder, Muriel, 138

Oblonski, Mary, 412

Office of Federal Contract Compliance (OFCC), 131

Ohio, nursing-home organizing in, 362–63

Old age. *See specific topics*

"Older Americans: Facts and Potential," 50–57

Older Americans Act, 234, 280, 293, 360, 408, 413

Older Americans Legal Action Center, 446–47

"Old People Talk About Death," 151–57

Old people write of aging, 171–77
"On Being Involved," 176–77

"Open Letter to a Young Doctor, An," 137–39

Operation Brown Bag, 436–37

Oppenheimer, Peter, 367

Oregon
activity of Gray Panthers in, 311

newspapers for elders in, 424–25
seniors lobbying in, 371–74
visitors' program in, 415
Oregon Center for Gerontology, 370
Organizing of elderly, 310–13, 347–63
retirement planning and, 406–7
See also Community involvement;
Political activity
Oriol, William, 293
Ossofsky, Jack, 53
"Nourishing the Minds of the
Aging," 257–66
Osteoporosis, 244

Palace, Lilly, 215, 219, 222–26
Palmore, Erdman, 141
Palm Springs, California, employment
program in, 432–33
Part-time work
and Harris poll on aging, 118
need for, 280, 303
pensions and, 233
programs for, 433–34
proposals for, 237–39
Pate, Adlai, Jr., 356
Paull, Irene, 120–22
"Everybody's Studying Us," 120–21
"I Hate to Be Called a Senior
Citizen," 121–22
Peak, Daniel T., 53
Pell, Samuel, 8
Pennsylvania
geriatric center in, 358
Geriatric Program Fair in, 425
legal program in, 445–46
Pension Reform Act of 1974, 252, 311
Pensions
ageism and, 355
economics of aging and, 67
financing of, 251–52
Gray Panther investigation of,
311–12
part-time work and, 233
retirement planning and, 401–2
Percy, Charles, "Destruction of the
Old," 7–11
Personal Security System, 252
Personnel placement for seniors,
376–80
Pets, medical aid for, 460–61
Pharmacists, Gray Panther survey of,
311
Pharmacy, seniors-owned, 448–49
Pharmacy program, mail-order, 348–51
Philadelphia Geriatric Center, 358–59
Phoenix, The (newspaper), 424–25
Physical aging, 77–78
Physical fitness for elders, 450

Physicians
attitudes of, toward elders, 137–39
sex and, 205–6
fear of dying and, 159
Gray Panther survey of, 310–11
Poetry workshop for elderly, 209–28
Policy, national, on aging, proposal for,
250–56
Political activity, 309, 347–63
education and, 367–68, 370–75
of Gray Panthers, 135, 310–13, 348,
352–54
voting patterns of elderly and,
277–78
young-old and, 48
See also Advocacy
Politics of aging, 370–71
and Harris poll on aging, 111–14
Population statistics for elderly, 50–52,
67, 241–42, 276
Portland, Oregon
activity of Gray Panthers in, 311
visitors' program in, 415
Portrayal of elderly in media, 353
combating stereotypes in, 423–24
and Harris poll on aging, 114–15
Poverty
ageism and, 83–84
black aged and, 282
and Harris poll on aging, 107
proposal for elimination of, 251–52
Powerlessness and aging in ghetto, 18
Powledge, Tabitha M., "Death as an
Acceptable Subject," 158–60
President's Task Force on the Mentally
Handicapped, The, 9
Productivity, attitudes toward, 7, 29, 93
Professionalism and working with eld-
erly, 231–32, 236
Professionals, retired, program for,
364–65, 426–27, 433
Project Elderly Person, 444–45
Prosthetics, research in, 244
Psychology Today (magazine), 158
Public attitudes toward elderly, 91–119
See also Ageism
Public policy on aging, proposal for,
250–56
"Putting Our Heads to the 'Problem'
of Old Age," 58–62

Quinlan, Karen, 141, 158, 160

Racial discrimination, 281–83
ageism and, 297–98
sexism and, 126, 128–30
aging in ghetto and, 26–27
Radio programs for seniors, 422
Ramsey, Paul, 158

Reagan, Ronald, 235
Recreation, programs in, 456–58
    See also Leisure
Red Cross, 411, 416
Reissman, Frank, 54
Religious involvement of elderly, 104–5
Repair, home
    as part-time work for elderly, 237
    programs in, 441–42
Repairs on Wheels, 441–42
Republican administrations (national),
        attitudes toward elderly of, 277
Research
    on aging, 244–49, 256
    on retirement, 331–38
Research on Aging Act of 1974, 248
Respect for elderly
    changing patterns in, 58–62
    and Harris poll on aging, 109
Respite care, 438
Responsibility and aging, 155
Resting vs. work, 302–3
Retired professionals, program for,
        364–65, 426–27, 433
Retired Senior Volunteer Program,
        236, 418
Retirement, 302–3, 315–41
    age of, 302
        drop in, 48–49
        Social Security and, 56
    ageism and, 83–84
        sexism and, 124–28
    attitudes toward, 56, 317–24, 331–38
        aging in ghetto and, 22–23
        and Harris poll on aging, 111–13
    economics of aging and, 66–73
    and Harris poll on aging, 111–13
    health of elderly and, 145–46
    mandatory, 317–41, 354–56
        ageism and, 233, 327–30
        attitudes toward, 317–24, 326–37
        danger of, 303, 331–41
        elimination of, 252–53, 346, 354
        and Harris poll on aging, 111–12
        health of elderly and, 145–46
        sexism and, 126–28
    planning for, 400–7
    right to work and, 232–33
    voluntary, 325
Retirement communities, 308
"Retirement Planning Classes in Los
        Angeles," 400–7
Revolution, rationale for, 299–300
Rhode Island, transportation service in,
        411
Richter, Curt, 335
Riley, Matilda White, "Most of the
        Problems of Aging Are Not Bi-
        ological, but Social," 63–65

"Rise of the Young-Old, The," 47–49
Robbery, fear of, 38–39
Rockefeller, Nelson, 361
Roentgen, Wilhelm Konrad, 248
Roles, social, right to, 253
Rose, Rae Edith, 166–67
Rosenfeld, Albert, "The Willy Loman
        Complex," 331–38
Rosenfeld, Dina, 209–10
Rosenfeld, Vera, 212–15, 218–26
Rosenstein, Jean, 7
Rubinstein, Artur, 333
Rudin, Rose, "Getting Older . . .
        Older . . . Old," 171–72
Rural health screen, 451–52
Rural transportation project, 459
Russia. See Soviet Union

Sacramento, California, nutrition pro-
        gram in, 435
St. Louis, Missouri, Gray Panther ac-
        tivity in, 312–13
Salk, Lee, 332
Samp, Robert, 334
San Francisco, California, housing pro-
        gram in, 438
San Mateo County, California, nutri-
        tion program in, 435–36
Santa Cruz, California, nutrition pro-
        gram in, 436–37
Satisfactions, life
    and Harris poll on aging, 109–11
    retirement planning and, 402
Saul, Shura, "An Open Letter to a
        Young Doctor," 137–39
Saunders, Cicely, 396, 398
Schaie, Warner, 294
Schoenberger, Joseph, 366–67
Schottland, Sarah, 367
Schreiber, Anna C., 12–14
Schreiber, Martin E., 359–60
Segregation, age, 63–64
    See also Ageism
Self-health, program in, 447
Self-image
    and Harris poll on aging, 102–4,
        106–11
    identity crisis and, 298–99
    improving, 387–88
Self-pity and aging, 178, 180
Self-pride and aging in ghetto, 17–18
Self-reliance
    aging in ghetto and, 18
    resources for, 408–21
    See also Independence
Selye, Hans, 336
Senate, United States
    Small Business Subcommittee of, 40

Special Committee on Aging of, 11, 293
Subcommittee on Long-Term Care, 361
Senility, 9–10, 79
and myths of aging, 52–53
"Senior Actualization and Growth Explorations (SAGE)," 387–95
Senior AIDES program, 280
Senior citizen centers, 420
and Harris poll on aging, 105–6
utilization of, 261
Senior citizen groups, popularity of, 276
See also specific groups
"Senior Citizens' Declaration of Independence, The," 273–75
Senior Edition (newspaper), 424
"Senior Lobby: A Model for Senior/Student Action," 370–75
"Senior Personnel Placement," 376–80
Seniors' fairs, 425
Seniors-owned pharmacy, 448–49
Senior Worker Action Programs (SWAP), 418
Sensitivity course on dying, 432
Serve and Enrich Retirement by Volunteer Experience (SERVE), 418
Service Corps of Retired Executives (SCORE), 418
Services. *See* Home services; Legal services; Social services; Transportation services
Setlow, Carol, 54
Sex, 9–10, 205–8
compounding impact of age on, 123–39
maintaining interest in, 305–7
and self-image of elderly, 103
"Sex and the Aging," 205–8
Sexism and ageism, 123–36
Share-a-Fare, 458–59
Share-a-Home Association, 358
Shepherd's Center, 381–86
Shock, N. W., 138
Shopping lounges, 458
Skills Exchange, 441–42
Sloan, Margaret, 130
Smith, Samuel Hopkinson, 200
Social roles, right to, 253
Social Security, 345–47
attitudes toward, 35
aging in ghetto and, 18
and Harris poll on aging, 113
financing of, 251, 345–46
as income mainstay, 278–79
inflation and, 347
regulations for, benefits
life expectancy and, 252

marriage and, 8, 132, 306
racial discrimination and, 282, 284–85, 298
retirement age and, 56
sexism and, 131–33
retirement planning and, 402
voluntary, 325
Social Security checks and crime, 39
Social services
comprehensive, supply of, 254
vs. independence, 231–33, 238
Social utilities vs. nursing homes, 255
Social work training for elders, 425–26
Sociogenic aging, 78–82
Sociology of age, 63–65
Sommers, Trish
"Compounding Interest of Age on Sex, The," 123–36
"Free-Lance Agitator Confronts the Establishment, A," 231–40
Sontag, Susan, 1–2
Soroptimist Club, 449
South Providence, Rhode Island, transportation service in, 411
Soviet Union
mandatory retirement and, 355
number of elderly in, vs. U.S., 287
Sparkman, John, 124
Springfield, Massachusetts, activity of Gray Panthers in, 311–12
Sprinkle, Gladys, 356
Standards, double, and ageism and sexism, 125–28
Statistics, population, for elderly, 50–52, 67, 241–42, 276
Stein, Edith, "What Is Ageism?" 89
Stereotypes of elderly
combating, in media, 423–24
in health care system, 137–39
Stieglitz, Alfred, 303
Storandt, Martha, 292, 294
Stratification, age, 63
Stress and retirement, 334–38
Students
involvement of, in senior lobbying, 370–75
medical, interest of, in gerontology, 142
Suicide rate and unemployment, 331–32
Supplemental Security Income (SSI), 278, 347
Sweden
mandatory retirement and, 355
part-time work and pensions in, 233
"System Makes It Unhealthy to Be Old, The," 140–48

Tai Chi, 391

Tardive dyskinesia, 248–49
Task Force on Older Women of National Organization of Women, 135
Taxes
  advocacy and, 350
  retirement planning and, 402
Taxi plan, Share-a-Fare, 458–59
Tax work-off program, 442–43
Telephoning services, 416
Television
  portrayal of elderly on, 114–15
  programs on aging on, 423
Terry, Robert, 124
Tests, means, elimination of, 238
Texas
  legal program in, 446
  mental health program in, 428–29
  nutrition program in, 437–38
Therapy
  grief, groups, 429–30
  in-home mental health, 430
  See also Mental health
Thornton, Susan, "An Inventory of Innovative Programs," 422–61
Time, use of, and mental health of elderly, 183
Tocqueville, Alexis de, 60
Toffler, Alvin, 304, 306
"To Find the Answers," 241–49
"Toward a National Policy on Aging," 250–56
Townsend, Francis, 347–48
Transitions, life-course, 64
Transportation Remuneration Incentive Program (TRIP), 459
Transportation services, 410–12, 458–60
  home services and, 383
  problem of, 280
  proposals for, 237
Triage, Inc., 452
Twain, Mark, 333
Tyhurst, James, 332

Unemployment
  and Harris poll on aging, 117–18
  statistics of, for elderly, 51
  suicide rate and, 331–32
  See also Retirement
United Presbyterian Residence, 12–15
United States
  Forest Service of, and part-time work program, 434
  Senate of
    Small Business Subcommittee of, 40
    Special Committee on Aging of, 11

    Subcommittee on Long-Term Care of, 361
  See also specific topics
Utilities, social, vs. nursing homes, 255
Utility bills, Gray Panther forum on, 312

Vacation apartment swap, 457
"Value impact forecasters," elderly as, 304
Van Hayek, Frederick, 124
Vasey, Wayne, 294
Vidal, David, "'Healthy' Elderly Face Transfer," 12–15
Visiting Nurse Association, 414
Visitors' programs, 414–15
Voluntary retirement, 325
Volunteerism, 234–36, 418–19
Voting patterns of elderly, 277–78

Waltons, The (television program), 114, 115
Waring, Joan, "Most of the Problems of Aging Are Not Biological, but Social," 63–65
Washington (state)
  education program in, 368
  home-health care program in, 414
Washington, District of Columbia, housing program in, 440–41
Watkins, Beverly T., "Gerontology Comes of Age," 291–95
Weg, Ruth, 291–93
Weinberg, Jack, 7
Weiss, Jay, 337
Welk, Lawrence, 115
Wesley, John, 384
"What Is Ageism?" 89
"What's Inside of You, It Shines Out of You," 209–28
White, Whitney, "A Lamp at Dusk: Adjusting Puts Peace into Growing Old," 200–4
White House Conference on Aging, 147, 250, 277, 381
White House Office on Aging, proposal for creation of, 250–51
Whitman, Walt, 219–21
Wichita, Kansas, transportation service in, 411
Widowhood, 127
Williams, Nancy, "'I Want to Go Home': A Very Old Lady Dies in Style," 161–65
"Willy Loman Complex, The," 331–38
Winter Park, Florida, housing program in, 358
Wisconsin, housing program in, 359
Wise, Harold, 387

Women
  ageism and sexism and, 123–36
  black, 19–22
    ageism and sexism and, 128–30
  population statistics for, 50–51
  sexual interests of, 205–6, 306
Work, 232–39, 301–3
  ageism and, 233–36, 325–30, 339–41,
    354–57
  attitudes toward, 55–57
    aging in ghetto and, 20–23, 81–82
    dignity and, 84–86
    and Harris poll on aging, 117–19
  part-time
    and Harris poll on aging, 118
    need for, 280, 303
    pensions and, 233
    programs for, 433–34
    proposals for, 237–39
  resting vs., 302–3
  retirement planning and, 401
  right to, 232–33, 252–53, 301

  senior personnel placement and,
    376–80
  volunteerism vs., 418–19
Work force
  and Harris poll on aging, 117–19
  keeping elderly out of, 233
  statistics of elderly in, 51
Work-off program, tax, 442–43
World Health Organization (WHO),
  145
Wyden, Ron, 311
  "Senior Lobby: A Model for Sen-
    ior/Student Action," 370–75

Yoga, 390
Young, Robert, 114–15
Young-old, 47–49, 346–47

Zimmerman, Joe, 414–15
Zucker, Beatrice, 216–24
Zweben, Andrew P., 14